TAXMANN®'S

Demystifying ESG

A Comprehensive Guide for Environmental-Social-Governance Integration and Practice

Dr. Garima Dadhich
Dr. Ravi Raj Atrey

2024

Price : ₹ 695

Published by :
Taxmann Publications (P.) Ltd.

Sales & Marketing :
59/32, New Rohtak Road, New Delhi-110 005 India
Phone : +91-11-45562222
Website : www.taxmann.com
E-mail : sales@taxmann.com

Regd. Office :
21/35, West Punjabi Bagh, New Delhi-110 026 India

Printed at :
Tan Prints (India) Pvt. Ltd.
44 Km. Mile Stone, National Highway, Rohtak Road
Village Rohad, Distt. Jhajjar (Haryana) India
E-mail : sales@tanprints.com

Dedicated to the entire human race which existed, living now and will come on the planet to witness the life here...

"Being responsible today is not an option, it is an unwritten mandate for each one of us in the new age of responsibility."

- Dadhich & Atrey

Acknowledgements

Parents owe a responsibility not only to nurture the children but also to secure a bright future to them, they expect that their children will excel in their lives. This expectation takes form of increased motivation to children when they grow-up. We would like to acknowledge our parents' expectations, dedications, compromises and continuous blessings which guide each step we take, and as a result this book could be possible. We respectfully acknowledge Dr. Shri Vallabh Sharma and Smt. Aruna Sharma, Shri Avinash Atrey and Smt. Usha Atrey.

Role of parents in present age (the age of responsibility) becomes more important when the world community expect that we leave a sustainable future and more liveable planet earth for our children, grand-children and upcoming generations. Hence, it becomes important to understand the aspects of sustainability and framework of ESG not only in the context of business but also what is expected from individuals in their various spheres of life. We would like to acknowledge efforts and emotions of each and every parent for securing a bright future for their children and will expect that such efforts will not only end at mere securing a livelihood and luxury in their lives but collectively to secure sustainability of planet earth as a home for their children.

We would also like to acknowledge contribution of Surabhi, Advait, Advita Pandey, Avyan and Ravi Pandey for their support in family, their compromise and encouragement in the journey of writing this book.

We also acknowledge the encouragement by Shri Rao Inderjit Singh, Hon'ble Cabinet Minister of State (I.C.) - Planning, Statistics and Programme Implementation, MoS – Corporate Affairs and writing a message for this book. We are also thankful to Shri Praveen Kumar, Director General & CEO, Indian Institute of Corporate Affairs for his guidance and also encouraging the readers with his message.

We would like to convey sincere thanks to the publisher M/s Taxmann Publications Pvt. Ltd. for their efforts and contribution in proofreading and bringing out this book in a time-bound manner.

Last but not the least, we would also like to thank the readers of our earlier books on ESG and CSR for their motivating words received through different means and their expectations to bring a publication on ESG Fundamentals, which made the foundation of present book.

Garima Dadhich
Ravi Raj Atrey

About the Authors

Prof. Garima Dadhich

Prof. Garima Dadhich is an internationally recognised Scholar in the stream of ESG. She is Associate Professor & Founder Head of the School of Business Environment at the Indian Institute of Corporate Affairs, where she ideated the one and only Certified ESG Professional: Impact Leader Programme to nurture the ESG as a profession in India, she also heads National Foundation for Corporate Social Responsibility and Centre for Business & Human Rights at IICA. She holds a PhD in Corporate Governance, and LLM in Commercial & Corporate Laws from the Queens Marry University, London. She has obtained various professional certifications from Cambridge University, Harvard University, Centre for Effective Dispute Resolution, World Sustainable Finance Association in Law Sustainable Finance, Dispute Resolution & Board Effectiveness. She has undertaken various research projects for the Ministry of Corporate Affairs and has provided policy support to the Government.7

Dr. Ravi Raj Atrey

Dr. Ravi Raj Atrey is a well acclaimed scholar and a diversified professional. He has authored the book 'Exploring CSR' where he propounded the famous 'Tree Model of CSR'. He holds PhD in CSR, and masters level degrees in Economics, Social Work, Business Administration, Human Rights, and International Law & Diplomacy. Dr. Atrey has been behind various social and governance reform movements in the country. During his two decades of rich experience with several Ministries, Civil Society Organizations, Academic Institutions,

Consulting & Corporate Firms, he worked in the areas of Good Governance, Human Rights, Social Development, CSR, Sustainability & ESG. He presently works as the Chief Programme Executive with the School of Business Environment, Indian Institute of Corporate Affairs.

Other Books by Authors

- Benchmarking ESG & CSR: A Compendium of Best Practices in Environmental, Social & Governance (ESG) and Corporate Social Responsibility (CSR) in India (2022)
- Exploring Corporate Social Responsibility: Fundamentals & Implementation (two editions 2017 & 2020)

राव इन्द्रजीत सिंह

RAO INDERJIT SINGH

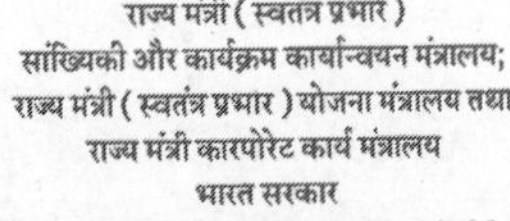
राज्य मंत्री (स्वतंत्र प्रभार)
सांख्यिकी और कार्यक्रम कार्यान्वयन मंत्रालय;
राज्य मंत्री (स्वतंत्र प्रभार) योजना मंत्रालय तथा
राज्य मंत्री कारपोरेट कार्य मंत्रालय
भारत सरकार

Minister of State (Independent Charge) of the
Ministry of Statistics and Programme Implementation;
MOS (I/C) of the Ministry of Planning and
MOS in the Ministry of Corporate Affairs
Government of India

Azadi Ka Amrit Mahotsav

MESSAGE

I am glad to learn that Dr. Garima Dadhich and Dr. Ravi Raj Atrey from Indian Institute of Corporate Affairs (Ministry of Corporate Affairs) have come out with this book on 'Demystifying Environmental-Social-Governance' (ESG). ESG is one of the most important aspects for Corporates to adopt in today's new age of functioning of corporate sector where carrying out developmental activities through 'Corporate Social Responsibilities' framework is essentially required under the Companies Act. I hope the new perspectives, theories and practical insights presented in the book shall be of great importance to corporates of all kind, size and sectors.

My best wishes to both the authors and readers.

(Inderjit Singh)

132, NITI Aayog, Parliament Street, New Delhi - 110001
Tel. : 011-23096561/62/63 Fax : 011-23096713

Residence : 6, Lodhi Estate, New Delhi - 110003
Telefax : 011-24643265, 24643266

Praveen Kumar, IAS (Retd.),
(Former Secretary to Govt. of India)
Director General & CEO
प्रवीण कुमार, भा.प्र.से (सेवानिवृत्त)
(पूर्व सचिव, भारत सरकार)
महानिदेशक एवं मुख्य कार्यकारी अधिकारी

Indian Institute of Corporate Affairs
Ministry of Corporate Affairs
Government of India
भारतीय कॉर्पोरेट कार्य संस्थान
कॉर्पोरेट कार्य मंत्रालय
भारत सरकार

MESSAGE

Re-imagining the future, particularly the visionary and philosophical base of embracing change, is one of the most important responsibilities we have to owe. This book on 'Demystifying ESG' presents the readers with some of the innovatively propounded theories and models of ESG and concepts like 'New Age of Responsibility', 'Corporate Social Revolution', and 'Originality Approach' etc.

I recommend this book as an essential read for a varied range of readers, those who wish to understand the basic concepts, want to go deep into intellectual debate, and want to adopt and practice ESG in their organizations.

I also appreciate efforts of the Authors - Dr. Garima Dadhich and Dr. Ravi Raj Atrey in the work behind bringing out this publication and wish them all the best.

(Praveen Kumar)

November 30, 2023

प्लॉट नम्बर-6, 7 और 8, सेक्टर-5, आईएमटी मानेसर, जिला-गुरूग्राम (हरियाणा)-122052
Plot No.-6,7 & 8, Sector-5, IMT Manesar, Distt. Gurugram (Haryana)-122052
Tel: +91-124-2292333 | dg.ceo-iica@nic.in | Website: iica.nic.in

Preface

ESG is a buzz word these days. It is to be seen as an alarming word also to our own existence. The Environmental-Social-Governance Framework commonly known as the 'ESG' is to be adopted by all types of businesses to be competitive and sustainable. There are many dilemmas associated with the adoption, integration, practice and reporting of ESG particularly in Indian context. This book presents the conceptual understanding on basic aspects of ESG as well as specific in-depth knowledge on each component of E, S & G. It gives a step-by-step guide on how to begin ESG journey in a company. This book will be a great learning experience for the Sustainability & ESG Professionals, budding Students in this sector, Non-Financial Audit & Assurance Professionals, Members of the Board, Investors, Consumers, Employees, and for other such stakeholders to the business.

Some of the unique features of this book are that the authors have propounded a "New Theory of Responsibility – creation of responsible capitalism, towards a new age of responsibility..", authors have also propounded the "Originality Approaches" for the businesses to integrate ESG in true sense to reap benefits of doing good. A new "Solar System Model of ESG" has also been propounded and presented by the authors in this book. The book provides readers a unique opportunity to grasp the most important aspects of ESG specifically in Indian context.

Chapter 1 on ESG - Definitions, Theories & Models compiles some of the standardised Definitions of ESG and after analysis redefines ESG as per the Indian context; it provides a comprehensive view on global as well as Indian evolution of the ESG as a concept; presents existing ESG Theories and propounds a new theory of responsibility; it provides the readers various models of ESG and also propounds new solar system model of ESG.

Chapter 2, ESG in India provides a comprehensive understanding on evolution of ESG in India and various instruments available for integration, practice, measurement, rating and reporting. It focuses ESG in Indian context and defines the NGRBC, BRSR, BRSR Core, BRSR Lite, regulatory regime of ESG in India and role of key institutions. Some of the key ESG trends and issues in India have also been explained.

Chapter 3 is on beginning with ESG journey in an organization. It focuses on how to conduct ESG baseline, peer benchmarking, materiality assessment, develop required policies, set targets and KPIs, monitor and measure performance, ESG audit in Indian context, participate in ESG index, report ESG including in value chain. It also talks about ESG and Branding, ESG and Investing, ESG and Profitability, ESG and Risk Mitigation, Measuring ESG against SDGs and other global goals among others. This chapter is an attempt to make learners equipped with the knowledge required to adopt and establish ESG related aspects in a company.

Chapter 4 is on Environmental Dimensions of ESG, it starts with the environmental risks to business, environmentally responsible investing, and also focuses on Indian regulatory mechanisms. It covers the key concepts like Climate Change, Carbon Accounting and Carbon Footprint calculation, decarbonisation solutions, Business and Biodiversity Conservations, Environmental Profit & Loss Account, Product Design, Life Cycle Assessment, Circular Economy, Environmentally Responsible Procurement & Cleaner Production. It also dwells upon key instruments like EIA, CRZ, EMP, SEA, EMS, ENVIS, CCTS, Eco-labelling etc.

Emphasis of Chapter 5 is on the Social Dimensions of ESG. It presents Social parameters under ESG including social risks to businesses, Diversity & Inclusion, Gender equity, Business & Human Rights, Community relations, Health & Safety, Corporate Social Responsibility & Product Safety etc. Information pertaining to key social impact certifications, Measurement and Audit tools has also been provided.

Chapter 6 Governance Dimensions of ESG (Governance) presents redefined corporate purpose in the new age of responsibility and revisits how corporate performance is conceived and assessed, it presents a shift towards cross sectoral leadership, Rights and duties of shareholders, an overview of Corporate Governance in Indian Law, Responsible Governance initiatives, building effective Boards, key leadership styles, transparency, Financial Disclosure, Feedback & Communication mechanisms, and risk management. Governance of sustainability issues, governance disclosure under key frameworks, global best practices in corporate governance have also been provided for the readers.

Chapter 7 deals with the summarising and way forward of ESG in India. It provides an overview on the key ESG targets, issues, challenges and achievements collectively in India, objectively verifiable benefits of adopting and disclosing ESG, summarises Indian developments and roles of key

Government institutions & sustainable development as a fundamental right, it also provides perspectives on ESG from sustainable value addition and sustainability champions.

We hope the book will demystify the various nuances of ESG and will help strengthen the responsible conduct of individuals, businesses and other entities.

Garima Dadhich

Ravi Raj Atrey

Endorsements

The need to adopt sound ESG practices is no longer just a desired goal, it is now a imperative for business sustainability. It is therefore essential that business organisations proactively adopt sustainable and good governance practices. Given this context, regulators and investors are increasingly mandating businesses to adhere to stringent ESG norms.

As ESG is still an evolving subject and new benchmarks are being set, publication of the book "Demystifying ESG" is timely and will provide a framework for practitioners. This book serves as a comprehensive guide and offers illustrations of good practices for businesses to follow. It will facilitate ESG to be factored in operating and investment decisions. I am confident that this will help adoption of responsible business practices so that future generations inherit a greener planet.

My compliments to Garima and Ravi Raj for their efforts in bringing out this publication.

- Ajay S. Shriram

Chairman & Sr. Managing Director, DCM Shriram Group

With the backdrop of the evolving ESG Framework applicable to businesses by investors, consumers, communities and other multiple stakeholders, Governments around the world are progressively mandating the ESG related aspects in business operations. This is becoming increasingly applicable to partners in the supply chain too. In such a scenario, the need for educating, building awareness, and providing guidance on how to embrace the ESG Framework is vital. I congratulate Dr. Garima Dadhich & Dr. Ravi Raj Atrey for bringing this timely publication on 'Demystifying ESG'.

- Naina Lal Kidwai

Chairperson, Rothschild & Co. India

Chairperson, India Sanitation Coalition

The requirements of the manufacturing intensive industries for adoption and practice of ESG is quite different from service sector industry. I hope the book 'Demystifying ESG' by Prof. Garima Dadhich & Dr. Ravi Raj Atrey will serve as a great piece of literature and guide to help corporate professionals to adopt and practice vital issues of sustainability within a well defined framework of ESG.

- Ramkrishnan Mukundan

Managing Director & CEO, Tata Chemicals Ltd.

The true vision of a sustainable world can be realized only when companies can act upon, track and monitor their carbon footprints, social impacts and ethical practices in a transparent manner. ESG Framework provides this opportunity to businesses. This book by Dr. Dadhich & Dr. Atrey is a great source of driving corporate sustainability.

- Raghunath Anant Mashelkar

Former Director General, Council of Scientific & Industrial Research (CSIR)

Climate change is one of the pressing issues today, tracking the carbon footprint of business activities is considered in investment decisions, and societal acceptance of business. In adopting strategies to solve societal challenges and providing the investment solutions, ESG framework has widely been accepted worldwide. Indian businesses are competing with the globe in not only expansion of markets but are gaining advantages by integrating ESG into core business. The book 'Demystifying ESG' authored by two finest minds in India gives another opportunity to businesses to review their ESG strategy and interventions and start a fresh to get more competitive advantages. My best wishes to Prof. Garima Dadhich & Dr. Ravi Raj Atrey.

- Prof. Cary Kronsinsky

Professor, Yale University

Businesses across sectors and geographies play a crucial role in driving sustainable development. To achieve this sustainable development in their core areas and the broader ecosystem that they operate in, businesses map their material issues in the areas of Environmental, Social and Governance and craft strategies to achieve set targets that are aligned with the Sustainable Development Goals. There are ESG Frameworks that not only help identify material issues and develop actionable strategies, but also ensure that businesses' contributions are distinctly measurable.

Disclosures of measurable impacts and outcomes can inspire broader local and global communities, and help build brands that exude goodwill, trust and admiration. The book 'Demystifying ESG' brings to life these and several other key aspects in an easy to consume language. Happy reading!

- Namita Vikas

Founder & Managing Director, auctusESG

It is heartening that Professor Dr. Garima Dadhich and Dr. Ravi Raj Atrey – both of whom are with the Indian Institute of Corporate Affairs (IICA), an establishment of the Ministry of Corporate Affairs (MCA) - have collaborated to put together this book, with the title, Demystifying ESG – A Comprehensive Guide for Environmental, Social and Governance Integration and Practice.

This is a timely book which provides a comprehensive overview of the evolving landscape of ESG in India. As stakeholders demand assurances from businesses – big and small alike – that business-actions related to the creation of value for customers and surpluses for shareholders will not adversely impact stakeholder-rights, as also their access to resources, there is a heightened need for the generation of all-round trust and transparency. The establishment of trust among stakeholders calls for systems and processes within enterprises to be created for all-round openness, and a culture of sustained business responsibility and sustainability reporting (BRSR). Only when businesses integrate all the above aspects in the warp and weft of their governance mechanisms, will stakeholders – and society - be assured that the activities of businesses are worthy of their support. The establishment of wholesome leadership practices and all-round good governance, are essential pre-requisites for the creation of sustainable businesses. The Boards of companies, as well as their executive leadership, must also make responsible business conduct a part of the DNA of their enterprises.

There is therefore an urgent need to generate awareness on all the vital aspects of Environmental, Social and Governance integration and practices among businesses. Furthermore, there is also a need to guide enterprises on how to implement ESG frameworks to achieve the important goals of enhancing societal trust, through a conscious pursuit of business responsibility and sustainability. I am confident that this book, by Dr. Dadhich and Dr. Atrey, will serve this need adequately. My congratulations to the authors for this timely release.

- Bharat Wakhlu

President, The Wakhlu Advisory

Former Resident Director (India), Tata Sons

Abbreviations

ASR	Asian Sustainability Rating
ATM	Atrey's Tree Model
BEE	Bureau of Energy Efficiency
BHR	Business and Human Rights
BRSR	Business Responsibility and Sustainability Reporting
BSE	Bombay Stock Exchange
CBD	Convention on Biological Diversity
CBDR-RC	Common But Differentiated Responsibilities and Respective Capability
CFCs	Chlorofluorocarbons
CITES	Convention on International Trade in Endangered Species
CMS	Convention on Migratory Species
CNA	Competent National Authority
COP	Conference of Parties
CPCB	Central Pollution Control Board
CRA	Community Reinvestment Act
CRZ	Coastal Regulation Zone
CSA	Corporate Sustainability Assessment
CSR	Corporate Social Responsibility
DJSI	The Dow Jones Sustainability World Index
EIC	Environmental Information Centre
EITs	Economies in Transition
ENVIS	Environmental Information System
EPR	Extended Producer Responsibility
ESG	Environmental-Social-Governance
EU	European Union

GHG	Greenhouse Gas
GMO	Genetically Modified Organism
GoI	Government of India
GRI	Global Reporting Initiative
HCFCs	hydrochlorofluorocarbons
IAIA	International Association for Impact Assessment
ICM	Indian Carbon Market
IICA	Indian Institute of Corporate Affairs
ILO	International Labour Organization
INCD	Intergovernmental Negotiating Committee
ISRO	Indian Space Research Organization
ISS	Institutional Shareholder Services
LCA	Life Cycle Assessment
LCI	Life Cycle Inventory
LCIA	Life Cycle Impact assessment
LDCs	Least Developed Countries
LiFE	Lifestyle for Environment
LMO	Living Modified Organism
MCA	Ministry of Corporate Affairs
MEI	Material ESG Issue
MoEFCC	Ministry of Environment, Forest and Climate Change
MoP	Meeting of the Parties
MoU	Memorandum of Understanding
NDC	Nationally Determined Contributions
NGO	Non-Governmental Organization
NGRBC	National Guidelines on Responsible Business Conduct
NSE	National Stock Exchange
NVG	National Voluntary Guidelines
ODS	Ozone depleting substances
OECD	Organisation for Economic Co-operation and Development
POP	Persistent Organic Pollutants
PPP	Policy, Plan and Programme
PRI	Principles of Responsible Investment
SCM	Supply Chain Management

SDGs	Sustainable Development Goals
SEA	Strategic Environmental Assessment
SEBI	Securities and Exchange Board of India
SRI	Socially Responsible Investment
UNCCD	United Nations Convention to Combat Desertification
UNCED	United Nations Conference on Environment & Development
UNFCCC	United Nations Framework Convention on Climate Change
UNGC	United Nations Global Compact
VCLT	Vienna Convention on the Law of Treaties
VUCA	Volatility-Uncertainty-Complexity-Ambiguity
LBI	Legally Binding Instruments
LBT	Legally Binding Treaties
PAPs	Project Affected Persons
R&R	Rehabilitation & Resettlement
RRM	Resettlement & Rehabilitation Management
PDF	Project Displaced Families
PAF	Project Affected Families
RBC	Responsible Business Conduct
OLGM	Operational-level Grievance Mechanisms
MSME	Micro, Small and Medium Enterprises
EoDB	Ease of Doing Business

Contents

CHAPTER 2

ESG IN INDIA

CHAPTER 3

BEGINNING WITH ESG JOURNEY

CHAPTER 4

E OF ESG (ENVIRONMENT)

CHAPTER 6

GOVERNANCE DIMENSIONS OF ESG

CHAPTER 7

ESG KEY TRENDS, CHALLENGES AND WAY FORWARD

ESG - DEFINITIONS, THEORIES & MODELS

CHAPTER 1

1.1 Genesis

Think about two scenarios, the one in which a business operates itself with ethical values, is responsible towards protecting the nature and planet, takes care of social needs, understands community expectations, is more humble towards its employees, adopts transparent policies and practices, has good governance structures, practices ethical sourcing, adopts clean manufacturing processes, adopts responsible branding and marketing strategies, supplies quality and sustainable products and services to consumers, and also cares about recycling of product at the end of its life.

The other scenario is an example of a business which adopts unethical practices starting from the setting-up of business units, acquiring land and other resources, resettlement and rehabilitation of habitants, procurement of raw materials, adversely impacting the environment and people without taking appropriate corrective measures, markets and communicates about products or services unethically, and has no appropriate conflict resolution modalities.

In the first scenario, purpose of the business is Sustainability. Whereas, in the second scenario, the only purpose remains profit maximization at any cost. Now, let's discuss these two scenarios further in detail:

The purpose of sustainability in the first case, leads to a business towards 'Trust'. The factor of trust is responsible for growth of a business, consumers intend to buy products and services from a company which is trustworthy, individual and institutional investors tend to invest their money in a trustworthy and stable business. Social acceptance of such business is very high. To achieve the purpose of sustainability, these businesses adopt a systematised framework for integration, practice, measuring impact, and make disclosures and reporting. This systematised framework is known as Environmental-Social-Governance (ESG) Framework.

The businesses who do not adopt ethical intent, policies and practices, may gain short-term benefits but in long-run these businesses are more prone to failure, there are many such examples in global as well as Indian History.

Main objective behind writing this book is to present the reasoning behind adoption of responsible business practices which leads to more responsible branding and business gains, whereas, irresponsible practices lead to business failures. The book also presents what ESG is? What is its philosophical and theoretical base? How a business adopts and integrates responsible conduct? How the ESG strategy and plans are prepared and impact is measured? And finally, what are the key aspects of efficient ESG reporting. It also deliberates in detail about each aspect of E, S and G and finally paves the way for future directions.

1.2 Defining ESG

1.2.1 Key definitions of ESG

According to Gartner Glossary:

> "Environmental, Social and Governance (ESG) refers to a collection of corporate performance evaluation criteria that assess the robustness of a company's governance mechanisms and its ability to effectively manage its environmental and social impacts. Examples of ESG data include the quantification of a company's carbon emissions, water consumption or customer privacy breaches. Institutional investors, stock exchanges and boards increasingly use sustainability and social responsibility disclosure information to explore the relationship between a company's management of ESG risk factors and its business performance."

According to Deloitte:

> "ESG stands for environmental, social and governance. These are called pillars in ESG frameworks and represent the 3 main topic areas that companies are expected to report in. The goal of ESG is to capture all the non-financial risks and opportunities inherent to a company's day to day activities."

According to CFA Institute:

> "ESG analysis has become an increasingly important part of the investment process. For investment professionals, a key motivation in the practice of considering Environmental, Social and Governance (ESG) issues as part of their financial analysis is to gain a fuller understanding of the companies in which they invest."

According to the Market Business News - Financial Glossary:

> "ESG stands for Environmental Social and Governance and refers to the three key factors when measuring the sustainability and ethical impact of an investment in a business or company. Most socially responsible investors check companies out using ESG criteria to screen investments. It is a generic term

used in capital markets and commonly used by investors to evaluate the behavior of companies, as well as determine their future financial performance."

According to the Paul, Weiss, Rifkind, Wharton & Garrison:

> "ESG grew out of investment philosophies clustered around sustainability and, thereafter, socially responsible investing. Early efforts focused on 'screening out' (that is, excluding) companies from portfolios largely due to environmental, social or governance concerns, while more recently ESG has favourably distinguished companies that are making positive contributions to the elements of ESG, premised on treating environmental and social issues as core elements of strategic positioning."

According to the Ecolytics:

> "ESG criteria are a subset of sustainable indicators linked to financial performance. ESG reports help investors avoid companies that could present greater financial risks because of their environmental record or other social or governmental practices."

According to the Leyla Acaroglu:

> "ESG is a non-financial reporting framework that covers several aspects of sustainability, whereas sustainability is about the social, economic and environmental factors that a company negatively impacts and can, in turn, create a positive impact on through changes to the way the company operates."

According to the Robeco:

> "ESG means using Environmental, Social and Governance factors to assess the sustainability of companies and countries. These three factors are seen as best embodying the three major challenges facing corporations and wider society, now encompassing climate change, human rights and adherence to laws."

1.2.2 Analysis of existing definitions

The key difference between ESG and sustainability is that ESG is a specific tool used to measure the performance of a company, while sustainability is a broad principle that encompasses a range of responsible business practices.

ESG criteria are a subset of sustainable indicators linked to financial performance. ESG reports help investors avoid companies that could present greater financial risks because of their environmental record or other social or governmental practices.

ESG means using Environmental, Social and Governance factors to assess the sustainability of companies and countries. These three factors are seen as best embodying the three major challenges facing corporations and wider society.

ESG is a non-financial reporting framework that covers several aspects of sustainability, whereas sustainability is about the social, economic and environmental factors that a company negatively impacts and can, in turn, create a positive impact on through changes to the way the company operates.

1.2.3 Redefining ESG

Be it global or Indian context, frameworks for adaptation and disclosures must have some specific and standard criteria and parameters. Post in-depth analysis of available understanding of ESG, Authors have presented below definition:

ESG is a fundamental responsibility of business to adapt, integrate and disclose its commitment towards sustainability. It enables businesses with a yardstick for their commitment towards stakeholders as mentioned in the solar system model. It also helps businesses towards monitor and measure of ESG practices which *inter alia* includes actions to combat climate changes, GHG emissions, deforestation, biodiversity preservation, reducing pollution, judicious usages of water, waste management, extended producer responsibility, customer relations, employee relations, labour, human rights, community, supply chains, responsible board, succession planning, compensation, diversity, equity and inclusion, regulatory compliance, corruption, and data hygiene etc.

1.3 Evolution of ESG as a Concept

ESG is an acronym used widely today not only in the world of business but in Governments also. The term ESG came into existence when Investors started considering Environmental, Social and Governance issues into account while investing in businesses. There are various events, developments and actions in the history which helped establishing present shape of ESG as a Framework.

1.3.1 Socially Responsible Investing (SRI)

We have observed that ESG was earlier derived from the Socially Responsible Investing (SRI). In the twentieth century, when investors were increasingly becoming more aware towards impact of the investment they are making, they started considering various ways to measure impact of investments in businesses. The term socially responsible investment was started using by investors during that time only.

1.3.2 The Community Reinvestment Act (CRA)

The Community Reinvestment Act was established in the Unites States of America with an objective to strengthen existing laws pertaining to investments requiring financial institutions to address social or community related issues into considerations before making investment related considerations. This law encourages depository institutions to help meet the credit needs of the communities in which they operate, including Low and Moderate Income (LMI) neighbourhoods, consistent with safe and sound banking operations.

1.3.3 Forum for Sustainable and Responsible Investment

Forum for Sustainable and Responsible Investment, was established as a Membership based Association in United States of America during mid 1980s with an objective to advance sustainable investing across all asset classes including the investment management and advisory firms, data and research firms, mutual fund companies, asset owners, financial planners and advisors, brokers, dealers, banks, credit unions, community development financial institutions and non-profit associations.

1.3.4 Who Cares Wins

In 2004, the term ESG was introduced in an UN Whitepaper, Who Cares Wins. Key recommendations of the report may be seen in graphical representation given below. Overall goals of the report are summarised as:

- Stronger and more resilient financial markets.
- Contribution to sustainable development.
- Awareness and mutual understanding of involved Stakeholders.
- Improved trust in financial institutions.

(Source: Who Cares Wins: Connecting Financial Markets to a Changing World, The Global Compact)

Figure 1.1: Goals of Who Cares Wins

1.3.5 Principles for Responsible Investment (PRI)

With a mission to create long term value by emphasis on an economically efficient, sustainable global financial system, this initiative was established by the United Nations Environment Programme Finance Initiative (UNEP FI) and United Nations Global Compact (UNGC). In early 2005, Kofi Annan, then-Secretary-General of the United Nations, asked a group of the world's top institutional investors to participate in a process for developing the Principles for Responsible Investment. A 20-person investor group drawn from institutions in 12 countries was supported by a 70-person group of experts from the investment industry, intergovernmental organisations and civil society.

The PRI is the world's foremost advocate of responsible investment, it comprehends the investing implications of Environmental, Social, and Governance (ESG) aspects and assists its global network of investor signatories in incorporating ESG considerations into their investment and ownership decisions.

According to the CEO and Chair of PRI Board—

> *"Including environmental, social and governance factors in investment decision making and ownership is no longer seen as a nice-to-do but a must-do. Investors are increasingly seeking to enhance their performance through more insightful evaluation of long-term risk factors, and by identifying new investment opportunities that take into account the rapidly evolving needs of their beneficiaries and clients."*

UNPRI provides a forum for investors to learn from one another, share best practises, and collaborate on responsible investing projects. It also provides guidance, research, and resources to help signatories effectively execute the principles. UNPRI strives to generate constructive change, support sustainable investing practises, and contribute to a more equitable and sustainable global economy by engaging investors internationally. Overall, UNPRI plays an important role in promoting ESG integration in investment decision-making, developing responsible ownership practises, and advocating for financial industry transparency and disclosure on ESG problems.

1.4 ESG Theories

A theory denotes the general idea or principles of a particular subject, it is an idea or set of ideas that tries to explain something. It is also an opinion or a belief that has either been tested on scientific parameters for generalization or has potentials to be generalised. Being a recent framework, ESG lacks specified theories, however authors have tried to compile the core ideation of ESG from the prevailing key developments in literature in an ecosystem where ESG as an independent stream took birth.

Several schools of thoughts had different theories on the structure of socio-economic modalities, these were coined as a guide to life, systems and structures for Governments, Businesses and also influenced living patterns of the individuals. Theories of capitalism, socialism etc. in the past and many conceptual developments recently have been considered in this section. Understanding and analysis of previous theories becomes essential to conclude a new theory on ESG denoting to the new age of responsibility.

1.4.1 Capitalism and Free Enterprise

We have observed different kinds of economic systems in theories and practice in different countries. Here we will talk about the Capitalist Economy and Free Market Economy and how these two economic systems influence ESG.

Capitalism is defined as an economic system in which the means of production, trade and industry are owned and controlled by private individuals or corporations for profit. It is also known as the free market economy or laissez-faire economy.

However, there are overlapping qualities in both these kinds of economic systems and the terms are sometimes used interchangeably in academic literature. Despite the fact that the Capitalist and Free-market systems arise from the same economic soil, there are some fundamental differences between the both:

- Capitalism includes personal ownership of property and open competition while a free-market system is ruled entirely by demand and supply with little to no government regulation.
- Many capitalistic nations have mixed economies where free market elements reign with considerable state oversight, taxation and regulations.
- The opposite of a free market economy is a planned, controlled, or command economy. The government controls the means of production and the distribution of wealth, dictating the prices of goods and services and the wages workers receive.

Capitalism is focused on the creation of wealth and ownership of capital and factors of production, whereas a free market system is focused on the exchange of wealth or goods and services.

1.4.2 Socialist Theory

Socialist Economy is defined as an economy in which the resources are owned, managed and regulated by the State. The central idea of this kind of economy is that all the people have similar rights and in this way, each and every person can reap the fruits of planned production.

Capitalist mode of production resulted in inequalities between the classes and imperialism across the globe. This led to the development of the antithesis of capitalism by Karl Marx and Frederich Engels.

The Socialist pattern of industrialization emphasizes co-operative enterprise and various forms of community enterprise that would benefit the public as a whole. Governments evolved with state control of the economy. These governments used public welfare as their reference point.

However, most socialists had an abiding fear of the state and state control as a possible source of intensification of exploitation rather than a solution to it.

1.4.3 The Capability Approach

We have witnessed that past few years have emphasised the Capability Approach while defining the Sustainable Development. Although we can trace some aspects of the capability approach back to, among others, Aristotle, Adam Smith, and Karl Marx, it is economist-philosopher Amartya Sen who pioneered the approach and philosopher Martha Nussbaum and a growing number of other scholars across the humanities and the social sciences who have significantly developed it.

The capability approach is a theoretical framework that entails two normative claims: first, the claim that the freedom to achieve well-being is of primary moral importance and, second, that well-being should be understood in terms of people's capabilities and functioning. Whether someone can convert a set of means - resources and public goods - into a functioning (*i.e.*, whether she has a particular capability) crucially depends on certain personal, socio-political, and environmental conditions, which, in the capability literature, are called 'conversion factors.'

The capability approach is considered the foundation of the Sustainable Human Development (SHD) paradigm and is considered appropriate to introduce environmental concerns within a holistic approach to sustainability (economic, social and environmental). There are mixed views among many other economists about the Capability Approach, some emphasize the transformative strength of the Capability Approach as an economically and politically people-centered approach and fundamental means to achieve the Sustainable Development. Some others perceive the Capability Approach to be a suitable framework to analyze the multiple links between human wellbeing and critical natural capital. These school of thought recommend Capability Approach as part of a normative and informative foundation for deliberative human development in a strong sustainability framework.

Economists also see the Capability Approach as a way to overcome the neglect of the human dimension, notably the human values and needs that characterize various ecosystem services analyses. It is further argued that the Capability Approach may serve as a theoretical framework to meet the ecological challenges of the Anthropocene. The term 'Anthropocene' is used to defined the time during which humans have had a substantial impact on our planet. Impact on planet in the sense of living in a new geological age, being part of a complex global system and impact of human activities on it.

1.4.4 Normative Dimensions of Sustainability

Normative refers to how things should be and what we should do. The answers to these questions, on the other hand, are based on our understanding of what is ethically valuable and desirable, in other words, what we should preserve to future generations as well. Sustainable development is therefore a normative concept. It is pertinent to mention that what we all consider 'sustainable' is entirely based on our values systems. Hence, issues of sustainability are to be addressed with related ethical considerations. "Ethical valuations are required to determine what should change in the current situation, or what normative goals and limits are required for human activity for the sake of sustainability". Ethics are required to justify the value and fair implementation of sustainability actions. An ethical analysis can also clarify the values and standards that sustainability measures assume and examine ethical assumptions critically.

We see that the Brundtland report's definition of sustainable development is also normative. It focuses on fairness between generations and the priority of the needs of the poor. The Brundtland report focuses on the division of material needs and living conditions. An ethical dimension has been proposed as an addition alongside the other sustainability dimensions, as sustainability issues are normative. The ethical side of sustainability can be divided further into material and procedural fairness.

1.4.5 The Economics of Sustainability

Major considerations while discussing the economics of sustainability is the debate of ideas in neo-classical school v/s ecological economics. The general consensus on sustainability among economists is based on the "constant capital rule", the notion of living off interest or income and not consuming capital.

There are different views of the economists on the definition of capital and what needs to be maintained and preserved. A "Strong Sustainability" view from ecological economics is contrasted with a "Weak Sustainability" view from neoclassical economics.

Key operational principle for sustainable economic activity is to keep capital intact. Here it is important to understand that there are three types of capital, *viz*. Man-made Capital, Human or Social Capital, and Natural capital.

Man-made capital includes all the tools, machines, buildings, technologies and infrastructure that enhance productivity, human or social capital in the economics is considered as the skills and knowledge of the workforce, whereas the earth and its living systems are considered as the natural capital.

Weak sustainability is about maintaining total capital stock without regard to proportions, with one kind of capital being substitutable for another. Weak sustainability advocates would acknowledge that natural capital is indeed depreciating like losing arable land, topsoil, fisheries; depleting groundwater, polluting watersheds, etc., but they subtract this depreciation from total investment in the economy.

Strong sustainability on the other hand treats natural capital on the assumption that man-made capital cannot be substituted for it. Strong sustainability rejects the idea that our built infrastructure adequately compensates future generations for ecological losses. Man-made capital cannot, regardless of price, replace the services and amenities provided by nature, most especially life-support services, like protection from UV radiation, climate regulation, the food chain, the balance between alkalinity and acidity, the storage, movement and purification of water, etc. Nature cannot, like other inputs to production, really be managed according to its marginal product. Its viability must be protected. If impaired, the unique services of ecological systems have no substitute.

1.4.6 The Ethical Economy

Ethical Economy describes the theory of the ethical preconditions of the economy and of business as well as the theory of the ethical foundations of economic systems. It analyses the impact of rules, virtues, and goods or values on economic action and management. Ethical Economy understands ethics as a means to increase trust and to reduce transaction costs. It forms a foundational theory for business ethics and business culture.

1.4.7 Theory of Inter-generational Justice

Here we consider the most popular definition of the development that the development which meets the needs of the present without compromising the ability of future generations to meet their own needs.

According to Stanford Encyclopaedia of Philosophy, ideas or questions like - Can prospective children be said to have an interest that their parents not act in a way likely to lead to their birth when the parents are in a position to know that the life of the child, should it be born, would fall below some relevant threshold of well-being, pose most pressing questions to the existence. The Procreational duty of omission says not to bring a person into existence unless the person will have "at least the ordinary chances of a desirable existence".

Equitable Intergenerational Transmission is based on two assumptions *viz.* Savings and Dissavings. It also considers three modalities in terms of Prohibition, Authorization, and Obligation. One of the arguments that 'the basic needs of the present should always take precedence over the basic needs of the future but the basic needs of the future should take precedence over the extravagant luxury of the present', provides an inside to the concept.

We can observe for example that both the utilitarians (a theory of morality that advocates actions that foster happiness and oppose actions that cause unhappiness) and the egalitarians (a person who advocates or supports the principle of equality for all people) include the generational savings obligation in their theories, the dissavings prohibition option has been taken seriously by egalitarians. It summarises that the standard approach to sustainable development as Brundtland views it is by no means the only option.

Brundtland's definition of the Sustainable Development "..Development is only said to be sustainable if it meets the needs of the present without compromising the ability of future generations to meet their own needs". In 1987, Brundtland Commission urged nations to improve present conditions without compromising the ability of future generations to meet their needs. Against the background of this appeal for sustainable development, there is a call for intergenerational justice, under a sufficientarian framework. It is normally stressed to consider sufficientarianism as a valid alternative to egalitarianism for achieving resource justice.

The theory of Inter-generational Justice considers the aspects, analysis and critiques of indirect reciprocity, mutual advantage, utilitarianism, lockean proviso, egalitarianism, and the Brundtland's sufficientarianism.

1.4.8 Sustainable Freedom

Redefining Sustainable Development, the concept of 'Sustainable Freedom' was propounded by Amartya Sen, the Capability Approach has also recently been reframed by Amartya Sen. Redefining the Sustainable Development as the Sustainable Freedom, Sen has described that on the one hand, we are authentically free to meet our needs for food, shelter and movement whilst, on the other, we are not preventing future generations from enjoying at least the same freedoms.

Interestingly, the concept of Sustainable Freedom has received little attention in the literature linking Capability Approach and Sustainable Development. However, the concept of Sustainable Freedom seems important from two directions. Firstly, Amartya Sen's theory of Sustainable Freedom denotes an evolution of his framing of sustainability that is based on Brundtland which aims at unite countries in pursuit of sustainable development. Secondly, the aim of this concept of Sustainable Freedom is to provide a vision of sustainability broader than the previously propounded concepts.

1.4.9 Redefining Capitalism

Barton et.al in their edited book 'Redefining Capitalism' have narrated various perspectives to CSR and Sustainability integration into current economic systems in practice. Andrew Crane and Dirk Matten in a write-up 'The Changing role of the corporations in society' led us to the idea of re-imagining capitalism. The 3P framework leads to a systematic change through Purpose of the Corporation, Performance in Social Impact, and Partnerships in cross sector leaderships. According to Crane & Matten, the idea that the Capitalism is to be seen as a perspective of social system also and not mere from an economic and political system perspective, it leads towards thinking beyond the conventional ideas of capitalism. The degree to which rights of shareholders be mirrored with certain duties of ownership, the broader concept of corporate performance on the degree of how free markets to be, and engagement with partners to replace market structures in stakeholder relations are some of the core ideas reimagining capitalism from the Crane & Matten.

Capitalism in its current form has already gone through multiple changes in different geographies and nations since the idea and practice of Capitalism was evolved. Today, we see certain forms of capitalisms which have been improvised from its original concept.

1.4.10 Propounding a New Theory of Responsibility

Since ages, human has been exploiting the natural resources available on planet earth. Whatever be the theory of initiation of human life on earth, since it very existence human was dependent on ecology, environment, natural and physical resources. Humans' core attribute to be in the groups and relations attracted emergence of various social institutions with a complex web of social relations. To cater the needs of increasing population, human race organized itself to produce necessary commodities, started barter systems which led to emergence of morden day economies.

The structured forms of societies, economies, market, and industrial organizations being witnessed today had a long history of evolution. Several patterns of practice as well as concepts were developed from time to time.

Capitalism leads to the creation of wealth but it advocates distinction between the haves and have-nots. Socialism fills the gap between rich and poor, but at the same time it wipes out the encouragement to work hard, due to which the country's Gross Domestic Product falls down and everyone turns out to be poor. Thus, as every coin has two aspects, it is very difficult to say which system is better than the other.

Other phenomenon like the capability approach, inter-generational justice etc. intend to reach to a solution to problems arised out of socialism and capitalism but limit to an extend in providing such solutions which are acceptable from different segments in theory and practice.

The new paradigms which are attracting each one of us to think and act towards sustaining our own existence, existence of our children, our grand children and our upcoming generations on the planet earth, also pressurising each one of us to come-up with innovative ways of living. Lifestyle for Environment is one of the important initiatives taken by India leading from the UNFCCC COP 26 'The Mission Life' was announced by the Government of India.

> *"LiFE envisions replacing the prevalent 'use-and-dispose' economy—governed by mindless and destructive consumption—with a circular economy, which would be defined by mindful and deliberate utilization. The Mission intends to nudge individuals to undertake simple acts in their daily lives that can contribute significantly to climate change when embraced across the world."*

This may be seen as only one aspect of the solution, but the problem of sustaining our existence is multi-fold and multi-dimensional. We need to think and route ourselves towards to root of the problem. Since the human existence has been witnessed on the earth, what has been core and fundamental factors behind all socio-economic-environmental problems? Mission Life focuses on individual actions, which seems into the right direction. Small steps lead to big changes at ideological level and revolutionize themselves.

We need to derive the root cause of problem and with this intent in mind, a 'New Theory of Responsibility' has been propounded by Atrey & Dadhich.

The Theory of Responsibility is presented as below:

Before entering to the core discussions of the theory, let's understand few basic conceptual arguments first:

Ethical Behaviour at the core of individual mindset

The structures in which we live have certain patterns of interactions among individuals. At the core, in any organization these are the individuals who play key role in defining culture, norms, identity, image and perception. Learning of individuals, which we say 'Conditioning' in psychological terms, becomes part of the ongoing cultural and related practices. The core thinking in this theory is that when individual mindsets are filled with the ethical dimensions of taking decisions and adopting it in their day-to-day conduct, the results will be charismatic in the sense of taking responsibility towards sustainability.

Link between Responsibility and Ethics

No one can imagine that an 'Ethical Person' cannot be a 'Responsible Person'. It is not only an assumption but there are several studies conducted in different streams which reflect that people with ethical mindsets do not intend to harm the surrounding. Though ethics are subjective and may change as per prevailing socio-cultural practices and norms, despite that being ethical may be seen in those local contexts. Linkages of responsible behaviours applies on individuals and organizations both. Organizations following ethical principles are seen responsible towards environment and society and in their internal practices and communication with external stakeholders as well.

Responsibility as a Mandatory Compulsion

We have evolved to our present stage of development after crossing several ages. We started from stone age, iron age, industrial age, technology age, and now heading into the 'Age of Responsibility'. Being responsible is no more an option for those living at this planet presently, its compulsion. If people and organizations will not follow responsible behaviour towards the environment, towards social structures and institutions, towards the way and patterns of living, they may not be able to leave the planet habitable to their upcoming generations to their children and grand-children. Being responsible has become an unwritten mandate.

Individual Responsible Behaviour to Collective Impact

The institutions, the organizations, the corporates and industries are led and run by individuals collectively. A group of individuals in organizational settings is avid by the rules, norms, and culture of the specified organization. On the other hand, it may also be appropriate to say that the cultures and norms of an organization are evolved and practiced by individuals. It is the collective intent and adoption of ethical and responsible conduct of individuals, which decides and reflects an organization's intent to be responsible and makes an impact on what an organization does. In the context of a business, the collective impact reflects through the Board's priorities, Corporate Policies, Code of Conducts which are defined by individuals at top levels. Entire organization with responsible intent adopts and follow the agenda set by top leadership. In that way individual responsible behaviours of people in various hierarchies collectively decide the organizational responsible conduct.

Organizational Responsibilities v/s Individual Ethics

We have seen that organizational responsibilities in terms of Environment, Social and Governance are discharged collectively by ethically oriented individuals coupled with the right intent policies, rules and norms in an organization. In that context, ethically motivated individuals both at the level of leadership roles as well as those who implement the policies, play an important role in discharging organizational responsibilities of E, S & G. The entire gamut of ESG system is based on the Ethics, be it Environmental, Social or Governance. This is 'Ethics' due to which all components of the ESG Business Ecosystem are balance-fully connected. It validates the role of ethics and moral values in deciding responsible business conduct.

The Age of Responsibility

As we enter into the age of responsibility, it is imperative to follow responsible business conduct. It is the collective effort of all of us to decide our future. How each individual learns, equipped herself/himself, and performs the ethical and responsible behaviour within the framework of ESG in organizational contexts will set the tone of our collective future.

The Theory

Hypothesis: The theory is based on a hypothesis that the Individual Ethical Behaviour leads to desired outcomes of Sustainability/ESG.

Assumption: The assumption here is that once an individual is ethical in his / her conduct, has adopted ethical principles in his / her core personality, he /she will do all the actions as per rationale and logical thoughts. These actions will not harm the social structures and institutions, the environment and other ecosystems around a human-being in areas of influence.

The Originality Approach: Today, we all intend to achieve the aims of sustainability by attributing some of the standard principles on organizations. These principles are derived from different global, regional, national, sector, stakeholder specific frameworks, guidelines and instruments of sustainability. These principles or suggestive actions are understood to attribute on organizations to follow and disclose certain practices, in many cases the examples of green washing are also evident where organizations intend to showcase what has not been implemented in its true sense, just to either attract stakeholders or investments. On the contrary if the ethical or responsible behaviour is integrated in the core philosophy of organizations, and values are at the core of the purpose and existence of the organization, the organizations will follow an 'Originality Approach' and will act in responsible manner by its core essence. There will not be any need of just cosmetic actions or green washing. Atrey's Tree Model of CSR (Atrey, 2020) provides a comprehensive and revolutionary perspective and model to integrate responsible conduct at the roots of businesses.

> "Ethics in ESG is to not making profit on the cost of any stakeholders".
>
> *-Dadhich & Atrey*

How to Integrate & Practice the Responsible Conduct

Organizations are not merely made of buildings and machines, the real soul of the organizations lies in the people and its policies. By adopting policies on required aspects of E, S & G does not ensure that the organization will be ethical and responsible in its conduct. Integrating the responsible business philosophy, ethical and value-based conduct and sustainable development goals as envisaged through the Atrey's Tree Model is the beginning of a journey of sustainability and responsible conduct. The success of all such integration will depend further from two dimensions, first at Governance level while establishing or restructuring the business as per the ESG needs, the question arises that how much the people leading corporate governance are ethical by themselves, unless the individuals leading the organization are not ethical there is probability that they will find the ways to escape the responsibilities in some way or other. Whereas once we make sure through adopting different means that the people at leadership are ethical, chances will be more that the organization will lead the sustainability in original sense. On the other hand, once the roots of business are established, processes are mainstreamed with sustainability, various policies are in place, the next step is to execute all these in true sense which is possible when all the people associated with the business are of ethical conduct. Once the individuals are ethical, they will lead their personal and professional lives following with ethical principles and responsible conduct, thereby leading to the responsible organizations.

Creation of Responsible Capitalism - towards an age of responsibility

Now the question arises that how it will create a broader responsiblism leading from the individual to organizations to the nations? We have understood that how the ethically imbibed individuals will co-create ethical and responsible organizations with originality approach. The acceptance of '..ism' is from two dimensions, the first is that an ideology is propounded and the people, institutions, governments etc. start to accept and adopt it, the later is reverse in process, for the ease of doing actions and processes the revolutionary actions are adopted first and the literature adopts it as a concept later on.

We have seen that Capitalism and Socialism are two established economic systems, while more emphasis on socialism leads to less efficiency, poor economic growth and development, the capitalistic system leads towards more control in hands of business not only to determine the market trends but so-called attributions of the adverse impacts on human rights and social hierarchy.

A new way of living through adoption of responsible and ethical behaviour from individual levels to organizational and national levels will affect the economic systems in multiple and fundamental ways. The way of doing businesses will change, there will be more stakeholders' satisfaction, more shareholders' value, more responsible branding and acceptance among buyers, customers and investors. Owners and shareholders will not only share profits but also discharge their duties towards different stakeholders. Motive to make profit will be with purpose. Doing business for purpose will be the only purpose of doing business.

Examining the Theory

In the social sciences, a theory is usually an explanation of a set of phenomena, it can be untested/extensively tested and accepted on scientific rationale. A theory needs to be (*a*) substantiated, (*b*) explanatory, (*c*) predictive, and (*d*) testable. We will examine the key aspects of Theory of Responsibility on these parameters:

(*a*) **Substantiated** - A theory cannot be independent of prior work and evidence, there needs to be some justification of it, within previous work in the field. Present theory has been developed based on previous theoretical deliberations of capitalism, free-market, socialism, capability, economics of sustainability, inter-generational justice, normative dimensions of sustainability, Atrey's Tree model of CSR, and Atrey's Originality Approach etc.

(*b*) **Explanatory** - A theory needs to explain something about the scientific in it, describes the scientific relationships among various variables. The present theory not only explains key relevant arguments but also provides a detailed explanation on how individual ethical conducts leads to the organizational responsible conduct and thereby leading to the national revolution in adopting responsible capitalism within the new age of responsibility.

(*c*) **Predictive** - A theory needs to make predictions which may be examined. Present theory provides predictions in terms of responsible capitalism as a concept and success in adopting responsible conduct in its originality through individual revolution.

(*d*) **Testable** - A model can be tested, so that the theory itself can, in principle has a possibility of rejection also. Because for any theory to be sound there needs to be a genuine commitment to reject the theory of the tests. It is important for a theory there is either the intent or the logical possibility of interpreting evidences from different perspectives. The New Theory of Responsibility tries to adopt this principle and tests itself in different situations.

(*e*) **Coherence** - Another criterion to examine a theory is that it should have a coherence or elegance. It should answer the question that does the theory "feel" right? For this, Occam's Razor Principle may be applied, it says that if you have two competing ides to explain the same phenomenon, you should prefer the simpler one, ruling out excessively or unnecessarily complicated theories. The Theory of Responsibility has been dwelt upon simplicity in its approach and flow of ideas.

Limitations

The theory provides the recommendations for adopting ethical behaviour but fails to elaborate the ethical behaviour in individual will be applied?

Future Directions

In the management and social sciences, whether all of abovementioned criterion are essential to be tested may be a matter of debate. However, together they describe the common characteristics of typical theories. Considering all these facts we see that the 'New Theory of Responsibility' fits in its own being as a theory and can be accepted worldwide as a revolutionary step.

1.5 ESG Integration Models

The concepts are derived from the theories, model representation of theories and concepts gives a pragmatic understanding on the essence and acceptability of the concepts either in practice or with futuristic approach. Since the ESG is a comparatively new phenomena, earlier discussions on the subject were on the term 'Sustainability' and 'Corporate Social Responsibility (CSR)' etc.

In this section various models propounded by some of the prominent thinkers have been presented and analysed and a new 'Solar System Model of ESG' has been presented after the analysis.

The term 'social' in the Corporate Social Responsibility, as global concept, takes into account environmental, economic and governance aspects also apart from social. Hence, for the purpose of analysis in this section, the meaning of term CSR is in its global sense and not as per CSR definition given by the Companies Act, 2013 in India.

Before we go depth into understanding different ESG-CSR-Sustainability Models, let's understand what a Model is and what are key characteristics or components of a model?

What a model is?

Models are simplified representation of a fact, reality or any situation. We construct a model to conceptualize a system, chalk out problems and issues and prioritize it, suggest a strategy for interventions and finally widely implemented after evaluating the performance.

Models are classified based on the specific purpose and sustainable development based models are broadly study into quantitative models, pictorial visualization, conceptual, standardizing and physical models.

1.5.1 Carroll's Model

Carroll's Pyramid Model was introduced first in the year 1991. Four key responsibilities of business and their hierarchy were explained in this model. These four responsibilities were Economic, Legal, Ethical and Philanthropic. The model is in a pyramid shape having various responsibilities from bottom to top aligned in order of importance. These responsibilities have also been linked with the expectations by society and other stakeholders and also actions required by business to fulfil these (Schwartz & Carroll, 2003). The graphical presentation of the Carroll's Pyramid Model as cited in Masoud (2017) is as under:

Figure 1.2: Carroll's Pyramid Model

Figure 1.3: Carroll's Modified Classic Pyramid Model

Carroll, in his model, kept various responsibilities in hierarchical order of importance. The economic responsibility was kept at the core of the business pyramid explaining that "profit making is the core responsibility for a business to survive and it is foundation for all other responsibilities" (Schwartz & Carroll, 2003). Carroll has kept Legal, Ethical and Philanthropic responsibilities of the business respectively in an order of less importance. (Atrey, 2020)

Carroll's Modified Classic Pyramid Model is based on certain additional considerations and explanations on various responsibilities of business. "In due course of time, Carroll revisited his pyramid model and carried out changes in the earlier model's description. Carroll has come up with a modified Classic Pyramid Model after bringing out following changes in the earlier version of Pyramid Model" (Atrey, 2020):

> Carroll changed the term 'Foundation for all Other Responsibilities' to 'Required by the Society' under the economic responsibilities of business. Under the description of legal responsibilities, the term 'Play by the rules of Game Right' was changed with 'Required by the Society'. Further, narration of 'Obligation to do what is right' was changed with 'Expected by Society' under the ethical responsibilities. In the Philanthropic Responsibility, 'To improve Quality of Life' was replaced with 'Desired by the Society'. He also described the term 'Be Ethical' as 'Do what is just and fair; avoid harm'.

1.5.2 Visser's Pyramid Model

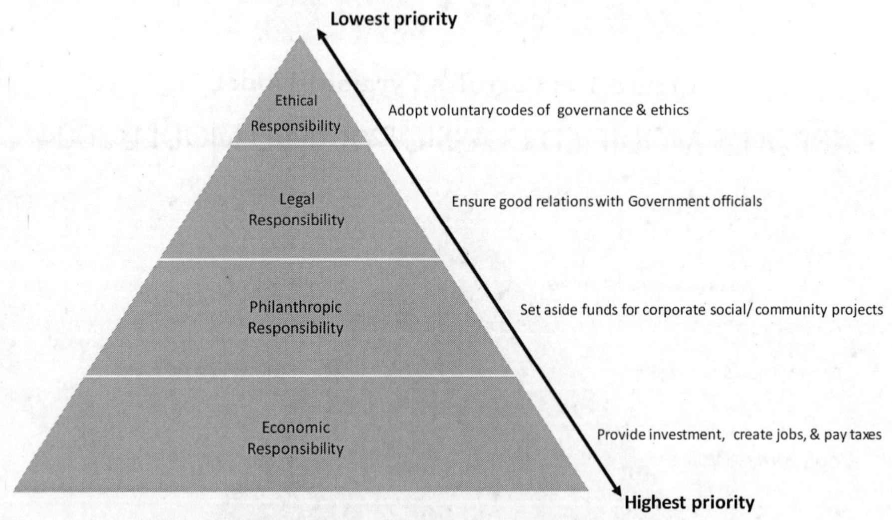

Figure 1.4 : Visser's Pyramid Model of CSR

Visser's Pyramid Model of CSR (as cited in Masoud, 2017) is also based on a Pyramid. Various responsibilities of business have been arranged in the order of priority in this model also. In this model, economic responsibility has been given highest priority and ethical responsibility at the lowest. The graphical presentation of the model is given in Figure 1.4.

While comparing the Visser's Pyramid Model with the Carroll's Model, the major changes observed are change of order of responsibilities such as the philanthropic responsibility in Visser's model has been placed next to the economic responsibility, whereas in the Carroll's model philanthropic responsibility was at the least priority for businesses.

1.5.3 International Pyramid Model

Masoud (2017) has propounded the International Pyramid Model of CSR. This model is also a pyramid shape model based on prioritisation of responsibilities of business. This model, contrary to Visser's model once again places the philanthropic responsibility at the lowest priority for business. The graphical presentation of the model is given as under (Masoud, 2017):

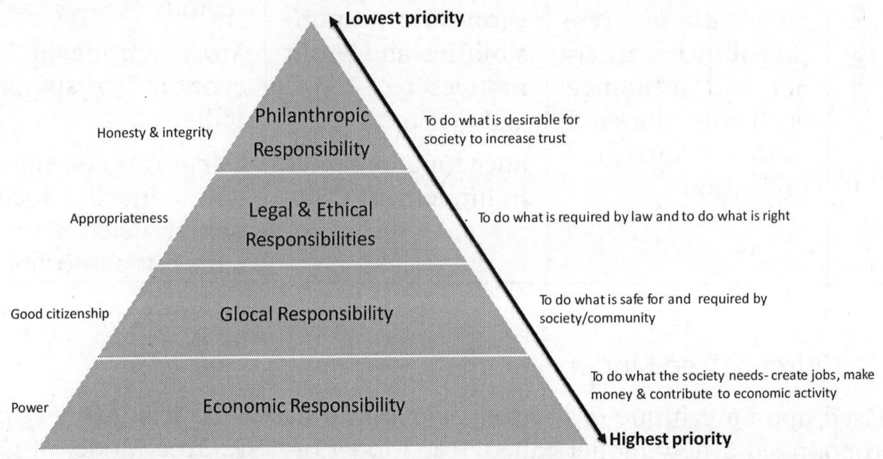

Figure 1.5: International Pyramid Model of CSR

The International Pyramid Model not only differs in the arrangement of priorities in the pyramid but also description of expectations and obligations of the businesses have been slightly different if compared with the earlier models. A new layer of glocal responsibilities has also been presented in this model (Atrey, 2020).

1.5.4 Analysis of Three Pyramid Models

A comparative analysis of three pyramid models on CSR *viz*. Carroll's Model, Visser's Model and International Model in terms of their merits and demerits has been done by Atrey (2020) as under:

Table : Analysis of three Pyramid Models on CSR

	Carroll's Model	Visser's Model	International Model
Merits	Established Modern CSR Concept	Focus on developing countries	Glocal drivers of CSR Power Structure in Society Legal and Ethical responsibilities as drivers of CSR
Demerits	Generated within the United States of America Global applicability is challengeable How different responsibilities interact and influence each other does not address cultural obligation	Tested in African countries Less Pressure of Good Conduct More emphasis on economic responsibilities and profit motives No practical guidance for companies to implement CSR	No comparative empirical study has been conducted. Order of layers may differ in different regions More emphasis on economic responsibility Corporate competitive context - focus not on society's problems but on profits

(Source: Atrey, 2020)

1.5.5 Atrey's Tree Model

Based upon a critique of the earlier pyramid-based models, Atrey (2020) propounded a new model called Tree Model of CSR. Tree Model of CSR consists of elements required for a tree to grow like Soil of available Natural and Physical Resources, Resources needed to grow, Roots, Timber, Branches, Fruits and Seeds. A description of the tree, its various components, their functions and inter-connections are presented as under (Atrey, 2020):

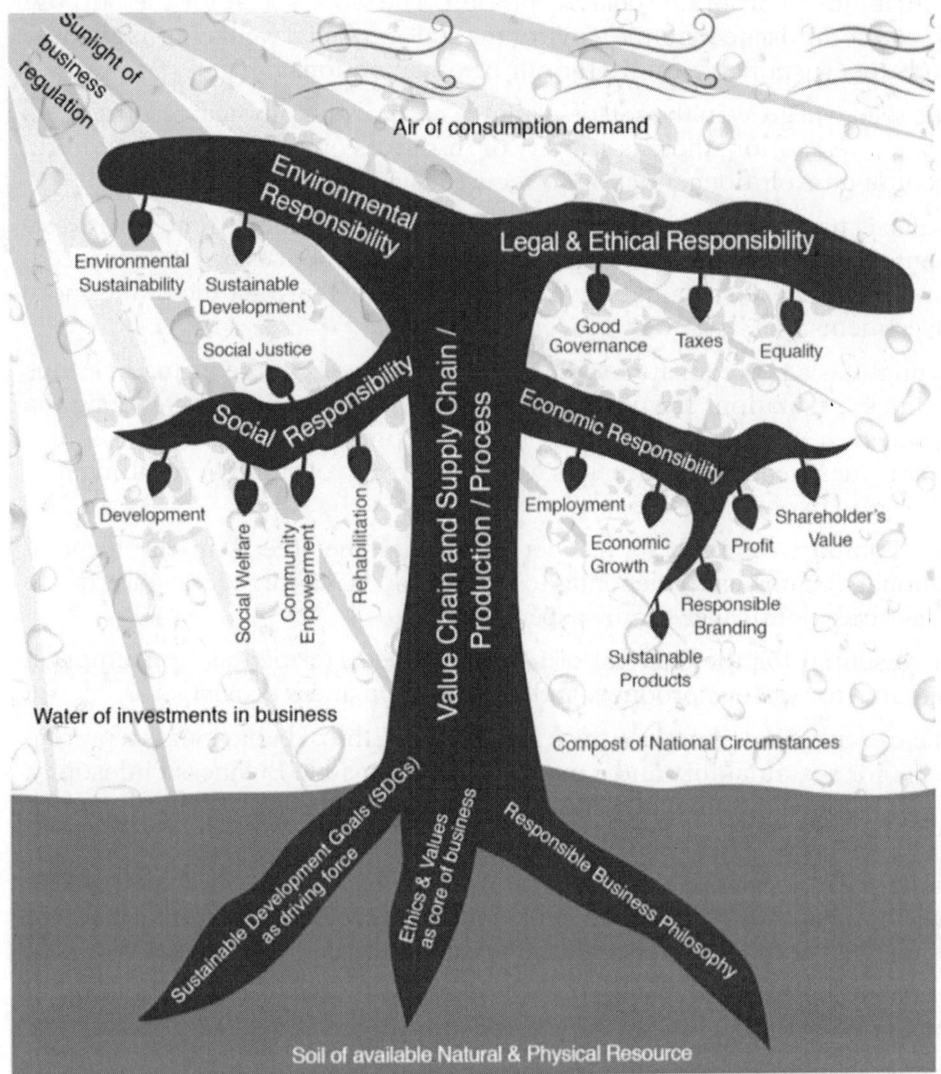

(Source: Atrey, Exploring Corporate Social Responsibility - Fundamentals and Implementation Ed. II, 2020)

Figure 1.6: Atrey's Tree Model

Seed for the tree will be comprised of economic, environmental and social sustainability. The seed is termed as 'Corporate Social Revolution'. It is called corporate social revolution because when the fruits on the tree will grow and will be utilised, these will leave sustainable footprints for future generations. Each seed will grow again in its respective sphere and will contribute to corporate social revolution. The word social for the purpose of seed comprises economic, environmental and social wellbeing as all these leads to a sustainable future for our next generations.

The seed will grow in the soil of available natural and physical resources. As a perceived notion, there is scarcity of resources on earth, it poses requirement of a revolutionary action to secure a sustainable future.

Water is in the form of investments in businesses. Global trend for investments towards businesses adopting sustainable practices has been noticed. An eco-system of sustainability for businesses will attract more and more investments.

Sunlight as a prerequisite for the growth of a tree is in the form of various business regulations from the Government. The direct relation among the business growth and regulations has been presented, *i.e.*, more complex the business regulations are, less will be the reach of sunlight resulting into poor growth of the business.

The compost required for proper growth of the tree is in the form of national circumstances denoting to the socio-cultural practices, governance structures, political economy aspects, etc.

Air essential for the survival of a tree has been termed as 'consumption demand' for various products and services a business provides.

The tree is enrooted in the Ethics and Values. Ethical behaviour is a prerequisite for sustainability and a motive for Responsible Business Philosophy. Sustainable Development Goals (SDGs) also work as a driving force for alignment of business activities with sustainability.

Value chain and supply chain of a business based on ethics, sustainable development and responsible behaviour are termed as timber of the tree which will be reflected through the manufacturing or service delivery.

Branches of the tree have been symbolised with various responsibilities of the businesses including social, economic, environmental, legal, ethical, etc.

Fruits, which the tree will produce, are symbolised with Economic Sustainability, Profit, Economic Growth, Shareholders' Value, Sustainable Products, Responsible Branding, Employment Creation, Good Governance, Contribution to Taxes, Equality, Social Sustainability, Social Justice, Social Development, Social Welfare, Community Empowerment, Rehabilitation, Environmental Sustainability, Sustainable Development, etc.

The responsibilities of business were presented as layers of importance for businesses in earlier pyramid-based models of CSR. In the tree model, these responsibilities have equal weightage with driving their roots from ethics/ values—Sustainable Development and Responsible Behaviour.

This model is ethical and value driven model of CSR. Responsible behaviour of the companies is attributed at each step of business activity. There is no emphasis on more or less importance of different layers as given in earlier models, all layers / aspects of business are equally important in this model. The model also aligns CSR with SDGs and initiates Corporate Social Revolution.

It is to be noted that here the term CSR denotes its attributes in global context where the CSR is used interchangeably with Sustainability and ESG. The Term Social in CSR from a global perspective incorporates environmental, economic, governance and other such aspects also.

1.5.6 Three Pillar Model of Sustainability

Sustainable Development is considered as the new paradigm of development. Sustainable Development consists of three key aspects namely Economic, Social and Environmental. These three aspects are also called 'Three Pillars Sustainability' or 'Three Dimensions of Sustainability' or 'Three Circles Model of Sustainability'. It is based on basic aspects of human society, but does not explicitly take into account 'human quality of life'. The environmental factor focuses on sustainable business processes, the societal factor on stakeholder and employee relations and the economic factor on the business's bottom line. Together, these three intertwined forms of sustainability enable businesses to take proactive, solutions-oriented approaches to complicated supply chain and procurement processes.

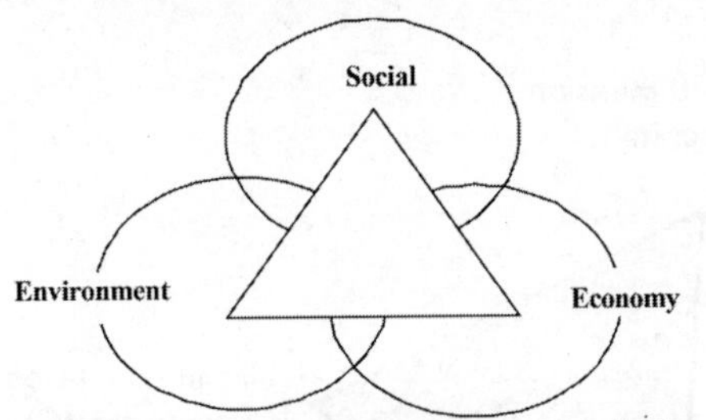

Figure 1.7 : Three Pillar Model of Sustainability

1.5.7 The Capital Stock Model of World Bank

The 'Capital Stock Model' (World Bank, 1994) expresses that "if we live only off the interest and not the capital, the basis of prosperity is maintained - however, if we consume the substance, our means of existence is endangered in the long term". It talks about ecological capital (the planning process includes biodiversity, landscape, mineral resources, clean air and healthy water) and Human and social capital (equates to health, social security, social cohesion, freedom, justice, equality of opportunity and peace).

The model proposed the following equation:

Capital Stock of Sustainable Development (CSD) = Capital Stock of the Environment (CEn) + Capital Stock of the Economy (CEc) + Capital Stock of the Society (CS).

1.5.8 The Prism Model of Stenberg

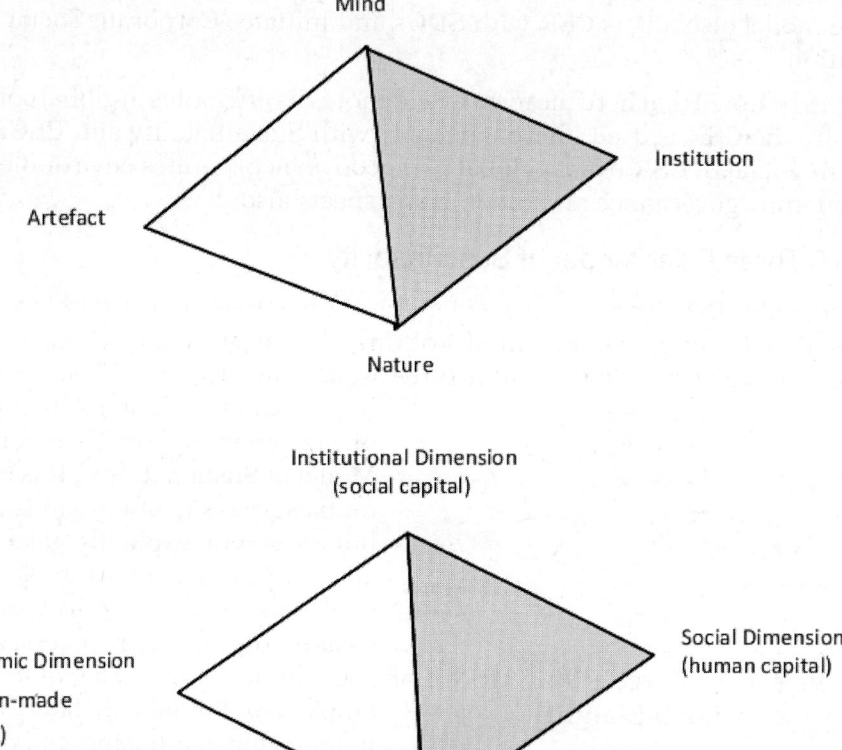

Figure 1.8: Prison Model

Stenberg (2001) proposed prisms models of sustainable development. The prism stipulates four dimensions *viz.* economic dimension (man-made capital), environmental dimension (natural capital), and social dimension (human capital) as the base for institutional dimension (social capital). Two versions of the prism model. *(Source: Stenberg (2001).*

1.5.9 The Egg Model (The Egg of Sustainability) by IUCN

The International Development Research Centre (IDRC, 1997) proposes the 'egg of sustainability' which originally designed in 1994 by the International Union for the Conservation of Nature (IUCN).

The egg of sustainability illustrates the relationship between people and ecosystem as one circle inside another, like the yolk of an egg. This implies that people are within the ecosystem, and that ultimately one is entirely dependent upon the other.

Hypothesis of IUCN:

Sustainable development = human wellbeing + ecosystem well being

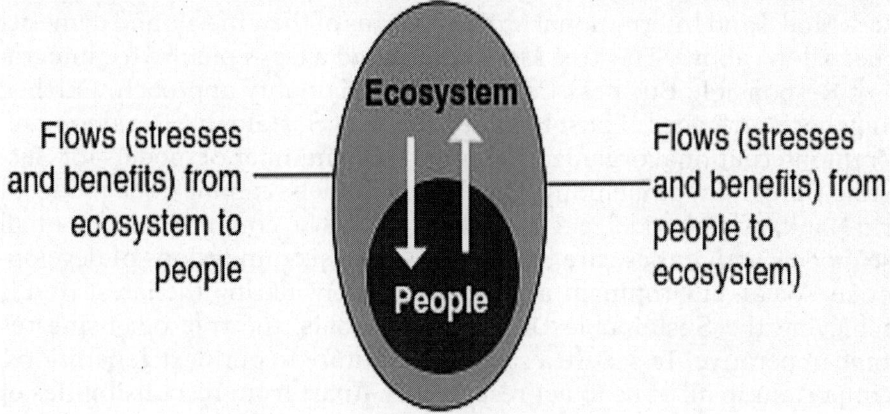

Figure 1.9: Egg Model

Social and economic development can only take place if the environment offers the necessary resources: raw materials, space for new production sites and jobs, constitutional qualities (recreation, health, etc.). Ecosystem is therefore to be regarded as a super-ordinated system to the other dimensions of the triangle or prism models: social, economic and institutional. These latter can only prosper if they adapt themselves to the limits of environmental carrying capacity.

As with any equation, the above hypothesis of IUCN appears to be too simple. It implies that the environment is not the super ordinate system, because it allows that sustainable development can occur if human well-being goes up more than ecosystem well-being falls. Thus, the equation does not show that humanity's wellbeing depends on ecosystem well-being and sustainable development as a whole.

There are three significant components of sustainable development *i.e.* economic, ecological and socio-cultural. They have a strong cyclic connection.

A sustainable economy requires a good ecological resilience or capacity for recovery where the socio-cultural domain bridges the two, people usually forget. Thus, most definitions refer to the viability of natural resources and ecosystems over time, and to maintenance of human living standards and economic growth.

It is also learnt that, after globalization, we the human created a second nature called human made material world which is as important as the old natural world. This second nature is threatening the planet's nature by affecting economy, society and the environment.

1.5.10 Summarising the previous Models

A comparative analysis of three pyramid models on CSR *viz.* Carroll's Model, Visser's Model and International Model in terms of their merits and demerits has been done above. The Tree Model presented a fresh picture for integration of Responsible Business Conduct with originality approach. Further, during the few decades of post Brundtland era of Sustainable Development, different international organization proposed a number of models for Sustainable Development including three pillar models, capital stock model of World Bank, prism model, egg model of IUCN. The common feature of all these models is that these are based on three basic dimensions of development *i.e.* social, environment and economy. Considering the latest trends in achieving the Sustainable Development Goals, the role of businesses become imperative. To secure a sustainable future to our next generations, it is important to all of us to act responsibly. Apart from responsibilities of the Governments and the Individuals, the Responsible Business Conduct is also seen as a major contributor. A new thinking towards adoption of responsible behaviour has been presented by the authors in a new model of ESG, 'The Solar System Model of ESG'.

1.5.11 New Solar System Model of ESG

As the Environmental-Social-Governance (ESG) is a recent phenomenon, direct theories on it are found rarely in the literature. We observe that models on various responsibilities of businesses have been described above which also denotes corporate initiatives in sustainability or ESG space. To be more precise on ESG integration in businesses the authors (Dadhich & Atrey) have propounded a new solar system model of ESG which is presented as under:

Model Assumptions

For the purpose of this model, we assume that:

(*i*) We consider the Business as a Solar System.

(*ii*) In the solar system the planets are at appropriate distance from each other so as to maintain the astronomical equilibrium.

(*iii*) Planets in this solar system are - Employees, Community, Consumers, Investors, Regulators, Value Chain, etc.

(*iv*) We consider Sun as Business Environment.

(*v*) ESG is considered as the Gravitational Force.

(*vi*) We can interchangeably use the terms solar-system and the universe for the ease of discussion.

The Rationale

Aspects of businesses are interconnected and balanced as a solar system. The Solar system *i.e.* Businesses are surviving only as a result of following the rules of the solar system. Gravity plays an important role in defining the rules or law of solar system.

The Gravitational Force is ESG

The model is based on the assumption that the entire gamut of Business is connected as a solar system and the gravitational force which is enduring the business is 'ESG'. This is 'ESG' due to which all components of the Business Ecosystem (referred as solar system) are balanced. The model has its key focuses on the assumption that 'profit first' approach of business should be altered with the 'people first' approach of the business.

The ESG Way of Doing Business

As the theory of 'New Age of Responsibility' has been propounded by the authors earlier in this chapter, which guides the businesses to be responsible in their actions, here the attempt has been made to establish an irrefutable connection between the Business and ESG in the same context of responsibility.

The Universal Twin Flame Connection of Business & ESG

The universe witnesses not only material aspects but the invisible energies behind the material aspects also. If we try to see scientifically also, we find that E = mc2, equation in German-born physicist Albert Einstein's theory of special relativity that expresses the fact that mass and energy are the same physical entity and can be changed into each other.

We all know that the universe is made of Atoms. Looking at construct of an Atom, an electron is either a wave or a particle in terms of possibility. The agency of transforming possibility into actuality is consciousness. At the core of consciousness - Purpose and Profit are two parts of the electron. Based on these assumptions, the electrons of consciousness at both the levels, the universal consciousness and individual consciousness, are divided into two parts, the Purpose and Profit while we describe the model. In this Atom, Proton is ESG, Neutron is Investment, and Electron is comprised of Business.

Gravity v/s Atom

ESG is considered as the gravitational force in the solar system model. The planets tug on the Sun just as it tugs on the planets. The best reference frame to describe motion within the solar system is that of the barycenter - the centre of mass. This is the real point that everything in the solar system is orbiting. On the largest scales, it's only gravity that determines the motion of everything, including us, as we move through the Universe. The gravitational force tugging between two bodies depends on how massive each one is and how far apart the two lies.

It is important to understand how gravity affects atoms in the universe? Gravity affects atoms the same way it affects all other matter. Every atom creates its own gravitational field which attracts all other matter in the universe. If you put a lot of atoms together, like in a planet or a star, all of the little gravitational fields add together, creating a much stronger pull. It is governed by one simple law of General Relativity.

In the essence, it is the ESG which plays the role of gravity in a Business Solar system which creates a gravitational pull of every atom of business. So, the relativity Law of ESG to Business defines the atomic pull leading the businesses towards goals of sustainability.

Inertial Measurement Unit (IMU)

Inertial Measurement Unit (IMU), is an electronic device that measures and reports acceleration, orientation, angular rates, and other gravitational forces. Now, we may think how to we should measure the impact of gravitational force within the purview of Solar System Model of ESG? For The purpose of measuring impact of ESG on business as well as its various entities, aspects and equations, we intend to use the Key Performance Indicators (KPIs) developed based on Business Responsibility and Sustainability Reporting Framework. So, the KPIs work as IMU for measuring the impact of gravity in ESG Solar system.

The Analysis

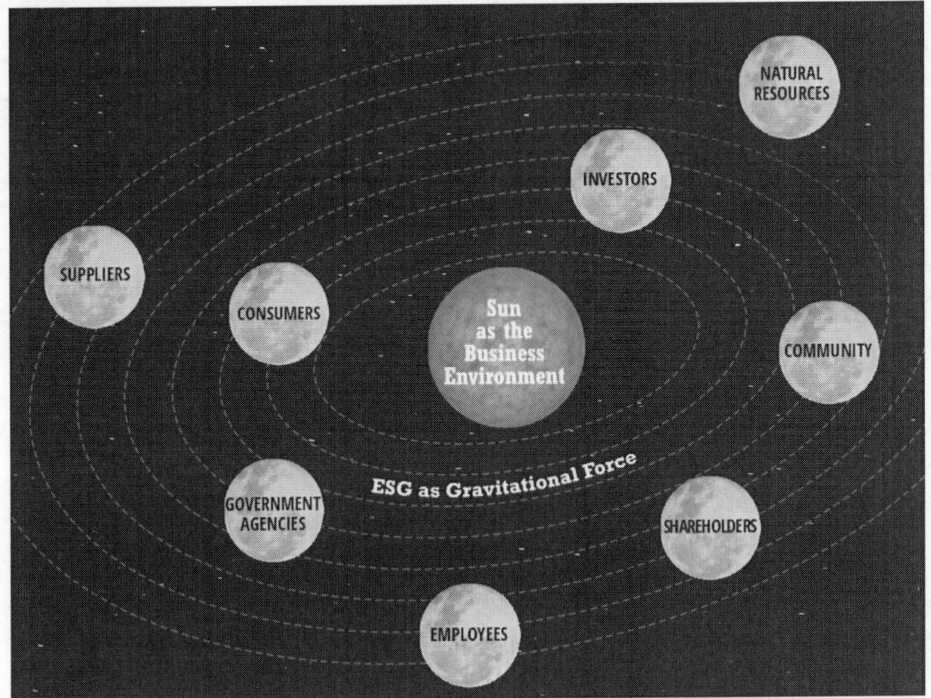

Figure 1.10: Solar System Model of ESG

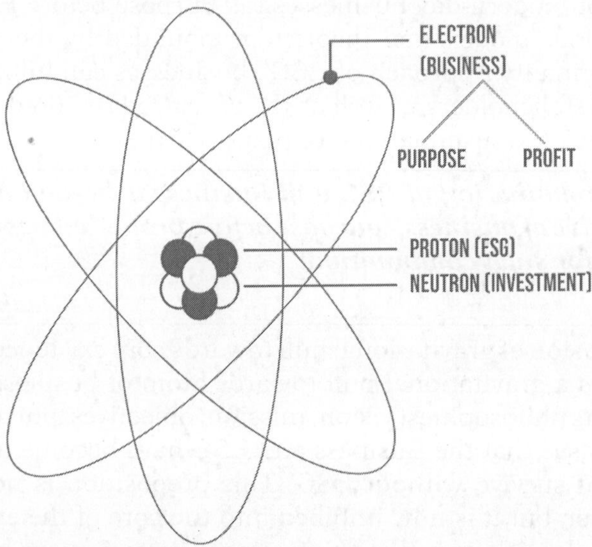

Figure 1.11: Atom of Business Ecosystem

As we all are aware that the businesses are deeply connected with the environmental, social and governance concerns, a systematised ESG preposition creates value to a business ecosystem. Here we once again come back to the discussions on the Atoms of which the universe or the solar system is made of, for the purpose of the model, we have already assumed that the Atom in the Business Solar system, looking from reverse composition of the atom, we see that an atom in the business solar system is generated from the two-dimensional conciseness that is Purpose and Profit.

Here it is important to mention that in the new age of responsibility running business as stand-alone with mere profit-making motives is not possible.

> ***"Being responsible today is not an option, it is an unwritten mandate for each one of us in the new age of responsibility."***
>
> *- Dadhich & Atrey*

Though many countries have mandated the ESG related disclosures in structured manner, in many others have such other relevant law which derive the mandate towards ESG related aspects. On an important note, it is not about the mandate by law but these days it is an unwritten mandate for businesses to be responsible towards their actions and impacts on environment and society at large. Today, not only due to pressure of law, but also an increased pressure from the investors which compel the businesses to be ethical, responsible and to adopt sustainable practices. Consumers, Communities and many such stakeholders demand the businesses to be responsible towards their actions and impact. ESG paves a way for businesses to be responsible and becomes an integral part of doing business, it is in the DNA of modern-day businesses (as Purpose before Profit). As we see in the previous models and theories propounded by the authors, following the 'Originality Approach of ESG', businesses can fulfil the desired expectations of stakeholders as well as the core need required for business existence towards the sustainability of planet earth.

> ***"Purpose of combination of ESG and Business is beyond mere profit-making objective of business, 'purpose before profits' comes an obvious phenomenon for such combination."***
>
> *- Dadhich & Atrey*

From the dimension of gravitational pull towards core existence of business the ESG creates a gravitational pull towards atom of business, defined in this context as its philosophies, vision, mission, objectives, purpose, policies etc. We thereby see that the Business and ESG have become integral part, business cannot survive without ESG. This preposition is not only seen at the outer layer, but it is now imbibed into the core of the existence of a business. That's how we say that the Business Solar System has the combination of Purpose and Profit a microest possible particles of their atoms which is the universal consciousness as described earlier in this model as an electron is either a wave or a particle in terms of possibility, the agency of transforming possibility into actuality is consciousness.

At the core of consciousness - Purpose and Profit are two parts of the electron. With this universal business consciousness, when individual businesses come into existence, they follow the same root.

Here we may measure the impact of gravity *i.e.* ESG based on the KPIs which take roots from the BRSR or NGRBC Frameworks in India or other globally recognised instruments including the indicators defined against the Sustainable Development Goals.

1.6 Summary of the Chapter

In this chapter we have studied some important definition of ESG and a new definition propounded by the authors, we had also studied global evolution of the ESG as a concept. ESG Theories section provided an overview on the key traditional as well as concurrent concepts and presents a New Theory of Responsibility propounded by the authors. This chapter also explained various models of ESG and also presented a New Solar System Model of ESG to the readers.

ESG IN INDIA

CHAPTER 2

We will study the evolution of ESG in India in this chapter, a detailed understanding on each Indian Instrument pertaining to ESG is presented while describing it in the process of evolution only. Key ESG Trends and Issues in Indian Context have also been presented. It is also pertinent to understand that when we consider evolution of ESG in Indian Context, we study among others:

- National Voluntary Guidelines on Social, Environmental, and Economic Responsibilities of Business (NVGs), 2011
- Business Responsibility Report (BRR), 2012
- National Guidelines on Responsible Business Conduct (NGRBC), 2019
- Business Responsibility and Sustainability Reporting (BRSR)
- BRSR CORE and LITE Versions.

2.1 ESG Evolution in India

The National Voluntary Guidelines on Social, Environmental, and Economic Responsibilities of Business (NVGs) were published in 2011 by the Ministry of Corporate Affairs, Government of India. It offered guidance to companies on what constituted ethical business behaviour. SEBI brought out the Business Responsibility Report (BRR) requirement in 2012 which was on disclosures on responsible business, to be done based on the NVGs. Following global developments, the NVGs were revised in 2018 in order to bring them in line with the Sustainable Development Goals (SDGs), the United Nations Guiding Principles on Business & Human Rights (UNGPs), as well as the emerging global issues. Hence, NVGs were revised and new guidelines were released namely, National Guidelines on Responsible Business Conduct (NGRBC) in 2019 following extensive stakeholder consultations. The NGBRC was developed to help companies adopt the concept of responsible behaviour beyond the requirements of regulatory compliance.

A Committee on Business Responsibility was constituted for finalising Business Responsibility Reporting formats for listed and unlisted companies. Report of this Committee recommended that BRR be updated to BRSR. Based on the NGRBC and report of the Committee on Business Responsibility Reporting, SEBI notified the BRSR format. The disclosures as per the BRSR framework were made mandatory for the top 1000 listed companies (by market capitalisation) in India from FY 2022-23, while the disclosures were voluntary for FY 2021-22 for these companies.

SEBI has also introduced the 'BRSR Lite Framework' for unlisted companies, which covers the essential aspects of ESG reporting for any kind of businesses in country. It is expected that the reporting requirement may be extended by the Ministry of Corporate Affairs to unlisted companies above a specified threshold of turnover or paid-up capital. Further, the Committee recommends that smaller unlisted companies below this threshold may, to begin with, adopt a Lite version of the format, on a voluntary basis.

The BRSR Core framework is a new regulatory framework for enhancing the ESG disclosures by India's top 1,000 listed entities. It was introduced by the Securities and Exchange Board of India (SEBI) on March 29, 2023, as a subset of the wider Business Responsibility and Sustainability Reporting (BRSR) framework that SEBI had launched in May 2021. The Gazetted notification came on 12 July 2023 and it prescribes the disclosure and assurance requirements for BRSR Core ESG disclosures for value chain, and assurance requirements. Now listed companies are also expected to mandatorily undertake Reasonable Assurance of BRSR Core, it has been notified that 150 top companies will undertake in FY 23-24, 250 in 24-25, 500 in 25-26 and 1000 in FY 26-27.

Table : Evolution of Business Responsibility Frameworks in India

Year	Initiative
2007	Ten Points Charter by the Hon'ble Prime Minister;
2009	Voluntary Corporate Social Responsibility Guidelines;
2011	Endorsement of United Nations Guiding Principles on Business & Human Rights by India;
2011	Ministry of Corporate Affairs issued National Voluntary Guidelines (NVGs) on Social, Environmental and Economic Responsibilities of Business;
2012	SEBI mandates top 100 listed companies by market capitalization to file Business Responsibility Reports (BRR) based on NVGs;
2014	Introduction of the CSR Provisions in the Companies Act, 2013;
2015	SEBI extends BRR reporting to top 500 companies by market capitalization;
2019	Ministry of Corporate Affairs released the National Guidelines on Responsible Business Conduct (NGRBC).

Figure 2.1: ESG Evolution in India

2.1.1 Ten Point Charter

In May 2007, the then Prime Minister of India, Shri Manmohan Singh, proposed a Ten Point Charter for Business that included: the inclusive employment and humane treatment of workers, investments in communities, ethical practices in all business dealings, investments in environment-friendly practices and technology, promotion of socially-responsible media and advertising, responsible consumption, and promotion of enterprise and innovation. This was in response to contemporary media and civil society reports of high-profile cases of social, environmental and economic violations by businesses and the resultant negative impacts on different stakeholders and on economic activity. At the same time, business needed to positively contribute more actively to the national goals of inclusive growth and sustainable development.

2.1.2 Voluntary Corporate Social Responsibility Guidelines

All the issues in ten point's charter remained relevant and found place in the voluntary Corporate Social Responsibility Guidelines-released by the Ministry of Corporate Affairs in 2009. The guideline, in its preamble, outlines the context, state that the 21st century is characterised by unprecedented challenges and opportunities arising from globalisation, including the desire for inclusive growth and the imperatives of climate change. The guidelines comprise six core elements:

(*a*) Care for all stakeholders

(*b*) Ethical business practice

(*c*) Respect for Worker's Rights and Welfare

(*d*) Respect for Human Rights

(*e*) Respect for the Environment

(*f*) Activities for Social and Inclusive Development.

Guidelines Drafting Committee

Based upon stakeholder feedback for a more comprehensive guideline, the Indian Institute of Corporate Affairs (IICA) was tasked by the Ministry of Corporate Affairs to undertake the process of 'review and elaboration' of the Guidelines, and a multi-stakeholder Guidelines Drafting Committee (GDC) was constituted in 2009, its mandate was as under:

(*a*) To formulate a draft framework guideline for social, environmental responsibilities of business, which would be offered to enterprises for voluntary adoption with wide applicability across all enterprises, irrespective of their size, and that the guidelines serve to ultimately enhance the performance of business.

(*b*) To specifically ensure that the framework addresses the concerns of Inclusive Growth and Sustainability.

Further, the GDC was encouraged to 'draw insights from good-practices and international norms and frameworks, as well as from national resources in as much as they help to address Indian particularities. In particular, the GDC took cognizance of key international and national resources focussing on business responsibility and sustainability issues which included:

(*a*) The International Standards Organisation (ISO)'s Corporate Social Responsibility Guideline (ISO 26000), as an example of a voluntary, holistic and certifiable standard

(*b*) The UN Global Compact, as an example of a UN-sponsored voluntary code for companies

(*c*) The OECD Guidelines for Multinational Enterprises, as an example of State-sponsored and supported initiative

(*d*) The Global Reporting Initiative (GRI), as an example of a holistic voluntary disclosure and reporting framework for companies

(*e*) Bureau of Indian Standards (BIS): IS 16000, as an example of a domestic workplace standard

(*f*) Department of Public Enterprises- CSR & (Community Development) Guidelines, as an example of state-driven guidelines for community development initiatives by companies in the public sector.

2.1.3 National Voluntary Guidelines

Ministry of Corporate Affairs released National Voluntary Guidelines (NVGs) on Social, Environmental and Economic Responsibilities of Business in 2011. NVGs comprise inter-related and inter-connected Nine Principles. Each of the nine Principles is explained through a Brief Description and accompanied by attendant Core Elements. the principles can be broadly aggregated as Social (P3, P4, P5, P8 and P9) Environmental (P2, P6 or Governance (P1 and P7). The Social can be further sub-divided into stakeholder-specific principles (P3, P8 and P9) and cross-cutting ones (P4 and P5).

Principle 1: Businesses should conduct and govern themselves with Ethics, Transparency and Accountability

Principle 2: Business should provide goods and services that are safe and contribute to sustainability throughout their life cycle

Principle 3: Businesses should respect and promote the well-being of all employees

Principle 4: Businesses should respect the interests of, and be responsive towards all its stakeholders, especially those who are disadvantaged, vulnerable and marginalized

Principle 5: Businesses should respect and promote human rights

Principle 6: Businesses should respect, protect, and make efforts to protect and restore the environment

Principle 7: Businesses, when engaged in influencing public and regulatory policy, should do so in a responsible manner

Principle 8: Businesses should support inclusive growth and equitable development

Principle 9: Businesses should engage with and provide value to their customers and consumers in a responsible manner.

(Ministry of Corporate Affairs, 2011)

2.1.4 Business Responsibility Reporting (BRR)

Business Responsibility Report (BRR) was introduced in India as part of the Annual Reports for the top 100 listed companies based on market capitalization in 2012. The format of BRR was based on the National Voluntary Guidelines (NVGs) issued by the Ministry of Corporate Affairs. The evolution of Business Responsibility Reporting in India can be traced back to the Corporate Voluntary Guidelines in 2009 and the endorsement of United Nations Guiding Principles on Business & Human Rights by India in 2011. The Committee on Business Responsibility Reporting proposed two formats for disclosures: a comprehensive format and a Lite version is a disclosure of adoption of responsible business practices by a listed company to all its stakeholders. This report is applicable to all types of companies including manufacturing, services, etc. The report is important considering the fact that these companies have accessed funds from the public, have an element of public interest involved, and are obligated to make exhaustive disclosures on a regular basis.

2.1.5 Transition from NVGs to NGRBC

The Ministry of Corporate Affairs (MCA), Government of India, released a set of guidelines in 2011 called the National Voluntary Guidelines on the Social, Environmental and Economic Responsibilities of Business (NVGs). This was expected to provide guidance to businesses on what constitutes responsible business conduct. In order to align the NVGs with the Sustainable Development Goals (SDGs) and the 'Respect' pillar of the United Nations Guiding Principles (UNGP) the process of revision of NVGs was started in 2015. After, revision and updation, the new principles are called the National Guidelines on Responsible Business Conduct (NGRBC). As with the NVGs, the NGRBC has been designed to assist businesses to perform above and beyond the requirements of regulatory compliance.

In 2017, Ministry of Corporate Affairs took a considered view, that given the various significant international and national developments had taken place related to the business responsibility domain and since sufficient time had elapsed since the NVGs were released 2011, the NVGs should be updated to include such developments, which may include: the UNGPs, the UN SDGs, Paris Agreement on Climate Change, Ratification in 2017 of ILO Core Conventions 138 and 182 on child labour, SEBI's 2012 notification for Annual BR Reports and the Ministry of Corporate Affairs' notification in the Companies Act, 2013 mandating companies to undertake CSR among others. Emerging global risks in respect of ESG were also considered. Accordingly, the review exercises and multi-stakeholders' consultations were organized throughout the country and comments were sought from public and stakeholders. After considering due processes, the National Guidelines for Responsible Business Conduct (NGRBC) came into shape as an update/ new version to the NVGs.

The primary rationale for the update is to capture key national and international developments in the sustainable development agenda and business responsibility field that have occurred since the release of the NVGs in 2011. Some of the key drivers behind the emergence of NGRBC are listed below:

- Core Conventions 138 and 182 on Child Labour by the International Labour Organization (ILO)
- SEBI Annual Business Responsibility Reports (ABRRs)
- Section 135 of the Companies Act, 2013
- The UN Guiding Principles for Business and Human Rights (UNGPs)
- UN Sustainable Development Goals (SDGs)
- Paris Agreement on Climate Change (2015).

The NGRBC are designed to be used by all businesses, irrespective of their ownership, size, sector, structure or location. It is expected that all businesses investing or operating in India, including foreign multinational corporations (MNCs) will follow these guidelines. Furthermore, the NGRBC reiterate the need to encourage businesses to ensure that not only do they follow these guidelines in business contexts directly within their control or influence, but that they also encourage and support their suppliers, vendors, distributors, partners and other collaborators to follow them.

2.1.6 National Guidelines on Responsible Business Conduct (NGRBC)

Government of India launched National Voluntary Guidelines on Economic, Social and Environmental Responsibilities of Business in 2007 which were revised in 2009 and 2011. The next revision was introduced as the National Guidelines on Responsible Business Conduct of Business, replacing the earlier guidelines. (Ministry of Corporate Affairs, Govt. of India, 2018).

Nine principles for performance disclosures are:

(*a*) Ethical, Transparent and Accountable conduct

(*b*) Provide goods and services in sustainable and safe way

(*c*) Promote the well-being of all employees including those in value chain

(*d*) Respect the interests of all shareholders

(*e*) Promote human rights

(*f*) Protect and restore the environment

(*g*) Transparent engagement in public policy

(*h*) Inclusive growth and equitable development

(*i*) Provide value to their consumers responsibly

(Ministry of Corporate Affairs, 2019)

A notion about the NGRBC among the readers may be that NGRBC is a business responsibility reporting tool. No doubt that NGRBC provide a framework of reporting also but it is not its mere function. NGRBC is a step by step guide for adopting responsible business conduct by a business. The NGRBC are designed to be used by all businesses, irrespective of their ownership, size, sector, structure or location. It is expected that all businesses investing or operating in India, including foreign multinational corporations (MNCs) will follow these guidelines. Correspondingly, the NGRBC also provide a useful framework for guiding Indian MNCs in their overseas operations, in addition to aligning with applicable local national standards and norms governing responsible business conduct.

Considering the national and international developments in the domain of RBC, the nine principles of NVGs have been modified and words such as sustainable, integrity, and respect were included in NGRBCs. This highlights the MoCA commitment towards the advancement of RBC. While NVGs had 48 Core Elements in the updated NGRBC there are 53 Core Elements.

2.1.7 Changes between NVG & NGRBC

An overview of modifications is presented in the table below:

	NGRBC 2019	NVG 2011
1.	Businesses should conduct and govern themselves with integrity in a manner that is ethical, transparent and accountable	Businesses should conduct and govern themselves with Ethics, Transparency and Accountability

	NGRBC 2019	NVG 2011
2.	Businesses should provide goods and services in a manner that is sustainable and safe	Businesses should provide goods and services that are safe and contribute to sustainability throughout their life cycle
3.	Businesses should respect and promote the well-being of all employees, including those in the value chain	Businesses should promote the well being of all employees
4.	Businesses should respect the interests of and be responsive to all its stakeholders	Businesses should respect the interests of, and be responsive towards all stakeholders, especially those who are disadvantaged, vulnerable and marginalised
5.	Businesses should respect and promote human rights	Businesses should respect and promote human rights
6.	Businesses should respect and make efforts to protect and restore the environment	Business should respect, protect, and make efforts to restore the environment
7.	Businesses, when engaging in influencing public and regulatory policy, should do so in a manner that is responsible and transparent	Businesses, when engaged in influencing public and regulatory policy, should do so in a responsible manner
8.	Businesses should promote inclusive growth and equitable development	Businesses should support inclusive growth and equitable development
9.	Businesses should engage with and provide value to their consumers in a responsible manner	Businesses should engage with and provide value to their customers and consumers in a responsible manner

The NGRBC are the framework that companies can use to integrate RBC practices into their operations and strategy in order to keep pace with the rapidly changing business environment and thrive in the uncertain world we live in.

2.1.8 Key Features of NGRBC

- The NGRBC consist of two chapters and an expanded set of annexures*
- NGRBC Principles have been updated, but they have retained the articulation and description of NVGs.

- More emphasis on Core elements of the principles
- Practical guidance to businesses to adopt NGRBC
- Practical guidance on implementation of NGRBC
- Business case for MSMEs has been given
- Updated Business Responsibility Reporting (BRR) Framework
- Serves as a tool for the companies to assess company's initiatives towards responsible business conduct
- Serves as tool to identify opportunities to improve responsible business conduct
- Serves as a framework for regulators to develop disclosure formats.

*The Guidance has following annexure:

- Guidance on adoption of NGRBC
- Guidance for Micro, Small and Medium Enterprises
- Business Responsibility Reporting Framework
- SDGs mapped against NGRBC
- Business Case Matrix
- Guidance for businesses on using BRRF as a self-assessment tool
- Indicative Mapping of Indian Laws and Principles against NGRBC
- Resources and reference list.

2.1.9 Nine Principles of NGRBC

Principle 1 - Businesses Should Conduct and Govern Themselves with Integrity, and in a Manner that is Ethical, Transparent and Accountable

This Principle recognizes that ethical behaviour in all operations, functions and processes, is the cornerstone of businesses guiding their governance of economic, social and environmental responsibilities. The Principle emphasizes that disclosures on business decisions and actions that impact stakeholders form the fundamental basis of operationalizing responsible business conduct and should be accessible to all relevant stakeholders. It recognizes that businesses are an integral part of society and that they will hold themselves accountable for the effective adoption, implementation, and the making of disclosures on their performance with respect to the Core Elements of these Guidelines. The Principle further emphasizes that the governance structure of the business should ensure this, in line with SDG 16 *i.e.* peace, justice, strong institutions. Essential indicators of this principle are based on awareness generation in the value chain and among multi-stakeholders, complaints arise, their disposal and unmet fiscal and social obligations. The leadership indicators support in disclosures and disseminating the disclosures.

Principle 2 - Businesses should provide goods and services in a manner that is sustainable and safe

This Principle recognizes the proposition of SDG 12, that sustainable production and consumption are interrelated, contribute to enhancing the quality of life and towards protecting and preserving earth's natural resources. The Principle further emphasizes that businesses should focus on safety and resource-efficiency in the design and manufacture of their products, and use their products in a manner that creates value while minimizing and mitigating its adverse impacts on the environment and society through all stages of its life cycle, from design to final disposal. Over time, businesses should embrace the idea of circularity in all its operations. In order to do so, the Principle encourages businesses to understand all material sustainability issues across their product life cycle and value chain. The performance disclosure indicators for this principle includes goods and services incorporating environmental and social concerns, risks and opportunities, investment, raw material and processes adopted and impact of products across value chains.

Principle 3 - Businesses should respect and promote the well-being of all employees, including those in their value chains

This Principle encompasses all policies and practices relating to the equity, dignity and well-being, and provision of decent work (as indicated in SDG 8), of all employees engaged within a business or in its value chain, without any discrimination and in a way that promotes diversity. The principle recognizes that the well-being of an employee also includes the well being of her/his family. Some of the Disclosure indicators under this principle are - complaints received and resolved, status of the employee associations, child and forced labour in value chains, wages and wage ratio, harassment and safety at workplace, skill upgradation of employees among others.

Principle 4 - Businesses should respect the interests of and be responsive to all its stakeholders

This Principle recognizes that businesses operate in an eco-system comprising a number of stakeholders, beyond shareholders and investors, and that their activities impact natural resources, habitats, communities and the environment. The Principle acknowledges that it is the responsibility of businesses to ensure that the interests of all stakeholders, especially those who may be vulnerable and marginalized, are protected. The Principle further recognizes that businesses have a responsibility to maximize the positive impacts and minimize and mitigate the adverse impacts of its products, operations, and practices on all their stakeholders. Essential disclosure indicators are related to the list of stakeholder groups, processes, local engagements, frequency of engagement, marginalized groups etc.

Principle 5 - Businesses should respect and promote human rights

This Principle recognizes that human rights are rights inherent to all human beings, and that everyone, individually or collectively, is entitled to these rights, without discrimination. It further recognizes that human rights are inherent, inalienable, interrelated, interdependent and indivisible. The Principle is inspired, informed and guided by the Constitution of India and the International Bill of Rights and recognizes the primacy of the State's duty to protect and fulfil human rights. The Principle is further informed and guided by the UN Guiding Principles on Business and Human Rights in its articulation of the responsibility of businesses to respect human rights. It affirms that the responsibility of businesses to respect human rights requires that it avoids causing or contributing to adverse human rights impacts, and that it addresses such impacts when they occur. The Principle urges businesses to be especially responsive to such persons, individually or collectively, who are most vulnerable to, or at risk of, such adverse human rights impacts. Some of the indicators in reporting under this principle are - training on human rights, human rights policies and their coverage, stakeholders groups for reporting human rights violations, corrective actions, human rights due diligence etc.

Principle 6 - Businesses should respect and make efforts to protect and restore the environment

This Principle recognizes that environmental responsibility is a prerequisite for sustainable economic growth and for the well-being of society. The Principle emphasizes that environmental issues are interconnected at the local, regional and global levels, which makes it imperative for businesses to address issues like pollution, biodiversity conservation, sustainable use of natural resources and climate change (mitigation, adaptation and resilience) in a just, comprehensive and systematic manner. These are aligned with SDGs 11, 13, 14 and 15. The Principle encourages businesses to assess environment impacts of its products and operations and take steps to minimize and mitigate its adverse impacts where these cannot be avoided. The Principle encourages businesses to adopt environmental practices and processes that minimize or eliminate the adverse impacts of its operations and across the value chain. The Principle encourages businesses to follow the Precautionary Principle in all its actions. Essential disclosure indicators for the principle are - potential risks on environment and good practices in reuse, recycling and reduction the risks, collective action, specific contribution, and creation of new business product/service etc.

Principle 7 - Businesses, when engaging in influencing public and regulatory policy, should do so in a manner that is responsible and transparent

This Principle recognizes that businesses operate within specified national and international legislative and policy frameworks, which guide their growth and also provide for certain desirable restrictions and boundaries. The Principle recognizes the legitimacy of businesses to engage with governments for redressal of a grievance or for influencing public policy. The Principle emphasizes that public policy advocacy must expand public good. Disclosures related to the affiliations with trade bodies, industry associations, political parties, monetary contributions, public policy advocacy positions, and corrective actions related indicators are done.

Principle 8 - Businesses should promote inclusive growth and equitable development

This Principle recognizes the challenges of social and economic development faced by India, and builds upon the national and local development agenda as articulated in government policies and priorities. This is particularly significant in zones affected by social disharmony and low human development. The Principle recognizes the value of the energy and enterprise of businesses and encourages them to innovate and contribute to the overall development of the country with a specific focus on disadvantaged, vulnerable and marginalized communities, as articulated in Section 135 of the Companies Act, 2013. The Principle also emphasizes the need for collaboration amongst businesses, government agencies and civil society in furthering this development agenda in line with SDG 17. The Principle reiterates that business success, inclusive growth and equitable development are interdependent. Disclosure indicators are - social impact of business operations, contribution to vulnerable and marginalized sections of society, relations with local communities, CSR interventions as per the Companies Act, 2013, etc.

Principle 9 - Businesses should engage with and provide value to their consumers in a responsible manner

This Principle is based on the fact that the basic aim of a business entity is to provide goods and services to its consumers that are safe to use, and in a manner that creates value for both. The Principle recognizes that consumers have the freedom of choice in the selection and usage of goods and services, and that the enterprises will strive to make available products that are safe, competitively priced, easy to use and safe to dispose of, for the benefit of their consumers. The Principle also recognizes that businesses should play a key role, along with other relevant stakeholders, in mitigating the adverse impacts that excessive consumption of its products may have on the overall well-being of individuals, society and our planet, in line with SDG 12. Some of the disclosure indicators are - adverse impact of goods or service in public domain, consumer complaints, advertising, delivery, corrective actions, international/national product label and certifications, etc.

2.1.10 Business Case of NGRBC

NGRBC serves as a tool and framework for companies in India through which companies may navigate their journey towards sustainable and responsible business existence. It not only guides companies to align their initiatives with SDGs but also aligns with various ESG reporting prevailed worldwide.

National Guidelines on Responsible Business Conduct indicates the benefits of adopting and integrating the abovementioned principles into core business philosophy and activities. As such the benefits of adopting NGRBCs may be categorized in following points:

(*a*) Revenue growth and market access

(*b*) Cost savings and productivity

(*c*) Access to capital

(*d*) Risk Management

(*e*) Facilitation of legal compliances and licenses to operate

(*f*) Human Capital

(*g*) Brand value and reputation

Principle-wise analysis of benefits of adopting NGRBC on the above points has been presented in the table below:

Principle	Revenue growth and market access	Cost savings and productivity	Access to capital	Risk management/ license to operate	Human capital	Brand value/ reputation
1. Integrity, Ethics, transparency, accountability	New customers; Business partner of choice		Good governance practices are attractive to investors, banks, financial markets	Positively seen by communities, NGOs, local governments, regulators	Attract and retain quality employees	Positively seen by customers, regulators, media
2. Safe and sustainable goods and services	New customers; Customer loyalty	Efficiency gains in supply chain and production	Lower risk perception is attractive to investors and lenders	Reduced risk of action from regulators and consumer activists	Attract and retain quality employees	Enhanced brand value

Principle	Revenue growth and market access	Cost savings and productivity	Access to capital	Risk management/ license to operate	Human capital	Brand value/ reputation
3. Well-being of employees		Increased productivity; high morale; reduced absenteeism		Improved labour relations leading to less disruptions	Attract and retain quality employees	Employer of choice
4. Respect and responsiveness to all stakeholders	New customers; Customer loyalty	Efficiency gains across procurement, production distribution, after-sales	Good governance practices are attractive to investors and banks	Positively seen by stakeholders - communities, NGOs, governments, regulators	Attract and retain quality employees	Positively seen by customers, regulators, media
5. Respect and promote Human rights	Access to international capital and developed country markets	Enhanced productivity	Good governance practices are attractive to investors, banks, financial markets	Positively seen by communities and NGOs; Lower risk of non-compliance	Attract and retain quality employees	Positively seen by customers, regulators, media
6. Respect, protect and restore the Environment	Business partner of choice, especially for sustainability-oriented buyers	Lower operating costs in the long term; less danger of "externalities" emerging as liabilities.	Lower risk perception is attractive to investors, banks, financial markets	Positively seen by communities, NGOs, governments, regulators; Lower risk of non-compliance	Attract and retain quality employees	Positively seen by customers, regulators, media
7. Responsible and transparent policy advocacy				Positively seen by governments, regulators, NGOs		Positively seen by customers, regulators, media

Principle	Revenue growth and market access	Cost savings and productivity	Access to capital	Risk management/ license to operate	Human capital	Brand value/ reputation
8. Promote inclusive growth and equitable development	Potential for market expansion and acquisition of new customers	Lower costs of ensuring business continuity	Lower risk perception is attractive to investors and lenders	Enhanced governmental support to initiatives; improved relations with communities	Potential source of trained employees	Positively seen by customers, regulators, media
9. Provide value to consumer responsibly	New customers; Customer loyalty		Growth prospects attractive to investors	Lower risk of consumer action	Talent will be drawn towards growing firm	Customers perceive brand and firm favourably

2.1.11 SDGs mapped against NGRBC

National Guidelines on Responsible Business Conduct (NGRBC) presents the Sustainable Development Goals mapped against the NGRBC Principles. The chart as given in the NGRBC document demonstrates an indicative alignment SDGs and relevant principles of the NGRBC. With each of its nine principles mapped to the relevant SDGs, NGRBC were created to cater to the need for an India-specific guideline that meets global best practice and Indian realities.

It is pertinent to mention that the materiality assessments to ascertain various social, environmental and governance issues of businesses are conducted worldwide. The SDGs provide a useful framework for companies to undertake their materiality assessment. Using the SDGs, in conjunction with existing reporting frameworks, not only ensures completeness of the materiality exercise, but also lends credibility to the process of prioritizing sustainability actions and engaging with stakeholders.

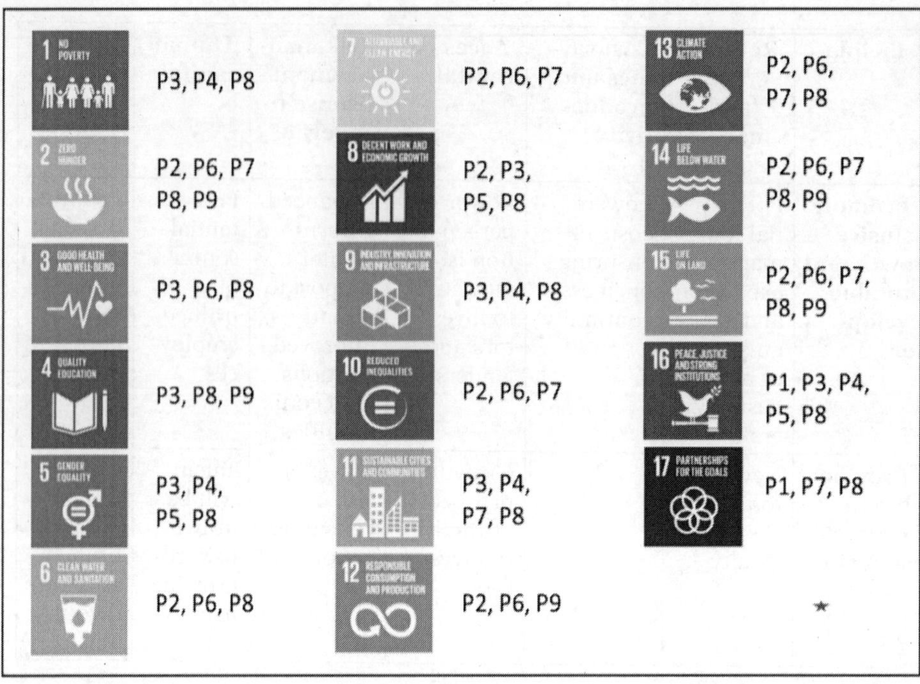

(Ministry of Corporate Affairs, 2018)

Figure 2.2: SDGs mapped against NGRBCs

2.1.12 Business Responsibility & Sustainability Reporting (BRSR)

The Committee on Business Responsibility was constituted for finalising Business Responsibility Reporting formats for listed and unlisted companies. Report of the Committee on Business Responsibility Reporting recommended that BRR be updated to BRSR. Based on the NGRBC and report of the Committee on Business Responsibility Reporting, SEBI notified the BRSR format. The disclosures as per the BRSR framework were made mandatory for the top 1000 listed companies (by market capitalisation) in India from FY 2022-23, while the disclosures were voluntary for FY 2021-22 for these companies.

India is gradually moving towards developing regulations around ESG. With the introduction of the Business Responsibility and Sustainability Report (BRSR) framework, SEBI has joined a group of countries to have released comprehensive and mandatory sustainability reporting frameworks. The BRSR framework is aligned with international reporting frameworks such as GRI, IIRC, SASB, TCFD, SDGs, etc. The BRSR is based on the mother document 'NGRBC' which was developed by Indian Institute of Corporate Affairs (IICA) for the Ministry of Corporate Affairs after long process of multi-stakeholders consultations. From the Financial Year 2023-24, SEBI has mandated the top 1000 listed companies by market capitalization to make disclosures as per BRSR framework as part of their annual report.

BRSR requires listed entities to disclose their performance on various ESG parameters, such as environmental impact, social responsibility, governance practices, cyber security, stakeholder engagement, etc. The BRSR framework is expected to enhance the transparency and accountability of businesses and enable investors and other stakeholders to make informed decisions based on ESG factors.

As Business Responsibility and Sustainability Reporting (BRSR) is now mandatory on top one thousand listed companies by market capitalization with effect from Financial Year 2022-23, this has led the corporate functioning in India to a new era of sustainability. It is also noteworthy that India became first country in the world to make Corporate Social Responsibility (CSR) mandatory by introducing amendments in the Companies Act, 2013. The efforts of the Government were praised by stakeholders as role of corporates in achieving the goals of inclusive development and to address the long pending structural social problems were seen as a revolutionary step in the country. Mandating the BRSR will be another glorious step in Indian history of corporate initiatives.

The BRSR Framework was introduced by the Government with intent to bring greater transparency through disclosure on Environment, Social and Governance (ESG) related aspects. Securities and Exchange Board of India (SEBI) came into existence to protect the interests of investors in securities and to promote the development of, and to regulate the securities market. SEBI first introduced sustainability reporting for listed companies in terms of BRR in 2012. SEBI increased the limit from 500 to 1000 companies in 2019, eligible companies (listed in recognised stock exchanges) were expected to mandatorily publish the Business Responsibility Report (BRR) as part of their annual reports for Financial Year 2019-20. A notification was released in August 2020 introducing new requirements, accordingly companies are required to prepare and submit report on ESG aspects, as per the reporting framework of BRSR. It was initially kept voluntarily for Financial Year 2021-22 and has been mandated with effect from 1st April 2022. Many challenges are envisaged in respect of the new reporting requirements from the point of view of corporates and mandating the BRSR. On the one hand responsible companies are welcoming the mandate, there are a few genuine challenges experienced by some corporate representatives.

Generally, most of the top listed companies are already complying with international frameworks such as GRI, SASB, IR etc. due to their global presence including value chains and are doing non-financial reporting. Thus, the real challenges may be identified once BRSR is applicable to other companies including SMEs. But is also pertinent to highlight that there are lot of existing statutes which independently required is closures about the environment, social and governance aspects, thus there can be some synchronisation of such reporting in BRSR. Further, BRSR puts lot of emphasis on governing body that indicates the importance of such non-financial disclosures. This highlights the dire need to sensitize and build capacity of business leaders to understand the subject in spirit which indicates the crucial role of government think-tanks such as Indian Institute of Corporate Affairs to help businesses understand and made disclosures on BRSR. There may also be a possibility in coming times about sectoral disclosures such as separate set of standards for manufacturing industry, service industry, and further classifying into other sub-sectors like FMCG, Retail, Mining, Power, Pharma, Automobile, Textile etc. Further there may be need for separate disclosures based on specific requirement of varied stakeholders.

There are certain benefits of mandating BRSR not only to the investors but to the businesses, customers, society as a whole and sustainability of the planet. Rationale behind introducing initiatives like BRSR is three dimensional, one the one hand investors want their money to be utilized in sustainable manner, on the other hand aware consumers also influence the demand and buying behaviour of sustainable products and services, thirdly it is question of survival of businesses when there will be threat to habitable planet, people will have less consumption demand and future businesses will affect adversely. Investors remain curious to know where their money is being utilized and what impact is it making? Alarming adverse affects of industrialization on sustainability of our Planet has been a key consideration before investors. Looking at the importance of the Sustainable Investments, various countries have come up with modalities to attract investors in responsible businesses. India was one of the countries who introduced the ESG reporting ahead of time. Taking the initiatives at next steps, a Task Force has also been formed by the Indian Government under the Chairmanship of Secretary, Deptt. of Economic Affairs, Ministry of Finance to layout a concrete roadmap to bolster India's sustainable Finance architecture.

Ethics and sustainability are two sides of the same coin. Can you imagine that if an individual or an organization adopts ethical practices, ethics are imbibed in the core of their thought process and philosophy, can they harm anyone or anything? Threats to the ecology, social balances, country's growth and planet's sustainability are emerged out of unethical practices, when for mere enhancing the profits, human rights are violated, natural resources are exploited, and adverse practices are adopted and many spheres of corporate functioning. Ethics as core and deep-rooted philosophy has potential to convert businesses into more ethical and sustainable entities. Businesses today also need to adopt Sustainable Development Goals as the driving force for their actions only then they will be able to practice responsible business.

It is well understood that the eco-system for businesses to operate is determined by the available natural and physical resources, national or regional circumstances and business regulations, consumption demand, type and availability of investments. The whole value chain and supply chain of businesses including the manufacturing and services delivery mechanisms affects the sustainability issues. If the businesses adopt ethics and values as core of their operations, Sustainable Development Goals as their driving force, and responsible business philosophy imbibed in their actions, businesses will be able to discharge their economic, legal, ethical, social and environmental responsibilities more effectively. It will not only result into more profits but will also ensure economic growth and sustainability, enhanced shareholders' value, more sustainable and responsible products and branding, good governance, social justice and sustainability, environmental sustainability and will ensure more sustainable development.

Ethical philosophies and principles will not only promote businesses as sustainable entities but such adoption will also result into more transparent Governance systems at national levels and more strengthened democracies. Sufferings of individuals, problems of social structures, issues in economic growth and environmental sustainability will be addressed more effectively and we will be in a better position to co-create a better world for our next generations. Commitment of the Indian Government towards strengthening the sustainability eco-system brings India at the forefront of global initiatives.

2.1.13 BRSR Lite

SEBI has also introduced the 'BRSR Lite Framework' for unlisted companies, which covers the essential aspects of ESG reporting for any kind of businesses in country. This has the Essential and Leadership category of questions, but fewer in number, and seeks information which such companies should be able to provide. The implementation of reporting requirement should be done in phases so that smaller companies have the time to adapt and learn from the larger ones. With regard to listed entities, reporting may be done by the top 1000 listed companies (by market capitalisation) as applicable presently or as prescribed by SEBI. Prior to implementing the reporting requirements for listed entities, SEBI may also adopt the due process of consultation. The reporting requirement may be extended by MCA to unlisted companies above a specified threshold of turnover or paid-up capital. Further, the Committee recommends that smaller unlisted companies below this threshold may, to begin with, adopt a Lite version of the format, on a voluntary basis.

2.1.14 BRSR Core

Further, progressing step ahead, listed companies shall mandatorily undertake Reasonable Assurance of BRSR Core gradually (150 in FY 2023-

24, 250 in 2024-25, 500 in 2025-26 and 1000 in FY 2026-27). The BRSR Core framework is a new regulatory framework for enhancing the ESG disclosures by India's top 1,000 listed entities. It was introduced by the Securities and Exchange Board of India (SEBI) on March 29, 2023, as a subset of the wider Business Responsibility and Sustainability Reporting (BRSR) framework that SEBI had launched in May 2021. The Gazetted notification came on 12 July 2023 and it prescribes the disclosure and assurance requirements for BRSR Core ESG disclosures for value chain, and assurance requirements.

- BRSR Core aims to reduce the number of ESG parameters from over 800 to less than 50, making it easier for companies to report on their ESG performance and for investors and other stakeholders to assess their ESG risks and opportunities.
- BRSR Core requires companies to disclose their ESG performance for their value chain, *i.e.*, suppliers, customers, and other business partners. SEBI has also prescribed the assurance requirements for BRSR Core and value chain disclosures, which include obtaining external assurance from an independent auditor or a qualified professional.
- BRSR Core is a subset of the BRSR Comprehensive framework, which was introduced in May 2021 as a voluntary disclosure regime based on the National Guidelines on Responsible Business Conduct (NGRBC).
- BRSR Core consists of 49 indicators that cover the nine principles of NGRBC and are aligned with international standards such as GRI, SASB, TCFD, and SDGs.
- The BRSR Core framework also requires these entities to disclose their ESG performance for their value chain, which includes their suppliers, customers, distributors, and other stakeholders that are relevant to their business. The value chain disclosures are based on a set of 15 indicators that cover environmental, social, and governance aspects.
- The entities must obtain assurance from an independent external auditor on the BRSR Core disclosures from FY 2023-24 onwards and on the value chain disclosures from FY 2024-25 ahead. The assurance should be in accordance with the International Standard on Assurance Engagements (ISAE) 3000 (Revised) or any other equivalent standard.

If we talk about the ambit of the BRSR Core, the format covers following nine attributes:

(*a*) Greenhouse Gas Footprints

(*b*) Water Footprint

(*c*) Energy Footprint

(*d*) Embracing Circularity
(*e*) Enhancing Employee well-being and safety
(*f*) Enabling Gender diversity in business
(*g*) Enabling inclusive development
(*h*) Fairness in dealing with customers and suppliers, and
(*i*) Openness of Business

An analysis of BRSR Core Attributes with the key indicators and questions of BRSR is given as under:

Attribute	Indicator	BRSR question
GHG Footprint	Scopes 1 and 2 - Absolute & Intensity	P6, Q7, E
Water Footprint	Consumption - Absolute & Intensity; Discharge by level of treatment	P6, Q3, E
Energy Footprint	Total, Intensity: Renewables	P6, Q1, E
Waste Management	Waste generated - Total (by type) & Intensity; Waste recovered - Total & Intensity; Waste disposed by nature of disposal	P6, Q8, E
Employee Well-being	Spending % to revenue; Safety	P3, Q1(*c*) & Q11, E
Gender Diversity	Women's wages to total; POSH complaints	P5, Q3(*b*) & Q7, E
Inclusive Development	Sourcing from MSMEs; Job creation in small towns	P8, Q4 & Q5, E
Fair Engagement with Customers, Suppliers	Data breaches; Accounts Payable in days	P9, Q7, E P1, Q8, E
Openness of business	Related party purchases, loans, investments	P1, Q9, E

The BRSR Core framework aims to provide more reliable, comparable, and consistent information on the ESG performance of the listed entities to the investors and other stakeholders. It also intends to encourage the entities to adopt responsible business practices and improve their ESG performance across their value chain. BRSR Core applicability timeline to top listed entities is as follows:

Financial Year	Applicability of BRSR Core to top listed entities (by market capitalization)
2023-24	Top 150 listed entities
2024-25	Top 250 listed entities
2025-26	Top 500 listed entities
2026-27	Top 1000 listed entities

Disclosures for **value-chain** shall also be made by the listed companies as per BRSR Core as part of their annual reports. Value chain shall encompass the top upstream and downstream partners of the listed entity, cumulatively comprising 75% of its purchases/sales (by value) respectively.

2.1.15 Benefits of adopting BRSR

India's response to the emerging trend of responsible business and ESG investing may be seen in terms of the Business Responsibility and Sustainability Reporting (BRSR) Framework. The BRSR is designed with the intention of having quantitative and standardized disclosures on ESG parameters to enable comparability across companies, sectors and trends. This aligns with global trends where many countries are committing to mandatory corporate disclosures on environmental, climate and other ESG relate aspects. Initiating the BRSR reporting for organisations that are mandated and the ones that are not, will have the following benefit -

- It promotes standardized disclosures on ESG parameters relevant in Indian context and sustainability-related risks and opportunities among listed companies in India;
- It aids the Businesses to better demonstrate their sustainability objectives, position and performance to the stakeholders;
- It furthers businesses' long-term value creation;
- It increases the ability of investors to make informed ESG-related decisions;
- The exercise provides an opportunity to check for one's readiness on critical indicators regulators may be looking to evaluate;
- Provide a standardised format to assess one's performance across peers, industries or even complementing sectors;
- BRSR can be the first step towards sustainability reporting for organisations, that have so far not plunged into it;
- Publishing BRSR also requires the organisations to establish or streamline internal systems and processes, and build capability of the staff that can set the path for future;

- As a mid-to-long term outcome, corporates can look to lower cost of capital, improved stock performance & valuations, efficient operational practices and overall reputation gains.

2.2 Regulatory Regime of ESG in India

Apart from mandate of BRSR on top 1000 listed companies (by market capitalization), regulations pertaining to the ESG in India are found in various legislations, there is no single source of legislation which can be claimed as the ESG legislation.

2.2.1 List of Important ESG related Law, Regulations and Guidelines

Some of the important law in India which relate with the ESG regime are:

- The Factories Act, 1948
- Environment Protection Act, 1986
- Air (Prevention and Control of Pollution) Act, 1981
- Water (Prevention and Control of Pollution) Act, 1974
- Hazardous Waste (Management, Handling and Trans-boundary Movement) Rules, 2016
- Companies Act, 2013
- Securities and Exchange Board of India (Listing Obligations and Disclosure Requirements) Regulations, 2015 (Listing Regulations)
- Prevention of Money Laundering Act, 2002
- Prevention of Corruption Act, 1988
- The Bureau of Indian Standard Act, 2016
- Micro Small & Medium Enterprises Development Act, 2006
- Right to Information Act
- Competition Act
- Laws with respect to labour welfare like the payment of minimum wage, bonus, gratuity, welfare activities, health and safety, etc. such as:
  - The Employees' State Insurance Act, 1948
  - The Minimum Wages Act, 1948
  - The Industrial Disputes Act, 1947
  - The Plantation Labour Act, 1951
  - The Mines Act, 1952

- The Employees' Provident Funds and Miscellaneous Provisions Act, 1952
- The Trade Union Act

Some other relevant rules and guidelines are also presented below:

- CSR expenditure of 2% of profit mandated under the Companies Act, 2013.
- India's Nationally Determined Contribution (NDC) under the Paris Accord, 2015.
- Target of 175GW of renewables capacity by 2022.
- Perform, Achieve and Trade (PAT) scheme introduced for energy intensive industries.
- Bharat Stage VI auto emission norms advanced to April 2020.
- Extended producer responsibility mandated under E-Waste Management Rules, 2016.
- Batteries Management Rules, 2016.
- Plastics Waste Management (Amendment) Rules, 2018.
- Hazardous and Other Waste (M&T) Rules, 2018.
- National Guidelines on Responsible Business Conduct, 2019.
- Business Responsibility & Sustainability Report mandated for top 1000 listed

Some of the specific examples are:

Rule 8 of the Companies (Accounts) Rules, 2014 and Section 134(3)(*m*) of the Companies Act requires that the board's report among others must contain details of efforts made by the company on the conservation of energy and the equipments used in this process, including any steps taken or the impact on the conservation of energy, steps taken to utilise alternate sources of energy, investment in energy conservation equipment and absorption, etc.

Section 166 of the Companies Act specifies the duties of a director of a company, which also includes aspects like to act in good faith in order to promote the objects of the company for the benefit of its members as a whole, and in the best interests of the company, its employees, the shareholders, the community and for the protection of the environment, and Exercise due-diligence etc.

Section 135 of the Companies Act read with the Companies (Corporate Social Responsibility Policy) Rules, 2014 makes it mandatory for companies with a specified net worth, turnover or net profit to constitute a Corporate Social Responsibility (CSR) committee to oversee the CSR policy and activities. Eligible companies are required to annually spend at least 2% of their average net profits of the last three financial years on CSR. The board's report shall disclose the composition of the CSR committee, content of the CSR policy, an explanation for any unspent amount, etc.

Regulation 17(1)(*b*) of the Listing Regulations on the Board of Directors of listed companies stipulates that one-third of the board of a listed entity shall be composed of independent directors in case the chairperson is a non-executive director and not a promoter or related to a promoter or a person occupying a management position; otherwise, at least half of the board should be composed of independent directors.

Section 149 of the Companies Act requires eligible companies to have a female director in certain cases. Additionally, **Regulation 17(1)(*a*) of the Listing Regulations** requires the top 1,000 listed entities (based on market capitalisation) mentions to have an independent, female director on their boards.

Section 177 of the Companies Act requires the board of every listed company and certain classes of public companies to constitute an audit committee consisting of a minimum of three directors, with independent directors forming a majority. Additionally, **Regulation 18 of the Listing Regulations** requires that at least two-thirds of a listed entity's audit committee members are independent directors; however, in case of a listed entity having outstanding superior voting right equity shares, all members must be independent directors. It also requires that the chairperson of the audit committee shall be an independent director.

Section 178 of the Companies Act requires the board of every listed company and certain classes of public companies to constitute a Nomination and Remuneration Committee (NRC) consisting of three or more non-executive directors, of which not less than half shall be independent directors. The chairperson of the company (whether executive or non-executive) may be appointed as a member of the NRC but shall not act as chair. Additionally, **Regulation 19 of the Listing Regulations** requires that at least two-thirds of the directors on the NRC of a listed entity must be independent, and the chairperson of the NRC must be an independent director.

Various aspects of ESG are covered under these pieces of legislation in a fragmented manner. Indigenisation of ESG is largely found in the form of National Guidelines on Responsible Business Conduct (NGRBC) and Business Responsibility and Sustainability Reporting (BRSR).

2.2.2 Role of the Ministry of Corporate Affairs

The Ministry of Corporate Affairs, Government of India has also taken steps to promote ESG disclosures by companies, it has recommended to align BRSR reporting with the MCA-21 Data. Section 135 of the Companies Act, 2013 also mandates eligible companies to spend 2% of their average net profits of the last three financial years on CSR activities, which was an important milestone towards social sustainability. Ministry has also launched National CSR Data Portal and National CSR Exchange Portals. Indian companies have set ambitious targets to reduce their carbon footprint, increase their renewable energy consumption, improve their diversity and inclusion practices, and enhance their stakeholder engagement among many such ESG related initiatives. Ministry of Corporate Affairs and other regulators like SEBI are acting promptly to release ESG related mandate and policies. Country seems on the right track to embrace ESG as a key driver of business growth and value creation. However, there is still scope for improvement in terms of standardisation, verification, and assurance of ESG data and disclosures. There is also a great need for awareness generation among Board level and C-Suite Executives and also among other business stakeholders including in MSMEs on the importance and business case of ESG integration.

By introducing the National Voluntary Guidelines on Social, Environmental and Economic Responsibilities of Business and also an updated version of National Guidelines on Responsible Business Conduct (NGRBC), the Ministry has played an important role in the ESG domain. The Securities and Exchange Board of India (SEBI) has mandated Business Responsibility and Sustainability Reporting (BRSR) on top 1000 listed companies by market capitalization. The foundation of BRSR is inspired by the Ministry of Corporate Affairs' Report on Business Responsibility Reporting (BRR) and National Guidelines on Responsible Business Conduct. Ministry's contribution in promoting Good Corporate Governance has further facilitated ease of doing business in the country. Government lays strong emphasis on the reinforcement of 'minimal government & maximum governance', public trust and ease of doing business. The Government has repealed over 25000 compliances and nearly 1500 union laws. The Amrit Kaal will focus on the next phase of Ease of Doing Business (EoDB 2.0) and Ease of Living and the government following the goal of 'trust-based governance' to improve the productive efficiency of capital and human resources. In the sphere of Corporate Social Responsibility (CSR), the Ministry of Corporate Affairs has also introduced more comprehensive provisions in the recent past. Companies' contribution to the social development has gained traction in the country and its leading towards a revolution in the global history.

2.3 Key ESG Trends & Issues in India

Sustainable Development is Fundamental Right of the people. The Supreme Court of India held that sustainable development is to be treated as an integral part of life under article 21 of the Constitution of India. Hence, complying with the principle of sustainable development is a constitutional mandate. Today ESG has also become an unwritten mandate for companies. Not only global investors and buyers demand businesses to adopt sustainable practices in the business value chains but the customers also demand products and services which have sustainable background. Sustainability is not limited to protection of environment as it is generally understood but it consists of social and governance aspects of company's performance too.

A country's collective performance in ESG is positively linked with per capita GDP also. Hon'ble Finance Minister of India in the budget for 2022-23 demonstrated a continuing effort by the Government of India towards a more sustainable resilient economy. The underlying objective of the Government is also to create a space where India emerges as one of the fastest growing nations in the world to integrating a strong ESG framework across industries while aligning with the 17 UN Sustainable Development Goals. Government encourages the ESG propaganda which projects a framework of global acceptance, making India a liberal and attractive nation for trade and global supply chains.

Our Prime Minister Shri Narendra Modi announced the 'Amrit Kaal' for our nation on 75th Independence Day celebration under Azadi Ka Amrit Mahotsav. Government's aim to fulfil vision India@100 by achieving specified milestones in Amrit Kaal includes - Focus on growth and all inclusive welfare, promoting technology development, energy transition and climate action, virtuous cycle starting from private investment, crowded in by public capital investment.

India is world's third largest green house gas emitter. India has also pledged to become a net-zero carbon emitter by 2070 at the recent COP 26 meeting, enterprises need to implement sustainable measures and take actions on ESG without any further delay. As individuals also, we have a great responsibility on our shoulders, until individual mindsets doesn't change, massive revolutions are challenging. All of us also have to discharge our Individual Social Responsibly (ISR) only than our country will be prosperous and will attain goals of inclusive and sustainable development.

Most of the companies are not designed with ESG integrated into their core strategic vision. It is practiced as compliance or an obligatory requirement. If India must do its business globally it has to integrate ESG in the supply chain. Lack of awareness, readiness, and financial strength of MSMEs is also one of the important issues. SEBI has not issued the detailed list of KPIs for BRSR Core, there are around 49 indicators yet. Data collection and disclosure is one of the principal challenges in the ESG space. Companies also need to take up capacity-building initiatives across their facilities and consider digital solutions to improve data collection and reporting. Some of the important trends are listed as under:

- Circular Economy
- GHG Protocol

- Greenwashing
- Carbon Footprint Calculation and Disclosure
- Sustainable Land Use
- Biodiversity
- Human Rights
- Modern Slavery
- COVID-19
- Just Transition
- Diversity, Equity & Inclusion
- Decent Work
- Ethics & Transparency
- Anti-Corruption
- Nomination of Directors
- Executive Pay
- Tax Fairness
- Responsible Political Engagement
- Sustainable Finance
- ESG Impact Measurement
- Sustainable Supply Chain
- Expanding Regulatory Changes

Relevant topics pertaining to each aspects of E, S, & G have been described in the respective chapters in this book. Some of the crosscutting trends and issues are explained below:

2.3.1 Sustainable Finance

In today's changing world, businesses are realizing their impact on society and the environment. It is now crucial for businesses to prioritise not only profitability but also the well-being of the planet. Sustainable finance is an important aspect of responsible business practices. It involves considering Environmental, Social, and Governance (ESG) factors when making financial decisions, aligning financial interests with sustainability goals. It seeks to fuse profit with purpose. Sustainable finance not only addresses the ethical concerns but also brings commercial benefits. It includes practices like green bonds, impact investing, and ESG screening. The core principle is that businesses, investors, and financial institutions can contribute to positive environmental and social outcomes while ensuring long-term financial stability. This shift reflects the consensus that responsible finance is essential for the future well-being of businesses and the planet.

Approximately half of the world's GDP relies on nature in some way, but as nature diminishes, there is a significant risk of economic loss. This emphasizes the significance of sustainable finance, and therefore the rationale is based on the recognition of pressing global challenges that require immediate attention. Several recent global events and conferences, such as the G20 Summit under India's presidency and the SDG Summit in New York, have boosted the push for sustainable finance and responsible business conduct. The decrease in funding for SDGs, highlighted at the SDG summit, has contributed to a greater emphasis on sustainable finance, which is crucial at this time. Sustainable finance, at its core, acknowledges the urgency of preserving the environment and addressing environmental degradation and climate change. It aims to allocate financial resources to project and initiatives that minimize environmental harm, conserve natural resources, and mitigate the negative impact of economic activities on our planet. Moreover, it embraces social responsibility by directing investments towards projects that promote social inclusion, reduce inequality, and improve human well-being. This encompasses initiatives in education, healthcare, affordable housing, and poverty alleviation, all of which contribute to a more equitable and fair society.

Sustainable finance refers to any form of financial service integrating Environmental, Social and Governance (ESG) criteria into the business or investment decisions for the lasting benefit of both clients and society at large. Sustainable Finance is a critical tool for driving responsible business practices. We need to identify and embrace strategies and best practices for towards sustainable finance, and also need to address challenges and opportunities associated with the adoption of sustainable finance. Some of the key terms used under the domain of sustainable finance as sustainable funds, green bonds, impact investing, microfinance, active ownership, credits for sustainable projects and development of the whole financial system in a more sustainable way. Some of the synonyms used in general are climate finance, green finance etc. Terminologies used in sustainable finance may sometimes be perceived differently in different countries organizations and context.

The two main financial instruments in sustainable finance are equity and debt. In the early stages of a project, equity financing is the main investment method used, and investors receive an ownership interest (stocks or shares) in the project in return for the amount of capital they invest.

Here we will get some insights on Sustainable Investment in India. While observing the estimate value of sustainable investment by Asset under Management (AuM) India 2021-2026, we find that in 2021, the total value of sustainable investments by Private Equity (PE)/Venture Capital (VC) assets under management in India was estimated to be around 19 billion U.S. dollars. The value is expected to grow to around 125 billion U.S. dollars in the next five years.

Sources of Sustainable Finance

- **Corporations** are the largest source of climate-related funding, both through CSR initiatives and their investments in multiple sectors including renewable energy, transportation and infrastructure.
- **Banks** provide a significant proportion of the financial resources that can be mobilized for green investments.
- **International Financial Institutions** support the scaling-up of green investments by testing new ways of financing, channelling funds toward sustainable development through mechanisms such as green bonds, and influencing global financial governance to give more support to sustainable development. These include green investment banks and development banks, which provide funding for sustainability- and development-related projects respectively.
- **International/Inter-governmental Organizations** like the United Nations, the OECD and the G20 provide limited finance but set the agenda on sustainability issues at the international level and help coordinate sources of funding.
- **Climate Funds** such as the Green Climate Fund, Adaptation Fund, Global Environment Facility and Climate Investment Funds, are multilateral funds for climate change adaptation and mitigation projects, funded through contributions from individual countries.
- **National Governments** determine the amount of public funding earmarked for green investments, as well as institutional support for them. They can also support the design of dedicated domestic investment vehicles such as national climate and environmental funds.
- **Central Banks and Regulatory Authorities** can also guide the actions of the financial sector through policies and regulations that define what can be considered a sustainable investment or require companies to disclose their climate risks.
- **Institutional Investors**, such as pension funds, sovereign wealth funds and insurers, are another important group of private-sector financiers.
- **Stock Exchanges** also often specialize in green and sustainable investments. For example, the Luxembourg Green Exchange (LGX), attached to the Luxembourg Stock Exchange, operates as a dedicated platform for green, social and sustainable securities.

EU Regulations

Some of the regulations pertaining to Sustainable Finance in the European Union are as under:

- **Taxonomy Regulation (TR)**

  To achieve the objectives of the 'European Green Deal', the Taxonomy Regulation (TR), commonly known as EU Taxonomy, was enforced as legal a framework *vide* EU Regulation No. 2020/852 on 12 July 2020. EU Taxonomy provides a classification system to define environmentally sustainable economic activities to create a common understanding of the sustainability. It applies to financial markets, financial products which are defined by the SFDR, it also applies to the issuers of corporate bonds and also to the undertakings as prescribed under the scope of the CSRD.

- **Sustainability related Disclosures in the Financial Services Sectors (SFDR)**

  Sustainability-Related Disclosures in the Financial Services Sectors (SFDR) applies to Financial Market Participants (FMPs) and also on Financial Advisors. This regulation was notified *vide* EU regulation No. 2019/2088 and became applicable step-by-step, starting from 10 March 2021. The regulation has the objective to create harmonized rules on the transparency expected from FMP and Financial Advisors and they must specify sustainability-related information on websites, in pre-contractual documentation and in periodic reports at entity and product level.

- **Corporate Social Responsibility Directives (CSRD)**

  The Corporate Social Responsibility Directive (CSRD) (Delegated Regulation (EU) 2022/2564) entered into force on 5 January 2023. It replaces the Non-Financial Reporting Directive (NFRD). The CSRD applies to all companies and/or groups that are based in the EU, regardless of the origin or domicile of the parent company.

- **AIFMD, UCITS, SOLVENCY II, IDD AND MIFID II**

  To harmonise sustainability-related disclosure requirements, the EU amended AIFMD, UCITS, Solvency II, IDD and MiFID II. The new measures integrated sustainability risks and factors into the existing directives. Most of these amendments started to be applicable from August 2022. The measures under MiFID II applied from August 2022 (sustainability risks and factors, sustainability preferences) respectively 22 November 2022 (product governance obligations).

EU Sustainable Investing Standards

A number of standards exist to aid investors in evaluating and differentiating between financial products described as sustainable:

- Eurosif Transparency Code
- Febelfin Quality Standard and Label
- FNG-Label for Sustainable Mutual Funds
- FNG Sustainability Profiles and Transparency Matrix
- Luxflag ESG label
- Nordic Swan Ecolabel for Investment Funds
- Greenfin Label
- Label ISR

Global ESG ETF Assets

Here we will consider Assets and Share of Sustainable Funds Worldwide. To calculate the ESG Exchange Traded Funds we adopt following formula:

ESG - ETF = ESG Exchange Traded Funds

Exchange-traded funds, or ETFs, are collections of stocks and bonds. Investors can purchase shares of an ETF, which invest according to specific objectives. ETFs are similar to mutual funds in that they're a group of stocks and bonds. Investors can buy shares of either mutual funds or ETFs, but ETFs differ from mutual funds in two key ways.

First, ETFs can be bought or sold throughout the trading day. They trade like stocks on major exchanges. Mutual funds can only be bought or sold once per day.

The second key difference is pricing. ETF prices fluctuate throughout the day as they are bought and sold. Mutual funds are priced once daily on their net asset value.

Financing for Sustainable Development Framework

In the new age of responsibility, it is important to understand the core principles and concepts that guide sustainable finance. How to expand sustainable investments to meet the objective of the 2030 Agenda and the Paris Agreement has also been a key challenge before the investors' community. Exploring the solutions, identifying institutional and market barriers to sustainable finance is important in that context alongwith real-world case study illustrating the economic benefits of sustainable finance in diverse sectors. The question arises how businesses can incorporate sustainable finance into their financial decision-making? Identifying key performance indicators and metrics to assess the impact of sustainable finance on business growth in this context is important to measure the impact. Exploring the investor's perspective at ESG factors and sustainable finance when making investment decisions, discovering the role of regulatory bodies and government incentives in promoting sustainable finance, and exploring the plans and policies deliberated and executed during the G20 summit pertaining to the future of sustainable finance are some of the important topics to deliberate.

Europe continued to dominate as the largest sustainable fund market, with assets of $2.1 trillion as of December 2022. That represented 83 per cent of global sustainable fund assets, up 2 per cent from the 2021 market share. Green finance is gaining momentum in the Indian economy as a crucial tool for transitioning toward net zero emissions. The integration of environmental considerations into financial decision-making is crucial for sustainable development. Initiatives like green bonds, carbon pricing, and sustainable investment strategies are driving the shift toward a greener economy in India. As one of the world's largest emitters of greenhouse gases, India requires a budget of over US$10t to accomplish its net zero emissions target by 2070. Several measures are underway in the public and the private sector, leading to increased investment and financing opportunities. One of them being green finance— a sustainable or responsible finance that effectively finances projects with environmental benefits, such as reducing greenhouse gas emissions, improving energy efficiency, or enhancing the circular economy.

Invest India

Being the national investment promotion and facilitation agency, Invest India plays a pivotal role in achieving India's SDG targets. Invest India not only adopts SDGs as a key driver of its investment promotion lifecycle but also conceptualizes, curates and helps execute bespoke projects targeted at specific SDGs. More importantly, Invest India has deployed a series of tools and enablers to make the SDG orientation stick across the investment ecosystem and among its various government and non-government stakeholders.

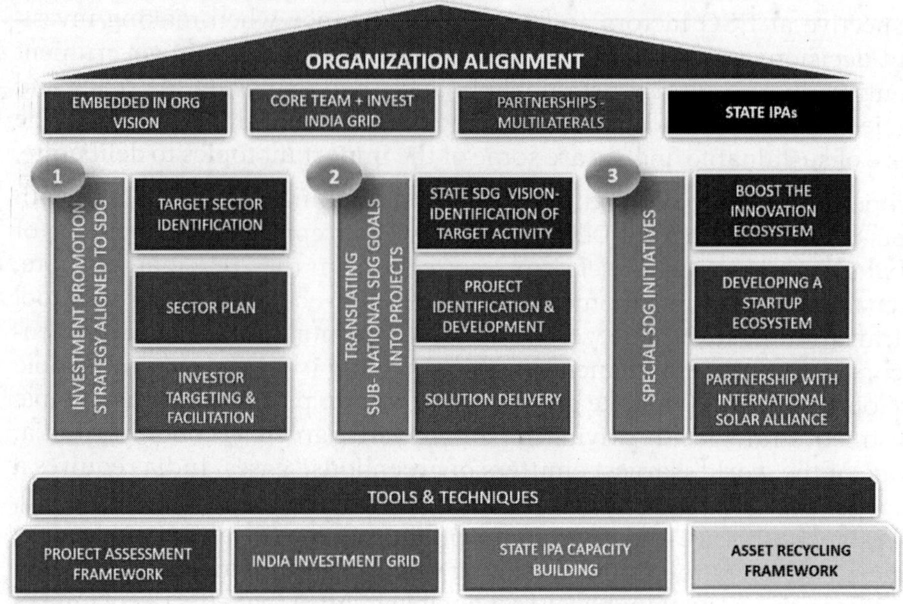

(Source: http://investindia.gov.in)

Figure 2.3: Invest India Sustainability Framework

ESG Project Assessment Framework

Developing a project pipeline involves assessing the sustainability impact of investible projects from the selected sectors. The project assessment will need to be carried out against an adopted definition and criteria of sustainable FDI. The framework is based on a broad set of sustainability characteristics that encompass economic, environmental, social and governance criteria. There are 21 indicators of sustainability under this framework, these indicators have been prioritised by giving weighted score of either 1, 2 or 3 points based on their priority. Indicators with higher score indicate higher priority in the sustainability matrix.

Sustainability Matrix

Economic		Environmental		Social		Governance	
Capital Investment	3	Pollution Controls	3	Labour Rights	2	Local Management	1
Employment	3	Low Carbon Footprint	3	Skills Enhancement	2	Supply Chain Standards	1
Local Business Linkages	2	Water Usage	1	Public Health Benefits	2		

Economic		Environmental		Social		Governance	
Technology Transfer/R&D	2	Biodiversity Protection	1	Poverty Alleviation (Income Equity)	1		
Infrastructure Development	3	Energy Efficiency	1	Entrepreneurship	3		
Exports	2	Waste Management	2	Housing	1		
		Land Management	1				

Above weighted score in total become 15 for economic, 12 for environment, 11 for social and 2 for governance, amounting to total 40 against which an FDI proposal will be assessed against the above criteria and marked out of the total score of 40. Any project proposal achieving a score of 75% (30 or above), can be classified as a sustainable project in investment promotion activities.

Sustainable Finance not only opens up many opportunities but also poses so many questions to all of us - what strategies can drive the adoption of financial tools like green bonds and carbon markets for green technology while also ensuring transparent and accountable climate finance practices? What regulatory frameworks and policies can support the development of sustainable finance initiatives? What role can fintech and blockchain technology play in advancing sustainable finance and improving transparency? How can financial education and literacy be leveraged to promote sustainable investing and responsible financial behaviour? What are the major challenges to scaling up social impact investments and how do we solve it? How can we effectively address the capacity building gaps in sustainable finance, particularly for MSMEs, while focusing on their specific needs, even when resources and expertise are limited? How can governments collaborate with the private sector to accelerate the sustainable finance? What specific areas within sustainable finance practices do you believe require the most immediate improvement or attention, and what strategies or initiatives can be employed to address these challenges effectively? What are the next steps and future trends in sustainable finance, and how can stakeholders prepare for them? We leave these as food for thought and exploration till we release a new book specifically on the Sustainable Finance with more detailed response to these questions.

2.3.2 Supply Chain Sustainability

Supply chain sustainability is defined as embedding environmental, social or corporate governance considerations as raw materials are sourced, converted to products and delivered to market.

Supply-chain sustainability is also the impact a company's supply chain in promoting human rights, fair labour practices, environmental progress and anti-corruption policies.

Here we need to understand what a sustainable value chain is also. A sustainable value chain is a mix of product development and the supply chain process - from the sourcing of raw materials to delivering the final product to the completion of the product lifecycle and back to the source, with the aim of minimal environmental or social impact. Therefore, sustainable value chain management ensures achieving sustainability goals through the business while maximizing the benefits for concerned stakeholders.

Sustainability in supply chain management is the ability to maintain the standardized processes without affecting the environment. Supply chain sustainability aims to reduce the impact of factors affecting the environment like pollutants, deforestation, ozone depletion and global warming.

Supply chain management focuses on speed, cost, reliability, optimization, and continuous improvement of the supply chain. Global supply chain sustainability efforts focus on goals that are environment friendly, improve resource optimization and retain or increase ROI at the same time. Sustainable chain management is put into practice right from the procurement of goods and services to delivering the right products at the right time.

Sustainable supply chain is a strategic business decision that includes sustainable sourcing, production, packaging, and optimized, responsible delivery of produced goods. SCM sustainability efforts under an enterprise's corporate social responsibility activities also drive green operations and result in cost savings and an improved supply chain over the long term.

There are the 10 easy to implement and easy to follow best practices for a sustainable supply chain:

- Supplier Code of Conduct
- Green Packaging
- Sustainable Transportation
- Ethical Sourcing
- Waste Reduction
- Life Cycle Assessment
- Product Design

- Stakeholder Engagement
- Reporting and Transparency

There are three key elements of a sustainable supply chain:

- **Environmental Responsibility:** It involves protecting the environment from potential harm caused due to supply chain activities like production, storage, packaging, transportation and other minute operations.
- **Financial Responsibility:** It addresses the financial needs of the firm. Financial markets include shareholders, employers/employees, customers, clients, business partners, domestic institutions and financial institutions.
- **Social Responsibility:** It involves principles, ethics, morals and philanthropic expectations of the society from a business. This means every person in a sustainable supply chain is treated fairly, equally and in line with human rights requirements.

BRSR Core & Supply Chain Sustainability

Considering the role of the supply chain in day to day business operation of large companies, SEBI has decided to introduce the BRSR Core for assurance by listed companies in its recent notification dated May 10, 2021. Based on the recommendations of the ESG Advisory Committee and pursuant to public consultation, the Board further decided to introduce disclosures and assurance for the value chain of listed entities, as per the BRSR Core.

Some key deliberations like importance of responsible procurement and its critical role in promoting ESG principles, challenges and opportunities that businesses encounter in implementing responsible procurement practices within their supply chains, and strategies that businesses shall entail in complying with the new BRSR Regulations with respect to the adoption of BRSR core by the supply chain, are important in context of supply chain sustainability or responsible procurement practices.

To adopt the sustainable practices in a company as well as to promote this adoption at broader level, there are some pertinent questions to be addressed. Some of the pertinent questions like - How can companies in India ensure ethical sourcing in their supply chains, considering the complexities and diversity of the supplier base? What are the best practices for supplier due diligence and risk assessment? And can technology and data analytics be leveraged to trace the origins of raw materials and ensure ethical sourcing? are important to deliberate.

How can supply chains or MSMEs overcome financial and resource limitations to invest in making itself ESG-compliant? How can the larger companies/corporates support their supply chain in the process to becoming

ESG-compliant supply chains? Are there financial incentives or support mechanisms available for supply chains looking to adopt ESG practices? What strategies can help them optimize their resource allocation for sustainable supply chain initiatives?

How can technology and digital tools be leveraged to enhance transparency and sustainability in the supply chains of companies? What could be the Strategy/ies for the MSME to keep track of the data related to the different parameters of the BRSR core? What digital platforms and solutions are accessible and cost-effective for MSMEs? How can technology help in real-time monitoring and reporting of ESG-related metrics and performance?

What are the success stories of listed companies that started small but successfully expanded their ESG practices as they grew? Can partnerships with larger corporations or industry associations play a role in scaling ESG practices for the supply chain?

How can companies build resilient supply chains that can adapt to disruptions and climate-related challenges while upholding ESG standards? What are the risks posed by climate change, and how can companies address them in their supply chains? What risk management strategies are practical for companies in India to ensure supply chain resilience?

What mechanisms can be established to facilitate the exchange of ESG knowledge and skills among big companies and supply chains in India? Can industry associations or government bodies play a role in creating platforms for knowledge sharing and capacity building? How can successful companies share their experiences and mentor others on ESG integration?

Business Responsibility and Sustainability Reporting (BRSR) Core was introduced by the Securities and Exchange Board of India (SEBI) with the primary focus of improving environmental and social governance across supply chains. BRSR Core is a limited set of nine ESG parameters: GHG emissions, water consumption and discharge, R&D and capital expenditure on technologies to improve environmental and social impacts, circularity and waste management, employee well being and safety, gender diversity, inclusive development, fairness in engaging with customers and suppliers, and openness in business dealings with trading houses, dealers, and related parties.

The SEBI has highlighted three core aspects of BRSR Core:

- Reporting entities will get it third party certified under a 'reasonable assurance' scope;
- It will be extended to supply chain disclosures;
- ESG rating providers will issue a separate rating based on it.

The framework provides that a listed entity should report the parameters as per BRSR Core for their value chain to the extent it is attributable to their business with that value chain partner. Key highlights of the ESG disclosures and assurance for value chain are given below:

Applicability: The ESG disclosures for the value chain is applicable to the top 250 listed entities (by market capitalisation), on a comply-or-explain basis from FY 2024-25.

Composition of Value Chain: As per BRSR Core, value chain encompass the top upstream and downstream partners of a listed entity. Such reporting may be segregated for upstream and downstream partners or can be reported on an aggregate basis.

Reporting Format: Disclosures for value chain should be made by the listed entity as per BRSR Core, as part of its annual report.

Limited Assurance: The abovementioned companies should obtain limited assurance on a comply-or-explain basis from FY 2025-26.

2.4 Summary of the Chapter

Indian context of ESG as well as its evolution in India has been explained in terms of the Ten Point Charter, Voluntary CSR Guidelines, NVGs, NGRBC, BRSR, BRSR Core, and BRSR Lite etc. A transition from NVGs to NGRBC has been explained in detail including the key changes between both versions of the guidelines. Further, emphasising on the NGRBC as a key instrument of ESG in India, its key features alongwith nine principles have been presented to the readers. Mapping of NGRBC against the Sustainable Development Goals (SDGs) and a Business Case of NGRBC is also explained. Explanation of Business Responsibility and Sustainability Reporting (BRSR) has been provided with its adaptation benefits. Regulatory regime of ESG in India has been briefly narrated by aligning it with some important and relevant Indian Laws. In end, key ESG Trends and Issues have been enlisted, most of these issues are part of upcoming chapters in this book. Aspects of Sustainable Finance and Sustainable Supply Chain have been narrated in detail.

CHAPTER 3

BEGINNING WITH ESG JOURNEY

3.1 Introduction

Existence of Businesses is primarily based on profit maximization, however, in a changing era, investors, shareholders and other stakeholders expect that businesses should strive to make the world a better place as they generate those profits. To do this, companies need to make an ESG business strategy. As an Impact Leader/Sustainability/ESG Professional, you may be expected to develop an ESG business strategy of your company or a company you might be providing such services.

The ESG knowledge, logic, legal instruments, guidelines, toolkits, standards etc. to be used in developing an ESG Business Strategy for companies of different level/size/sector etc. has been presented in this chapter. It is also pertinent to mention that in case a company already has its ESG strategy, you may redevelop it with your expert point of view. To do so, the ESG Business Strategy is developed keeping following stages as indicative format:

- **Develop a baseline on ESG programmes, policies and matrix available in the Company** (some of the indicative issues are - Health and Safety, Environmental Performance, Energy, Ethical Sourcing, Diversity and Inclusion, Social Impact programmes, etc.)
- **Understand What your peer companies are doing** (understand benchmarking ESG)
- **Set ESG Goals for your Company** (define process to be adopted in setting the goals, institutional arrangements, genesis of the work, materiality assessment, rationale for the goals, stakeholders' engagement in setting goals, finalise qualitative and quantitative goals, etc.)
- **Implementation modalities** (Prepare a plan and implementation strategy, set milestones and monitoring indicators, MIS, review modalities, employee engagement, capacity building, etc.)

- **How to communicate your ESG philosophy and actions** (modalities for disclosures, standards/guidelines/frameworks to be adhered, communication strategy, etc.)

A detailed set of information, analysis and methodology has been presented in this chapter on each of the above mentioned framework for developing ESG Business Strategy, its implementation, disclosure and communication.

3.2 How to conduct Baseline

An ESG baseline assessment is used to gather information on the ESG reality of a company prior to instituting initiatives and programmes that aim to address ESG topics.

An ESG baseline assessment is used to gather information on the ESG reality of a company prior to instituting initiatives and programmes that aim to address ESG topics. It should be every company's starting point in the ESG journey wherein they determine where they are currently before envisioning where they wish to go. Most importantly, it creates a basis for comparison, so that initiatives and programmes can be analyzed for their effectiveness in reference to this benchmark. Without a proper baseline, a company is unable to monitor progress and improvements over a period of time.

It is also important to understand how an ESG Baseline Assessment differs from a Materiality Assessment and why both are important? The materiality assessment informs which elements should be included in the baseline assessment by providing visibility around the importance of various ESG topics (both positive and negative impacts) to your organization and its stakeholders.

A baseline on ESG programmes, policies, and matrix can be developed by conducting a comprehensive assessment of a company's current ESG practices. This assessment should evaluate the company's policies and programmes related to environmental sustainability, social responsibility, and corporate governance. The following are some key steps that can be taken to develop a baseline on ESG in a company:

- Review the company's annual report and sustainability reports: This can help provide insights into the company's ESG policies, programmes, and metrics. Companies often include information on their ESG performance, initiatives, and targets in these reports.
- Conduct interviews with key stakeholders: Interviews with senior management, employees, and customers can help gain a better understanding of the company's ESG practices, including the effectiveness of existing policies and programmes.
- Review industry benchmarks: Industry benchmarks can help determine how a company's ESG practices compare to its peers. This can

provide insights into areas where the company can improve its ESG performance.

- Evaluate ESG performance metrics: Assessing key performance indicators (KPIs) related to ESG can help identify areas where a company needs to improve. Common ESG KPIs include carbon emissions, water usage, employee turnover, and diversity metrics.
- Review relevant policies and procedures: Reviewing relevant policies and procedures, such as the company's Code of Conduct, Environmental Policy, and Human Rights Policy, can help identify areas where the company is addressing ESG risks and opportunities.

Based on the above steps, a baseline can be developed that outlines the company's current ESG practices, including its strengths and weaknesses. This can be used as a starting point to develop a comprehensive ESG strategy that aligns with the company's goals and values.

3.3 How to do Peer Benchmarking

ESG benchmarking gives context to a company's ESG performance through comparison across peers in the industry. It uses ratings/scores to give this context. However, as there remains no universal standard for ESG scoring, benchmarking can sometimes be difficult.

Information on a company's ESG progress is helpful, but it means little without a broader industry-based context. Stakeholders cannot asses a company's or an entire industry's performance if they can't understand how each entity compares against the other. Thus, the peer benchmarking is seen an important step in ESG journey. Practically, benchmarking is crucial in assessing what works and doesn't work in your ESG strategy. ESG benchmarking gives context to a company's ESG performance through comparison across peers in the industry. It uses ratings/scores to give this context. However, as there remains no universal standard for ESG scoring, benchmarking sometimes becomes difficult.

Important steps to be followed in benchmarking are:

- Step 1 - Aggregate all ESG information in one place
- Step 2 - Pinpoint Peers' ESG goals with Company Documents
- Step 3 - Uncover the Strategy behind Peers' Goals

Elaborative steps are presented below:

(*a*) Define the purpose of the benchmark and the most effective strategy to achieve that purpose.

(*b*) Identify the audience and understand their expectations ahead of time.

(*c*) Establish the scope of the benchmark
(*d*) Designate who will manage the benchmarking process
(*e*) Categorize the types of criteria that will be used to evaluate the sustainability performance.
(*f*) Determine the evaluation structure of the benchmark. Is it mandatory or aspirational? Is there an option to implement scoring? Are you including progress models?
(*g*) Specify how the benchmarking process or programmes will be implemented.
(*h*) Stipulate how the results will be communicated.

By benchmarking ESG, a company can gain a better understanding of its ESG performance relative to its peers and set targets for improvement. This can help enhance the company's reputation, reduce risks, and create long-term value for stakeholders.

3.4 Materiality Assessment

"Materiality assessment is the identification of issues impacting the businesses which a reasonable investor may consider while making investment decisions. This information may also be used by multi-stakeholders to assess the business for various engagements."

- Dadhich & Atrey

3.4.1 How to do Materiality Assessment

ESG materiality is assessed by corporate companies by conducting a materiality assessment, which is an exercise that helps organizations determine which environmental, social, and governance factors are relevant and important to an organization and its stakeholders. This includes measuring the organizational impact of each factor in consideration to determine which factors should be prioritized.

There are different approaches to conduct a materiality assessment, but some common steps are:

- Creating a steering committee of cross-functional executives to be accountable for the ESG strategy's creation and execution.
- Identifying specific stakeholders, such as employees, customers, suppliers, investors, regulators, and communities, and engaging them to understand their perspectives on the most critical ESG issues.
- Compiling a list of material ESG issues, based on stakeholder feedback, benchmarking with peers, and consulting global or cross-issue frameworks, such as the Global Reporting Initiative or the Sustainability Accounting Standards Board.

- Assessing the significance and urgency of each ESG issue, both from a financial and a broader impact perspective, and plotting them on a materiality matrix.
- Validating and reviewing the results of the materiality assessment, and using them to inform the ESG strategy, goals, and reporting.

A materiality assessment is not a one-time activity, but rather a continuous process that should be updated regularly to reflect the changing ESG landscape and stakeholder expectations. A materiality assessment can help corporate companies to focus on the ESG issues that matter most to their business and society, and to communicate their ESG performance and progress effectively.

3.4.2 Double Materiality

Double materiality assessment determines which Environmental, Social and Governance factors to disclose based on their actual or expected effect on business value. It consider both impact materiality and financial materiality. Double Materiality is one of the most important tool for materiality assessment for most of the companies.

Impact materiality includes externalities which means inside-out-impact by considering both positive and negative impacts on people, planet and society over short, medium and long term period.

Financial materiality includes measuring, managing and reporting on ESG issues that have a positive or negative impact on Financial Performance of the Businesses.

Double Materiality also takes into consideration the "reverse impact" on the company by the stakeholders and the environment and ensures accountability to all stakeholders.

Dynamic Materiality refers to the fact that the impact of the environmental and social issues on businesses and *vice versa* are not static but can change over time. This means that the issues that are material today may not be material tomorrow. The reason for this dynamism as per a report from World Economic Forum entitles 'Embracing the new age of materiality' are; growth in evidence of impacts and transparency; escalating stakeholder action; Growing responsiveness by key decision makers; greater emphasis on ESG.

By understanding which Key performance indicators are material to their business and stakeholders, companies can develop more effective ESG strategies and initiatives. For an example, Data security and the percentage of female employees would be relevant indicators for a bank or a service oriented company but not for a power generation company. Similarly, employee injury rate or amount of GHG emission will be important for the power sector company. Once an organization has identified its material ESG issues, it can use this information to develop ESG strategies and initiatives to address these issues. For example, if an organization identifies climate change as a material ESG issue, it may develop a strategy to reduce its greenhouse gas emissions.

The organization should document its process of determining material topics. This includes documenting the approach taken, decisions, assumptions, and subjective judgments made, sources analysed, and evidence gathered. The approach for each step will vary according to the specific circumstances of the organization, such as its business model, sectors, geographic, cultural, and legal operating context, ownership structure, and the nature of its impacts. Given these specific circumstances, the steps should be systematic, documented, replicable, and used consistently in each reporting period. The organization's highest governance body should oversee the process and review and approve the material topics.

To conduct the material assessment, suggested key considerations are as under:

- ◆ Understand the organization's context – sector specific standards may be used
- ◆ Identify actual and potential impacts – topics and impacts specific to the industry sector
- ◆ Engage with relevant stakeholders
- ◆ Assess the significance of the impacts
- ◆ Test the material topics with experts
- ◆ Prioritise the most significant material topics
- ◆ Take management's approval
- ◆ Communicate material topics

3.4.3 Materiality Matrix and Mapping

A materiality matrix is a tool that helps companies identify and prioritize their most significant ESG issues. It is a two-dimensional chart that maps the importance of an issue to the company and its stakeholders against the impact of the issue on the company and its stakeholders. The materiality matrix is a crucial component of the materiality assessment process.

The materiality matrix is based on a structured methodology that involves stakeholder engagement, peer benchmarking, and international ESG frameworks. This is a good practice that ensures the relevance and validity of the material topics identified. Materiality is a dynamic concept that evolves and is influenced by changes in the business environment and stakeholder expectations.

The materiality matrix shows the relative importance of each topic to the business and the stakeholders, based on a scoring system. The topics are plotted on a two-dimensional graph, where the x-axis represents the importance to the business and the y-axis represents the importance to the stakeholders. The topics are also color-coded according to the type of capital they are linked to, such as human, social, natural, manufactured, and intellectual capital. This is a useful way to visualize the materiality assessment and to communicate the results to internal and external audiences.

A materiality matrix is a tool that helps companies identify and prioritize the sustainability issues that are most relevant to their business and stakeholders. It is usually presented as a two-dimensional graph, where the horizontal axis represents the degree of stakeholder interest or concern, and the vertical axis represents the degree of business impact or significance.

The different circle layers in a materiality matrix can represent different levels of materiality for each issue, depending on the position and size of the circle. For example, a large circle in the upper right corner of the matrix would indicate a high level of materiality, meaning that the issue is very important to both the business and the stakeholders. A small circle in the lower left corner would indicate a low level of materiality, meaning that the issue is not very important to either the business or the stakeholders.

The materiality matrix can also be used to classify the issues into four categories, based on the quadrant they fall into:

- **High Priority/Crucial ESG Issues**: These are the issues that have a high impact on the business and a high interest from the stakeholders. They are the most material issues that should be addressed and disclosed by the company.
- **Emerging/Important ESG Issues**: These are the issues that have a high impact on the business but a low interest from the stakeholders. They are the issues that may become more material in the future, as the stakeholder awareness and expectations increase.
- **Monitoring ESG Issues**: These are the issues that have a low impact on the business but a high interest from the stakeholders. They are the issues that the company should monitor and communicate with the stakeholders, as they may affect the reputation and trust of the company.
- **Low-priority ESG Issues**: These are the issues that have a low impact on the business and a low interest from the stakeholders. They are the least material issues that the company can manage internally or report voluntarily.

Materiality is not a one-size-fits-all concept. It is an extensive, nuanced, expensive and complex procedure that requires careful consideration of the company's unique circumstances. However, once the materiality matrix is assessed a company can draft its ESG strategy taking the matrix as a base for the upcoming three to five years. The matrix should be revised every three to five years. The analysis of the sustainability and annual reports of top Indian companies across different sectors to extract their materiality matrix and assessment.

3.5 Materiality Assessment Examples

3.5.1 National Thermal Power Corporation (NTPC) Materiality Matrix Analysis

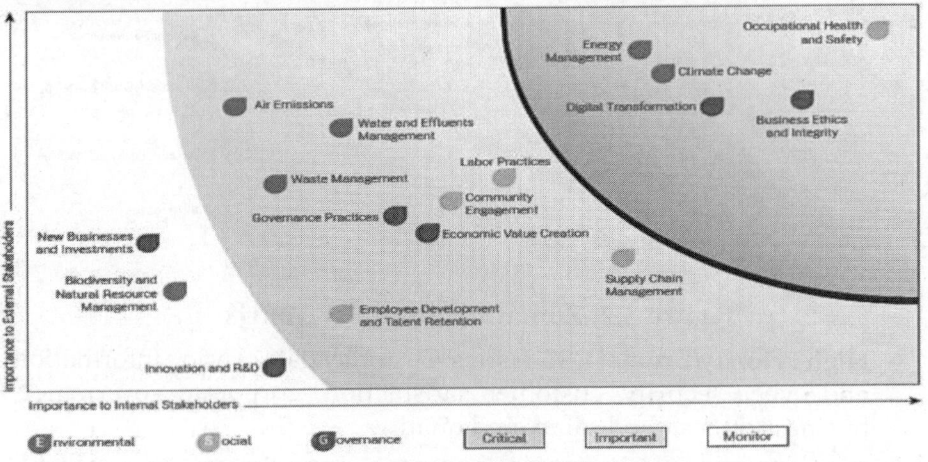

Figure 3.1: NTPC Materiality Matrix

- **High priority/Crucial ESG Issues**: Occupational Health and Safety, Energy Management, Climate Change, Business Ethics and Integrity and Digital transformation.
- **Emerging/Important ESG Issues**: Air Emissions, Water and effluents management, Waste management, Labour practices, community engagement, supply chain management, employee development and talent retention, governance practices and economic value creation.
- **Monitoring ESG Issues**: New businesses and investments, Innovation and R&D, Biodiversity and Natural Resource management.
- **Low-priority ESG Issues**: Null
- The NTPC materiality matrix covers a wide range of ESG issues that are important for the power sector, such as climate change, energy management, water and effluents management, air emissions, occupational health and safety, business ethics and integrity, labour practices, community engagement, and governance practices. These

topics reflect the key impacts and risks that NTPC faces as a leading power company in India, as well as the opportunities and expectations that it has to create value for its stakeholders.

3.5.2 Zomato Ltd.

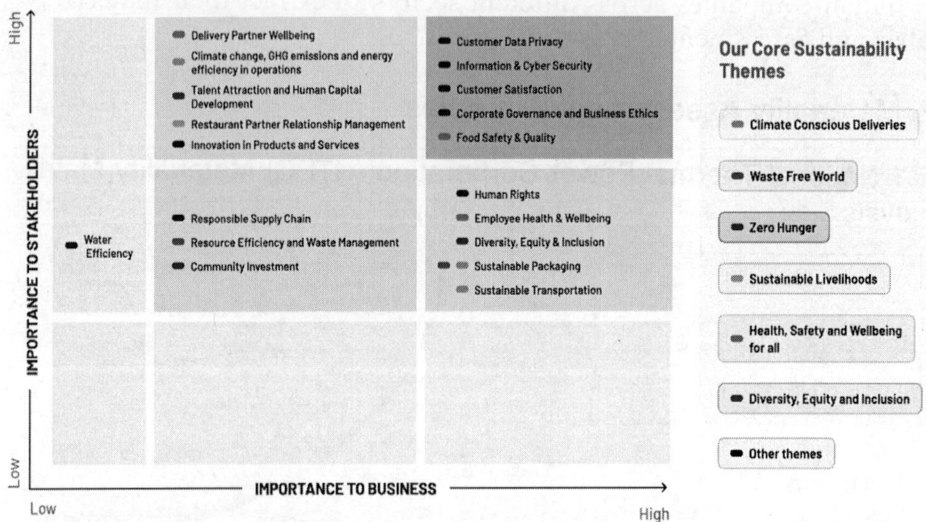

Figure 3.2: Zomato Materiality Matrix

- **High Priority/Crucial ESG Issues**: Customer data privacy, Information and cyber security, customer satisfaction, corporate governance, business ethics, food safety and quality.
- **Emerging/Important ESG Issues**: Human Rights, Employee Health and well-being, diversity-equity and Inclusion, sustainable packaging and sustainable transportation.
- **Monitoring ESG Issues**: Delivery partner well-being, climate change, GHG Emissions and energy efficiency and operations, talent attraction and human capital development, restaurant partner relationship management and innovation in products and services.
- **Low-priority ESG Issues**: Responsible supply chain, resource efficiency and waste management and community investment.
- **Least priority ESG Issues:** Water Efficiency.

3.5.3 Bharti Airtel Ltd.

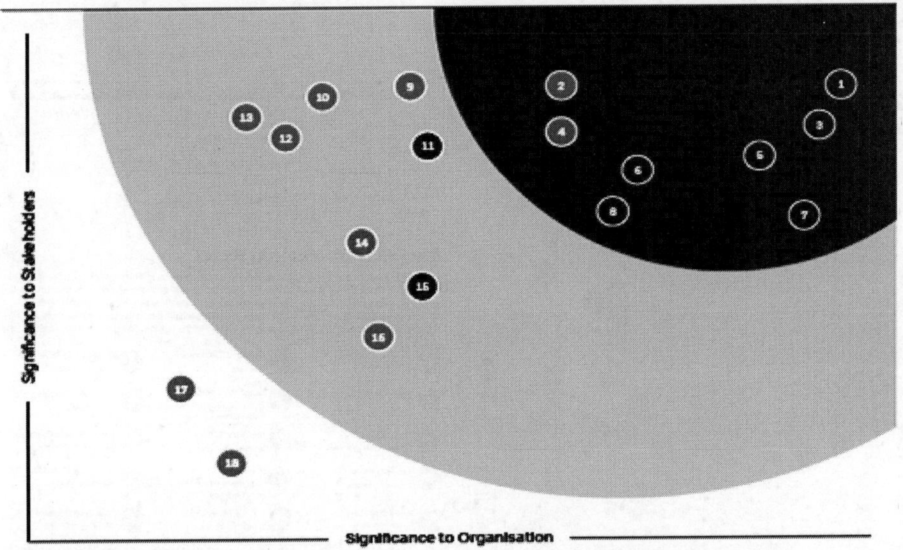

1. Information security and customer data privacy
2. Talent attraction and human capital development
3. Corporate Governance and business ethics
4. Climate change, energy efficiency and emission reduction
5. Enhancing customer experience and satisfaction
6. Network quality, expansion and transformation
7. Regulatory compliance
8. Innovation of product and services
9. Employee health and well-being
10. Diversity and inclusion
11. Sustainable supply chain management
12. Promoting human rights
13. Corporate citizenship and community development
14. Resource efficiency and waste management
15. Fair marketing and advertising
16. Digital inclusion and enhanced access to ICT
17. Water efficiency
18. Green ICT solutions

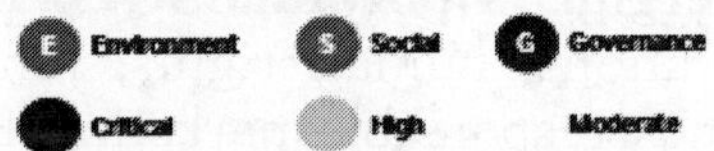

Figure 3.3: Airtel Materiality Matrix

- **High Priority/Crucial ESG Issues**: Information Security and customer data privacy, talent attraction and human capital development, corporate governance and business ethics, climate change, energy efficiency and emission reduction, enhancing customer experience and satisfaction, network quality, expansion and transformation and regulatory compliance.
- **Emerging/Important ESG Issues**: Employee Health and well-being, diversity and inclusion, sustainable supply chain management, promoting human rights, corporate citizenship and community development, resource efficiency and waste management, peer-marketing and advertising, digital inclusion and enhanced access to ICT.
- **Monitoring ESG Issues**: Water-efficiency and green ICT solutions.

3.5.4 ITC Ltd.

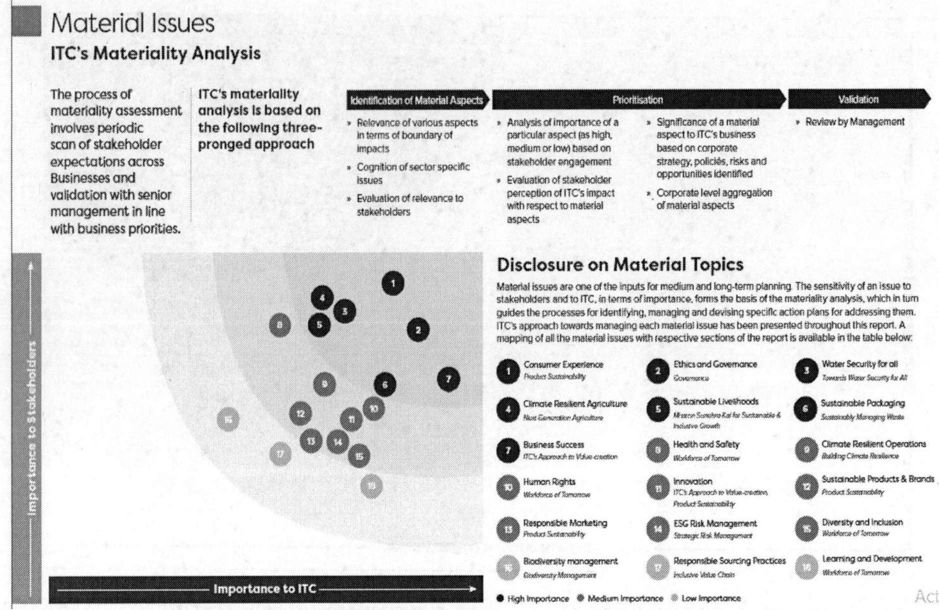

Figure 3.4: ITC's Materiality Analysis

- **High Priority/Crucial ESG Issues**: Consumer experience, ethics and governance, water security for all, climate resilient agriculture, sustainable livelihoods, sustainable packaging and business success
- **Emerging/Important ESG Issues**: Health and safety, climate resilient operations, human rights, innovation, sustainable products and brands, responsible marketing, ESG Risk management, Diversity and Inclusion.
- **Monitoring ESG Issues**: Biodiversity management, Responsible sourcing practices, learning and development.

3.5.5 Nestle

Materiality matrix

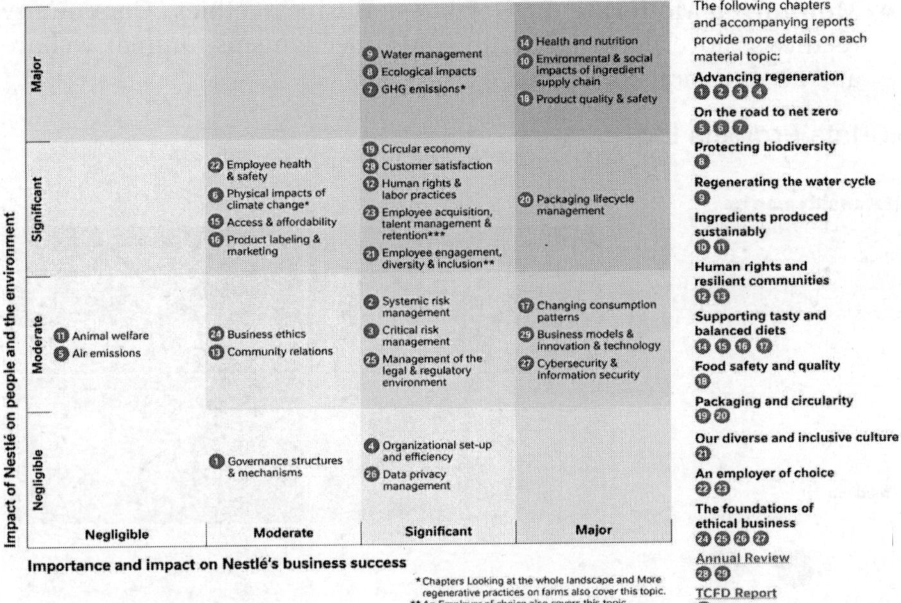

Our materiality process

Material topics selection	Establish external context	Stakeholder engagement	Materiality assessment	Review strategies	Publish in CSV and Sustainability Report
Sustainability Accounting Standards Board (SASB) aligned material topics selected	AI software analysis and analysis of environment	55 interviews conducted and surveys collected	Quantitative and qualitative input assessed	Identify risks and opportunities in results and adjust priorities accordingly	Share results internally and externally

Creating Shared Value and Sustainability Report 2022 7

Figure 3.5: Nestle Materiality Matrix

- **High Priority/Crucial ESG Issues/Major**: Health and Nutrition, Environmental and social impacts of the ingredients supply chain, product quality and safety, Water Management, Ecological Impacts, GHG-Emissions, packaging Life cycle management, changing consumption patterns, business models and innovation and technology, cyber security and information security.
- **Emerging/Important/Significant ESG Issues**: Circular Economy, customer satisfaction, human rights and labour practices, employee acquisition, talent management and retention, employee engagement, diversity and inclusion, systematic risk management, critical risk management, organizational setup and efficiency, data privacy

management and management of the legal and regulatory environment, Employee health and safety, physical impacts of climate change, access and affordability, product labelling and marketing.

- **Monitoring/Moderate ESG Issues**: Business ethics, Community relations, governance structures and mechanisms, animal welfare and air emissions.

3.5.6 Tata Projects Ltd.

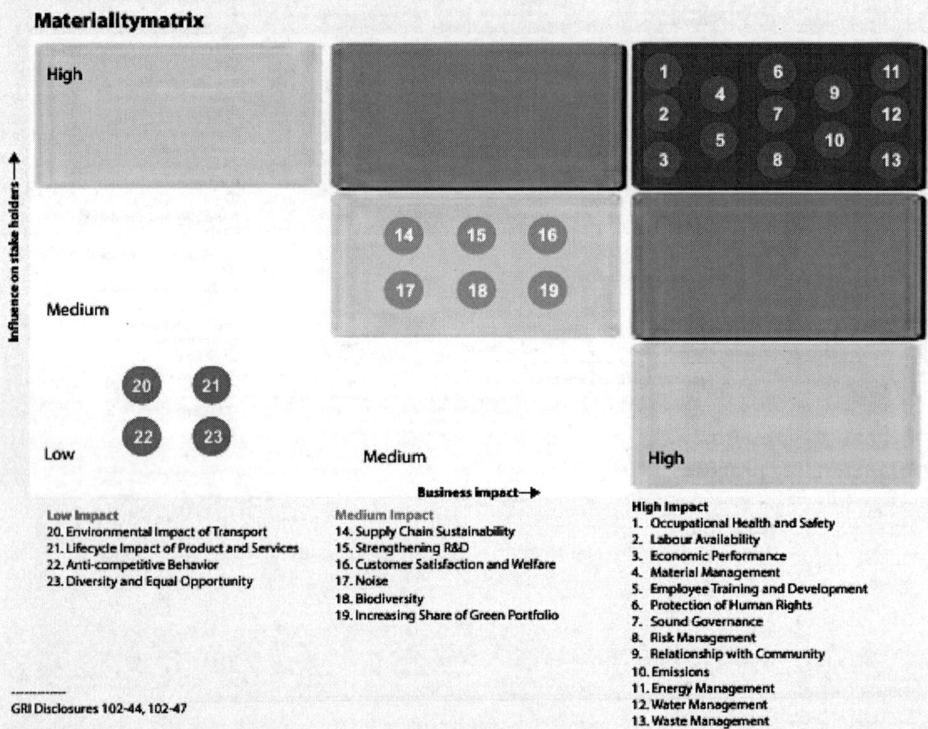

Figure 3.6: Tata Projects Materiality Matrix

- **High Priority /Crucial ESG Issues**: Occupational health and safety, labour availability, economic performance, material management, employee training and development, protection of human rights, sound governance, risk management, relationship with community, Emissions, energy management, water management and waste management.

- **Emerging/Important/Medium Impact ESG Issues**: Supply chain sustainability, strengthening R&D, Customer satisfaction and welfare, Noise, Biodiversity, Increasing Share of Green Portfolio.

- **Monitoring ESG Issues**: Environmental impact of transport, Lifecycle impact of product and services, anti-competitive behaviour and Diversity and Equal opportunity.

3.5.7 Philips Morris International

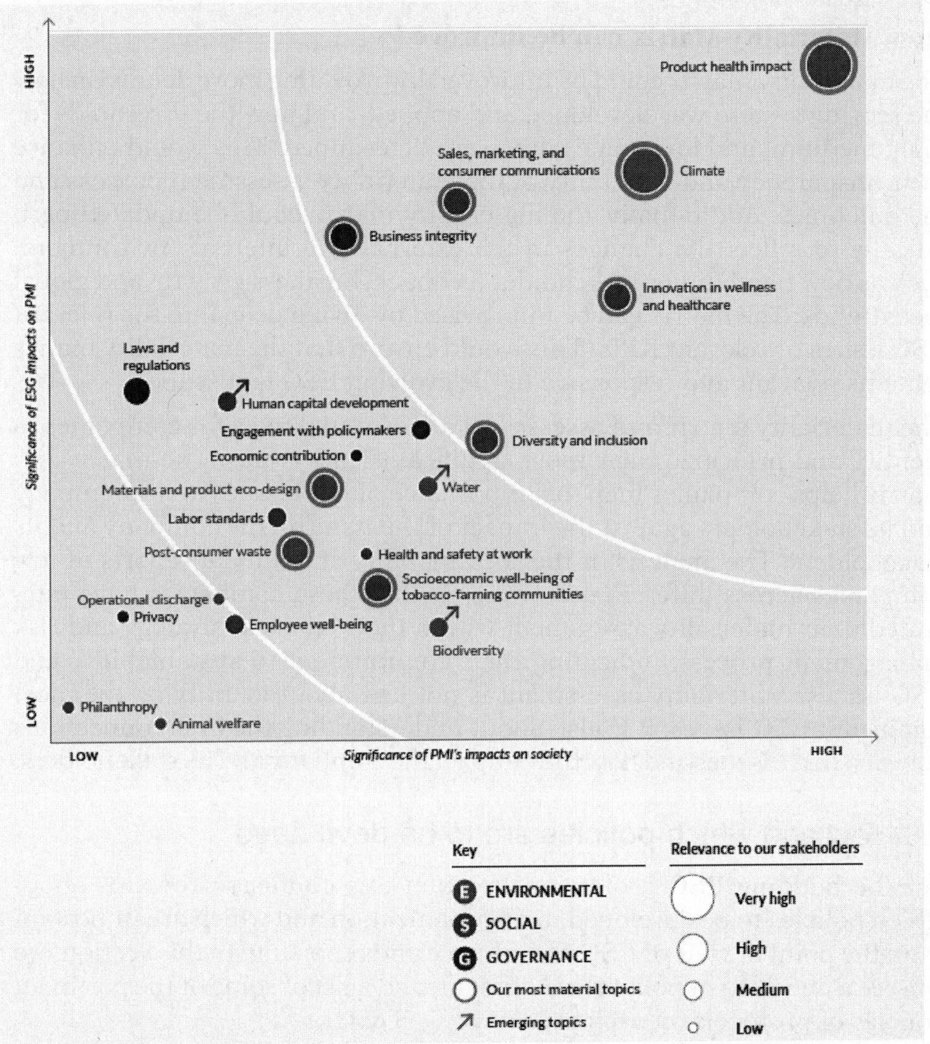

Figure 3.7: Philip Morris International Materiality Matrix

- **High Priority/Crucial ESG Issues**: Product Health Impact, Climate, Innovation in Wellness and Healthcare, sales marketing and consumer communication, business integrity, diversity and inclusion.
- **Emerging/Important/Medium Impact ESG Issues**: Water, Biodiversity, Materials and product eco-design, post-consumer waste,

laws and regulations, engagement with policymakers, economic contribution, human capital development, labour standards, health and safety at work and socio-economic well-being of tobacco farming communities.

- **Monitoring ESG Issues**: Employee well-being, operational discharge, privacy, animal welfare, philanthropy.

How Materiality Matrix can be improved

The materiality matrix could be improved by providing more details on how the scoring system was developed and applied, and how the thresholds for high, medium, and low materiality were determined. This would enhance the transparency and credibility of the materiality assessment process and the outcomes. Additionally, the materiality matrix could be updated periodically to reflect the changes in the external and internal environment, such as new regulations, stakeholder feedback, business growth, and global megatrends. The matrix can be improvised by diving deep into the relevant ESG issues or relevant KPIs. This would ensure that the materiality matrix remains relevant and responsive to the evolving ESG landscape.

The materiality matrix and assessment are essential tools for companies to identify and prioritize their most significant ESG issues. The materiality matrix helps companies map the importance of ESG issues to the company and its stakeholders against the impact of the issue on the company and its stakeholders. The analysis of the sustainability and annual reports of few companies across different sectors show that these companies have integrated their materiality assessment within their business strategy and risk management process, indicating their commitment to sustainability and ESG issues. Materiality assessment is not just about identifying the most significant ESG issues, it is also about understanding the interconnections between these issues and how they impact the company and its stakeholders.

3.6 How and which policies are to be developed

For the budding ESG professionals, often this confusion remains about which policies to be developed in an organization and which are important from the point of view of ESG compliance and reporting. In this section, we will see a checklist of policy development, and a list of some of the pertinent policies of protocols on each aspects of E, S & G.

3.6.1 Suggestive Checklist for Policies relevant to ESG in Business

The following is a checklist for policies and Protocols to be in place in a company:

- Has the business undertaken an exercise to map material risks and opportunities in relation to ESG?

- Does the company have a separate standalone ESG policy (*i.e.* in addition to an environmental or safety policy) which provides details of your approach and commitments to management of key ESG risks and opportunities? Please provide details.
- Does the organization have an environmental policy? If yes, has the environmental policy been implemented?
- Has a policy of Climate Change/action plan to reduce GHG emissions been formalized? If yes, are there steps for implementation included?
- Do you have a workplace harassment policy/Prevention of Sexual Harassment policy?
- Do you have a Business and Human Rights policy?
- Do you have a diversity and inclusion policy? Or are these aspects covered in your human resource policy?
- Does the company have a CSR policy?
- Do you have a responsible procurement policy and/or a supplier code of conduct which incorporates your ESG/sustainability expectations/ considerations?
- Does the company have a cyber security/data protection policy?
- Does the company have an IT policy which includes components of cyber security and data privacy?
- Does the company have a code of ethics?
- Does the company have a whistle-blowing policy?
- Does the company have Anti-bribery and Anti-Corruption (ABC) Policy in place?
- Does the company have a Enterprise Risk Management System in place?
- Does the company have a conflict of interest policy in place?
- Does the company have Code of Conduct for the members of the board of directors?
- Does the company have health & safety policy?
- Does the company have biodiversity conservation policy?

3.6.2 Business Policies for 'E' of ESG

Some of the pertinent policies and protocols in E of ESG may be:

- Assessment of Environmental impact
- Climate Change Mitigation, Resiliency and Adaptation
- Waste Management

- Air and water pollution
- Energy consumption
- Greenhouse gas emissions from energy and fuels used
- Carbon emissions and carbon footprint
- Natural resources and resource scarcity, including deforestation
- Biodiversity
- Circularity
- Sustainable Agriculture
- Nature based solutions
- Responsible Consumption

3.6.3 Business Policies for 'S' of ESG

Some of the pertinent policies and protocols in S of ESG may be:

- Employee Engagement
- Employee well-being initiatives
- Fair pay and living wages
- Diversity, equity and inclusion
- Workplace health and safety
- Fair treatment of customers and suppliers
- Responsible sourcing
- Supply chain sustainability
- Business and Human Rights policy
- Corporate Social Responsibility and community engagement
- Grievance Redressal Mechanism
- Memberships of industry associations
- Workplace harassment policy, Prevention of Sexual Harassment
- Cyber security, data protection policy
- Labour Rights
- Social Impact Investing

3.6.4 Business Policies for 'G' of ESG

Some of the pertinent policies and protocols in G of ESG may be:

- Composition of board of directors and the senior management
- Constitution of ESG Committee

- Board evaluation
- Executive Compensation
- Financial Transparency
- Various regulatory compliance
- Risk Management
- Data Privacy
- Ethical Business Practices
- Prevention corruption and bribery
- Conflict of interest and political lobbying
- Reputational risk
- Stakeholder Engagement Plan
- ESG Integration into business strategy
- ESG reporting and disclosures
- Developing ESG Impact Leadership

3.7 How to set Targets & KPIs

Key Performance Indicators (KPIs) are the foundation on which the ESG structure of any company is established. KPIs in an ESG report are specific metrics or measurements indicators used to assess and communicate an organization's performance on various parameters under three main components of ESG. These indicators help in performance and impact evaluation of a particular company and are crucial to judge how efficiently a company is meeting its ESG commitments. KPIs help stakeholders, such as investors, customers, employees, and the general public, understand the organization's sustainability efforts and track progress over time. Some of the key commonly adopted KPIs by the companies are:

3.7.1 Environmental KPIs

- **Carbon Emissions:** Metrics related to greenhouse gas emissions, such as CO2 emissions per unit of production or emissions reduction targets.
- **Energy Consumption:** Measures of energy use and efficiency, like energy intensity or the use of renewable energy sources.
- **Water Usage:** Metrics that quantify water consumption, conservation efforts, and water recycling rates.
- **Waste Management:** KPIs related to waste reduction, recycling rates, and hazardous waste disposal.

3.7.2 Social KPIs

- **Employee diversity:** Metrics on workforce diversity, including gender, ethnicity, and age.
- **Health and safety:** Measures of workplace safety, accident rates, and occupational health programmes.
- **Community engagement:** Indicators assessing a company's involvement in local communities, charitable contributions, and community development initiatives.
- **Employee satisfaction:** Surveys or assessments of employee well-being and job satisfaction.

3.7.3 Governance KPIs

- **Board diversity:** Metrics on the diversity of the board of directors and its committees.
- **Ethics and compliance:** Indicators related to the organization's adherence to ethical standards, codes of conduct, and legal compliance.
- **Anti-corruption efforts:** Measures to assess and report on anti-corruption policies, training, and incidents.
- **Shareholder engagement:** KPIs tracking interactions and engagement with shareholders on ESG matters.

3.7.4 Process of setting ESG goals

Setting ESG goals for a company involves a process that includes a materiality assessment, stakeholder engagement, and defining qualitative and quantitative goals. The following is a step-by-step process that can be adopted in setting ESG goals for a company:

- **Institutional arrangements:** The first step is to establish institutional arrangements for ESG goal setting. This may involve creating a dedicated ESG committee, appointing a chief sustainability officer, or assigning responsibility to existing committees.
- **Materiality assessment:** A materiality assessment is a process that identifies the ESG issues that are most significant to a company and its stakeholders. This involves analyzing the company's operations, value chain, and stakeholder expectations. The output of this assessment informs the selection of ESG goals that are most relevant to the company and its stakeholders.
- **Defining qualitative and quantitative goals:** Based on the materiality assessment and stakeholder engagement, qualitative and quantitative goals can be defined. Qualitative goals may include

commitments to reduce carbon emissions, increase diversity, or improve supply chain sustainability. Quantitative goals may include targets to reduce greenhouse gas emissions by a certain percentage, achieve a certain level of employee diversity, or increase the use of renewable energy.

- **Rationale for the goals:** The rationale for each ESG goal should be documented. This should include the business case for the goal, such as the benefits it will bring to the company and its stakeholders, as well as the risks and opportunities it addresses.
- **Stakeholder engagement in setting goals:** Stakeholders should be engaged throughout the goal-setting process to ensure that their expectations and priorities are taken into account. This may involve setting up a stakeholder advisory group, inviting stakeholder feedback on draft goals, and providing regular updates on progress towards the goals. Stakeholder engagement is a crucial part of setting ESG goals. This involves engaging with key stakeholders, such as employees, customers, investors, and NGOs, to understand their expectations and priorities. This can be done through surveys, focus groups, and stakeholder consultations.
- **Finalize qualitative and quantitative goals:** Once the ESG goals have been defined, they should be finalized and communicated to all stakeholders. This should include clear timelines for achieving the goals, as well as targets for measuring progress.

By following this indicative process, a company can set ESG goals that are aligned with its material issues and stakeholder expectations, and create long-term value for its stakeholders. It is also important to regularly review and update ESG goals as the company's material issues and stakeholder expectations change.

3.8 Implementation Modalities

Implementing an ESG plan requires a comprehensive strategy that includes setting milestones, monitoring indicators, engaging employees, building capacity, and establishing review modalities. The following is a step-by-step process for implementing an ESG plan:

- **Prepare a plan and implementation strategy:** The first step is to prepare a comprehensive ESG plan that includes specific goals, targets, and action plans for each area of focus (environmental, social, and governance). The implementation strategy should outline the steps required to achieve each goal and should include timelines, resource allocation, and roles and responsibilities.

- **Set milestones and monitoring indicators:** Milestones are specific targets that need to be achieved at various stages of the ESG plan implementation. Monitoring indicators are metrics that measure the progress towards achieving these milestones. The milestones and monitoring indicators should be established at the beginning of the implementation process and should be regularly reviewed and updated.
- **Establish an MIS:** An MIS (Management Information System) is a tool for tracking and reporting on ESG performance. The MIS should be designed to capture data on each ESG area of focus, and should include key performance indicators (KPIs) that align with the milestones and monitoring indicators. The MIS should also be user-friendly and accessible to all relevant stakeholders.
- **Employee engagement:** Employee engagement is critical to the success of ESG implementation. Employees should be trained on the ESG plan, their roles and responsibilities, and the expected outcomes. They should also be involved in the implementation process and encouraged to provide feedback and suggestions for improvement.
- **Capacity building:** Capacity building is an ongoing process that involves developing the skills and knowledge of employees and other stakeholders. This can include training on sustainability, social responsibility, and governance issues, as well as providing resources and support to enable them to take action on ESG goals.
- **Review modalities:** Regular reviews of ESG performance are critical to ensuring that the plan is on track and that adjustments can be made as needed. Review modalities should be established at the beginning of the implementation process and should include regular reporting on progress towards milestones, feedback from stakeholders, and an evaluation of the effectiveness of the ESG plan.

By following this process, a company can effectively implement its ESG plan and achieve its goals. It is important to communicate progress to stakeholders and to celebrate successes along the way to

3.9 Measuring ESG Performance

A recent report shows that 83% of consumers believe that it is important for companies to adopt ESG best practices. Additionally, 91% of business leaders feel that they have a responsibility to address ESG issues. Furthermore, 86% of employees prefer to work for a company that shares their views on such issues. By this rationale, and if we view the bedrock of any company's success as the people who form it, ESG in some form is the direction companies need to take to find growth pathways that align with a changing world.

The data reveals that when it comes to making purchasing decisions, consumers between the ages of 17 and 38 are twice as likely as older consumers to take into account ESG issues. This is not just a matter of personal opinions or feelings.

ESG trends are being noticed by investors, as assets under management in ESG funds have doubled between 2017 and 2020. This shift towards ESG is being seen in both passive funds that track ESG indexes and activist funds that purchase the entire market and then advocate for ESG issues through shareholder voting. Even organisations that prioritise financial metrics need to comprehend the impact of ESG on their sales and capital-raising abilities.

Investors typically use three approaches to compare ESG ratings:

- Comparing ratings with peers who manage similar portfolios.
- Using a standard industry benchmark index.
- Relying on their own historical and internal data.

3.9.1 How to measure ESG Performance

There isn't a single factor that determines the success of a company's ESG initiatives. To measure ESG, both quantitative and qualitative indicators are used, and each industry requires a customised approach. These are the essential steps for measuring ESG:

- Use industry-specific frameworks to identify the relevant metrics for your business. These metrics could include parameters like compensation for your employees, diversity on your board of directors, or greenhouse gas emissions
- Gather data on your company's performance through sources such as financial reports, reports from suppliers, and industry benchmarks
- Review and assess the company's trends, strengths, and weaknesses by analysing available data. It may be helpful to compare the findings with similar companies or sustainability standards
- Publish the ESG results on the website or share the ESG performance with relevant stakeholders

To enhance the performance, use the gained insights to create a plan that addresses any identified weaknesses. This should involve setting ESG targets and goals, with key performance indicators (KPIs) to measure progress, while implementing new policies and practices.

3.9.2 Tools for Measurement

- **ESG Ratings**: ESG ratings are aimed at evaluating the level of an organization's environmental, social, and governance risk exposure.

Essentially, it advises investors on how sustainable a company's business processes are and what measures they are employing to integrate sustainably into their operations. A high ESG rating or ESG score would demonstrate that the company either has sustainable values that it deems favourable or is proactive about guarding itself as well as the environment against environmental or governance risks like pollution. It is intended to provide information to market participants (investors, analysts, and corporate managers) about the relation between corporations and non-investor stakeholders interests.

- **ESG Index**: When the concept of a stock index is combined with ESG criteria, we get an ESG index. It consists of companies that meet certain sustainability criteria and excludes or underweight less sustainable companies.
- **ESG Audit & Assurance**: It helps organizations in navigating the continuously evolving regulatory landscape concerning ESG reporting requirements and emerging best practice. In order to facilitate the verification process, SEBI has introduced assurance requirements as per the BRSR Core that specifies the data and approach for reporting and assurance.
- **ESG Survey**: It highlights views on continued importance of sustainability and ESG practices. While one survey cannot capture the full breadth of sustainability and ESG initiatives under way in the business landscape, the questionnaire in each survey should aim to assess the ESG aspects of a company such as ESG strategy and practices for making informed decisions.
- **ESG Software Platforms**: To maintain high ESG performance, It is essential to implement a data management system and track key indicators such as energy use, water consumption, waste generation, and workplace health and safety metrics. Companies have various digital tools available to track and measure different ESG metrics. These tools can also help in benchmarking against industry peers, identifying areas for improvement and creating sustainability reports and disclosures.

3.10 How ESG Audit is done in Indian context

ESG auditing and accounting are crucial parts of ethical business operations. They concentrate on the governance, social, and environmental facets of a business's operations in addition to financial reporting. Through ESG audit, companies can show and validate their dedication to ethical and sustainable business practices by disclosing their performance in these areas.

Some of common pertinent question for the purpose of ESG Audit may be considered as under:

3.10.1 Environment

- Does the organization monitor energy consumption?
- In case the company is not tracking energy consumption, is there a plan that has been put in place to capture energy consumption?
- Total Energy consumption - Direct (fuels burned in captive power plants, diesel usage in backup generators, etc.)
- Total Energy consumption - Indirect (purchased from Grid, green electricity from third party vendor)
- Total renewable energy used
- GHG emissions within the organization - Scope 1 & 2
- Does our organization monitor waste consumption and recycling?
- Total waste generated within the organization - Plastic, E-waste, Hazardous (Bio-waste), Non-hazardous, Others
- % of waste recycled
- Does our organization monitor water consumption? What is total water consumption within organization? (Ground water, Surface Water, Municipal supply)
- % of water recycled within the organization

3.10.2 Social

- Number of Permanent/Full Time Employees
- Permanent Male Employees
- Permanent Female Employees
- Part-Time Employees/temporary employees/employees through third-party contracts
- Women in senior management/leadership positions
- Retention rate
- What is the net promoter score for employee satisfaction (eNPS)?
- Details on learning and development hours undertaken per employee (training hours)
- Training details separated by topic and hours for Male and Female Employees separately (Technical, Non-technical, Business ethics and integrity, Ethical standards such as Code of Conduct etc., Bribery and Corruption, Prevention of Sexual Harassment, etc.)

- Details on the complaints made by employees and other stakeholders for the sub-indicators like - Sexual Harassment, Discrimination at workplace, Child Labour, Forced Labour/Involuntary Labour, Wages, other human rights related issues etc.
- Details on pending resolutions for the complaints/grievances stakeholders for the sub-indicators like - Sexual Harassment, Discrimination at workplace, Child Labour, Forced Labour/Involuntary Labour, Wages, other human rights related issues etc.
- Health and Safety Performance: Lost time injury frequency rate for employees.
- Health and Safety Performance: Total number of fatalities.

3.10.3 Governance

- Details of Gender Diversity in business
- Details of instances involving loss/breach of data of customers as a percentage of total data breaches or cyber security breaches
- Details of related party transactions
- Details of executive pay
- How the stakeholders have been engaged?
- How the ESG performance is being tracked by the Board?

3.10.4 Indian ESG Audit and Assurance

In India, ESG Assurance and Audit is popularly done under following instruments:

- **Assurance in accordance with the BRSR Core**

  The BRSR Core is a framework for assurance and ESG disclosures for the value chain by listed entities in India. It was introduced by SEBI in July 2023 to enhance the quality and reliability of ESG information and reporting. The BRSR Core consists of a subset of the BRSR, which has nine ESG attributes and key performance indicators (KPIs) under each attribute. The BRSR Core aims to provide reasonable assurance by listed entities on their ESG performance and impact on their value chain. The BRSR Core applies to the top 500 listed entities by market capitalization from FY 2023-24 onwards. The BRSR Core requires these entities to obtain assurance from an independent assurance provider and disclose the assurance report along with the BRSR Core in their annual report. The BRSR Core is expected to improve the transparency and accountability of ESG disclosures and help investors and stakeholders make informed decisions.

◆ **ISO 26002 by Bureau of Indian Standards (BIS)**

ISO 26002 is a guidance standard developed by the International Organization for Standardization (ISO) that provides information and recommendations for integrating social responsibility into an organization's practices, policies and processes. It covers issues such as human rights, fair operating practices, environmental sustainability, consumer issues and community involvement.

We may summarise the aspects of ESG Audit as reflected in the figure below:

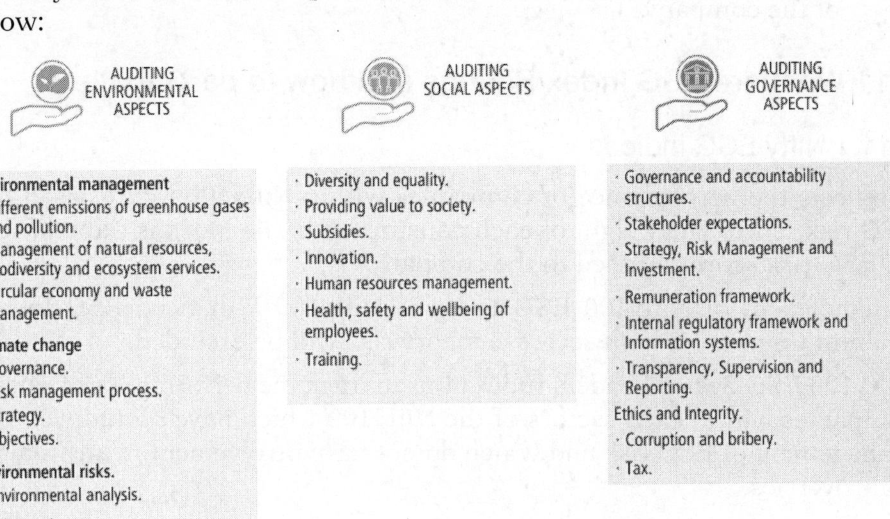

Figure 3.8 : Key Aspects of ESG Audit

3.10.5 Internal Audits and Role of Assurance

Internal Audit should benchmark its own capabilities and resources with those required to execute work, which in itself will depend on the actual nature of the business, the complexity of information, the maturity of ESG reporting roles and the dependence on third parties for information and expertise. Company should make sure ESG aspects are contemplated in internal audit's risk assessment methodology. Internal audit needs different skill sets and knowledge for ESG aspects, regular updates and capacity building of the team involved in internal audit is essential.

ESG Assurance plays a vital role in mitigating business risks, providing authenticity on what is being reported and ultimately gaining trust of stakeholders in the business. Following are key role of ESG Assurance:

- Ensuring that ESG aspects are integrated into the company's strategic and investment initiatives.
- Guaranteeing that executive remuneration is aligned with sustainability-related goals (ESG aspects).
- Guaranteeing coherent and transparent communication of these aspects to all interested parties.
- Ensuring the effectiveness of the approach to integrate the consideration of ESG aspects in the organizational structure and governance of the company.

3.11 What are ESG Index/Ratings and how to participate

3.11.1 Nifty ESG indices

It reflects the performance of companies within Nifty100 index based on ESG risk score. The weight of each constituent in the index is tilted based on ESG risk score assigned to the company.

Enhancement of Nifty100 ESG Index is Nifty100 Enhanced ESG Index wherein Companies with severe category risk will be excluded.

Nifty100 ESG Sector Leaders Index aims to track the performance of select companies within each sectors of the Nifty100 which have scored well on management of ESG risk and which do not have involvement in any major controversies.

3.11.2 Bloomberg ESG Ratings

It provides information on the environmental, social, and governance (ESG) performance of over 10,000 publicly listed companies globally. The service evaluates companies annually by collecting public ESG information disclosed by companies through Corporate Social Responsibility (CSR) or sustainability reports, annual reports, websites, and other public sources, as well as through direct contact with the companies. The data is checked and standardized, including 120 indicators for environmental, social, and governance, such as carbon emissions, climate change impact, pollution, waste disposal, renewable energy, resource depletion, supply chain, political contributions, discrimination, diversity, community relations, human rights, cumulative voting, executive compensation, shareholder rights, takeover defense, staggered boards and independent directors.

3.11.3 MSCI (Morgan Stanley Capital International) ESG Ratings

The MSCI ESG Ratings use a rules-based methodology that identifies the key issues, risks and opportunities facing an organization within the context of its industry vertical. MSCI ESG Research looks at 37 key ESG issues, divided into three pillars (environmental, social, and governance) and ten themes. The data is collected from various sources such as government databases, company disclosures, and macro data from academic, government, and NGO databases. Companies are systematically monitored and reviewed, and new information is reflected in updates in reports weekly. In-depth company reviews occur at least annually. Companies are also invited to participate in a formal data verification process before the publication of their ESG Ratings report. MSCI ESG Ratings are widely used by institutional investors such as BlackRock, State Street Global Advisors, Allianz Group, BMO Global Asset Management, and others.

3.11.4 Corporate Knights Global 100

The Corporate Knights Global 100 is an annual ranking of the world's most sustainable corporations, published in 2005. The ranking is conducted by Corporate Knights, a specialized media and investment research firm based in Toronto. Corporate Knights is an employee-owned B Corp that operates in three segments: Corporate Knights Magazine, Corporate Knights Research and Council for Clean Capitalism. The Global 100 ranking is based on a rigorous assessment of public companies with revenue over $1 billion and is based mostly on publicly disclosed data. The ranking is based on up to 24 Key Performance Indicators (KPIs) covering resource management, employee management, financial management, clean revenue & clean investment and supplier performance.

3.11.5 EcoVadis

The EcoVadis methodology aims to measure the quality of a company's sustainability management system through its policies, actions and results. The assessment evaluates 21 sustainability criteria that are grouped into four themes: Environment, Labour & Human Rights, Ethics and Sustainable Procurement. These criteria are based on international sustainability standards such as the UN Global Compact, the International Labour Organization (ILO) conventions, the Global Reporting Initiative (GRI) standards, the ISO 26000 standard, the CERES Roadmap, and the UN Guiding Principles on Business and Human Rights.

3.11.6 S&P Global Corporate Sustainability Assessment

The CSA evaluates firms by using surveys that include a blend of 80 to 100 questions that pertain to both cross-industry and industry-specific topics. Information from the CSA flows into the Dow Jones Sustainability Index family, which provides a ranking of ESG scores.

3.11.7 Sustainalytics

The Sustainalytics approach looks to provide a score based on understanding an organization's unmanaged ESG risk. A key part of the score is providing insight into what the company refers to as *Material ESG Issues (MEIs)*.

3.11.8 Fitch Ratings

Using its own proprietary scoring system, the Fitch Ratings approach ties an ESG score to credit rating decisions. Fitch Ratings Inc. is an American credit rating agency and is one of the "Big Three credit rating agencies", the other two being Moody's and Standard & Poor's. It is one of the three nationally recognized statistical rating organizations designated by the U.S. Securities and Exchange Commission in 1975.

3.11.9 Moody's

Formerly known as Vigeo Eiris, the Moody's ESG service provides scores and assessment of ESG initiatives. Moody's is well known in the financial services market for its bond rating services. Moody's does Credit risk analysis, deep ESG domain expertise and innovative technologies, ESG risk solutions to help address evolving business needs and inform better decisions through ESG scores and assessments.

3.11.10 Refinitiv

Refinitiv has its roots in Thomson Reuters ESG Scores and provides environmental, social and governance scores for global firms based on publicly reported data. LSEG is one of the world's leading providers of financial markets infrastructure and delivers financial data, analytics, news and index products to more than 40,000 customers in 190 countries. Fund innovation, manage risk at every point in the trade lifecycle are key areas of its work.

3.11.11 RepRisk

Using a combination of machine learning and human analysts, RepRisk claims it can help to identify and classify ESG risk as part of its scoring approach. RepRisk AG is an environmental, social, and corporate governance data science company based in Zurich, Switzerland, specializing in ESG and business-conduct risk research, and quantitative solutions.

3.11.12 ISS ESG

Institutional Shareholder Services (ISS) provides insight into the financial material information that can be contained in what is normally non-financial ESG disclosures. ISS is a leading provider of corporate governance and responsible investment solutions, market intelligence, fund services focused on ESG and governance risk mitigation as a shareholder value enhancing measure.

3.11.13 Asian Sustainability Rating

Asian sustainability rating (ASR) is a benchmarking tool developed by Responsible Research and CSR Asia, covering areas such as the Environment, Social and Governance (ESG) of leading listed companies in ten Asian countries including China, India, South Korea, Thailand, and Singapore among others. The Asian Sustainability Rating (ASR) is a simple, open source benchmarking tool, launched in October 2009 and currently covers the top 20 companies in ten Asian markets. The ASR was created by analysing the CSR disclosure of the companies against 51 indicators including the availability and communication of company policies and codes of conduct in relation to labour and human rights issues.

3.11.14 The Dow Jones Sustainability World Index

The Dow Jones Sustainability World Index, or DJSI World, is a global index consisting of the top 10% of the largest 2,500 stocks in the S&P Global Broad Market Index based on their sustainability and environmental practices. The index was started in 1999, and is maintained by S&P Dow Jones Indices in conjunction with Robeco SAM, a Zurich-based investment specialist that conducts detailed sustainability research on thousands of global market-cap leaders each year.

3.11.15 FTSE4Good

Launched in 2001, the FTSE4Good Index Series is useful for ESG (Environmental, Social and Governance) investors for benchmarking and identifying individual companies that adhere to desired corporate practices. To be included in the FTSE4Good Indices, companies must, for example, support human rights, have good relationships with the various stakeholders, make progress to become environmentally sustainable, ensure fair labour standards not only for their own company but for companies that supply them as well, and fight bribery and corruption.

3.11.16 EIRIS

EIRIS is a global leader in the provision of environmental, social, governance (ESG) research for responsible investors being operated by Vigeo Eiris. It was born from the merger of two entities, is rooted in Europe and is now positioned as a global player in ESG research. This status makes Vigeo Eiris a key stakeholder in building greater ESG awareness amongst civil society and local authorities, and in adapting companies' and investors' strategies and practices.

3.11.17 CSRHub

CSRHub provides access to corporate social responsibility and sustainability ratings and information on 18,424+ companies from 136 industries in 132 countries. CSRHub is a B Corporation, an Organizational Stakeholder (OS) with the Global Reporting Initiative (GRI), a silver partner with Carbon Disclosure Project (CDP), a founding member of The Alliance of Trustworthy Business Experts (ATBE) and supports both the Global Initiative for Sustainability Ratings (GISR) and the International Integrated Reporting Committee (IIRC). B Corps use the power of business to solve social and environmental problems. Unlike traditional corporations, B Corps agree to meet social and environmental performance standards, disclose their performance so that it is transparent, and include consideration of all stakeholder interests in their legal structure.

3.12 How to Communicate

Communicating your ESG philosophy and actions to stakeholders is an essential part of ESG management. Here are some steps to consider for communicating your ESG efforts:

3.12.1 Steps for ESG Communication

- **Disclosures:** Companies should disclose their ESG policies, goals, and performance through regular reporting. This reporting should be transparent, reliable, and relevant to stakeholders. Some common reporting frameworks that can be used include the Global Reporting Initiative (GRI), Sustainability Accounting Standards Board (SASB), and the Task Force on Climate-related Financial Disclosures (TCFD).
- **Standards/Guidelines/Frameworks:** Companies should adhere to relevant ESG standards, guidelines, and frameworks to ensure consistency and comparability of reporting. Some commonly used frameworks include the United Nations Sustainable Development Goals (UN SDGs), the Principles for Responsible Investment (PRI), and the United Nations Global Compact.
- **Communication Strategy:** Companies should have a communication strategy that outlines how they will communicate their ESG philosophy and actions to stakeholders. This should include identifying the target audience, the key messages, and the channels for communication (*e.g.*, annual reports, websites, social media). The communication strategy should also ensure that the company is presenting a consistent and coherent message across all communication channels.

- **Engagement with stakeholders:** Companies should engage with their stakeholders to understand their expectations and to communicate their ESG efforts. This engagement can be done through stakeholder meetings, surveys, focus groups, and other communication channels. Companies should also seek feedback from stakeholders on their ESG reporting and use this feedback to improve their reporting in the future.
- **Assurance:** Companies can provide assurance on their ESG reporting to enhance credibility and reliability. This can be done through independent audits or assurance services provided by third-party providers.

By following these steps, companies can effectively communicate their ESG philosophy and actions to stakeholders. This will help to build trust, enhance reputation, and create value for all stakeholders.

3.12.2 ESG Disclosure/Communication Checklist

A tentative checklist of the content to be included in the ESG related communications/disclosures may be:

General

- What are the most material ESG issues for the company in your view and how have you determined these?
- Details on how you may have contributed to helping achieve any of the UN Sustainable Development Goals.
- Disclosure of any legal processes with third parties, including (environmental) regulators, unions and/or individual employees.
- Describe measures in place to monitor supply chain risks.

Environmental

- Description of environmental/climate change policy
- Description of metrics used including current levels and any targets set in relation to greenhouse gas emissions (split between scope 1/2/3 if available)
- Energy consumption metrics and share of non-renewable versus renewable energy
- Water consumption and emissions to water metrics
- Waste generated including hazardous waste, and waste to landfill metrics
- Disclosure of sites/operations located in or near to biodiversity-sensitive areas
- Describe exposure to toxic or hazardous substances, emissions and waste

- Describe any policies for the sustainable sourcing of materials
- Details of any circular economy/recycling initiatives
- Describe exposure to single use plastics and any plastics recycling initiatives
- Disclosure of any environmental certifications.

Social

- Disclosure of policies to protect employees from hazardous waste (if applicable)
- Disclosure on occupational health and safety metrics, such as TRIR (Total Recordable Injury Rate) and LTIR (Lost Time Incident Rate), including historical tracking
- Information about employee turnover, well-being and satisfaction, (*e.g.* how this is gathered and measured), including if applicable for any contracted workforce
- Disclosure on diversity and inclusion statistics and targets, how these are measured, and their achievement historically, including gender pay gap information
- Details about employee training programmes
- Describe policies on human rights, employee legislation and modern slavery
- Describe policies and processes in place to monitor labour standards across the supply chain
- Details on how customer satisfaction is monitored and current performance
- Disclosure of performance on key customer metrics (*e.g.*, complaints, Net Promoter Score (NPS) and how this compares to peers
- Details on how product safety is monitored, including any information on product recalls or any other controversies
- Description of customer policies including adherence with regulatory requirements
- Details on how relationships with local communities are managed
- Policy and process for safeguarding data security and customer privacy
- Policy and process for managing customer information, including how and where it is stored
- Policy and process for dealing with cyber threats
- Disclosure of any governmental fines, reprimands, or other regulatory actions with respect to customer data.

Governance

- Describe how you manage compliance with applicable regulations, including competition legislation, and any other required industry practices.
- Describe current board composition and main criteria when constructing the board.
- Describe any targets and timeline for increasing diversity of the board.
- Disclosure on all control committees (*e.g.*, Audit, Remuneration, Investment), including involvement of independent directors.
- Disclosure of the metrics to which management remuneration is linked.
- Describe anti-corruption and anti-bribery policies and procedures, including whistle-blower policies, and provide information on any past significant incidents.
- Disclosure of the size of the financial control function and how this is adapted as the company grows.
- Disclose information on your auditor, including how long they have been in place, process for selecting the auditors, and any audit related issues in the past.
- Disclosure of your Revolving Credit Facility (RCF) and/or other material covenants including their current levels.
- Disclosure of details of any ESG linked financing.

3.13 ESG and Brand Reputation

Several researches have indicated that the Companies with a strong ESG practices score higher in terms of reputation and carry lower risk probability because they incorporate sustainability as a core value. This translates into steady and more sustainable performance for the business over the years. On the other hand, companies with a low ESG score due to irresponsible business practices expose investors to higher risks and greater potential for sudden shocks/losses over the long+term.

3.13.1 Key Concepts

Before going deep into the interrelation between ESG and Brand reputation, let's understand the key related terms.

Brand Identity

The brand identity is probably the most well represented branding pillar across all businesses because quite simply, very few businesses in the world don't have a logo of some kind. But the identity system itself is more than just a logo. The term *"system"* here refers to the individual visual elements of the brand all working together in cohesion. The visual branding elements (logo etc.) are designed to communicate the attributes of the brand.

Brand

A brand is an entity developed by a business to shape the perception and build the reputation of the business in the market.

Branding

Branding is the process of creating the brand identity of a company. This process also delivers materials that support the brand, like a logo, tagline, visual design, or tone of voice.

Brand Positioning

Positioning is the act of designing the company's offering and image to occupy a distinctive place in the mind of the target market.

Brand Building

Brand building is the process of marketing your brand, whether that be for the purpose of building brand awareness, promoting products, or simply connecting with your intended audience for the purpose of establishing a relationship with them in their day-to-day lives.

3.13.2 Brand Equity & its Measurement

Value that a specific brand adds to a product or service. Positive perception or emotional attachment that consumers have towards a brand, which can influence their purchasing decisions and overall loyalty to the brand. There are four dimensions of the brand equity.

- Brand loyalty
- Brand awareness
- Brand associations
- Perceived quality

It can positively raise the worth of a brand because as you build your brand equity, you achieve greater brand recognition and positive brand associations, which can boost revenue and brand loyalty. A brand can have value even if it has no equity.

There are different ways to measure the brand equity:

- Run surveys to learn your community's associations with your brand and assign scores.
- Use a brand equity index to compare your brand with your competitors.
- Analyze other financial metrics such as premium price, customer lifetime value, average transaction value, and rate of sustained growth.

- Monitor your brand perception and relevance among your target audience.

If we see some examples, in 2022, Coca-Cola's brand was valued at 97.9 billion U.S. Dollars and in 2021, the Starbucks brand was valued at approximately 13.01 billion U.S. dollars.

3.13.3 The Business Case

Customers are not only willing to pay more for a product with strong brand equity, they're also willing to stay loyal to a company over many years, while, routinely coming back to buy the product. It indicates that the more sustainable your business is, the more customers are willing to buy from you, and that they are willing to pay more too.

A few decades ago, a company was trusted if their products were liked by their customers. Today, a company is only trusted if its employees, customers and other stakeholders are satisfied with the economic, social, and environmental outcomes. Most companies have sustainability mandates that show the world that money is not the only reason that they are in business.

In recent years, sustainability has become essential in measuring brand equity due to its increasing influence on consumers' active consciousness and purchase decision. 2022 BCG survey of 11,971 people across eight countries found that consumers are taking the climate change crisis more seriously post-COVID-19 and have increased their preference for purchasing eco-friendly products.

3.13.4 How to establish, maintain & increase brand equity?

Today, every kind of business be it listed, large, medium, small or start-up, intend to publish its Sustainability Report to attract trust of different stakeholders and ensuring growth of business in today's *sustainability competition*. In India, top 1000 listed entities disclose their Sustainability/ESG efforts through the Business Responsibility and Sustainability Reporting (BRSR).

ESG Disclosures are the important tools for making different business stakeholders aware about what steps a company is taking to adopt responsible conduct.

3.14 ESG and Mitigating Risks

Global sustainability challenges such as flood risk and rising sea levels, privacy and data security, demographic shifts, and regulatory pressures, are introducing new risk factors for investors that may not have been seen previously. As companies face rising complexity on a global scale, investors may re-evaluate traditional investment approaches.

3.14.1 ESG Risk Assessment Checklist

A suggestive checklist for ESG Risk Assessment is placed below:

ESG Risk Assessment	Yes/No
Have you scoped your ESG-related policies and mandatory ESG compliance obligations?	
Do your existing policies meet your ESG objectives and obligations?	
Do you need to develop, redesign or overhaul your ESG policies?	
Have your policies been reviewed to ensure they appropriately mitigate ESG litigation risk?	
Have you undertaken a high-level flag ESG litigation risk review?	
Where ESG litigation risk is identified have you taken appropriate actions to mitigate this?	
Have you designed and implemented a roadmap to meet your ESG mitigation strategy?	
Have you benchmarked your ESG risks against current best market practices and your competitors?	
Have you mitigated your ESG litigation risk by drafting and implementing appropriately worded policies, practices and other ESG documentation?	
Have you identified and prioritised the mitigation of ESG risks associated with the key stakeholders and third parties for your business?	
Do you have an effective monitoring system to identify future ESG risks?	
Do you have a process for identifying the common "themes" that emerge concerning the nature and scope of ESG risks for different classes of stakeholder?	
Do you have a system to effectively monitor and mitigate ongoing/current ESG risks?	
Do ESG risks feature in your audit and assurance plan?	
Do ESG risks get considered by the board or executive/senior management team?	
Have you identified someone at board level responsible for ESG?	

3.14.2 Categorization of various Business Risks

Environment, Social and Governance (ESG) issues are crucial part of investment decision process, they affect the way investors invest. As a global engagement agenda, a list of issues that should be targeted in an attempt to change companies' behaviour for the better performance and to mitigate ESG related Business risks, is presented below, these risks can be categorised in four key categories:

Physical Risks

Damage to companies and assets because of the physical impact of volatile and extreme weather events, for example, heat waves, droughts, rising sea levels, storms or flooding.

Indirect Risks

Secondary financial impacts of extreme weather, for example, lower crop yields, borrowers defaulting on their loans, disruption to supply chains, political instability, insurance claims or losses, legal damages, or conflict.

Policy Risks

The financial impact if regulators react with carbon prices or caps on emissions, the withdrawal of subsidies or the support of renewables.

Transition Risks

The impact of changing valuations to businesses or assets as economies shift to renewable energy sources. This also includes stranded asset risk, whereby assets or businesses are written down to zero because of the transition.

3.14.3 Global Risk Reports

Every year, the World Economic Forum publishes a Global Risk Report, based on interviews with various members and other experts globally. The 2020 edition was released in January 2020 when COVID-19 was just emerging and had not grown into or recognized as a black swan event. Interestingly and somewhat presciently, the report identified "Infection Disease" as one of the 10 long-term risks over the next 10 years. Apart from this, what makes the Global Risk Report interesting is that out of the 10 risks, 7 were environmental and societal as can be seen from the figure below:

(Source: World Economic Forum, 2020)

Figure 3.9 : Long-term Risk outlook

What also very interesting is how the top 5 risks have moved over time to a point where the 5 top risks of 2020 are the 5 environmental risks! While extreme weather has remained consistently on top, issues like Climate Action Failure have become very important to businesses while others like Biodiversity Loss have made an appearance. Many of these are interlinked and these will be explored and discussed further in this session.

Another interesting data point is an annual Sustainability Leaders' Survey conducted by GlobeScan in partnership with the think-tank, Sustainability. The recently-published 2020 survey covers a diverse range of sustainability experts from corporations, NGOs, Academia, Services & Media and Government. In response to a question on which sustainable development issues were considered most urgent, the list, though longer than the WEF one, was similar with environmental ones like Climate Change, Biodiversity Loss, Plastic Waste, Water & Air Pollution being near the top. Interesting part is that the top Societal one was the same as WEF - Water Scarcity - followed by Poverty, Economic Inequality, Access to Education & Healthcare (both brought back into focus by COVID-19) and Food Security. Infectious Disease ranked in the middle but expectedly showed a big jump from 2019.

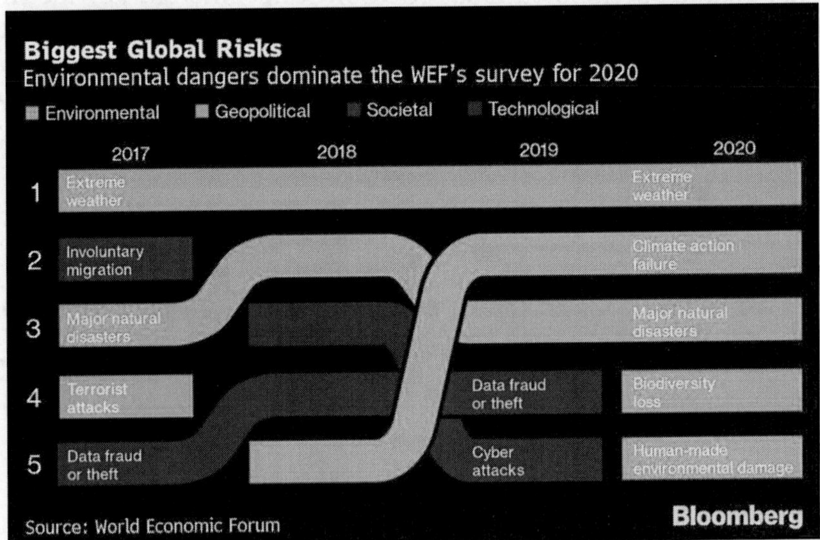

Figure 3.10 : Biggest Global Risks

What do all these studies indicate? Clearly, there is some convergence on the issues that the globe - and hence business - is facing currently (and this is likely to continue into the future). Many are therefore relevant in India too but given the realities here and some of the lessons from COVID-19, the 5 big mega-trends that will impact Indian businesses discussed here are:

- Climate Crisis;
- Natural Resources Scarcity - water, forest produce, minerals;
- Growing Inequality;
- Increasingly Unmanageable Pollution - water, air and solid waste;
- Informalisation of the workforce.

3.15 Measuring against Sustainable Development Goals

The specific methodology used to calculate an ESG score can vary depending on the rating agency or research firm. However, some common factors that are considered when determining a company's ESG score include:

Environmental: Greenhouse gas emissions, waste management, energy efficiency, water usage, biodiversity, and pollution.

Social: Labour practices, human rights, community relations, diversity and inclusion, health and safety, and product safety.

Governance: Board composition and diversity, executive pay, shareholder rights, business ethics, and transparency.

The 17 Sustainable Development Goals (SDGs) are not inherently divided into ESG categories since they are a broader set of goals defined by the United Nations for a sustainable future. However, if we attempt to categorize each SDG into Environmental, Social, and Governance groups based on their primary focus, here is a potential alignment:

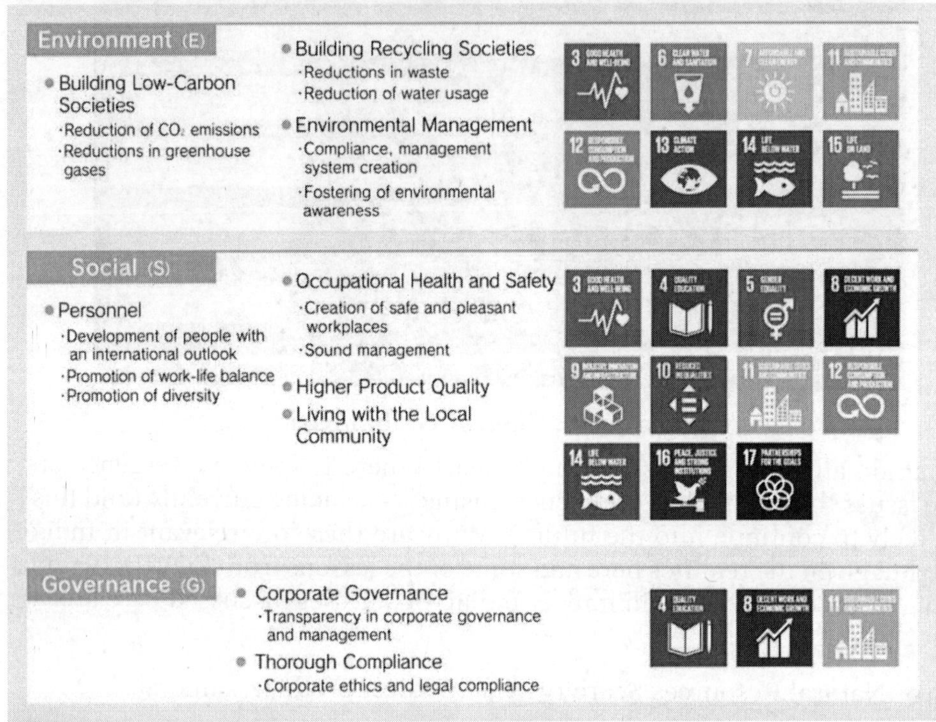

Figure 3.11 : ESG mapped with SDGs

Environmental:

- Goal 6: Clean Water and Sanitation
- Goal 7: Affordable and Clean Energy
- Goal 13: Climate Action
- Goal 14: Life Below Water
- Goal 15: Life on Land

Social:

- Goal 1: No Poverty
- Goal 2: Zero Hunger
- Goal 3: Good Health and Well-Being
- Goal 4: Quality Education
- Goal 5: Gender Equality

- Goal 10: Reduced Inequality
- Goal 11: Sustainable Cities and Communities
- Goal 16: Peace, Justice, and Strong Institutions

Governance:

- Goal 8: Decent Work and Economic Growth
- Goal 9: Industry, Innovation, and Infrastructure
- Goal 12: Responsible Consumption and Production
- Goal 17: Partnerships for the Goals

This categorization is somewhat arbitrary because many of the SDGs encompass elements that could fall under multiple ESG categories. For example, Goal 8 (Decent Work and Economic Growth) includes social aspects like employment but also has governance implications in terms of economic policies. Similarly, Goal 16 (Peace, Justice, and Strong Institutions) has a strong governance component but also underpins social stability.

3.16 Summary of the Chapter

In this chapter efforts have been made to equip the professionals to design ESG Business Strategy. We have discussed how to develop a baseline on ESG programmes, policies and matrix available in the Company, and understand what our peer companies are doing as benchmarking ESG for yourselves. We learned how to set ESG Goals for your Company, define process to be adopted in setting the goals, institutional arrangements, genesis of the work, materiality assessment, rationale for the goals, stakeholders' engagement in setting goals, and finalising qualitative and quantitative goals, etc. Under the implementation modalities, we discussed to prepare a plan and implementation strategy, set milestones and monitoring indicators, MIS, review modalities, employee engagement, capacity building, etc. For communicating ESG vision and actions, modalities for disclosures were discussed. We saw some of the examples of materiality assessment apart from its conceptual understanding. Lists of suggestive policies, KPIs, checklists for different functions have been provided. ESG Audit and Assurance in Indian Contact and Risk mitigation strategies were also discussed. Measuring ESG against Sustainable Development Goals, and an interrelation of ESG and Brand Reputation has also been narrated.

CHAPTER 4

E OF ESG (ENVIRONMENT)

4.1 Environmental dimensions of ESG

In the 1950s, with the establishment of global peace institutions after world war, the world arose to a new war, which was the fight against a triple planetary crisis. As the scientific community sensitised the global community to the realities of environmental degradation and the grave consequences of unhindered industrial development, a global movement for environmental protection under the overarching umbrella of sustainable development has been evolved. India, because of its unique challenges, remained highly susceptible to the planetary crises on account of changes in the climate, the increased pollution levels and the lack of attribution for the rampant increase in environmental pollution. In order to tackle the novel challenges posed by climate change mitigation and adaptation pressures and waste accumulation risks, the Government of India has introduced path-breaking regulatory mechanisms like Extended Producer Responsibility, Corporate Environment Responsibility, Carbon Markets Framework, Business Responsibility & Sustainability Reporting, enactment of various statutes, schemes, policies, and signatory to various international convention among others. The figure below also depicts the key aspects of environmental dimension of the ESG:

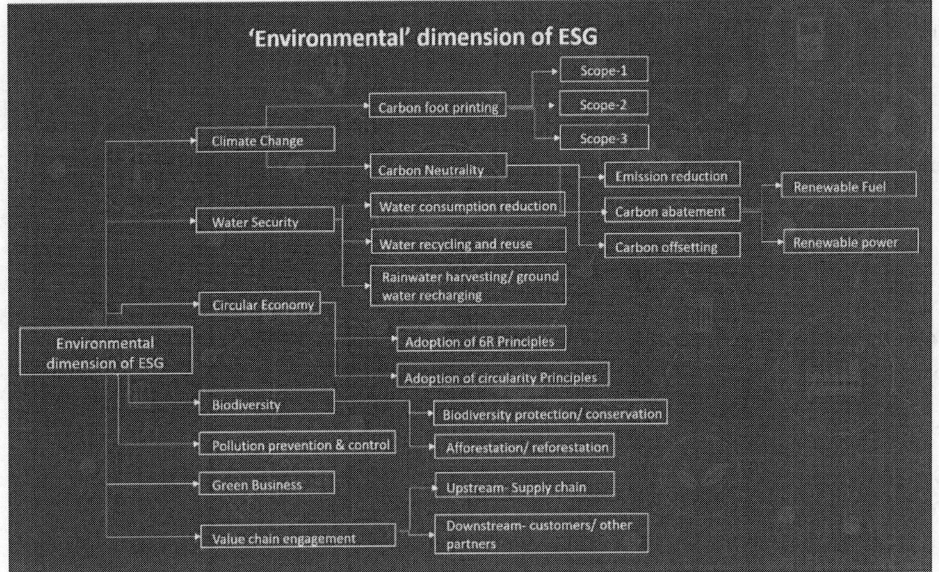

Figure 4.1: Environmental dimensions of ESG

We have studied in earlier chapters how important integration of ESG is into the Business functioning. We see that from the product design to manufacturing process, procurement, marketing, there are several environmental risks and associated opportunities for businesses. Adopting a sustainable product design, cleaner production process, adopting responsible procurement practices and a clean supply chain, adherence to the extended producer responsibility not only attract more investments but also benefits the business in multiple ways. Let's have a brief overview on these aspects.

4.1.1 Integrating ESG into Product Design

Business leaders see the rising demand for sustainable products as a growth opportunity. To address this demand, they have focused their efforts on two important trends that strongly influence the design of products. The first is conscious consumption or a shift in consumer preference towards sustainable products. Sustainable investment is the second trend, where investors consider ESG metrics as indicators of reduced business risk and improved financial performance.

Integrating ESG into Product Design is key to a Sustainable Future. Product design plays a pivotal role in shaping the world we live in. As consumer awareness about Environmental, Social, and Governance (ESG) issues continues to rise, there is a growing need to integrate ESG principles into product design. In this section, we explore present practices, relevant laws, the necessity of such integration, and the broader implications for businesses and society. Contemporary product design is witnessing a paradigm shift towards sustainability. Many companies are adopting eco-friendly materials, reducing waste in manufacturing, and implementing energy-efficient processes. Sustainable design practices aim to minimize environmental impact throughout a product's life cycle, from raw material extraction to disposal.

4.1.2 Cleaner Production

Cleaner production is a preventive, company-specific environmental protection initiative. It is intended to minimize waste and emissions and maximize product output. By analysing the flow of materials and energy in a company, one tries to identify options to minimize waste and emissions out of industrial processes through source reduction strategies. Improvements of organisation and technology help to reduce or suggest better choices in use of materials and energy, and to avoid waste, waste water generation, and gaseous emissions, and also waste heat and noise.

The concept was developed during the preparation of the Rio Summit as a programme of UNEP (United Nations Environmental Programme) and UNIDO (United Nations Industrial Development Organization) under the leadership of Jacqueline Aloisi de Larderel, the former Assistant Executive Director of UNEP. The programme was meant to reduce the environmental impact of industry. It built on ideas used by the company 3M in its 3P programme (pollution prevention pays).

Cleaner production is endorsed by UNEP's *International Declaration on Cleaner Production*, "a voluntary and public statement of commitment to the practice and promotion of Cleaner Production". Implementing guidelines for cleaner production were published by UNEP in 2001.

4.1.3 Responsible Procurement/Supply Chain

Responsible procurement integrates specifications, requirements and criteria that are compatible with the protection of the environment and society as a whole. It encompasses many issues beyond, for example, child labour or the use of harmful chemicals that can affect people or the environment. Commitment to responsible procurement ensures that a company's core sustainability values are throughout the life cycle of their products and services. Best practice would be to future-proof your company's responsible procurement and investments by implementing sustainable policies that increase their long-term viability. Responsible procurement can help companies protect their brand reputation as it requires them to develop robust risk management.

4.1.4 Environmental Risks & Opportunities to a Business

Business Risks and Challenges

Businesses face its own set of risks and challenges due to climate change, these risks may be divided ton transition risks and physical risks.

Transition risks are the risks associated with carbon-intensive business models in a rapidly decarbonizing economy.

Physical risks are risks and impacts on business operations due to acute or chronic changes in climate patterns.

Opportunities to Businesses

Climate Change risks also come with myriad opportunities to innovate for businesses to survive in present age, these opportunities may be seen as:

- New technology to tackle carbon sources
- New technology to adapt to the impacts of climate change
- New business models to tap into new market demands
- New tools to make informed corporate decisions

4.1.5 Environmentally Responsible Investing

Today, investors tend to invest their money in the businesses which are more environmentally responsible and are actually helping the environmental protection, restoration and rejuvenation. Though we have already studied about sustainable finance and ESG funds in an earlier chapter, it is important to mention here the specific focus on E of ESG *i.e.* environmental considerations in investment decisions. These investments aim to promote sustainable development, combat climate change, and foster responsible business practices. It is crucial to address pressing global challenges such as climate change, resource scarcity etc.

4.2 Corporate Environmental Responsibility (CER)

The term 'Corporate Social Responsibility' (CSR) is commonly known to all of us, particularly in India, where CSR is considered a little differently from what it is considered in almost rest of the world. Driving its patterns from CSR, the term Corporate 'Environmental Responsibility' (CER) is also seen as a revolutionary concept. We see that the term CSR is interchangeably used with Sustainability in business context globally, only India was an exception with redefining CSR as per the Companies Act, 2013. When the CSR is interchangeably used with sustainability, it takes care of a corporate's responsibility towards planet, environment, communities, stakeholders, employees and etc.

The concept of Corporate Environmental Responsibility comes under the aegis of Corporate Social Responsibility. According to the European Union, "Corporate Social Responsibility (CSR) is the process, whereby enterprises integrate social, environmental, ethical and human rights concerns into their core." Corporate Environment Responsibility (CER) refers to the duty of the company not to indulge in activities that may damage the natural environment in any manner.

However, it is equally important to learn the difference between the two in Indian Context. CSR spending by a company is linked to the profits earned by it as per the Companies Act, 2013. CER spending is related to the cost involved in the project/business activity. Hence the commitment in the latter is regardless of profit or loss endured by the company.

According to the Ministry of Environment, Forest and Climate Change, Government of India, summary record of the tenth (10th) meeting of expert appraisal committee held on 29th - 31st August, 2016 for environmental appraisal of industry-I sector projects constituted under EIA Notification, 2006:

The Company shall submit within three months their policy towards Corporate Environment Responsibility which shall *inter alia* address

(*i*) Standard operating process/procedure to being into focus any infringement/deviation/violation of environmental or forest norms/conditions,

(*ii*) Hierarchical system or Administrative order of the Company to deal with environmental issues and ensuring compliance to the environmental clearance conditions and

(*iii*) System of reporting of non-compliance/violation environmental norms to the Board of Directors of the company and/or stakeholders or shareholders.

It also mentions the key components/Terms of Reference of the Corporate Environmental Policy:

(*i*) Does the company have a well laid down Environment Policy approved by its Board of Directors? If so, it may be detailed in the EIA report.

(*ii*) Does the Environment Policy prescribe for standard operating process/procedures to bring into focus any infringement/deviation/violation of the environmental or forest norms/conditions? If so, it may be detailed in the EIA.

(*iii*) What is the hierarchical system or Administrative order of the company to deal with the environmental issues and for ensuring compliance with the environmental clearance conditions? Details of this system may be given.

(*iv*) Does the company have system of reporting of non-compliances/ violations of environmental norms to the Board of Directors of the company and/or shareholders or stakeholders at large? This reporting mechanism shall be detailed in the EIA report.

The Ministry has further incorporated the term in the Revised Draft EIA Notification 2020 prominently. Hence, it is expected that the term CER is likely to get recognition in India.

4.3 Indian Regulatory and Policy Mechanism

Businesses have been the predominant users and beneficiaries of the resources offered by the environment. On the other hand, they have one of the largest impacts or footprints on the environment as well. In this light, the regulations aimed at environmental protection, impact the businesses directly. The novel onus put on businesses for environmental stewardship by the Indian regulatory framework has led to an increased need to measure and report on their environmental footprints.

The G20 Delhi Declaration set the tone for greater corporate responsibility, especially with a special emphasis on green development pact for a sustainable future. Taking this momentum forward, the Indian regulatory framework for environmental protection has been evolving, and businesses are now required to comply with various novel environmental norms. With the introduction of concepts like Corporate Environment Responsibility (CER), Carbon Markets, and EPR, businesses continue to grapple with the right approach and guidance for complying with these environmental compliances. As measuring these environmental footprints of businesses is a complex process, involving multiple factors and metrics, this panel discussion aims to shed light on this critical issue and conclude with a guidance note on the dynamics of measuring the environmental footprints of the business under the regulatory framework in India. Some of the recent Environment Policies and Regulations announced by Government of India are presented below:

4.3.1 The Water (Prevention and Control of Pollution) Act, 1974

The Water (Prevention and Control) Act, 1974 was introduced to prevent and control water pollution and to restore and maintain the wholesomeness of water for the establishment. Enacted to combat water pollution, this Act empowers regulatory bodies to take measures for water purification and pollution prevention. As per the Act, two agencies were set up for controlling and preventing water pollution-

- Central Board- which means Central Pollution Control Board according to section 2(*b*)

- State Board- which means State Pollution Control Board according to section 2(*h*)

The Act establishes strict standards for the discharge of pollutants into water bodies, aiming to safeguard water quality, aquatic life, and public health. The legislation emphasizes the importance of sustainable water management and holds industries accountable for adhering to pollution control measures.

4.3.2 The Air (Prevention and Control of Pollution) Act, 1981

Addressing air pollution concerns, this Act grants regulatory authorities the power to set and enforce air quality standards. This act is seen as the first concrete step taken by the Government of India to combat air pollution. It targets various sources of air pollution, including industrial emissions and vehicular exhaust as it defines 'air pollutants' in Section 2(*a*) as any solid liquid or gaseous substance which may cause harm or damage the environment, humans, plants, animals or even damage property. A 1987 amendment to the act also added 'noise' in the list of harmful substances. With a focus on maintaining ambient air quality, this legislation plays a vital role in safeguarding public health and mitigating environmental impacts linked to air pollution.

4.3.3 Perform, Achieve and Trade (PAT) Scheme, 2012

The Perform, Achieve and Trade (PAT) Scheme, implemented by the Bureau of Energy Efficiency (BEE), focuses on improving energy efficiency in energy-intensive industries. Under the scheme, Designated Consumers (DCs) are given specific energy saving targets for a three-year cycle. Industries exceeding their energy efficiency targets receive tradable Energy Saving Certificates (ESCerts). This innovative market-based approach not only incentivizes industries to adopt energy-efficient technologies but also fosters a competitive market for energy savings, promoting a sustainable balance between industrial growth and environmental conservation.

4.3.4 CSR Expenditure under the Companies Act 2013

Section 135 of the Companies Act, 2013 mandates eligible companies to spend 2% of their average net profits from the preceding three financial years on Corporate Social Responsibility (CSR) activities. Schedule VII of the Act delineates specific areas for CSR spending, allowing companies to contribute to environmental initiatives such as afforestation, conservation of natural resources, and pollution control. This legislative provision is unique in its dual focus on corporate responsibility and environmental sustainability, emphasizing the integration of business interests with societal and ecological well-being.

4.3.5 India's Nationally Determined Contribution (NDC) - Paris Accord (2015)

India's NDC under the Paris Agreement outlines quantifiable goals for mitigating climate change. Key targets include reducing the emissions intensity of its GDP by 33-35% and achieving 40% cumulative electric power capacity from non-fossil fuel-based energy resources by 2030. The NDC reflects a nuanced approach, balancing economic growth with sustainable development, and highlights India's commitment to being a responsible global player in climate action. In August 2022, India updated its NDC. As per updated NDC, targets to reduce emissions intensity of its GDP has been enhanced to 45% by 2030 from 2005 level, and the target on cumulative electric power installed capacity from non-fossil fuel-based energy resources has been enhanced to 50% by 2030.

4.3.6 Target of 175GW Renewable Capacity by 2022

India set an ambitious target in 2015 as it aimed to significantly increase its renewable energy capacity. The plan included achieving 100GW of solar power, 60GW of wind power, 10GW of biomass, and 5GW of small hydro-power. This target was a landmark initiative, positioning India as a leader in the global transition to clean and sustainable energy sources, reducing dependence on conventional fossil fuels and addressing environmental concerns.

Today, India has 424 GW of power generation capacity which includes around 180 GW from non-fossil fuels and another 88 GW is in the works. The country has now a target of 500 GW of renewable energy capacity by 2030.

4.3.7 Plastics Waste Management (Amendment) Rules, 2016, 2018, and 2022

The original Rules which were introduced in 2016 with the purpose of phasing out single use plastic over the course of years and better management of plastic (solid) waste. Later, the Plastics Waste Management (Amendment) Rules in 2018 strengthens the Extended Producer Responsibility (EPR), making producers responsible for the end-of-life management of plastic products. The rules classifies plastics in following 4 categories-

- Category 1: Rigid plastic packaging will be included under this category.
- Category 2: Flexible plastic packaging of single layer or multilayer (more than one layer with different types of plastic), plastic sheets and covers made of plastic sheet, carry bags, plastic sachet or pouches will be included under this category.
- Category 3: Multi-layered plastic packaging (at least one layer of plastic and at least one layer of material other than plastic) will be included under this category.

- Category 4: Plastic sheet or like used for packaging as well as carry bags made of compostable plastics fall under this category.

It emphasizes reducing single-use plastics and encourages recycling. The rules represent a proactive step towards addressing the plastic pollution crisis, promoting responsible use, and fostering a circular economy by establishing a centralised online portal by Central Pollution Control Board (CPCB) for the registration as well as filing of annual returns by producers, importers, brand-owners, and plastic waste processors of plastic packaging waste. Environmental compensation will be levied based upon polluter pays principle, with respect to non-fulfilment of EPR targets by producers, importers and brand owners, for the purpose of protecting and improving the quality of the environment and preventing, controlling and abating environment pollution.

4.3.8 E-Waste Management Rules, 2016

Extended Producer Responsibility (EPR) under the E-Waste Management Rules, 2016 places the responsibility on producers of electronic goods for the proper disposal and management of electronic waste. Producers are required to collect a specific percentage of the electronic waste generated from their products and channel it to authorized recyclers. This regulation encourages sustainable product design, reduces the environmental impact of electronic waste, and establishes a structured approach to e-waste management.

4.3.9 Batteries Management Rules, 2016

The Batteries Management Rules, 2016 incorporate EPR principles, obligating battery producers to manage the entire life cycle of batteries. This includes the establishment of collection centers, recycling facilities, and safe disposal methods. These rules aim to minimize the release of hazardous substances from batteries, promote eco-friendly battery technologies, and ensure the environmentally safe disposal of batteries.

4.3.10 Hazardous and Other Waste (M&T) Rules, 2018

The Hazardous and Other Waste (M&T) Rules, 2018 provide a comprehensive regulatory framework for the management and handling of hazardous waste. By categorizing hazardous waste and prescribing guidelines for its treatment, storage, transportation, and disposal, these rules aim to minimize environmental and health risks associated with hazardous waste. The rules underscore the importance of responsible waste management practices in industries dealing with hazardous substances.

4.3.11 Coastal Regulation Zone (CRZ)

Under the section 3 of Environment Protection Act, 1986 of India, Coastal Regulation Zone notification was issued in February, 1991 for the first time, for regulation of activities in the coastal area by the Ministry of Environment and Forests. As per the latest notification the CRZ-IIIA areas will have No Development Zone (NDZ) of 50 metres from the High Tide Line (HTL) as compared to the 200 metres as stipulated in the notification of 2011. The CRZ-IIIB areas however will have a no development zone of 200 metres from the HTL. The notification also proposes a no development zone of 20 metres for all islands. The ecologically vulnerable areas identified on the basis of Environment Protection Act, 1986 are to be managed in partnership with coastal communities and fisherfolks. For the purpose of pollution abatement in coastal areas, the development of treatment facilities is proposed under the regulation in CRZ-IB areas.

4.3.12 National Guidelines on Responsible Business Conduct (2019)

The National Guidelines on Responsible Business Conduct, issued in 2019, provide a comprehensive framework for ethical and sustainable business practices. Covering diverse areas including the environment, these guidelines encourage businesses to integrate responsible conduct into their operations. They emphasize human rights, environmental sustainability, and inclusive development, urging companies to adopt practices that go beyond profit-making and contribute positively to society and the environment.

4.3.13 Bharat Stage VI Auto Emission Norms (April 2020)

Bharat Stage VI (BS-VI) norms mandate stringent emission standards for vehicles, aligning with global standards. These norms specifically target pollutants like Nitrogen Oxides (NOx) and particulate matter, addressing the environmental impact of vehicular emissions. The implementation of BS-VI norms has led to the adoption of advanced emission control technologies, signalling a transformative shift in the automotive industry towards cleaner and greener transportation.

4.3.14 The Polluter Pays Principle

Polluter Pays Principles is a globally well recognized and a much celebrated environment law principal. The Polluter Pays Principle imposes liability on a person who pollutes the environment to compensate for the damage caused and return the environment to its original state regardless of the intent.

In India, there are several case laws which define polluter pays principles' scope and applicability. Some of these are presented as under:

> **Indian Council for Environmental Legal Action v. Union of India 2011**
>
> In this case, the polluter pays principle was applied for the first time in India, the court tried to define the polluter pays principle and its scope. Justice Dalveer Bhandari and justice H.L. Datta said, "the polluter pays principle demand that the financial cost of preventing or remedying the damage caused by pollution

should lie with the undertaking which cause the pollution or produce the good which cause the pollution.

Vellore Citizens Welfare Forum v. Union of India 1996

In this case the Supreme Court declared that the polluter pays principle is part of the environmental juris produce of India. The court held that the polluting tanneries were liable to pay for the past pollution generated by them. The polyester Prince principal the court observed 'the polyester Prince principal as interpreted by this quote means that the absolute liability 4 harmful to the environmental extend not only to compensate the victim of pollution.

M.C. Mehta v. Kamal Nath 1997

This case also known as Span Motel Case the court opened that 'one who pollutes the environment must pay to reserve the damage caused by his act'. It was proved thát the motel administration changed the course of the river in order to save the model from future floods. The court held that the motel should pay compensation by way of cost for the restitution of the environment and ecology of the area.

M.C. Mehta v. Union of India 1987

This case also known as drum gases leak case Shri Ram food and fertilizer is subsidiary of Delhi cloth mill limited was manufacturing caustic chlorine and oleum at a plant surrounded by physically polluted colonies Environmentalist and lawyer, M.C. Mehta requesting the Supreme Court for the immediate closure and relocation of the industrial complex. On the 4th of December 1985, one month after the petition was filed oleum head lead from the complex into the surrounding community resulting in one fertility and many injuries. Justice P.N. Bhagwati writing for a constitution branch discussed the need for the development of the polluter pays principle in the Indian sustainable development. The court also discussed the concept of strict liability and absolute liability citing the famous Rylands v. Flethcher case.

4.3.15 Extended Producer Responsibility (EPR)

Extended Producer Responsibility (EPR) is a policy approach where producers take responsibility for the entire life cycle of their products, including disposal. This concept has been incorporated into various environmental laws in India to address specific waste streams.

Producers are expected to create and submit an Extended Producer Responsibility (EPR) strategy to the relevant regulatory bodies. This plan details their approach to managing e-waste, which includes collection, transportation, recycling, and awareness raising.

India is moving forward with environmental sustainability at a fast pace, as are many other countries. Compliance with Extended Producer Responsibility (EPR) is an essential component of this journey. An EPR policy holds manufacturers accountable for managing post-consumer waste as well as the complete lifecycle of their products. This article offers thorough guidance on EPR compliance in India.

Extended Producer Responsibility (EPR) guidelines specify the obligations and conditions that producers, importers, and brand owners must meet to comply with EPR laws. In recognition of the variety of products and their effects on the environment, these guidelines are adjusted to various product categories and waste streams.

EPR compliance is an essential component of ethical waste management. Once registered, firms must carry out their EPR responsibilities, which include putting in place collection systems, recycling facilities, and eco-friendly waste disposal techniques. Meeting recycling goals and routinely reporting waste management actions to regulatory bodies are requirements for compliance. Penalties and legal repercussions may follow non-compliance. Companies must prioritise sustainability, resource conservation, and circular economy principles to achieve EPR compliance.

4.3.16 Business Responsibility & Sustainability Report

Mandated by SEBI, the Business Responsibility & Sustainability Report (BRSSR) requires the top 1000 listed companies to disclose their Environmental, Social, and Governance (ESG) performance. This reporting mandate enhances transparency and accountability, fostering sustainable business practices. It provides stakeholders with valuable insights into a company's commitment to sustainability and responsible business conduct, encouraging a culture of continuous improvement in environmental performance. The reporting framework tries to cover all the relevant parameters of ESG (Environment, Social, Governance) to ensure the ownership of corporates. The BRSR report format will consist of three sections:

- *General disclosures:* The objective of this section is to obtain basic information about the company - size, location, products, number of employees, CSR activities, etc.
- *Management disclosures:* In this section, the company is required to disclose information on policies and processes relating to the NGRBC Principles concerning leadership, governance, and stakeholder engagement. Wherever relevant, companies have been asked to provide links to their websites where these policies are available.
- *Principle-wise disclosures:* Responses to this section indicate how a company is performing in respect of nine Principles and Core Element of the NGRBCs. This section requires companies to demonstrate their intent and commitment to responsible business conduct through actions and outcomes.

The reporting framework is continuously evolving as it continues to increase parameters to be disclosed through BRSR core and also expanding the scope of BRSR disclosures to the value chain of specified companies.

4.3.17 Environmental Information System (ENVIS) of MoEFCC

Realising the importance of Environmental Information, the Government of India, in December, 1982, established an Environmental Information System (ENVIS) as a plan programme. The focus of ENVIS since inception has been on providing environmental information to decision makers, policy planners, scientists and engineers, research workers, etc. all over the country. Since environment is a broad-ranging, multi-disciplinary subject, a comprehensive information system on environment would necessarily involve effective participation of concerned institutions/organisations in the country that are actively engaged in work relating to different subject areas of environment. ENVIS has, therefore, developed itself with a network of such participating institutions/organisations for the programme to be meaningful. It has following objectives:

- to build up a repository and dissemination centre in Environmental Science and Engineering
- to gear up state-of-the-art technologies of information acquisition, processing, storage, retrieval, and dissemination of information of an environmental nature; and
- to support and promote research, development and innovation in environmental information technology.

4.3.18 Carbon Credit Trading System

The Ministry of Power, Government of India notified the Carbon Credit Trading Scheme, 2023, to develop the domestic carbon market as the country aims at decarbonising the economy and has committed to cut emissions by 45% from the 2005 levels by 2030. In the pursuit of a greener and sustainable future, India has taken a momentous step by introducing the Carbon Credit Trading Scheme (CCTS). This pioneering scheme, brought into effect through the Energy Conservation (Amendment) Bill, 2022, empowers the Central Government to establish a carbon trading framework.

With the CCTS, India aims to create a thriving domestic carbon market, encouraging industries and entities to reduce their carbon emissions through a market-based approach. As India endeavours to combat climate change and achieve its emission reduction goals, a comprehensive analysis of the potential, challenges, and the road ahead for this innovative carbon credit trading scheme is imperative.

The concept of emissions trading revolves around the notion of countries trading excess emission units to aid others in meeting their emission targets. India's carbon market has been gradually evolving, gaining substantial impetus from the Ministry of Power through the introduction of the CCTS. This visionary scheme lays out the organisational architecture required to establish and operationalise the domestic carbon market in India. Key constituents of the scheme include the India Carbon Market Governing Board, the administrator, the registry, the trading administrator, and more. At the heart of the CCTS lies the active participation of industries, which are strategically positioned to contribute significantly to India's ambitious emission reduction goals. The Ministry of Power has been entrusted with the crucial task of identifying designated consumers, including energy-intensive industries, and assigning them specific carbon emissions targets.

4.3.19 Detailed Procedure for Compliance Mechanism under CCTS

The Bureau of Energy Efficiency (BEE) has issued a draft detailing the procedures for a compliance mechanism under the Carbon Credit Trading Programme in India. In this document, so far as the GHG targets are concerned, the trajectory is based on NDC commitments, tech potential, and costs. Obligated entities get sector-specific reduction targets. Compliance Cycle has been mentioned as 3-year trajectory with annual targets, and obligated entities should ensure compliance. This initiative will have global impact in terms of push for India to mitigate carbon emission through market driven approach. The draft is entitled as 'Detailed Procedure for Compliance Mechanism under CCTS'. Compliance mechanism as per the draft is as under:

- The Carbon Credit Trading Scheme envisages the Compliance Mechanism, whereby the registered entities which are notified under the compliance mechanism are called as 'Obligated Entity'.
- The Ministry of Environment, Forest and Climate Change (MoEFCC) shall notify the GHG Emission intensity targets in terms of tons of carbon dioxide equivalent (tCO2e) per unit of equivalent product for each cycle of defined trajectory for the considered obligated entities.
- The obligated will be notified an annual target for a three-year trajectory period and on completion of trajectory period, the targets shall be revised.
- The Obligated Entity notified in any trajectory period shall comply for each annual year (compliance cycle) with the GHG emission intensity targets assigned to it.
- The obligated entity who exceeds the targeted GHG emission intensity in any compliance cycle are entitled for issuance of the Carbon Credit Certificates based on the difference in the achieved GHG emission intensity and targeted GHG emission intensity for the production quantity in the relevant compliance cycle.
- The obligated entity who fails to achieve the targeted GHG emission intensity in any compliance cycle are entitled to purchase the Carbon

Credit Certificates based on the difference in the achieved GHG emission intensity and targeted GHG emission intensity for the production in the relevant compliance cycle.

- The obligated entities can purchase the CCC to meet the GHG emission intensity targets in each compliance cycle.
- The illustration given below shows that the Obligated Entity 'A' are issued CCC on achieving the GHG emission intensity greater than the target GHG emission intensity while the Obligated Entity 'B' is entitled to purchase the CCC to meet their GHG emission intensity targets from Indian Carbon Market.

4.3.20 Draft Eco-Labelling Rules

The Ministry of Environment, Forest and Climate Change, Government of India has notified the new draft Ecomark Certification Rules, 2023. The Rules provide a comprehensive framework for developing and implementing the Ecomark certification scheme for labelling products which have lesser adverse impacts on the environment, with the objective to encourage the consumers to adopt such products, thereby supporting the principles of LiFE (Lifestyle for Environment).

The key requirement under the Rules is the need for products to meet specific environmental criteria and quality standards for certification. Producers, exporters and importers of products seeking Ecomark certification will need to apply to Central Pollution Control Board (CPCB) and submit relevant documentation. CPCB will verify compliance with eco-labelling criteria for the award or renewal of certificate of products under the Rules.

4.3.21 Lifestyle for Environment

Environmental degradation and climate change are global phenomena where actions in one part of the world impact ecosystems and populations across the globe. Estimates suggest that if requisite action is not taken against the changing environment, approximately 3 billion people globally could experience chronic water scarcity. The global economy could lose up to 18% of GDP by 2050.

Over the last two decades, several macro measures have been implemented globally to address environmental degradation and climate change, including policy reforms, economic incentives and regulations. Despite their enormous potential, actions required at the level of individuals, communities and institutions have received limited attention.

Changing individual and community behaviour alone can make a significant dent in the environmental and climate crises. According to the United Nations Environment Programme (UNEP), if one billion people out of the global population of eight billion adopt environment-friendly behaviours in their daily lives, global carbon emissions could drop by approximately 20 per cent.

In this context, the concept of 'Lifestyle for the Environment' (LiFE) was introduced by the Government of India at COP26 in Glasgow on 1st November 2021, calling upon the global community of individuals and institutions to drive LiFE as an international mass movement towards "mindful and deliberate utilisation, instead of mindless and destructive consumption" to protect and preserve the environment. LiFE puts individual and collective duty on everyone to live a life that is in tune with Earth and does not harm it. Those who practice such a lifestyle are recognised as Pro Planet People under LiFE.

Changing our lifestyle, however, is not easy. Our habits are deeply ingrained in our daily lives and are continually reinforced through several elements of our environment. Translating our intention to do good for the environment is not always easy to translate into action. However, it is not impossible. By taking one action at a time and making one change daily, we can change our lifestyle and inculcate long-term environment-friendly habits. Studies suggest that practising an action for a minimum of 21 days helps make it a habit.

In that context, the LiFE 21-Day Challenge is launched to enable Indians to take one simple environment-friendly action per day for 21 days and eventually develop an environment-friendly lifestyle. It is a challenge to change one small thing in your life daily and become Pro Planet People.

4.4 Environment Specific International Instruments

Business operations in a particular country are governed by various national and international aspects. While the national aspects most often are seen in terms of national regulations, guidelines, relevant rules and norms etc. whereas international guidelines, rules, convections, covenants, treaties, etc. provide framework for the aspirational actions. As we understand that international treaties and conventions etc. are in many cases enacted as a law/guidelines in a country and in that context become mandatory to obey or comply with.

Environment related international instruments (law, treaties, covenants, conventions, guidelines, key events, etc.) have been presented in this section. Some are directly relevant to business operations while some are obligations of the National Governments to take actions. Obligations of National Governments pertaining to environment cannot be fulfilled in isolation without active contribution of the business community. Some of the important instruments are presented below:

4.4.1 Ramsar Convention

Also known as the 'Convention on Wetlands', it is the intergovernmental treaty that provides the framework for the conservation and wise use of wetlands and their resources. The Convention was adopted in the Iranian city of Ramsar in 1971 and came into force in 1975. Since then, almost 90% of UN member states, from all the world's geographic regions, have acceded to become "Contracting Parties". Every three years, representatives of the contracting parties meet as the Conference of the Contracting Parties (COP). The convention works on **three pillars** that define the purpose of the Ramsar Convention:

- **Wise Use** - To work towards the wise use of all wetlands.
- **List of Wetlands of International Importance** - Designate suitable wetlands under the Ramsar List to effectively manage those.
- **International Cooperation** - To bring cooperation internationally over the transboundary wetlands, shared wetland systems and shared species.

As per the broad definition of Ramsar Convention, "Wetlands are areas of marsh, fen, peat land or water, whether natural or artificial, permanent or temporary, with water that is static or flowing, fresh, brackish or salt, including areas of marine water the depth of which at low tide does not exceed six metres." Examples of Wetlands are:

- Marine and coastal areas
- Estuaries
- Lakes and rivers
- Marshes and peatlands
- Groundwater and human-made wetlands such as rice paddies, shrimp ponds, and reservoirs.

India became one of the signatories of the Ramsar Convention on 1st Feb. 1982. India has recently added 11 new wetlands to the list of Ramsar sites, and with that, the total number of Ramsar sites in India has reached to total of 75 Ramsar sites. All these sites cover a total area of 13,26,677 hectares in the country. List is given below:

- Tampara Lake in Odisha.
- Hirakud Reservoir in Odisha.
- Ansupa Lake.
- Yashwant Sagar in Odisha.
- The Chitrangudi Bird Sanctuary in Madhya Pradesh.

- Suchindram Theroor Wetland Complex in Tamil Nadu.
- The Vaduvur Bird Sanctuary in Tamil Nadu.
- Kanjirankulam Bird Sanctuary, situated in Tamil Nadu.
- Thane Creek in Maharashtra.
- The Hygam Wetland Conservation Reserve in Jammu and Kashmir.
- Shallbugh Wetland Conservation Reserve in Jammu and Kashmir.

4.4.2 Stockholm Convention

Stockholm Convention on Persistent Organic Pollutants is an international environmental treaty, signed on 22 May 2001 in Stockholm and effective from 17 May 2004, aims to eliminate or restrict the production and use of Persistent Organic Pollutants (POPs) to protect human health and the environment from chemicals that remain intact in the environment for long periods, become widely distributed geographically, accumulate in the fatty tissue of humans and wildlife, and have harmful impacts on human health or on the environment.

Exposure to Persistent Organic Pollutants (POPs) can lead to serious health effects including certain cancers, birth defects, dysfunctional immune and reproductive systems, greater susceptibility to disease and damages to the central and peripheral nervous systems. Persistent Organic Pollutants are carbon-based organic chemical substances that display the following properties once they are released into the environment:

Lifespan - They remain in the environment for long periods of time counted in years.

Distribution - The natural carriers like soil, water and air distribute it throughout the environment.

Food Chain - They become a part of the food chain by getting accumulated in the fatty tissue of living organisms including humans.

Toxicity - They are termed as toxic for both humans and wildlife.

Bioaccumulation - The POPs get accumulated in the fatty tissues and its concentration gets magnified. The species including at the higher level of the food chain absorb greater concentrations of POPs and carry it along.

Effect - The exposure to POPs can cause:

- Cancer
- Allergies
- Hypersensitivity
- Damage to the central and peripheral nervous systems

- Reproductive disorders, and
- Disruption of the immune system
- Endocrine disruptors.

Parties to the convention have agreed to a process by which persistent toxic compounds can be reviewed and added to the convention, if they meet certain criteria for persistence and transboundary threat. The first set of new chemicals to be added to the convention was agreed at a conference in Geneva on 8 May 2009. As of September 2022, there are 186 parties to the convention (185 states and the European Union). Notable non-ratifying states include the United States, Israel, and Malaysia.

It requires parties to adopt a range of control measures to reduce and, where feasible, eliminate the release of POPs. For intentionally produced POPs, parties must prohibit or restrict their production and use, subject to certain exemptions such as the continued use of DDT. The Stockholm Convention also requires parties to restrict trade in such substances. For unintentionally produced POPs, the Stockholm Convention requires countries to develop national action plans to address releases and to apply "Best Available Techniques" to control them. The Stockholm Convention also aims to ensure the sound management of stockpiles and wastes that contain POPs.

4.4.3 CITES

Convention on International Trade in Endangered Species (CITES) of Wild Fauna and Flora, also referred as the Washington Convention, is a multilateral treaty to protect endangered plants and animals from the threats of international trade. It was drafted as a result of a resolution adopted in 1963 at a meeting of members of the International Union for Conservation of Nature (IUCN). The convention was opened for signature in 1973 and CITES entered into force on 1 July 1975. Its aim is to ensure that international trade (import/export) in specimens of animals and plants included under CITES, does not threaten the survival of the species in the wild. This is achieved via a system of permits and certificates. CITES affords varying degrees of protection to more than 38,000 species.

Representatives of CITES nations meet every two to three years at a Conference of the Parties to review progress and adjust the lists of protected species, which are grouped into three categories with different levels of protection:

- **Category I**: Includes the world's most endangered plants and animals, such as tigers and gorillas. International commercial trade in these species, or even parts of them, is completely banned, except in rare cases such as scientific research.

- **Category II**: Contains species like corals that are not yet threatened with extinction, but which could become threatened if unlimited trade were allowed. Also included are "look-alike" species that closely resemble those already on the list for conservation reasons. Plants and animals in this category can be traded internationally, but there are strict rules.
- **Category III**: Species whose trade is only regulated within a specific country can be placed in this category if that country requires cooperation from other nations to help prevent exploitation.

CITES also brings together law enforcement officers from wildlife authorities, national parks, customs, and police agencies to collaborate on efforts to combat wildlife crime targeted at animals such as elephants and rhinos. Many marine species that are traded internationally are highly migratory—meaning they swim long distances, often crossing national boundaries. Their conservation can only be achieved if nations work collaboratively. That's where CITES comes in. The agreement provides a legal framework to regulate the international trade of species, ensuring their sustainability and promoting cooperation among CITES members, also known as CITES Parties.

4.4.4 Convention on Biological Diversity (CBD)

The Convention on Biological Diversity (CBD), known as the Biodiversity Convention, is a multilateral treaty. Its objective is to develop national strategies for the conservation and sustainable use of biological diversity, and it is often seen as the key document regarding sustainable development. The Convention has three main goals:

- Conservation of biological diversity (or biodiversity);
- Sustainable use of its components; and
- Fair and equitable sharing of benefits arising from genetic resources.

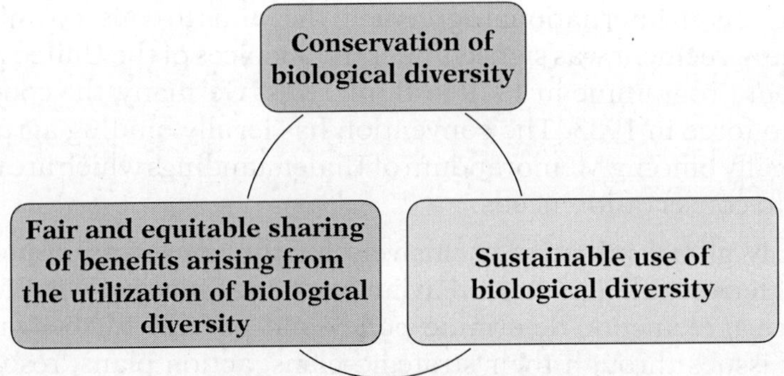

Figure 4.2: Goals of CBD

The Convention was opened for signature at the Earth Summit in Rio de Janeiro on 5 June 1992 and entered into force on 29 December 1993. The United States is the only UN member state which has not ratified the Convention. It has two supplementary agreements, the Cartagena Protocol and Nagoya Protocol. It covers biodiversity at all levels: ecosystems, species and genetic resources. It also covers biotechnology, including through the Cartagena Protocol on Biosafety. In fact, it covers all possible domains that are directly or indirectly related to biodiversity and its role in development, ranging from science, politics and education to agriculture, business, culture and much more.

The Secretariat of the Convention on Biological Diversity is based in Montreal, Canada. Its main function is to assist governments in the implementation of the CBD and its programmes of work, to organize meetings, draft documents, and coordinate with other international organizations and collect and spread information.

The Geneva Meeting of CBD 2023 took up the call by governments, made in CBD 2022 Meeting held in Montreal, Canada, to:

- affirm the need for further enhancing the role and participation of indigenous peoples and local communities in the work of the Convention and the implementation of its Kunming-Montreal Global Biodiversity Framework; and
- advance their discussions on the development and operationalization of a multilateral mechanism, including a global fund, for the sharing of benefits from the use of digital sequence information (DSI) on genetic resources.

4.4.5 Bonn Convention

The Convention on the Conservation of Migratory Species of Wild Animals, also known as the Convention on Migratory Species (CMS) or the Bonn Convention is concerned with conservation of wildlife and habitats on a global scale. It is an international agreement that aims to conserve migratory species. The agreement was signed under the auspices of the United Nations Environment Programme in 1979 in Bonn, West Germany, the convention entered into force in 1983. The convention has legally binding agreements and non-legally binding Memorandum of Understandings which are tailored according to conservation needs.

It is the only global initiative exclusively for the conservation and management of terrestrial, aquatic and avian migratory species. The CMS, and its daughter agreements, determine policy and provide further guidance on specific issues through their strategic plans, action plans, resolutions, decisions and guidelines. Its fundamental principles are:

- The Parties acknowledge the importance of migratory species being conserved and of Range States agreeing to take action to this end whenever possible and appropriate, paying special attention to migratory species the conservation status of which is unfavourable, and taking individually or in co-operation appropriate and necessary steps to conserve such species and their habitat.
- The Parties acknowledge the need to take action to avoid any migratory species becoming endangered.
- In particular, the Parties:
  - should promote, co-operate in and support research relating to migratory species;
  - shall endeavour to provide immediate protection for migratory species included in Appendix I; and
  - shall endeavour to conclude Agreements covering the conservation and management of migratory species.

India has been a part of the Bonn Convention since 1983. Some of the important migratory species in India are:

- Amur Falcons
- Bar-headed Geese
- Black-necked cranes
- Marine turtles
- Dugongs
- Humpback Whales

4.4.6 Montreal Protocol

The Montreal Protocol on Substances that Deplete the Ozone Layer, adopted on 16 September 1987, is the landmark multilateral environmental agreement that regulates the production and consumption of nearly 100 man-made chemicals referred to as Ozone Depleting Substances (ODS). When released into the atmosphere, those chemicals damage the stratospheric ozone layer, Earth's protective shield that protects humans and the environment from harmful levels of ultraviolet radiation from the sun.

The Montreal Protocol phases down the consumption and production of the different ODS in a step-wise manner, with different timetables for developed and developing countries. Under this treaty, all parties have specific responsibilities related to the phase out of the different groups of ODS, control of ODS trade, annual reporting of data, national licensing systems to control ODS imports and exports, and other matters. Developing and developed countries have equal but differentiated responsibilities, but most importantly, both groups of countries have binding, time-targeted, and measurable commitments.

We all understand what ozone layer is what its importance is:

- It is a layer in the earth's stratosphere that contains high levels of ozone.
- This layer protects the earth from the Sun's harmful UV radiation. It absorbs 97 - 99% of the UV radiation from the Sun.
- In the absence of the ozone layer, millions of people would be affected by skin diseases including cancer and weakened immune systems.
- UV radiation would also affect the environment adversely leading to decreased productivity.
- Fauna on earth is also adversely affected by ozone layer depletion.

Ozone Layer Depletion refers to the thinning of the protective ozone layer in the atmosphere. It happens when certain chemicals come into contact with ozone and destroy it. Chemical compounds that cause ozone layer depletion are called Ozone Depleting Substances (ODSs). Some examples of ODSs are chlorofluorocarbons (CFCs), hydrochlorofluorocarbons (HCFCs), carbon tetrachloride, methyl chloroform, hydrobromofluorocarbons, halons, etc. The indiscriminate use of these chemicals causes ozone layer depletion. These ODSs are also powerful Greenhouse Gases (GHGs) and have a long life as well. There are a few natural causes also which cause ozone depletion such as volcanic eruptions, sunspots, and stratospheric winds. However, these do not cause more than 1 - 2% of the ozone depletion.

4.4.7 Kyoto Protocol & Doha Amendment

The Kyoto Protocol implemented the objective of the UNFCCC to reduce the onset of global warming by reducing greenhouse gas concentrations in the atmosphere to "a level that would prevent dangerous anthropogenic interference with the climate system". The Kyoto Protocol applied to the seven listed greenhouse gases (Nitrogen trifluoride was added for the second compliance period during the Doha Round) viz.:

- Carbon dioxide (CO_2),
- Methane (CH_4),
- Nitrous oxide (N_2O),
- Hydrofluorocarbons (HFCs),
- Perfluorocarbons (PFCs),
- Sulfur hexafluoride (SF_6),
- Nitrogen trifluoride (NF_3).

The Protocol was based on the principle of common but differentiated responsibilities: it acknowledged that individual countries have different capabilities in combating climate change, owing to economic development, and therefore placed the obligation to reduce current emissions on developed countries on the basis that they are historically responsible for the current levels of greenhouse gases in the atmosphere. The Kyoto Protocol was adopted on 11 December 1997. Owing to a complex ratification process, it entered into force on 16 February 2005. Currently, there are 192 Parties to the Kyoto Protocol.

In short, the Kyoto Protocol operationalizes the United Nations Framework Convention on Climate Change by committing industrialized countries and economies in transition to limit and reduce greenhouse gases (GHG) emissions in accordance with agreed individual targets. It only binds developed countries, and places a heavier burden on them under the principle of "common but differentiated responsibility and respective capabilities", because it recognizes that they are largely responsible for the current high levels of GHG emissions in the atmosphere.

The Doha Amendment, which establishes the Kyoto Protocol's 2013-2020 second commitment period, has received the required number of ratifications to enter into force. The emission reduction commitments of participating developed countries and economies in transition (EITs) became legally binding. The Amendment sets a goal of reducing greenhouse gas (GHG) emissions by 18% compared to 1990 levels for participating countries. This, according to the UNFCCC, "represents an increase from an average reduction of 5% compared to 1990 levels" during the Kyoto Protocol's first commitment period from 2008-2012. The protocol presents its mechanism in three ways as presented in figure below:

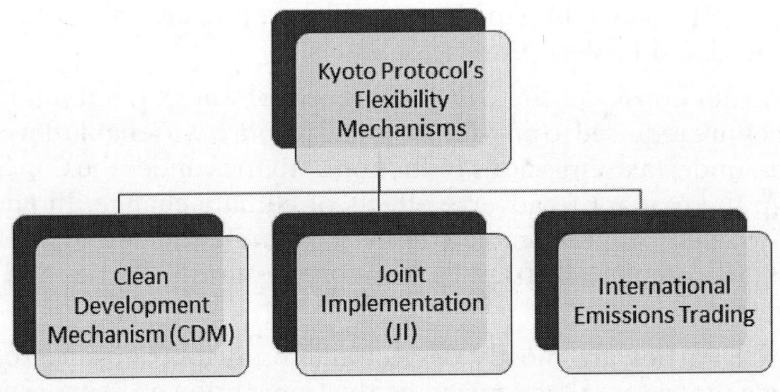

Figure 4.3 : Mechanisms of Kyoto Protocol

4.4.8 United Nations Framework Convention on Climate Change (UNFCCC)

The United Nations Framework Convention on Climate Change (UNFCCC) established an international environmental treaty to combat "dangerous human interference with the climate system", in part by stabilizing greenhouse gas concentrations in the atmosphere. It was signed by 154 states at the United Nations Conference on Environment and Development (UNCED), informally known as the Earth Summit, held in Rio de Janeiro from 3 to 14 June 1992. Its original secretariat was in Geneva but relocated to Bonn in 1996. It entered into force on 21 March 1994.

The treaty called for ongoing scientific research and regular meetings, negotiations, and future policy agreements designed to allow ecosystems to adapt naturally to climate change, to ensure that food production is not threatened and to enable economic development to proceed in a sustainable manner.

India ratified the UNFCCC in 1993. The nodal agency for the UNFCCC in India is the Ministry of Environment, Forests and Climate Change (MoEFCC). Since India is a developing country, it is not required to adhere to GHG mitigation commitments because of its relatively smaller emissions and also because of lesser technical and financial capacities. India has been a big champion of the principles of Equity and Common But Differentiated Responsibilities and Respective Capability (CBDR-RC) at the Convention. This is primarily based on the belief that developed countries have largely been responsible for the huge emission levels, owing to their being industrialized decades before the other countries.

The Convention divides countries into three main groups according to differing commitments:

Countries in first category are in Annex I which include the industrialized countries that were members of the OECD, plus countries with Economies in Transition (EIT), including the Russian Federation, the Baltic States, and several Central and Eastern European States.

Annex II Parties consist of the OECD members of Annex I, but not the EIT Parties. They are required to provide financial resources to enable developing countries to undertake emissions reduction activities under the Convention and to help them adapt to adverse effects of climate change. In addition, they have to "take all practicable steps" to promote the development and transfer of environmentally friendly technologies to EIT Parties and developing countries.

Non-Annex I Parties are mostly developing countries. Certain groups of developing countries are recognized by the Convention as being especially vulnerable to the adverse impacts of climate change, including countries with low-lying coastal areas and those prone to desertification and drought. Others countries that rely heavily on income from fossil fuel production and commerce, feel more vulnerable to the potential economic impacts of climate change response measures. The Convention emphasizes activities that promise to answer the special needs and concerns of these vulnerable countries, such as investment, insurance and technology transfer.

The 49 Parties classified as Least Developed Countries (LDCs) by the United Nations are given special consideration under the Convention on account of their limited capacity to respond to climate change and adapt to its adverse effects. Parties are urged to take full account of the special situation of LDCs when considering funding and technology-transfer activities.

A scientific study carried on greenhouse gas emissions from the time period 1850 to 2012 estimated that the US, China and the European Union would contribute to 50 per cent of temperature increase by 2100. The total emissions' share in the given time period of the US, European Union, and China is 20%, 17%, 12% respectively. On the other hand, India is responsible for only 5%.

From its inception in 1992, the UNFCCC has led to the adoption of a number of subsequent agreements. It has spurred the development of key infrastructure and policies at the international and national levels that serve as cornerstones of today's climate action, including measuring and tracking and reporting emissions and impacts; generating knowledge and research; and building the capacity to address the causes and effects of climate change.

4.4.9 United Nations Conference on Environment and Development (UNCED), Rio Conference, Earth Summit

The United Nations Conference on Environment and Development (UNCED), which is also known as the Rio Conference or the Earth Summit, was a major event in the history held in Rio de Janeiro in 1992. Earth Summit was created as a response for member states to cooperate together internationally on development issues after the Cold War. Due to issues relating to sustainability being too big for individual member states to handle, Earth Summit was held as a platform for member states to collaborate on these issues.

It highlighted how different social, economic and environmental factors are interdependent and evolve together, and how success in one sector requires action in other sectors to be sustained over time. The primary objective of the 'Earth Summit' was to produce a broad agenda and a new blueprint for international action on environmental and development issues that would help guide international cooperation and development policy in the twenty-first century.

The 'Earth Summit' concluded that the concept of sustainable development was an attainable goal for all the people of the world, regardless of whether they were at the local, national, regional or international level. It also recognized that integrating and balancing economic, social and environmental concerns in meeting our needs is vital for sustaining human life on the planet and that such an integrated approach is possible.

The conference also recognized that integrating and balancing economic, social and environmental dimensions required new perceptions of the way we produce and consume, the way we live and work, and the way we make decisions. This concept was revolutionary for its time, and it sparked a lively debate on how to ensure sustainable development.

This summit led to the development of the following documents:

- Rio Declaration on Environment and Development
- Agenda 21
- Forest Principles

The first document called the Rio Declaration, in short, contained 27 principles that were supposed to guide countries in future sustainable development. Agenda 21 is an action plan concerning sustainable development, but it is non-binding. The Forest Principles is formally called Non-Legally Binding Authoritative Statement of Principles for a Global Consensus on the Management, Conservation and Sustainable Development of All Types of Forests. It makes many recommendations for conservation and sustainable development forestry and is non-binding.

4.4.10 UNCCD

When land is degraded or plagued by drought, it loses its capacity to sustain life, which leads to a range of consequences from crop failure to migration and conflict. The United Nations Convention to Combat Desertification (UNCCD) was established in 1994 to protect and restore our land and ensure a safer, just, and more sustainable future.

The UNCCD is the only legally binding framework set up to address desertification and the effects of drought. There are 197 Parties to the Convention, including 196 country Parties and the European Union. The Convention - based on the principles of participation, partnership and decentralization - is a multilateral commitment to mitigate the impact of land degradation, and protect our land so we can provide food, water, shelter and economic opportunity to all people.

Tackling desertification took centre stage at the seminal 1992 United Nations Conference on Environment and Development (UNCED) - also known the Earth Summit - held in Rio de Janeiro. The Rio Conference called on the United Nations General Assembly to establish an Intergovernmental Negotiating Committee (INCD) to prepare, by June 1994, a Convention to Combat Desertification. In December 1992, the General Assembly agreed and adopted resolution 47/188 on this matter, and the UNCCD was established in 1994. Total 197 countries and the European Union are now Parties to the Convention. The Conference of the Parties (COP), which is the Convention's supreme governing body, held its first session in October 1997 in Rome, Italy.

India ratified the Convention to Combat Desertification in December 1996. The nodal ministry for the convention in India is the Ministry of Environment, Forest and Climate Change. India faces a huge desertification problem. According to a report by ISRO, 29% of the land in India is degraded. The 14th Conference of Parties (COP) to the UNCCD was held in India in 2019 in Greater Noida with theme "Restore Land, Sustain Future". It is also pertinent to mention that India is part of the Bonn Challenge, which is an international effort to bring 150 million hectares of the world's degraded and deforested land into restoration by 2020, and 350 million hectares by 2030.

4.4.11 Basel Convention

The Basel Convention on the Control of Transboundary Movements of Hazardous Wastes and their Disposal was adopted on 22 March 1989 by the Conference of Plenipotentiaries in Basel, Switzerland, in response to a public outcry following the discovery, in the 1980s, in Africa and other parts of the developing world of deposits of toxic wastes imported from abroad.

Awakening environmental awareness and corresponding tightening of environmental regulations in the industrialized world in the 1970s and 1980s had led to increasing public resistance to the disposal of hazardous wastes - in accordance with what became known as the NIMBY (Not In My Back Yard) syndrome - and to an escalation of disposal costs. This in turn led some operators to seek cheap disposal options for hazardous wastes in Eastern Europe and the developing world, where environmental awareness was much less developed and regulations and enforcement mechanisms were lacking. It was against this background that the Basel Convention was negotiated in the late 1980s, and its thrust at the time of its adoption was to combat the "toxic trade", as it was termed. The Convention entered into force in 1992.

The Basel Convention aims to protect the environment by bringing measures to control and regulate hazardous and other waste disposals. The negotiations for the convention were started in the late 1980s under the auspices of the United Nations Environment Programme (UNEP). Salient Points of Basel Convention are:

- It came into force in 1992.
- The Basel Convention secretariat is situated in Geneva, Switzerland.
- It applies Prior Consent Approval procedure to regulate the transboundary movement of the hazardous and other wastes.
- Non-parties cannot transport hazardous waste to and from each other unless specially agreed. Basel Convention states such transportation, illegal.
- The member nations to the convention are required to have domestic legislation for both prevention and the punishment of the illegal trafficking of such hazardous wastes.
- It ensures that the member nations control the generation, storage, transportation, treatment, reuse, recycling, recovery and final disposal of hazardous wastes.
- Conference of Parties (COP) is a primary organ of the Basel Convention and is responsible to make decisions about the operations of the convention. It meets biennially.

4.4.12 Rotterdam Convention

The Rotterdam Convention (formally, the Rotterdam Convention on the Prior Informed Consent Procedure for Certain Hazardous Chemicals and Pesticides in International Trade) is a multilateral treaty to promote shared responsibilities in relation to importation of hazardous chemicals. The convention promotes open exchange of information and calls on exporters of hazardous chemicals to use proper labelling, include directions on safe handling, and inform purchasers of any known restrictions or bans. Signatory nations can decide whether to allow or ban the importation of chemicals listed in the treaty, and exporting countries are obliged to make sure that producers within their jurisdiction comply.

The Rotterdam Convention establishes a prior informed consent ("PIC") procedure to ensure that restricted hazardous chemicals are not exported to countries that do not wish to receive them. The PIC procedure does not ban or restrict any chemicals, nor does it mean that any individual country must automatically prohibit their import. Parties implement the PIC procedure through extensive information exchange, priority attention to national decisions on imports, and obligations related to export controls.

The objectives of the Convention are:

- to promote shared responsibility and cooperative efforts among Parties in the international trade of certain hazardous chemicals in order to protect human health and the environment from potential harm;

- to contribute to the environmentally sound use of those hazardous chemicals, by facilitating information exchange about their characteristics, by providing for a national decision-making process on their import and export and by disseminating these decisions to Parties.

The Convention creates legally binding obligations for the implementation of the Prior Informed Consent (PIC) procedure. It built on the voluntary PIC procedure, initiated by UNEP and FAO in 1989 and ceased on 24 February 2006. Following are the provisions covered under the Rotterdam Convention:

- The convention covers those pesticides and industrial chemicals that are banned or severely restricted.
- Any concern related to pesticides and industrial chemicals promotes their inclusion on Annex III of the convention.
- Annex III other than comprising chemicals that need PIC, also may contain those chemicals and pesticides that present a risk under conditions of use in developing countries or countries with economies in transition.
- A decision guidance document (DGC) contains all the information regarding the chemicals mentioned under Annex III.
- With respect to the chemicals under Annex III, the member parties have the following choices:
  - To allow its import
  - To disallow its import
  - To allow its import with some conditions
- A country that imports chemicals has to formulate decisions that are trade-neutral.

4.4.13 Cartagena Protocol on Biosafety

The *Cartagena Protocol on Biosafety to the Convention on Biological Diversity* is an international treaty governing the movements of living modified organisms (LMOs) resulting from modern biotechnology from one country to another. It was adopted on 29 January 2000 as a supplementary agreement to the Convention on Biological Diversity and entered into force on 11 September 2003.

On 29 January 2000, the Conference of the Parties to the Convention on Biological Diversity adopted a supplementary agreement to the Convention known as the Cartagena Protocol on Biosafety. The Protocol seeks to protect biological diversity from the potential risks posed by living modified organisms resulting from modern biotechnology. It establishes an advance informed agreement (AIA) procedure for ensuring that countries are provided with the information necessary to make informed decisions before agreeing to the import of such organisms into their territory. The Protocol contains reference to a precautionary approach and reaffirms the precaution language in Principle 15 of the Rio Declaration on Environment and Development. The Protocol also establishes a Biosafety Clearing-House to facilitate the exchange of information on living modified organisms and to assist countries in the implementation of the Protocol.

In accordance with the precautionary approach, contained in Principle 15 of the Rio Declaration on Environment and Development, the objective of the Protocol is to contribute to ensuring an adequate level of protection in the field of the safe transfer, handling and use of 'living modified organisms resulting from modern biotechnology' that may have adverse effects on the conservation and sustainable use of biological diversity, taking also into account risks to human health, and specifically focusing on transboundary movements (Article 1 of the Protocol, SCBD 2000).

India is a party to the Cartagena Protocol (ratified in 2003). The nodal agency (Competent National Authority-CNA) in the country for the implementation of the Protocol is the Ministry of Environment, Forest and Climate Change (MOEF&CC), Government of India. Regarding setting up of procedures for regulating LMOs, India was one of the early movers in the development of a biosafety regulatory framework, way back in 1989, and has a systematic and structured science-based regulatory system. In the Indian regulations, the terms Genetically Engineered Organism or Genetically Modified Organism are used, which are synonymous with LMOs. In India, series of guidelines are available for risk assessment and risk management of GMOs.

4.4.14 UN - REDD

Three UN agencies - United Nations Environment Programme (UNEP), United Nations Development Programme (UNDP) and Food and Agriculture Organization of the United Nations (FAO) - have collaborated in the establishment of the UN-REDD Programme, a multi-donor trust fund that allows donors to pool resources and provide funding with the aim of significantly reducing global emissions from deforestation and forest degradation in developing countries. Since the programme was launched in 2008, the UN-REDD Programme has been supporting 65 partner countries across Africa, Asia-Pacific, Latin America and the Caribbean and has been the largest international provider of REDD+ readiness assistance in terms of funding, expertise and geographical scope.

Since 2008 the UN-REDD Programme has been supporting 65 partner countries in their nationally led efforts to become "REDD+ ready" and qualify for results-based payments. As of today, UN-REDD countries have submitted forest emissions reductions equal to taking 150 million cars off the road for a year. And UN-REDD has channelled and mobilized more than USD 1 billion since inception. Within the UN-REDD Programme, UNEP leads on private sector engagement, safeguards, knowledge management and communications.

As with other approaches under the UNFCCC, there are few prescriptions that specifically mandate how to implement the mechanism at national level; the principles of national sovereignty and subsidiarity imply that the UNFCCC can only provide guidelines for implementation, and require that reports are submitted in a certain format and open for review by the convention. There are certain aspects that go beyond this basic philosophy - such as the 'safeguards', explained in more detail below - but in essence REDD+ is no more than a set of guidelines on how to report on forest resources and forest management strategies and their results in terms of reducing emissions and enhancing removals of greenhouse gases. However, a set of requirements has been elaborated to ensure that REDD+ programs contain key elements and that reports from Parties are consistent and comparable and that their content are open to review and in function of the objectives of the convention.

4.4.15 Copenhagen Summit

The United Nations Climate Change Conference, commonly known as the Copenhagen Summit, was held at the Bella Centre in Copenhagen, Denmark, between 7 and 18 December 2009. The conference included the 15th session of the Conference of the Parties (COP 15) to the United Nations Framework Convention on Climate Change (UNFCCC) and the 5th session of the Conference of the Parties serving as the Meeting of the Parties (CMP 5) to the Kyoto Protocol. According to the Bali Road Map, a framework for climate change mitigation beyond 2012 was to be agreed there.

The 15th session of the Conference of the Parties to the UNFCCC and the 5th session of the Conference of the Parties serving as the Meeting of the Parties to the Kyoto Protocol took place in Copenhagen and was hosted by the Government of Denmark. Also sitting were the 31st sessions of the Subsidiary Body for Implementation (SBI) and the Subsidiary Body for Scientific and Technological Advice (SBSTA), the 10th session of the Ad hoc Working Group on Further Commitments for Annex I Parties under the Kyoto Protocol (AWG-KP), and the 8th session of the Ad hoc Working Group on Long-term Cooperative Action under the Convention (AWG-LCA).

The basic terms of the Copenhagen Accord were brokered directly by a handful of key country leaders on the final day of the conference. It took nearly another full day of tense negotiations to arrive at a procedural compromise allowing the leaders' deal to be formalized over the bitter objections of a few governments. Key elements include:

- an aspirational goal of limiting global temperature increase to 2 degrees Celsius;
- a process for countries to enter their specific mitigation pledges by January 31, 2010;
- broad terms for the reporting and verification of countries' actions;
- a commitment by developed countries for $30 billion in 2010-2012 to help developing countries; and
- a goal for mobilizing $100 billion a year in public and private finance by 2020.
- The accord also called for the establishment of a new Green Climate Fund.

The Conference was an exceptional event that attracted unprecedented participation and resulted in:

- Attendance by 120 Heads of State and Government, a raising climate discussions to a new level.
- More Record numbers of participants including 10,500 delegates, 13,500 observers, and coverage by more than 3,000 media representatives.
- Intensive negotiations characterized by over 1,000 official, informal and group meetings among Parties.
- Observers discussed climate change in more than 400 meetings and media attended over 300 press conferences.
- A vibrant programme of over 200 side events. Over 220 exhibits from Parties, UN, IGOs and civil society. A total of 23 decisions adopted by the COP and the CMP.

4.4.16 The Nagoya Protocol

The Nagoya Protocol on Access to Genetic Resources and the Fair and Equitable Sharing of Benefits Arising from their Utilization to the Convention on Biological Diversity is an international agreement which aims at sharing the benefits arising from the utilization of genetic resources in a fair and equitable way. It entered into force on 12 October 2014, 90 days after the date of deposit of the fiftieth instrument of ratification.

This protocol is a legal framework for the implementation of one of the objectives of the Convention on Biological Diversity, which is the fair & equitable sharing of benefits arising out of the utilization of genetic resources. The protocol was adopted in 2010 in Nagoya, Japan. It entered into force in

October 2014. The objective of the protocol is the fair and equitable sharing of benefits coming from the utilization of genetic resources and helping in the conservation & sustainable usage of biodiversity. The protocol creates obligations for members to incorporate measures in respect of access to genetic resources, sharing of benefits, and compliance. It is one of the important environmental protocols of the world.

The Nagoya Protocol applies to genetic resources that are covered by the CBD, and to the benefits arising from their utilization. The protocol also covers traditional knowledge associated with genetic resources that are covered by the CBD and the benefits arising from its utilization.

Its aim is the implementation of one of the three objectives of the CBD: the fair and equitable sharing of benefits arising out of the utilization of genetic resources, thereby contributing to the conservation and sustainable use of biodiversity.

The Nagoya Protocol establishes a framework that helps researchers' access genetic resources for biotechnology research, development and other activities, in return for a fair share of any benefits from their use. This provides the research & development sector with the certainty they need to invest in biodiversity-based research. Indigenous and local communities may also receive benefits through a legal framework that respects the value of traditional knowledge associated with genetic resources.

4.4.17 Kigali Agreement

The Kigali Amendment to the Montreal Protocol is an international agreement to gradually reduce the consumption and production of hydrofluorocarbons (HFCs). It is a legally binding agreement designed to create rights and obligations in international law.

The Montreal Protocol was originally created to preserve and restore the ozone layer; participating countries agreed to phase out chlorofluorocarbons (CFCs), gases that had been causing ozone depletion. HFCs do not contain chlorine, so they do not cause ozone depletion, and therefore have been replacing CFCs under the Protocol. However, HFCs are powerful greenhouse gases that contribute to climate change, so this amendment adds HFCs to the list of chemicals that countries promise to phase down. Some of the important Facts about Kigali Agreement are:

- After coming into force in 1989, the Montreal Protocol has undergone many amendments.
- The Kigali Amendment is the 8th amendment.
- It happened during the 28th Meeting of Parties when the 197 member countries signed the agreement to amend the Montreal Protocol.

- It is so named because it happened in Kigali, the capital of Rwanda in October 2016.
- According to the terms of the Amendment, the signing countries are expected to decrease the manufacture and usage of hydrofluorocarbons (HFCs) by about 80-85% from their baselines until 2045.
- This will curb global warming (by arresting global average temperature rise to 0.5 degrees Celsius) by the year 2100.
- The Kigali Amendment to the Montreal Protocol on Substances that Deplete the Ozone Layer entered into force on 1st January 2019, following ratification by the required number of countries.
- The agreement aims to phase down HFCs by reducing its manufacture and consumption.
- HFCs are used as replacements for chlorofluorocarbons (CFCs) and hydrochlorofluorocarbons (HCFCs) since they (HFCs) do not have any impact on the depletion of the ozone layer.
- However, HFCs are powerful greenhouse gases.
- The Montreal Protocol is made even more potent in the fight against greenhouse gases with the Kigali Amendment.

4.4.18 Minamata Convention

The Minamata Convention on Mercury is an international treaty designed to protect human health and the environment from anthropogenic emissions and releases of mercury and mercury compounds. The convention was a result of three years of meeting and negotiating, after which the text of the convention was approved by delegates representing close to 140 countries on 19 January 2013 in Geneva and adopted and signed later that year on 10 October 2013 at a diplomatic conference held in Kumamoto, Japan. The convention is named after the Japanese city Minamata. This naming is of symbolic importance as the city went through a devastating incident of mercury poisoning. It is expected that over the next few decades, this international agreement will enhance the reduction of mercury pollution from the targeted activities responsible for the major release of mercury to the immediate environment.

Mercury pollution is a global problem that requires global action. It moves with air and water, transcends political borders, and can be transported thousands of miles in the atmosphere. The United States is significantly reducing its use and emissions of mercury, but domestic efforts alone are not sufficient to address the effects of global mercury pollution on the U.S. population. According to some estimates, global sources contribute about 70 percent of mercury deposited in the contiguous United States, although the percentage varies geographically. These global sources include natural sources, re-emitted mercury, and man-made emissions from other countries. The Minamata Convention on Mercury is an opportunity for the global community to address this mounting problem before it gets worse. Over the next decades, implementation of this international agreement will help reduce mercury pollution from the specific human activities responsible for the most significant mercury releases to the environment.

As per the official definition under the Convention, the objective of the Minamata Convention is "to protect the human health and the environment from the anthropogenic emissions and releases of mercury and mercury compounds."

- The Convention contains, in support of this objective, provisions that relate to the entire life cycle of mercury, including controls and reductions across a range of processes, products, and industries where mercury is used, emitted or released.
- The Convention also includes provisions relating to mercury mining, its export and import, storage, and disposal.
- The Treaty also covers areas such as the identification of at-risk populations, improving healthcare facilities, and training healthcare personnel to better tackle mercury-related ailments and diseases.

Areas covered under the Convention are:

- Mercury supply sources and trade
- Manufacturing processes in which mercury or mercury compounds are used
- Mercury-added products
- Emissions to air
- Artisanal and small-scale gold mining
- Releases to land and water
- Mercury wastes
- Environmentally sound interim storage of mercury, other than mercury waste
- Health aspects
- Contaminated sites

4.4.19 Conference of Parties (CoPs)

Various Conference of Parties (CoPs) have been organized till date hosted by different countries and resulting in either evolving of some new international environmental instruments or tracking progress on strategies on existing ones. Some of the CoPs have been described above as part of the discussions on several Conventions and other initiatives.

According to the United Nations Climate Change, the COP is the supreme decision-making body of the Convention. All States that are Parties to the Convention are represented at the COP, at which they review the implementation of the Convention and any other legal instruments that the COP adopts and take decisions necessary to promote the effective implementation of the Convention, including institutional and administrative arrangements.

A key task for the COP is to review the national communications and emission inventories submitted by Parties. Based on this information, the COP assesses the effects of the measures taken by Parties and the progress made in achieving the ultimate objective of the Convention.

The COP meets every year, unless the Parties decide otherwise. The first COP meeting was held in Berlin, Germany in March, 1995. The COP meets in Bonn, the seat of the secretariat, unless a Party offers to host the session. Just as the COP Presidency rotates among the five recognized UN regions - that is, Africa, Asia, Latin America and the Caribbean, Central and Eastern Europe and Western Europe and Others - there is a tendency for the venue of the COP to also shift among these groups.

It is to be noted that 27 summits of COP has already conducted. 28th Summit *i.e.* COP 28 is happening this year in Dubai, UAE from 30th November to 12th December 2023. A summary of the COPs held till date is presented in below table:

Table : Details of various COPs

Session	Conference	Location
COP 28	UN Climate Change Conference - United Arab Emirates	Dubai, United Arab Emirates
COP 27	Sharm el-Sheikh Climate Change Conference - November 2022	Sharm el-Sheikh, Egypt
COP 26	Glasgow Climate Change Conference - October-November 2021	Glasgow, United Kingdom of Great Britain and Northern Ireland
COP 25	UN Climate Change Conference - December 2019	Madrid, Spain
COP 24	Katowice Climate Change Conference - December 2018	Katowice, Poland
COP 23	UN Climate Change Conference - November 2017	Bonn, Germany
COP 22	Marrakech Climate Change Conference - November 2016	Marrakech, Morocco

Session	Conference	Location
COP 21	Paris Climate Change Conference - November 2015	Paris, France
COP 20	Lima Climate Change Conference - December 2014	Lima, Peru
COP 19	Warsaw Climate Change Conference - November 2013	Warsaw, Poland
COP 18	Doha Climate Change Conference - November 2012	Doha, Qatar
COP 17	Durban Climate Change Conference - November 2011	Durban, South Africa
COP 16	Cancún Climate Change Conference - November 2010	Cancun, Mexico
COP 15	Copenhagen Climate Change Conference - December 2009	Copenhagen, Denmark
COP 14	Poznan Climate Change Conference - December 2008	Poznan, Poland
COP 13	Bali Climate Change Conference - December 2007	Bali, Indonesia
COP 12	Nairobi Climate Change Conference - November 2006	Nairobi, Kenya
COP 11	Montreal Climate Change Conference - December 2005	Montreal, Canada
COP 10	Buenos Aires Climate Change Conference - December 2004	Buenos Aires, Argentina
COP 9	Milan Climate Change Conference - December 2003	Milan, Italy
COP 8	New Delhi Climate Change Conference - October 2002	New Delhi, India
COP 7	Marrakech Climate Change Conference - October 2001	Marrakech, Morocco
COP 6-2	Bonn Climate Change Conference - July 2001	Bonn, Germany
COP 6	The Hague Climate Change Conference - November 2000	The Hague, Netherlands
COP 5	Bonn Climate Change Conference - October 1999	Bonn, Germany
COP 4	Buenos Aires Climate Change Conference - November 1998	Buenos Aires, Argentina

Session	Conference	Location
COP 3	Kyoto Climate Change Conference - December 1997	Kyoto, Japan
COP 2	Stockholm Convention, 1996	Geneva, Switzerland
COP 1	Global Environment Facility, 1995	Berlin, Germany

(Source: UNFCCC)

4.5 Climate Change

Earth systems are increasingly becoming unpredictable, with drastic shifts in regional climate, will come all kinds of impacts, risks and instabilities like drought, floods, glacier loss, ocean acidification, wildfires, heavy rain, sea-level rise, and heat extremes etc.

Climate Change is the defining issue of our time and we are at a defining moment. From shifting weather patterns that threaten food production, to rising sea levels that increase the risk of catastrophic flooding, the impacts of climate change are global in scope and unprecedented in scale. Without drastic action today, adapting to these impacts in the future will be more difficult and costly. Recent events have emphatically demonstrated our growing vulnerability to climate change. Climate change impacts will range from affecting agriculture - further endangering food security - to sea level rise and the accelerated erosion of coastal zones, increasing intensity of natural disasters, species extinction, and the spread of vector-borne diseases.

Impacts of the climate change affect the human existence in multiple ways. It affects social and economic systems in terms of coastal flooding, extreme weather damage, infrastructure wear & tear, and transition or physical risks. It affects food systems from the angle of availability of water, agriculture and food production, fishery sustainability, and animal productivity. It affects human health due to extreme weather induced illness, malnutrition, heat, air pollution, infectious disease vectors, displacement and mental health etc. When we talk about affects on the environmental systems, we see how the climate change affects the terrestrial ecosystems, freshwater ecosystems, ocean ecosystems, biodiversity and food chains.

In India, the vulnerability assessment and adaptation studies of climate change were made in various areas such as water resources, agriculture, forests, natural eco-systems, coastal zones, health energy and infrastructure as a part of the Initial National Communication of India to the United Nations Framework Convention on Climate Change (UNFCCC). Further, the Expert Committee on Impact of Climate Change set up by the Ministry of Environment & Forests in June 2007 assessed the impact of climate change on six areas, namely water resources, agriculture, Natural Ecosystem, Health, Coastal Zone Management and Climate modelling. Reports of the Expert Committee were then prepared and a range of policies and programmes were initiated to address the problem of climate change in the context of sustainable development.

While the Paris Agreement on Climate Change in 2015 was a landmark as all countries acknowledged the danger and committed to do something about it, the current commitments - referred to as Nationally Determined Contributions or NDCs - do not ensure that we keep temperature rise well-below 2°C. It is therefore often referred to as a Climate Crisis. Countries were to meet in December 2020 to deepen these commitments but this meeting has been deferred to 2021 due to COVID-19.

The response to the Climate Crisis is broadly put into two buckets. The first, referred to as Mitigation means reducing the GHG emissions while the second, referred to as Adaptation, is about recognising the impacts of climate change and rejigging activities so that the adverse impacts are minimised. Adaptation includes building resilience. Mitigation is associated with specific targets for reduction of GHGs (and associated costs of doing this) while Adaptation is essentially about the costs incurred in adapting and building resilience.

Before going into what the Climate Change or Crisis is and how it will impact business, we need to understand few key concepts and terms used in the context. Having understood these concepts, it is important to understand how this impacts everyone's lives and threatens the future of business alongwith the creating possibilities of new opportunities.

4.5.1 Greenhouse Effect and Global Warming

Greenhouse gases let the sun's light shine onto Earth's surface, but they trap the heat that reflects back up into the atmosphere. In this way, they act like the insulating glass walls of a greenhouse. The greenhouse effect is the process through which heat is trapped near Earth's surface by substances known as 'greenhouse gases. The Greenhouse Effect refers to the fact that radiant heat from the sun is in short wavelengths which allows it to penetrate the glass in a greenhouse but when it reflects from the earth, the long wavelength radiant heat gets reflected by the glass, thus raising the temperature in the greenhouse. This same phenomenon happens on earth, where the atmosphere plays a role similar as that of the glass of a greenhouse; reflected radiation from the earth would ordinarily escape out of the atmosphere but when the atmosphere has large concentrations of gases like carbon dioxide, methane etc., it absorbs these radiations, gets warm and in turn radiates back to the earth, thus increasing the earth's temperature. That is why these gases are called *Greenhouse Gases* and some of these gases remain in the atmosphere and do not dissipate for centuries!

Greenhouse effect therefore gives rise to the phenomenon of Global Warming. Again, in normal circumstances, if the concentration of Greenhouse Gases (GHGs) in the atmosphere was a constant, the earth's temperature would reach an equilibrium and over time would reduce. However, as more and more GHGs are emitted, and since these dissipate very slowly, this state of disequilibrium will only make the earth hotter. What then is Climate Change? While it is used interchangeably with Global Warming, one way to think of it is that it is the effect of Global Warming which impacts long-term weather patterns or climate. So, while the average temperature of the earth rises, the changes in the climate causes huge disruptions in weather patterns resulting in extreme weather events - floods and droughts, extremely hot summers and surprisingly cold winters, etc.

4.5.2 How human and industrial activities contribute to climate change

Burning fossil fuels, cutting down forests and farming livestock are increasingly influencing the climate and the earth's temperature. This adds enormous amounts of greenhouse gases to those naturally occurring in the atmosphere, increasing the greenhouse effect and global warming.

Describing further, we may say that human activities contribute to climate change by causing changes in Earth's atmosphere in the amounts of greenhouse gases, aerosols (small particles), and cloudiness. The largest known contribution comes from the burning of fossil fuels, which releases carbon dioxide gas to the atmosphere. Greenhouse gases and aerosols affect climate by altering incoming solar radiation and outgoing infrared (thermal) radiation that are part of Earth's energy balance. Changing the atmospheric abundance or properties of these gases and particles can lead to a warming or cooling of the climate system.

Since the start of the industrial era from about year 1750, the overall effect of human activities on climate has been a warming influence. The human impact on climate during this era greatly exceeds that due to known changes in natural processes, such as solar changes and volcanic eruptions. Carbon dioxide, Methane, Nitrous oxide, Halocarbon gas concentrations, Water vapour, Aerosols etc. affects the environment due to industrial growth majorly. We may see causes for rising emissions through a pictorial representation below:

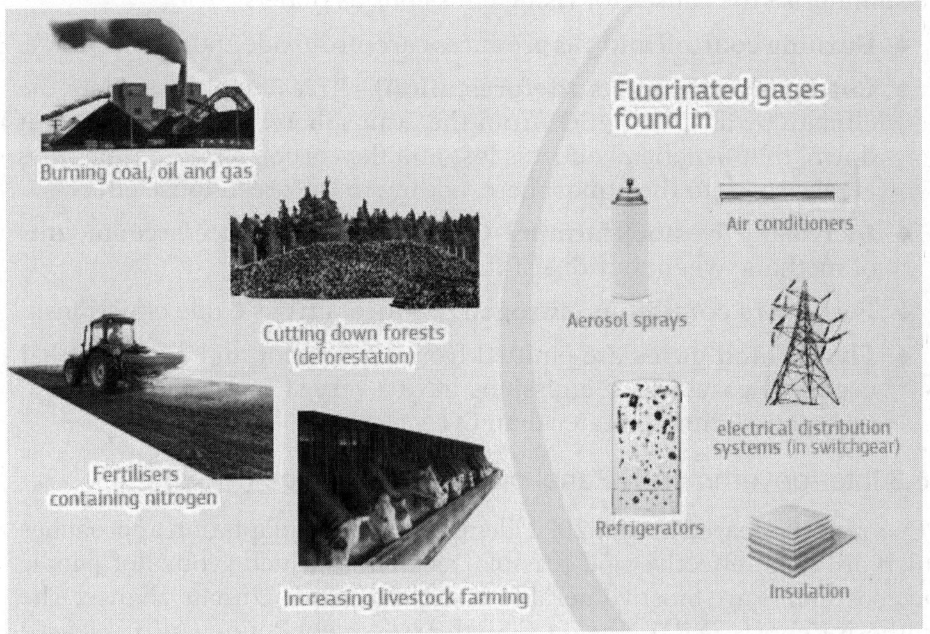

(Source: europa.eu)

Figure 4.4: Causes for Rising emissions

According to the European Commission, the main driver of climate change is the greenhouse effect. Some gases in the Earth's atmosphere act a bit like the glass in a greenhouse, trapping the sun's heat and stopping it from leaking back into space and causing global warming. Many of these greenhouse gases occur naturally, but human activities are increasing the concentrations of some of them in the atmosphere, in particular carbon dioxide (CO_2), methane, nitrous oxide and fluorinated gases.

CO_2 produced by human activities is the largest contributor to global warming. By 2020, its concentration in the atmosphere had risen to 48% above its pre-industrial level (before 1750).

Other greenhouse gases are emitted by human activities in smaller quantities. Methane is a more powerful greenhouse gas than CO_2, but has a shorter atmospheric lifetime. Nitrous oxide, like CO_2, is a long-lived greenhouse gas that accumulates in the atmosphere over decades to centuries. Non-greenhouse gas pollutants, including aerosols like soot, have different warming and cooling effects and are also associated with other issues such as poor air quality. Natural causes, such as changes in solar radiation or volcanic activity are estimated to have contributed less than plus or minus 0.1°C to total warming between 1890 and 2010.

We summarise the causes for rising emissions as under:

- **Burning coal, oil and gas** produces carbon dioxide and nitrous oxide.
- **Cutting down forests (deforestation) -** Trees help to regulate the climate by absorbing CO_2 from the atmosphere. When they are cut down, that beneficial effect is lost and the carbon stored in the trees is released into the atmosphere, adding to the greenhouse effect.
- **Increasing livestock farming -** Cows and sheep produce large amounts of methane when they digest their food.
- **Fertilisers containing nitrogen** produce nitrous oxide emissions.
- **Fluorinated gases** are emitted from equipment and products that use these gases. Such emissions have a very strong warming effect, up to 23000 times greater than CO_2.

4.5.3 Inter-governmental Panel on Climate Change (IPCC)

IPCC's report released in year 2022 identifies climate adaptation approaches which are most effective and feasible, as well as which groups of people and ecosystems are most vulnerable to the impacts of climate change. The Synthesis Report (SYR) of the IPCC Sixth Assessment Report (AR6) released in 2023, also summarises the state of knowledge of climate change, its widespread impacts and risks, and climate change mitigation and adaptation. Major takeaways from the report are:

- **Climate impacts are already more widespread and severe than expected -** Climate change is already causing widespread disruption in every region in the world with just 1.1 °C (2° F) of warming. Withering droughts, extreme heat and record floods already threaten food security and livelihoods for millions of people.
- **We are locked into even worse impacts from climate change in the near-term -** Even if the world rapidly decarbonizes, greenhouse gases already in the atmosphere and current emissions trends will make some very significant climate impacts unavoidable through 2040.
- **Risks will escalate quickly with higher temperatures, often causing irreversible impacts of climate change -** The report finds that every tenth of a degree of additional warming will escalate threats to people, species and ecosystems. Even limiting global warming to 1.5 °C (2.7° F) — a global target in the Paris Climate Agreement — is not safe for all.
- **Inequity, conflict and development challenges heighten vulnerability to climate risks -** Inequity, conflict and development

challenges such as poverty, weak governance, and limited access to basic services like healthcare not only heighten sensitivity to hazards, but also constrain communities' ability to adapt to climatic changes.

- **Adaptation is crucial. Feasible solutions already exist, but more support must reach vulnerable communities -** At least 170 countries' climate policies now include adaptation, but many have yet to move beyond planning into implementation. The IPCC finds that efforts today are still largely incremental, reactive and small-scale, with most focusing only on current impacts or near-term risks. A gap between current adaptation levels and those needed persists, driven in large part by limited financial support.
- **Some impacts of climate change are already too severe to adapt to** - The world needs urgent action now to address losses and damages. With the 1.1 °C of global warming the world is already experiencing, some highly vulnerable people and ecosystems are beginning to reach the limits of what they can adapt to. In some regions, these limits are "soft" — effective adaptation measures exist, but political, economic and social challenges hinder implementation. But in others people and ecosystems already face or are fast approaching "hard" limits to adaptation, where climate impacts are so severe that no existing adaptation measures can effectively prevent losses and damages.

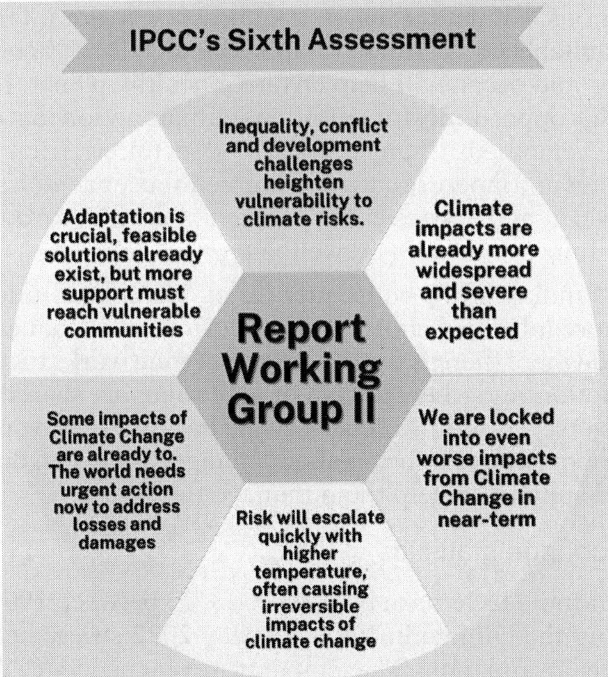

Figure 4.5: Key Takeaways from IPCC WG Report II

According to the IPCC Report "Climate justice is crucial because those who have contributed least to climate change are being disproportionately affected", it further says that "Almost half of the world's population lives in regions that are highly vulnerable to climate change. In the last decade, deaths from floods, droughts and storms were 15 times higher in highly vulnerable regions". The solution lies in climate resilient development. This involves integrating measures to adapt to climate change with actions to reduce or avoid greenhouse gas emissions in ways that provide wider benefits. There is sufficient global capital to rapidly reduce greenhouse gas emissions if existing barriers are reduced. Increasing finance to climate investments is important to achieve global climate goals.

Governments, through public funding and clear signals to investors, are key in reducing these barriers. Investors, central banks and financial regulators can also play their part. There are tried and tested policy measures that can work to achieve deep emissions reductions and climate resilience if they are scaled up and applied more widely. Political commitment, coordinated policies, international cooperation, ecosystem stewardship and inclusive governance are all important for effective and equitable climate action.

If technology, know-how and suitable policy measures are shared, and adequate finance is made available now, every community can reduce or avoid carbon-intensive consumption. At the same time, with significant investment in adaptation, we can avert rising risks, especially for vulnerable groups and regions. Climate, ecosystems and society are interconnected. Effective and equitable conservation of approximately 30-50% of the Earth's land, freshwater and ocean will help ensure a healthy planet. Urban areas offer a global scale opportunity for ambitious climate action that contributes to sustainable development. Changes in the food sector, electricity, transport, industry, buildings and land-use can reduce greenhouse gas emissions. At the same time, they can make it easier for people to lead low-carbon lifestyles, which will also improve health and wellbeing.

A better understanding of the consequences of overconsumption can help people make more informed choices. "Transformational changes are more likely to succeed where there is trust, where everyone works together to prioritise risk reduction, and where benefits and burdens are shared equitably". "We live in a diverse world in which everyone has different responsibilities and different opportunities to bring about change. Some can do a lot while others will need support to help them manage the change".

4.5.4 Climate change statistics in India

Temperatures in India have risen by 0.7 °C (1.3 °F) between 1901 and 2018, thereby changing the climate in India. In May 2022 severe heatwave was recorded in Pakistan and India. The temperature reached 51°C. We see some of the data and data sources reported by India as under:

Key trends in India

- Increase in surface temperature by 0.4°C over the past century.
- Warming trend along the west coast, in central India, the interior peninsula, and northeastern India.
- Cooling trend in northwest India and parts of South India.
- Regional monsoon variations: increased monsoon seasonal rainfall along the west coast, northern Andhra Pradesh and North-western India, decreased monsoon seasonal rainfall over eastern Madhya Pradesh, North-eastern India, and parts of Gujarat and Kerala.
- Observed trends of multi-decadal periods of more frequent droughts, followed by less severe droughts.
- Studies have shown a rising trend in the frequency of heavy rain events and decrease in frequency of moderate events over central India from 1951 to 2000.
- Records of coastal tide gauges in the north Indian ocean for the last 40 years has revealed an estimated sea level rise between 1.06-1.75 mm per year.
- The available monitoring data on Himalayan glaciers indicates recession of some glaciers.

Climate Change Data Sources in India

Different Ministries/Organisations/institutions collect and compile the data relating to different indicators of climate changes:

Indian Metrological Departments (IMD) is the nodal agency for cyclone warning and monitoring. IMD maintains a list of all depressions and cyclonic storms formed in Arabian Sea as well as Bay of Bengal for more than 50 years. This data is useful in identifying the areas prone to cyclones, storms, and land slides. The daily report of the data is available in the website of IMD (**www.imd.ernet.in**)

Centre Pollution Control Board (**www.cpcb.nic.in**) and State Pollution Control Board collects the data on different air pollutants like SO_2, NOx, SPM, RSPM at all the important locations throughout the country. CPCB also collects the data on green houses gases (GHG) for a few important locations.

Ministry of Home Affairs (www.mha.nic.in) is monitoring the data on damages due to heavy rains, flood and cyclone during South-West monsoon at State and district level, the month-wise data is also available.

Geological Survey of India (**www.gsi.gov.in**) is having a wide network of field level offices but presently there does not exists any dedicated network for landslide data collection. GSI are studying only the incidents reported by the district administration.

Central Water Commission (**www.cwc.nic.in**) has 147 flood forecasting sites in all the major river basins of the country.

Central Bureau of Health Intelligence (CBHI) is the National Nodal agency for Health Intelligence in the Directorate General of Health Services (Dte. GHS), Ministry of Health & Family Welfare, and Government of India. CBHI also functions as Collaborating Centre for World Health Organization, Family of International Classification (WHO FIC) in India & South East Asia Region (SEAR) countries. CBHI is committed to build an integrated health informatics platform which can provide reliable, accurate, and relevant national health information and enable evidence based policy formulation and decision making.

Department of Agriculture and Cooperation in Ministry of Agriculture (**www.agricrop.nic.in**) maintains the data on land use as per nine fold classification. It also maintains the data on area sown under different crops for different seasons. The impact of extreme temperature on production and productivity is also monitored by the agriculture department. Department of Agriculture and Cooperation does the coordination of relief measures necessitated by drought. It maintains the data on drought throughout the country.

Central Statistical Organisation (**www.mospi.gov.in**) publish 'compendium of Environment Statistics' which covers many indicators relating to climate change.

4.5.5 Net Zero

Setting and achieving net zero goals are crucial to maintaining the complex global systems we rely on today. As every tonne of CO_2 emitted contributes to global warming, all emissions reductions contribute to slowing it down. In order to stop global warming completely, CO_2 emissions have to reach net zero worldwide.

According to the University of Oxford, 'Net zero refers to a state in which the greenhouse gases going into the atmosphere are balanced by removal out of the atmosphere'.

Net zero is an ideal state where the amount of greenhouse gases (GHGs) released into the earth's atmosphere is balanced by the amount of GHGs removed. Decarbonization efforts are needed to reach net zero.

The term net zero is important because for CO_2, this is the state at which global warming stops. The Paris Agreement underlines the need for net zero. It requires states to 'achieve a balance between anthropogenic emissions by sources and removals by sinks of greenhouse gases in the second half of this century'.

A net-zero gain of GHG in the atmosphere is achieved when the level of GHG emissions released into the atmosphere is equal to the amount removed. This is also referred to as carbon neutrality.

CO_2 is a gas found in the Earth's atmosphere—and it's part of the planet's air, along with nitrogen, oxygen, methane, and other gases. CO_2 helps to trap heat, but too much of it can cause problems, such as heat waves or flooding. It occurs both naturally and as a byproduct of human activities such as burning fossil fuels. As we understand that the impact of the industrial activities on atmosphere is a major concern, it is expected that the industries must achieve net zero targets to avoid a permanently warmer planet, role of energy sector industries is seen more important in this scenario.

As we know that India has already committed to achieve Net Zero emission targets by 2070 as announced by Government. India is set to achieve its short term and long-term targets under the Panchamrit Action Plan, which is:

(*i*) reaching a non-fossil fuel energy capacity of 500 GW by 2030;

(*ii*) fulfilling at least half of its energy requirements via renewable energy by 2030;

(*iii*) reducing CO_2 emissions by 1 billion tons by 2030;

(*iv*) reducing carbon intensity below 45 per cent by 2030; and

(*v*) pave the way for achieving a Net-Zero emission target by 2070.

Role of businesses and business leaders is important in achieving the Net Zero targets in any country. As the momentum toward net zero becomes undeniable, investors, customers, and regulators have raised their expectations for companies. According to a report by McKinsey, nearly 90 per cent of emissions are now targeted for reduction under net-zero commitments, and financial institutions responsible for more than $130 trillion of capital have pledged that they will manage these assets along a 1.5°C commitment pathway.

4.5.6 Decarbonisation Solutions

It is important to understand various strategies to reduce carbon emissions effectively and sustainably. At COP26, India set out its plan to help slow down and halt global warming, with a 2070 net-zero target. While we support the global net-zero ambition of decarbonising by 2050, we see that only six of the major industrial sectors in India are responsible for about 70% of India's overall Carbon emissions, these are power, automotive, aviation, steel, cement and agriculture.

Baseline emissions, $MtCO_2e$[1], 2019

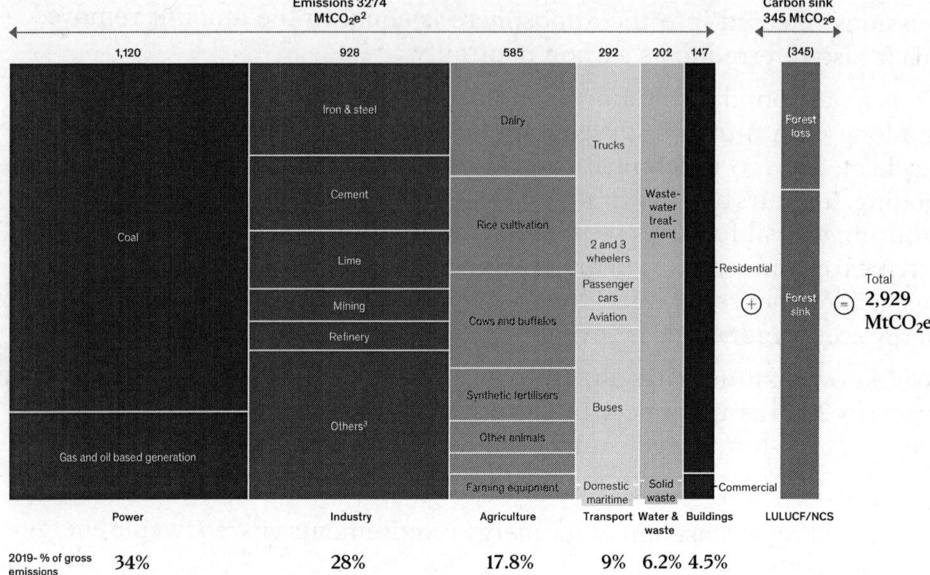

1. Converting GHGs into CO_2e assuming GWP-100 and AR5 methodology with India's BUR-3 reported emissions for 2016 as baseline.
2. Gross and net emissions for 2019 based on Climate Action Tracker overall emissions for India.
3. Others include: other industry oil & coal use, ammonia, aluminium, F-gases and ethylene.

(Source: McKinsey India Decarbonisation Scenario Explorer)

Figure 4.6 : India's Current Carbon Emission Mix

India has reduced its emissions intensity of GDP by 1.3 per cent per annum over the last decade, somewhat decoupling emissions from GDP growth. If we consider the challenges of adopting Carbon Tax in India, we find that India being a developing country, its development may largely depend on Oil & Energy Sectors, and in turn, carbon will be used. If India brings its own carbon tax, then there may be a challenge for Indian goods that are exported to the EU as the cost may increase, and ultimately the question of competitive advantages may arise, which may affect the exports.

All the businesses are affected by differently strategizing and implementing decarbonization. Some of the important sectors according to the McKinsey which are most affected for adopting the decarbonization are explained below:

- **Fossil Fuels**

  Combustion of fossil fuels produces 83 per cent of global CO_2 emissions. In the decarbonization journey for fossil-fuel industries, players are pursuing energy efficiency, driving electrification, and managing fugitive methane emissions (for example, those that escape through degraded flange joints, valve glands, or seals), among other actions. Oil and gas companies in particular are making the low-carbon transition by working several levers, including transforming into diversified energy players.

- **Power**

  Decarbonizing the power sector will require phasing out power generation from fossil fuels and adding capacity for low-emissions power to meet demand that's currently coming from economic development and the electrification of other sectors.

- **Mobility**

  Road transportation accounts for three-quarters of all mobility emissions, so decarbonizing it will be crucial. Efforts here could involve replacing vehicles that have internal-combustion engines with vehicles that have battery electric power or hydrogen fuel cells.

- **Industry**

  Steel and cement are core components of this category, and together they account for about 14 per cent of global CO_2 emissions. Decarbonization efforts might involve installing equipment for carbon capture and storage or switching to processes or fuels with low or no emissions.

- **Buildings**

  Decarbonizing the buildings and real-estate sector will involve improving energy efficiency (for instance, by using insulation) and replacing heating and cooking equipment powered by fossil fuels with low-emissions systems.

- **Agriculture and Food**

  A few actions can help reduce agricultural emissions. Using greenhouse-gas-efficient farming practices can aid in decarbonization, as can changes at a consumer level—for example, if people eat fewer ruminant animals (such as cows) that generate lots of methane.

- **Forestry and Land use**

  CO_2 emissions in this sector often come from land clearing and deforestation. What can curtail these emissions? Efforts could include halting deforestation and speeding up efforts to restore natural environments, such as forests, that can be a net sink for emissions.

- **New Energy Sectors**

  In the new energy sector like hydrogen and biofuels, there will be a lot of opportunities to expand low-emissions energy technologies. And even if expanding capacity and infrastructure for low-carbon fuels requires additional capital spending of $230 billion per year through 2050, the hydrogen and biofuels sectors could create around two million jobs by then.

It is important to note that these industry sectors together account for about 85 per cent of global GHG emissions through their operations or products.

4.5.7 India's National Action Plan on Climate Change

National Action Plan for Climate Change (NAPCC) is a Government of India's programme launched in 2008 to mitigate and adapt to the adverse impact of climate change. The action plan is designed and published under the guidance of Prime Minister's Council on Climate Change (PMCCC).

The National Action Plan on Climate Change (NAPCC) was released by the Prime Minister on 30th June 2008. It outlines a national strategy that aims to enable the country to adapt to climate change and enhance the ecological sustainability of India's development path. It stresses that maintaining a high growth rate is essential for increasing living standards of the vast majority of people of India and reducing their vulnerability to the impacts of climate change.

There are eight National Missions which form the core of the National Action Plan. They focus on promoting understanding of climate change, adaptation and mitigation, energy efficiency and natural resource conservation. These missions are:

(*a*) National Solar Mission

(*b*) National Mission for Enhanced Energy Efficiency

(*c*) National Mission on Sustainable Habitat

(*d*) National Water Mission

(*e*) National Mission for Sustaining the Himalayan Eco-system

(*f*) National Mission for a Green India

(*g*) National Mission for Sustainable Agriculture

(*h*) National Mission on Strategic Knowledge for Climate Change

The Principles of NAPCC are:

- Protecting the poor through an inclusive and sustainable development strategy, sensitive to climate change
- Achieving national growth and poverty alleviation objectives while ensuring ecological sustainability
- Efficient and cost-effective strategies for end-use demand-side management
- Extensive and accelerated deployment of appropriate technologies for adaptation and mitigation
- New and innovative market, regulatory, and voluntary mechanisms for sustainable development

- Effective implementation through unique linkages - with civil society, LGUs, and public-private partnerships

Key features of India's National Action Plan are:

- Protecting the poor and vulnerable sections of society through sustainable development sensitive to climate change
- Achieving national growth objectives through a qualitative change in direction, ecological sustainability, mitigation of greenhouse gas emissions.
- Efficient and cost effective strategies for end user Demand side Management.
- Technologies for adaptation and mitigation of greenhouse gases emissions.
- Promote sustainable development - Regulatory and voluntary mechanisms

4.6 Carbon Footprint Calculation & Trends

Carbon Accounting is a core component of tackling Climate Change. Before going into understanding of Carbon Accounting and Carbon Footprint Calculation, let's understand some of the important key terms pertaining to the subject:

4.6.1 Key Concepts

Carbon Footprint

Emissions impact from human activities, primarily carbon dioxide.

Carbon Neutrality

Achieving a balance between the amounts of carbon dioxide emitted and removed from the atmosphere.

Carbon Offset

Carbon Offset is compensating emissions by investing in projects reducing or capturing equivalent greenhouse gases, aiding environmental balance.

Carbon Sequestration

Carbon Sequestration is trapping CO_2 through methods like reforestation, soil improvement, or technology, helping reduce atmospheric carbon and combat climate change.

Carbon Trading

It's a market-based approach where companies can buy and sell permits that allow them to emit a certain amount of greenhouse gases.

Carbon Pricing

Putting a monetary cost on carbon emissions to incentivize businesses and individuals to reduce their carbon footprint.

Decarbonisation

Decarbonisation is a process of reducing carbon emissions from various sectors, such as energy, transportation, and industry, to mitigate climate change.

Carbon Disclosure

Carbon Disclosure is a process of reducing carbon emissions from various sectors, such as energy, transportation, and industry, to mitigate climate change.

Carbon Tax

Government levy on carbon emissions to encourage reduction and fund sustainability is known as the Carbon Tax.

Carbon Market

Carbon Market is a platform where carbon emissions are assigned a monetary value. There are two types of the Carbon Market, viz. Volatile Market and Compliance Market.

Carbon Accounting

It is crucial to accurately measure your carbon footprints and knowing the methods to offset or reduce it.

4.6.2 Carbon Footprint Calculation

Carbon Footprint Calculation or accounting is part of the broader term Greenhouse Gas (GHG) Accounting. Before beginning to understand the Greenhouse Gas Accounting, we need to understand what is the difference between the Carbon Accounting or Carbon Footprint Calculation and the Greenhouse Gas Accounting. Although the two terms are similar and often used interchangeably, there is a subtle but key difference. Carbon accounting refers only to carbon dioxide emissions, while GHG accounting refers to all greenhouse gases. We will have fair understanding of the GHG Accounting in next section.

4.6.3 Trends in Carbon Dioxide Emissions

Carbon dioxide emissions have risen dramatically after the industrial revolution took place globally. According to a study, most of the world's greenhouse gas emissions come from a relatively small number of countries. China, the United States, and the nations that make up the European Union are the three largest emitters on an absolute basis. Carbon dioxide emissions are primarily from the combustion of fossil fuels.

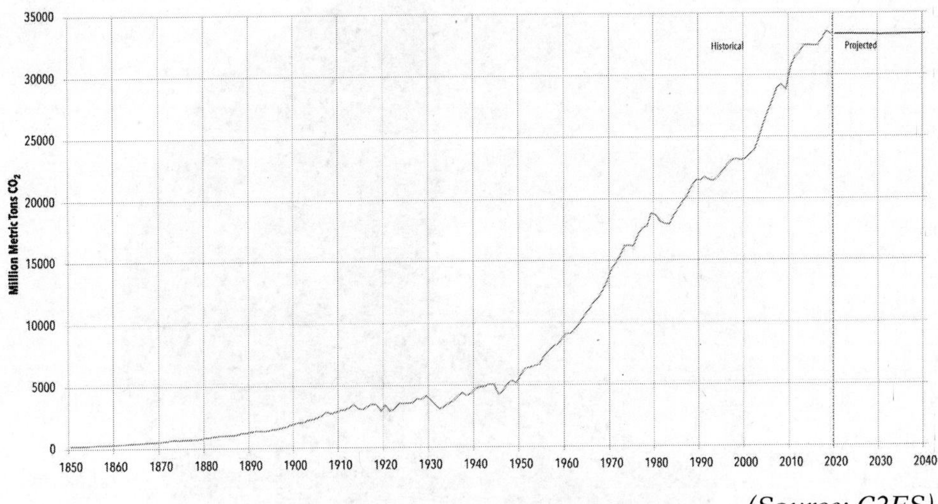

(Source: C2ES)

Figure 4.7: Global CO_2 Emissions 1850 - 2040)

In 2014, the top carbon dioxide (CO_2) emitters were China, the United States, the European Union, India, the Russian Federation, and Japan. These data include CO_2 emissions from fossil fuel combustion, as well as cement manufacturing and gas flaring. Together, these sources represent a large proportion of total global CO_2 emissions.

Emissions and sinks related to changes in land use are not included in these estimates. However, changes in land use can be important: estimates indicate that net global greenhouse gas emissions from agriculture, forestry, and other land use were over 8 billion metric tons of CO_2 equivalent, or about 24% of total global greenhouse gas emissions. In areas such as the United States and Europe, changes in land use associated with human activities have the net effect of absorbing CO_2, partially offsetting the emissions from deforestation in other regions.

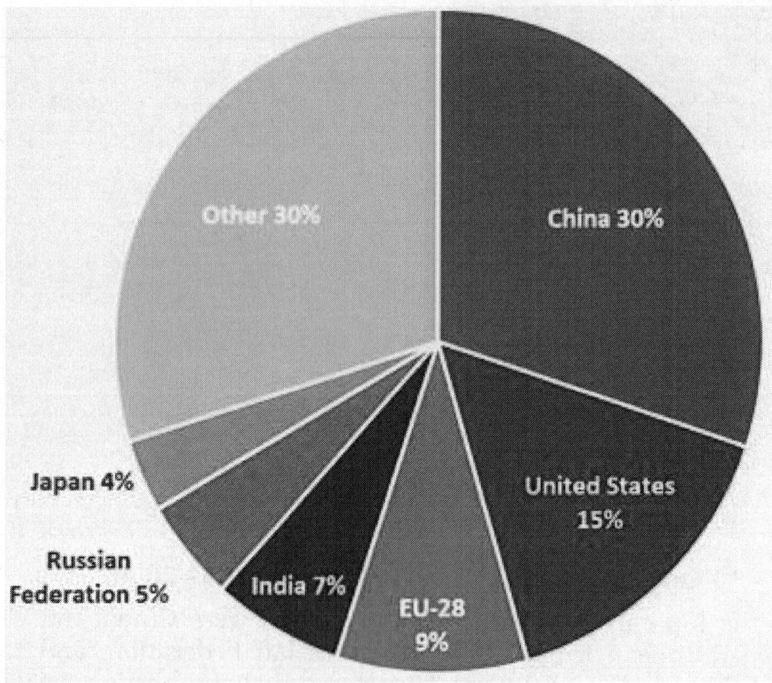

(Source: IPCC 2017)

Figure 4.8: CO_2 Emissions by Countries from Fossil Fuels

Sector-Specific Analysis of the Global CO_2 Emissions, 2019-2022:

As per IPCC, the Global CO_2 emissions by sector 2019-2022 based on the source IEA is a chart that shows the historical and projected emissions of carbon dioxide (CO_2) from different sectors of the global economy, such as power, industry, transport and buildings. The chart is based on the data and analysis from the International Energy Agency (IEA), which is a reliable and authoritative source of information on energy and climate issues. The chart reveals some interesting trends and insights about the global CO_2 emissions by sector:

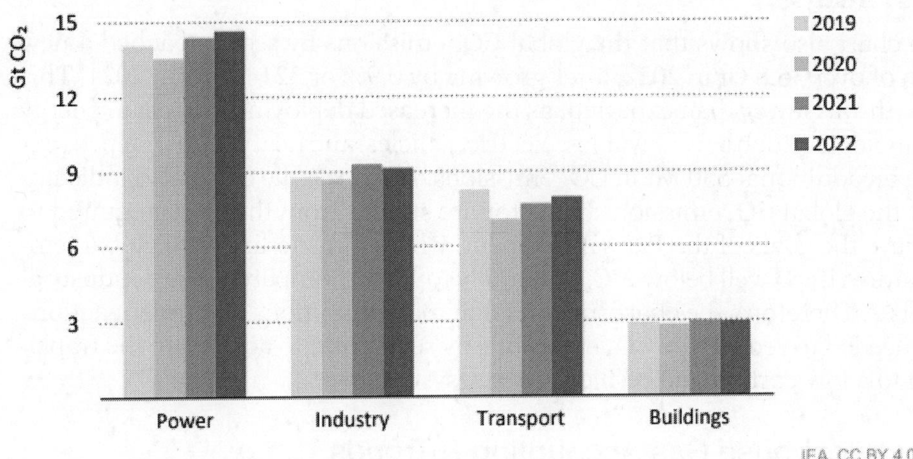

Note: Transport includes international bunkers.

(Sources: CO_2 Emissions in 2022 (windows.net))

Figure 4.9: Sector-wise Greenhouse Gas Emission

Power

The power sector is the largest source of CO_2 emissions, accounting for more than 40% of the total emissions in 2019-2022. The power sector emissions grew by 1.8% in 2021, but declined by 0.4% in 2022, mainly due to the reduced use of natural gas and coal for electricity generation.

Industry

The industry sector is the second largest source of CO_2 emissions, contributing about 25% of the total emissions in 2019-2022. The industry sector emissions increased by 2.4% in 2021, but decreased by 2.8% in 2022, largely due to the slowdown in industrial production, especially in China and Europe, amid the global energy crisis and supply chain disruptions.

Transport

The transport sector is the third largest source of CO_2 emissions, representing about 20% of the total emissions in 2019-2022. The transport sector emissions declined by 6.5% in 2020, but rebounded by 7.3% in 2021 and 2.5% in 2022, as the demand for road, rail and air travel recovered from the pandemic lows.

Buildings

The buildings sector is the fourth largest source of CO_2 emissions, accounting for about 10% of the total emissions in 2019-2022. The building sector emissions increased by 1.6% in 2020, 0.8% in 2021, and 1.9% in 2022, driven by the higher demand for heating and cooling in extreme weather conditions.

Chart Analysis

The chart also shows that the global CO_2 emissions by sector reached a new high of over 36.8 Gt in 2022, after growing by 0.9% or 321 Mt from 2021. This growth was lower than expected, as the increased deployment of clean energy technologies, such as renewables, electric vehicles, and heat pumps, helped prevent an additional 550 Mt in CO_2 emissions. However, the chart also indicates that the global CO_2 emissions by sector are still far from the levels required to achieve the goals of the Paris Agreement, which aims to limit the global temperature rise to well below 2°C, preferably to 1.5°C, compared to pre-industrial levels 2. Therefore, the chart suggests that more ambitious and urgent actions are needed to reduce the CO_2 emissions by sector and to accelerate the transition to a low-carbon and resilient energy system.

4.7 Greenhouse Gas Accounting & Trends

Greenhouse Gas Accounting refers to the process of calculating the total Greenhouse Gas (GHG) emissions produced directly and indirectly from business operations and other organizational activities. It is a framework of methods used to measure and track how much GHG an organization emits. The accounting process is used to track projects or actions aimed at reducing emissions in Industries such as Cement, Electricity, Fertilizers, Iron & Steel, Aluminium and Hydrogen.

> Before attempting to reduce carbon GHG emissions, one should understand how to measure and track these emissions.

The Greenhouse Gas Protocol is widely used as an accounting standard for companies. It helps organizations understand GHG emissions, their impacts, and the risks they present to the global economy. The protocol covers carbon accounting methodologies and best practices, informed by the GHG Protocol.

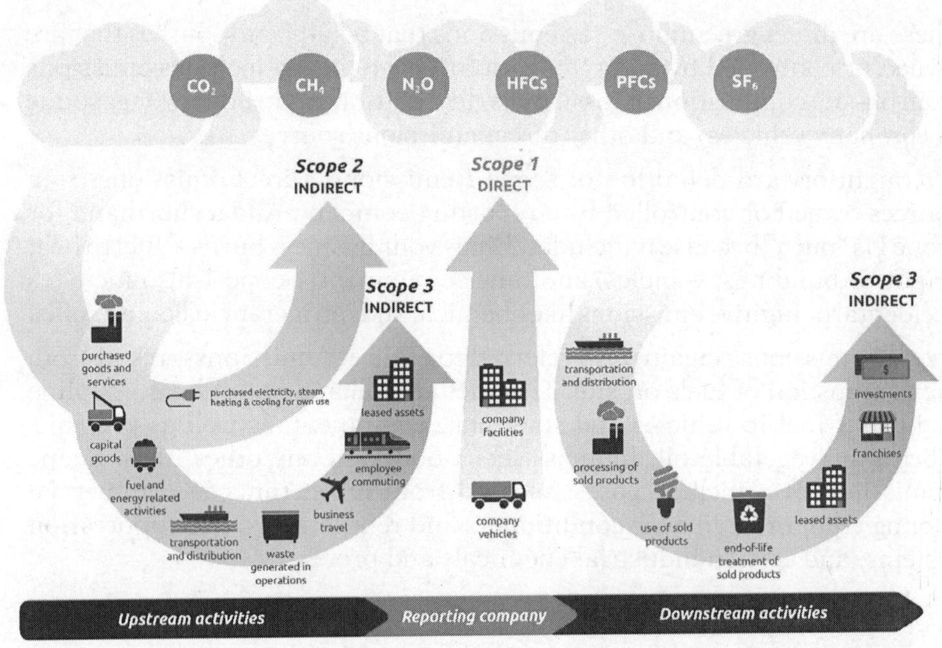

(Source: USEPA)

Figure 4.10: Tracking Climate Change

According to the U.S. EPA, transportation and electricity—two essential functions for most businesses—produce over half of greenhouse gas emissions (GHG emissions).

The Greenhouse Gas Protocol (GHG Protocol) divides emissions into three scopes:

Scope I Emissions - direct emissions from sources owned or controlled by a company

Scope II Emissions - indirect emissions from purchased electricity, steam, heat, and cooling

Scope III Emissions - all other emissions associated with a company's activities

In simpler words these three scopes are defined as Burn, Buy, Beyond. Scope-I is what you burn, Scope-II is energy you buy; and Scope-III is everything beyond that. Detailed description of each of the scopes of emissions are presented below with necessary information about calculation, measurement and accounting.

4.7.1 Scope-I Emissions

These are direct greenhouse gas emissions that result from sources that are owned or controlled by an organization. This typically includes emissions from on-site combustion of fossil fuels (like natural gas in boilers or gasoline in company vehicles) and other direct emissions sources.

A straightforward definition of scope I emissions: Direct emissions from sources owned or controlled by a reporting company. And a shorthand for scope I is "burn" because it includes things your business burns—fuel to heat or power buildings, vehicles, and other equipment. Scope 1 also includes accidental or fugitive emissions like chemical and refrigerant leaks and spills.

Scope I emissions—again, also referred to as direct emissions—result from the combustion of fuels on-site. This includes oil and natural gas, gasoline and diesel fuel in vehicles and stationary equipment, as well as propane, lubricants, vegetable oil, biomass like wood, and any other fuels. Scope I emissions also include gases released from refrigerants in commercial cooling equipment like air conditioners and refrigerators, fire suppression systems, and certain industrial chemicals and processes.

4.7.2 Scope-II Emissions

Scope II Emissions: These are indirect greenhouse gas emissions associated with the production of electricity, heat, or steam that an organization consumes. They result from the generation of the energy used by the organization but occur off-site. Scope 2 emissions are usually attributed to the organization based on their energy consumption and the emissions associated with the energy sources they use.

Scope II emissions are indirect emissions generated from purchased energy—including electricity, steam, heating, and cooling. A simple shorthand you can use to remember scope 2 is "buy" because your organization typically buys energy to run its operations.

Scope II emissions come from purchased electricity, steam, heating, or cooling. You can usually calculate scope 2 emissions based on the consumption outlined in energy bills. What we mean when we say steam, heat, and cooling: it must be generated off-site. Essentially it's what you purchase from a utility or other supplier—for instance, district heating and cooling, or steam used in industrial processes. It shouldn't be confused with heat you generate on-site by using a boiler or furnace or cooling your facility with an electricity-powered AC unit.

4.7.3 Scope-III Emissions

These are indirect GHG emissions that occur as a result of the organization's activities but are not owned or controlled by the organization. Scope 3 emissions can include emissions from purchased goods and services, business travel, employee commuting, and waste disposal.

Scope 3 emissions are likely to be the largest share of your carbon emissions—typically 80-90%. But what are scope 3 emissions? Essentially, all the carbon emissions indirectly generated by a business: business travel, employee commutes, waste disposal, purchased goods and services, the goods you produce, end-of-life disposal of your products, transportation, distribution, and more.

To get a holistic view of your total emissions sources, look both upstream and downstream, in other words, everything it takes to make and consume your product. On a whiteboard or digital brainstorming tool, visually map all the upstream and downstream activities that go into what you do, including:

Upstream emissions-producing activities (everything to produce your product)

- Goods and services you purchase
- Capital goods (like buildings, machinery, tools to make your product)
- How materials are transported and distributed to your manufacturing facility
- Waste generated in day-to-day operations
- Business travel
- Employee commutes
- Leased assets

Downstream emissions-producing activities (everything to consume your product)

- How your product gets to your customers via transportation and distribution
- Processing of sold products
- Use of sold products
- Disposal or recycling of sold products
- Franchises
- Investments

These scopes are part of the Greenhouse Gas Protocol, a widely accepted framework for measuring and managing greenhouse gas emissions. By categorizing emissions into these scopes, organizations can better understand their environmental impact and develop strategies to reduce their carbon footprint.

4.7.4 Trends in Greenhouse Gas Emissions

In respect of sources of the Greenhouse Gas Emissions, we see that the most significant sources in an organization may vary depending on the nature of its operations. However, some common sources for emitting concerned gases are:

Carbon dioxide (CO_2)

Fossil fuel use is the primary source of CO_2. CO_2 can also be emitted from direct human-induced impacts on forestry and other land use, such as through deforestation, land clearing for agriculture, and degradation of soils. Likewise, land can also remove CO_2 from the atmosphere through reforestation, improvement of soils, and other activities.

Methane (CH_4)

Agricultural activities, waste management, energy use, and biomass burning all contribute to CH_4 emissions.

Nitrous oxide (N_2O)

Agricultural activities, such as fertilizer use, are the primary source of N_2O emissions. Fossil fuel combustion also generates N_2O.

Fluorinated gases (F-gases)

Industrial processes, refrigeration, and the use of a variety of consumer products contribute to emissions of F-gases, which include hydrofluorocarbons (HFCs), perfluorocarbons (PFCs), and sulfur hexafluoride (SF_6).

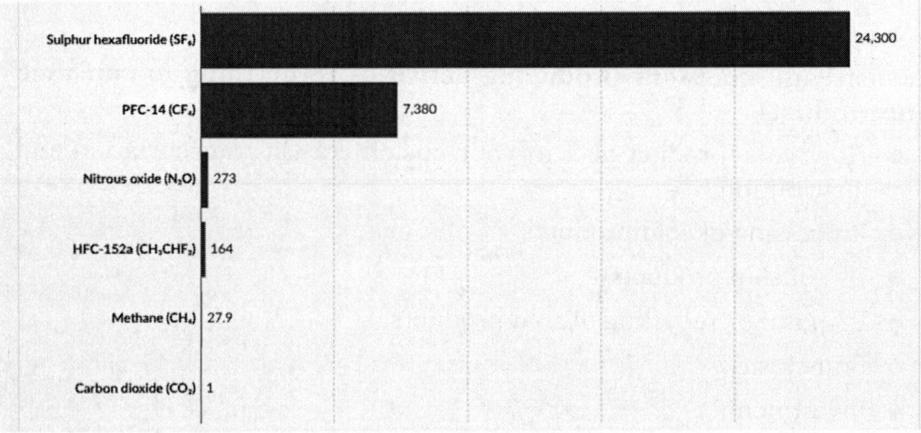

(Sources: Greenhouse gas emissions - Our World in Data)

Figure 4.11: Global Warming potential of greenhouse gases relative to CO_2

According to the Our World in Data, the GWP-100 values for various greenhouse gases are based on the latest report by the Intergovernmental Panel on Climate Change (IPCC), which provides multiple methods of calculating GWPs based on how to account for the influence of future warming on the carbon cycle. The GWP-100 values used in this report are calculated over a 100-year time horizon. Global warming potential measures the relative warming impact of one unit mass of the greenhouse gas relative to carbon.

The GWP-100 measures how much energy the emissions of 1 ton of a gas will absorb over a given period, relative to the emissions of 1 ton of carbon dioxide (CO_2). The larger the GWP-100, the more a given gas warms the Earth compared to CO_2 over that period.

Analysis of the data: The data shows the global warming potentials with a 100-year time horizon (GWP-100) for different greenhouse gases and countries or regions in 2021. The GWP-100 measures how much a given gas contributes to global warming over 100 years, relative to carbon dioxide (CO_2), which has a GWP-100 of 1.0. The data reveals that some gases, such as perfluoromethane (PFC-14) emits 7380 mt, Sulphur hexafluoride (SF_6) emit 24300 mt, Nitrous Oxide (N2O) emits 273 mt, HFC-152a emits 164 mt, Methane (CH_4) emits 27.9 mt, Carbon Dioxide (CO_2) emits 1 mt and have very high GWP-100 values, meaning that they have a much stronger warming effect than CO_2.

According to another study by the Centre for Climate and Energy Solutions - C2ES, we see that the top Greenhouse Gas emitter countries are China, United States and European Union, followed by India. We also see per capita Greenhouse Gas Emission highest in United States, followed by Russia, Japan, China, and European Union.

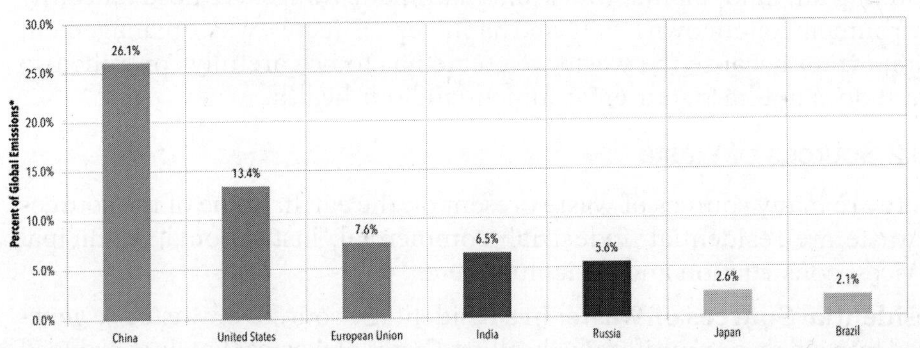

(Source: C2ES)

Figure: 4.12 Greenhouse Gas Emissions by Top Emitters 2018

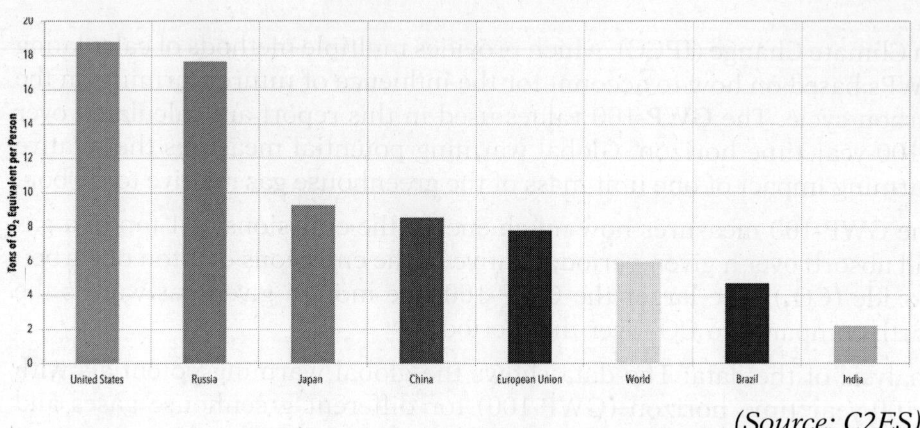

(Source: C2ES)

Figure 4.13 : Per Capita Greenhouse Gas Emissions 2018

4.8 Circular Economy (Re-use, recycling, recovery, reduce)

4.8.1 What is Waste

If any resource is not of use immediately or not of use in its present form or not of use because it has taken a different form or if it has a time value or if it is precious, rare or is depleting in availability for some and is of no use to others then we are generating something called a Waste. Waste is anything discarded, throwaway, rejected, surpluses, abandoned or released into the environment. Waste when thrown into bin, becomes a part of the environment - that's OUR environment, everything that surrounds you including air, land, plants, water and man-made things. We need a healthy environment for our own health and happiness. Effective waste management is important because the waste we create has to be carefully controlled so that it does not harm our environment and our health.

4.8.2 Sources of Waste

There are many sources of waste present on the earth. Some of the sources of waste are residential, industrial, commercial, institutional, municipal services, construction and agriculture, etc.

Residential Sources of Waste: In a resident the sources of waste are generated by a single or multifamily dwelling. Types of wastes that are produced by residences include - Food wastes, paper, cardboard, plastics, textiles, leather, yard wastes, wood, glass, metals, ashes, special wastes.

Industrial Sources of Waste: In industries mainly the waste is generated by power and chemical plants, heavy and light manufacturing machines, construction sites, etc. The main waste products that are produced in industries are, housekeeping wastes, packaging, food wastes, construction and demolition materials, hazardous wastes, ashes, etc.

Commercial Sources of Waste: Stores, hotels, restaurants, markets, office buildings etc. are the main generators of waste in commercial areas. The main waste products in commercial areas include paper, cardboard, plastics, wood, food wastes, glass, metals, special wastes, hazardous wastes, etc.

Institutional Sources of Waste: The main waste generating sources under this category includes Schools, hospitals, prisons, government centers etc. The main waste products are paper, cardboard, plastics, wood, food wastes, flass, metals, special wastes, hazardous wastes, etc.

Construction and demolition Sources of Waste: This category includes new construction sites, road repair, renovation sites, demolition of buildings, wood, steel, concrete, dirt, etc.

4.8.3 Preventing Waste

Below are some suggestions for the Reduction of Waste:

(*a*) Environmentally Responsible Procurement

(*b*) Cleaner Production

(*c*) ZERI Methodology by UNU Tokyo

(*d*) Life Cycle Assessment

4.8.4 Disposing Waste

Disposing Waste industrial wastes and household waste require different methods. Some of the common methods of waste disposals are mentioned below:

(*a*) Landfill

(*b*) Incineration

(*c*) Waste Compaction

(*d*) Biogas Generation

(*e*) Composting

(*f*) Vermicomposting

4.8.5 Treatment of Waste

The technology to burn waste has developed significantly over the past 50 years and incinerators are now much cleaner than they used to be. The energy released from burning the rubbish is often used to generate electricity. Even greater benefits can be gained by using the extra heat to heat nearby housing or offices. However, despite improvements in the operation of incinerators, there is strong public concern about health effects. And from a resource point of view, incineration may not be the best way to deal with our rubbish. Even if energy is obtained through the process, incinerating our rubbish may be a waste of valuable resources.

Two main systems operate to treat this material are:

A. Mechanical Biological Treatment

Residual mixed waste is mechanically sorted into recyclable materials; refuse derived fuel (RDF) and an organic fraction. The organic fraction is treated and used as soil conditioner; the RDF goes for further treatment and then used for Energy from Waste (EfW), for example gasification or pyrolysis. Some material is rejected and land filled.

B. Biological Mechanical Treatment

The residual, mixed, unsorted waste is homogenized and treated by part composting and drying. Sorting and treatment follows by using mechanical processes so that recyclate, RDF and soil conditioner streams, as well as the rejected fraction of residual waste, are produced.

4.8.6 Reuse

In a circular economy, people will be able to reuse nearly all products again and again. If a product is broken, it will be repaired. And if that is no longer possible, new products will be made from it. In a circular economy, waste is the new raw material. Reuse means the valuable materials we create keep their value across many lifetimes.

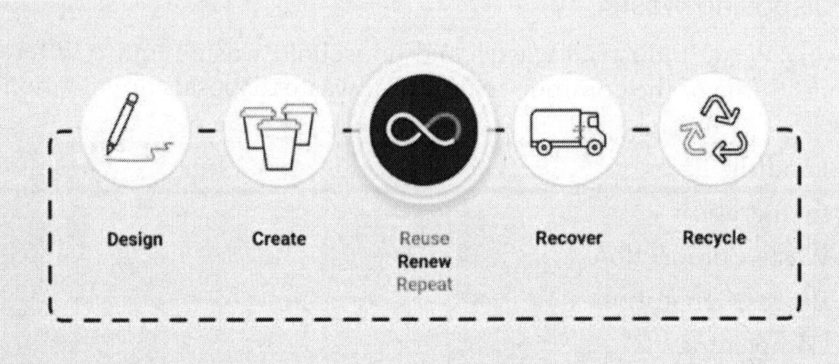

Figure 4.14: Reuse Process

Reuse is the action or practice of using an item, whether for its original purpose (conventional reuse) or to fulfil a different function (creative reuse or repurposing). It should be distinguished from recycling, which is the breaking down of used items to make raw materials for the manufacture of new products.

4.8.7 Recycling

Recycling refers to the process of collecting used materials which is usually considered as 'waste' and reprocessing them. In this process these used materials are sorted and processed to be used as 'raw materials' for the production of new products. Recycling varies from 're-use' in the sense that while re-use just means using old products repeatedly, recycling means using the core elements of an old product as raw material to manufacture new goods. Some of the most common items that are recycled are plastic, glass, paper, batteries, aluminum etc

The recycling process involves three stages. In the first stage the old products are collected and processed, where they are sorted, cleaned and made ready for recycling or manufacturing new products. The second stage involves the manufacturing of new products from the raw material obtained by the processing of the old products. Finally, the process ends with the purchasing of recycled goods by the consumers.

4.8.8 Recovery

Recovery is defined as any waste management operation that diverts a waste material from the waste stream which results in a certain product with a potential economic or ecological benefit.

Recovery mainly refers to the following operations:

- Material recovery, *i.e.* recycling;
- Energy recovery, *i.e.* re-use a fuel;
- Biological recovery, e.g. composting;
- Re-use.

4.8.9 Reduce

Waste Reduction refers to any activity which avoids the creation of waste. This can be achieved through the use of better design, improvements to manufacturing processes, or by influencing consumption patterns. Waste reduction sits at the top of the hierarchy and offers the greatest environmental gains. At the next level, once items have been used some products and materials can be re-used, either for the same or a different purpose. The third level of the hierarchy is recycling which entails bringing materials from a product back into use. It is important to distinguish between recycling, in which the material is reused in a form which has equal properties to its original form, and down-cycling, in which the material's properties are reduced and the material cannot be used in its original application. At the next level of the hierarchy, recovery, value can also be recovered by generating energy from waste materials. Finally, if none of the above options can be employed, waste should be disposed of.

4.9 Business and Biodiversity

Biodiversity, the variety of life on Earth, is critical to the health and sustainability of our planet. In India, a country known for its rich and diverse ecosystems, the intersection of business and biodiversity is of utmost importance. Business activities have a significant impact on the environment, and understanding the role of biodiversity in business is crucial for sustainable development.

Biodiversity contributes to businesses in several ways, including through ecosystem services, resource availability, and risk mitigation. Healthy ecosystems underpin the supply chain for many industries, and businesses that depend on natural resources or benefit from ecosystem services are directly impacted by biodiversity. Moreover, biodiversity conservation is increasingly seen as a responsible and sustainable business practice:

- Explore the ways in which businesses can positively impact biodiversity conservation.
- Discuss policy and regulatory frameworks that support the integration of biodiversity into business strategies.

Biodiversity refers to the variety and variability of life on Earth. 'Biodiversity' comes from two words: 'biological', which means relating to biology or living organisms, and 'diversity', meaning a range of different things or variety. Biodiversity conservation is one of the irrefutable action and subject for sustaining life on the earth.

Conservation of biodiversity -

- supports food security and sustained livelihoods through overall genetic diversity
- contributes to modern medicine and advancements in human health research and treatment
- helps maintaining functioning ecosystems, a steady food supply, and the multiple other benefits including aesthetics, recreation, and spiritual purposes
- ensures material welfare, security of communities, resilience of local economies and human health
- ensures the continuing existence of a wide-range of crops, etc.

The world is losing biodiversity at an ever-increasing rate as a result of human activity. Today, all types of business are expected to be aware of their responsibilities for conservation and protecting biodiversity. Awareness raising, capacity building, employee engagement, partnerships and cause related marketing are some of the important areas for businesses in this domain. Finding a common language, identifying target businesses, engaging businesses as well as SMEs, addressing ethical issues, building relevant partnerships, developing and disseminating a framework of action, and how can businesses participate etc. are some issues need immediate interventions. Convention on Biological Diversity provides action agendas, a global framework, and other such facilitations. India is also a party to the Convention. India ratified it in 1994. The Biological Diversity Act, 2002 was enacted for giving effect to the provisions of the Convention. To implement the provisions of the Act, the government established the National Biodiversity Authority (NBA) in 2003. Some of the important issues are as under:

Biodiversity, Climate & Related Policies for Businesses

- National & Global Policy Frameworks
- Awareness on Biodiversity, Climate Change & Land
- Business & Biodiversity Relationship

Business Commitment, Mapping Biodiversity & Ecosystem Services and Risk Management

- Business & Biodiversity
- Mapping of B&ES across Business Value Chain
- Introduction of Tools for Risk Mapping & Monitoring
- Risk management by No Net Loss Approach

Business Action, Nature-based Solutions & Value Chain Resilience

- Value of Nature for Business
- Company specific biodiversity policy and standard
- Nature-based solutions & building resilience
- Tool- Carbon Sequestration

Business Investments, Valuation & Reporting

- Natural Capital Reporting & ESG Investment
- Business investments for biodiversity conservation, climate mitigation & ecosystem restoration
- Tool-Valuation and Calculating Monetary/Non-Monetary Benefits & Return on Investments
- Business disclosures for biodiversity & Climate
- Open Discussion on Valuation, Benefits & Reporting

Some other key considerations in the context of the Business and Biodiversity Conservation are:

- **Biodiversity and Sustainable Supply Chains:** How businesses can ensure their supply chains promote biodiversity conservation.

- **Economic Benefits of Biodiversity:** Exploring the economic advantages of integrating biodiversity into business strategies.
- **Biodiversity Policies and Compliance:** Discussion on regulatory frameworks and compliance issues related to biodiversity.
- **Success Stories from Indian Businesses:** Showcase examples of businesses effectively incorporating biodiversity into their operations.
- **Collaborative Approaches:** How partnerships between businesses, government, and non-profits can enhance biodiversity conservation.

4.10 Life Cycle Assessment

Lifecycle Assessment is a method that assesses environmental impacts associated with all the stages of a product's life cycle, including raw material extraction and material processing, manufacture, distribution, use and end-of-life. The method is standardised and guided by ISO 14044:2006, which makes the results comparable globally and across products. However, it's not mandatory to conduct LCA in India, to date.

Life Cycle Assessment (LCA) sometimes also known as Life Cycle Analysis, is a methodology for assessing environmental impacts associated with all the stages of the life cycle of a commercial product, process, or service. For example, in case of a manufactured product, environmental impacts are assessed from raw material extraction and processing, through the product's manufacture, distribution and use, to the recycling or final disposal of the materials composing it. A Life Cycle Assessment involves a thorough inventory of the energy and materials that are required across the supply chain and value chain of a product, process or service, and calculates the corresponding emissions to the environment. LCA thus assesses cumulative potential environmental impacts. The aim is to document and improve the overall environmental profile of the product by serving as a holistic baseline upon which carbon footprints can be accurately compared.

Widely recognized procedures for conducting LCAs are included in the 14000 series of environmental management standards of the International Organization for Standardization (ISO), in particular, in ISO 14040 and ISO 14044. ISO 14040 provides the 'principles and framework' of the Standard, while ISO 14044 provides an outline of the 'requirements and guidelines'. Generally, ISO 14040 was written for a managerial audience and ISO 14044 for practitioners. As part of the introductory section of ISO 14040, LCA has been defined as the following:

> "LCA studies the environmental aspects and potential impacts throughout a product's life cycle (*i.e.*, cradle-to-grave) from raw materials acquisition through production, use and disposal. The general categories of environmental impacts needing consideration include resource use, human health, and ecological consequences."

Life cycle assessment (LCA) is sometimes referred to synonymously as life cycle analysis in the scholarly and agency report literatures. Also, due to the general nature of an LCA study of examining the life cycle impacts from raw material extraction (cradle) through disposal (grave), it is sometimes referred to as "cradle-to-grave analysis".

As stated by the National Risk Management Research Laboratory of the EPA, "LCA is a technique to assess the environmental aspects and potential impacts associated with a product, process, or service, by:

- Compiling an inventory of relevant energy and material inputs and environmental releases
- Evaluating the potential environmental impacts associated with identified inputs and releases
- Interpreting the results to help you make a more informed decision.

We may say that the LCA is a technique to assess environmental impacts associated with all the stages of a product's life from raw material extraction through materials processing, manufacture, distribution, use, repair and maintenance, and disposal or recycling. The results are used to help decision-makers select products or processes that result in the least impact to the environment by considering an entire product system and avoiding sub-optimization that could occur if only a single process were used. The goal of LCA is to compare the full range of environmental effects assignable to products and services by quantifying all inputs and outputs of material flows and assessing how these material flows affect the environment.

4.10.1 Stages of Product Life Cycle

There are five stages of product life cycle:

(*a*) Raw Material Extraction

(*b*) Manufacturing & Processing

(*c*) Transportation & Distribution

(*d*) Usage & Retail

(*e*) Waste Disposal/Recycling

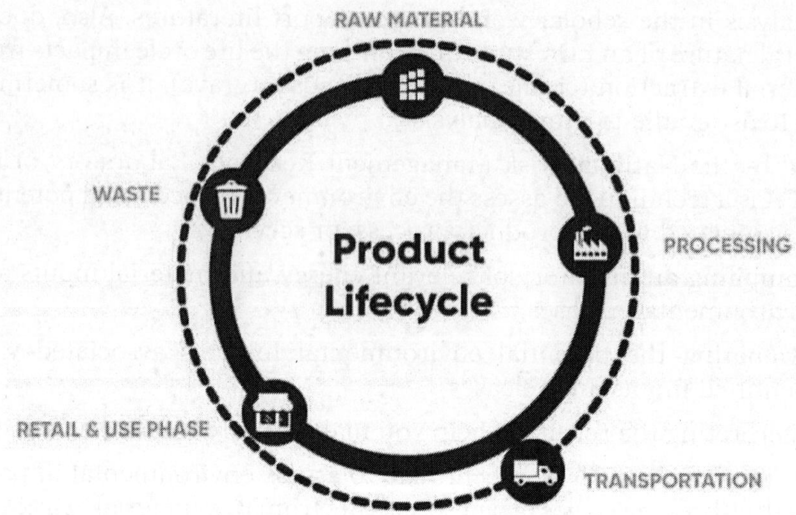

(Source: Ecochain)

Figure 4.15: Stages of Product Life Cycle

4.10.2 Approaches for Product Life Cycle Assessment

The approaches or models of product life cycle assessment are called from cradle-to-grave. Cradle as inception of the product with activities like sourcing raw material, whereas the grave is considered as the disposal of the product at the end of its life cycle.

Cradle-to-gate

Cradle-to-gate only assesses a product until it leaves the factory gates before it is transported to the consumer. This means cutting out the use and disposal phase. *Cradle-to-gate* analysis can significantly reduce the complexity of an LCA and thus create insights faster, especially about internal processes. Cradle-to-gate assessments are often used for environmental product declarations (EPD).

Cradle-to-grave

This stage measures the impacts from the raw material extraction to the end of the product's life. It is more comprehensive than the cradle-to-gate approach as it includes the use/maintenance and the disposal phase of the product.

Cradle-to-cradle

It is a concept often referred to within the Circular Economy. This stage measures the impact from the raw material extraction to when the product is recycled or reused and starts a new life cycle. It is considered the most comprehensive assessment of all the stages of a product's life cycle as it promotes the concepts of circularity, recyclability, and reuse, meaning the entire environmental impact of the product is assessed. This is also referred to as closed-loop recycling.

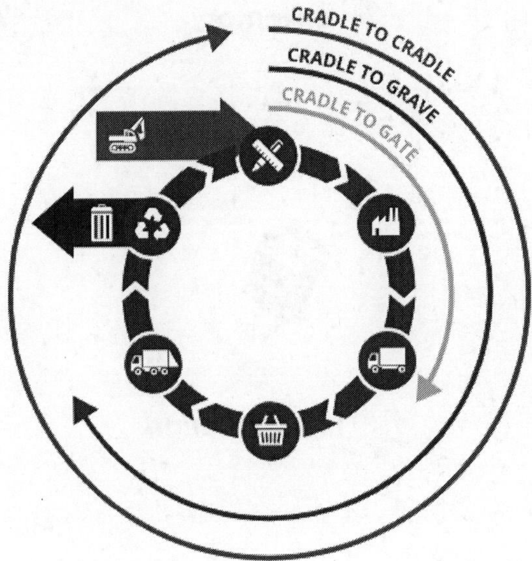

(Source: KPMG)

Figure 4.16: LCA Approaches

4.10.3 Phases of Life Cycle Assessment

A Life Cycle Assessment consists four phases:

- Definition of Goal and Scope
- Inventory Analysis
- Impact Assessment
- Interpretation

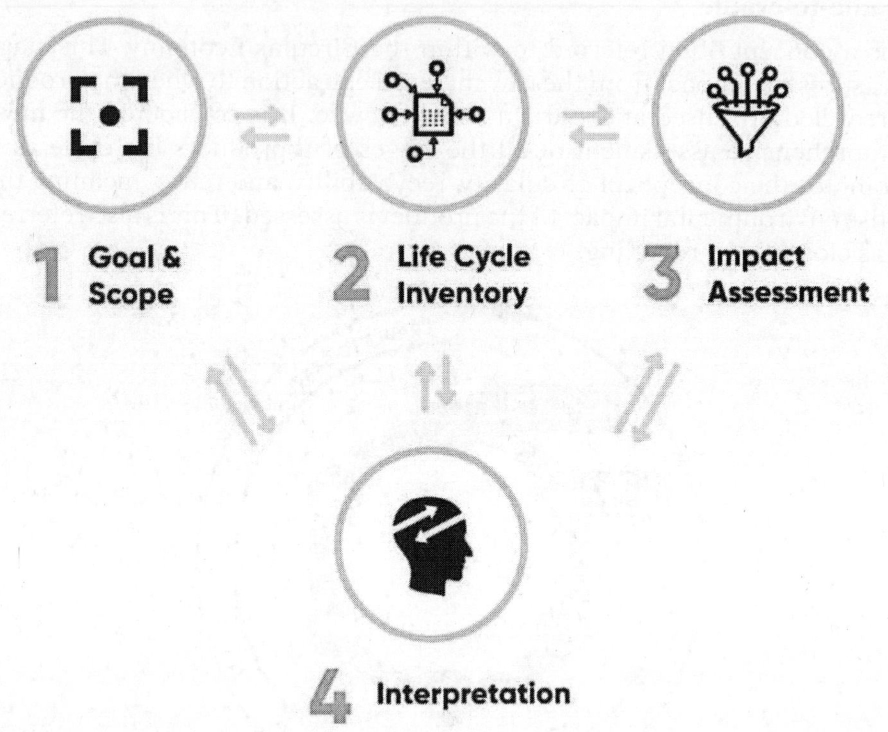

(Source: Echochain)

Figure 4.17: Phases of LCA

Phase 1: Definition of Goal and Scope

Phase 1 of Life Cycle Assessment includes defining the goal & scope of an LCA means defining what we want to analyze, how we want to analyze it, and how far we want to go with our analysis. Key questions like - What will we be assessing? Will it be a product? If so, how much of the product will we be assessing (functional unit)? What system will we be assessing in? are considered in this phase.

This defines our product life cycle, as well as the implications we will be analyzing. Also, we have to decide which Impact Categories we want to focus our assessment on. We might, for example, want to generate an Environmental Product Declaration for one of our products. If that is the goal, we have to build our assessment around the methods required by the political bodies, for example, the ministry of construction.

The value chain can go very deep. However, a certain depth might not be interesting for our analysis. We might, for example, decide, that we won't analyze the details of the pre-forms of our raw materials in-depth. Also, the social implications of the unit we are assessing might not be completely relevant. This is an extremely important step. Because an analysis can - in theory - never be fully finished. If we analyze a certain raw material, will we also examine the implications it has on the family of the worker who harvested it?

Phase 2: Life Cycle Inventory (LCI)

The LCI is the data collection phase of a Life Cycle Assessment. We collect the data and model it into input-output flows.

The Life Cycle Inventory Analysis (LCI) looks at the environmental inputs and outputs of a product or service. It is essentially the data collection phase of our LCA.

Here the goal is to quantify the environmental inputs and outputs - this means we measure everything that flows in and out of the system we defined in phase 1.

What could these inputs and outputs be?

- Raw materials or resources
- Different types of energy
- Water
- Emissions to air, land, or water by substance

Phase 3: Life Cycle Impact Assessment

After collecting the data in earlier phases, we assign it in the Life Cycle Impact Assessment (LCIA). There are 3 key tasks in this step.

Task 1: Selection of indicators and models

We defined our Impact Categories based on our goals earlier in phase 1. Impact Categories are what you want to measure your impact in. Now, we define these impact categories more precisely. There are many impact categories to choose from. Depending on the goal and scope of your analysis, different categories might apply.

Task 2: Classification

In this step of our Life Cycle Impact Assessment, we are sorting our Life Cycle Inventory and assigning it to our defined impact categories.

Task 3: Impact Measurement

In the last step of our impact assessment, we finally calculate all our equivalents. We sum them up in overall impact category totals.

Phase 4: Interpretation of our Life Cycle Assessment

What we want to interpret is also defined in the ISO norms defining the Life Cycle Assessment. According to ISO 14044:2006, following is what the interpretation of a Life Cycle Assessment should include:

- Identifying significant issues based on LCI and LCIA phase
- Evaluating the study itself, how complete it is, if it's done sensitively and consistently
- Conclusions, limitations, and recommendations

It means that we have to make sure we collected accurate data and took care of measuring and analyzing it correctly. Only then we can make recommendations - otherwise, we would literally be "jumping to conclusions"!

4.10.4 Relevant LCA Standards

A. ISO 14000: Environmental Management Standards

The ISO 14000 Environmental Management Standards are a family of standards. They define how companies and organizations manage their environmental responsibilities.

The following standards belong, as the numbers indicate, to this family. LCA software and any Environmental Management Software should comply with these standards, as does our own Environmental Intelligence Platform:

- **ISO 14001: Environmental Management System:** ISO 14001 defines the criteria Environmental Management Systems have to comply with. It ensures that environmental impacts are being measured and improved.
- **ISO 14021: Environmental Claims and Labels:** ISO 14021 defines how specific environmental claims have to be and how they have to be formulated and documented.
- **ISO 14040:2006: Life Cycle Assessment Framework:** ISO 14040:2006 defined the principles and framework of a Life Cycle Assessment. Many parts of this article are based on ISO 14040:2006.
- **ISO 14044: The Update:** ISO 14044 replaced earlier versions of ISO 14041 to ISO 14043.
- **ISO 14067: Quantifying carbon footprint:** ISO 14067 defines how the carbon footprint of products is quantified during a Life Cycle Assessment.
- **ISO 50001: Efficient Energy Management:** ISO 50001 defines Energy Management Systems.

B. EN 15804: European standard for Environmental Product Declarations (EPD) in the construction industry

EN 15804 defines the setup of Environmental Product Declarations in the construction industry.

C. PAS 2050 & GHG Protocol - Carbon Footprinting

PAS 2050 and the GHG Protocol are standards to define and measure emissions.

D. Life Cycle Accounting and Reporting Standard

This standard defines how the Life Cycle can be accounted for and reported on.

E. GRI data framework environment

The Global Reporting Initiative provides a framework to assess the environmental impact of companies and their supply chain.

F. European Energy Efficiency Directive (EED)

The European Energy Efficiency Directive is "a set of binding measures to help the EU reach its 20% energy efficiency target by 2020. Under the Directive, all EU countries are required to use energy more efficiently at all stages of the energy chain, from production to final consumption".

G. PEF (Product Environmental Footprint) and OEF (Organisation Environmental Footprint)

PEF and OEF are currently under development. With PEF and OEF, the European Commission aims to harmonize methodology for the calculation of the environmental footprint of products and organizations. The system has been under development for several years now, and will in the end provide a standardized impact assessment method, a database with background LCA data and calculation rules for different industrial sectors (PEFCRs).

4.11 Environmental Impact Assessment (EIA)

Here we talk about the measurement of Environmental Impact of a Company in direct operations and supply chain. Environmental Impact assessment (EIA) is the assessment of the environmental consequences of a plan, policy, programme, or actual projects prior to the decision to move forward with the proposed action.

It is a tool of environmental management forming a part of project approval and decision-making. Environmental assessments may be governed by rules of administrative procedure regarding public participation and documentation of decision making, and may be subject to judicial review. The purpose of the assessment is to ensure that decision-makers consider the environmental impacts when deciding whether or not to proceed with a project.

EIA is a process of evaluating the likely environmental impacts of a proposed project or development, taking into account inter-related socio-economic, cultural, and human-health impacts, both beneficial and adverse. UNEP defines EIA to be an analytical process that systematically examines the possible environmental consequences of the implementation of a given activity (project). In other words, EIA is a tool used to assess the positive and negative environmental, economic, and social impacts of a project. This is used to predict the environmental impacts of a project in the pre-planning stage itself so that decisions can be taken to reduce the adverse impacts.

The concept of EIA emerged in the 1960s and 1970s as a response to growing concerns about the environmental impacts of large-scale development projects. On 27 January 1994, the Union Ministry of Environment and Forests, Government of India issued the first EIA notification. The devastating effects of projects such as the construction of dams, highways, and industrial facilities on ecosystems and communities prompted the need for a systematic approach to assess and mitigate these impacts.

The importance of EIA has been recognized globally, leading to the development of international conventions and agreements that promote its implementation. The United Nations Conference on the Human Environment in Stockholm in 1972 was a significant milestone, emphasizing the need for environmental assessment in decision-making. Other notable agreements include the United Nations Framework Convention on Climate Change (UNFCCC) and the Convention on Biological Diversity (CBD), which highlight the importance of considering environmental impacts in various sectors.

EIA is the assessment of the environmental consequences of a plan, policy, programme, or actual projects prior to the decision to move forward with the proposed action. In this context, the term "environmental impact assessment" is usually used when applied to actual projects by individuals or companies and the term "strategic environmental assessment" (SEA) applies to policies, plans and programmes most often proposed by organs of state. It is a tool of environmental management forming a part of project approval and decision-making. Environmental assessments may be governed by rules of administrative procedure regarding public participation and documentation of decision making, and may be subject to judicial review.

The purpose of the assessment is to ensure that decision-makers consider the environmental impacts when deciding whether or not to proceed with a project. The International Association for Impact Assessment (IAIA) defines an environmental impact assessment as "the process of identifying, predicting, evaluating and mitigating the biophysical, social, and other relevant effects of development proposals prior to major decisions being taken and commitments made". EIAs are unique in that they do not require adherence to a predetermined environmental outcome, but rather they require decision-makers to account for environmental values in their decisions and to justify those decisions in light of detailed environmental studies and public comments on the potential environmental impacts.

General and industry specific assessment methods are following:

- *Industrial products* - Product environmental life cycle analysis (LCA) is used for identifying and measuring the impact of industrial products on the environment. These EIAs consider activities related to extraction of raw materials, ancillary materials, equipment; production, use, disposal and ancillary equipment.
- *Genetically modified plants* - Specific methods available to perform EIAs of genetically modified organisms include GMP-RAM and INOVA.
- *Fuzzy logic* - EIA methods need measurement data to estimate values of impact indicators. However, many of the environment impacts cannot be quantified, e.g. landscape quality, lifestyle quality and social acceptance. Instead, information from similar EIAs, expert judgment and community sentiment are employed. Approximate reasoning methods known as fuzzy logic can be used. A fuzzy arithmetic approach has also been proposed and implemented using a software tool (TDEIA).

The Ministry of Environment, Forests and Climate Change (MoEFCC) of India has been taking various initiatives in Environmental Impact Assessment in India. The main laws includes the Water Act, (1974), the Indian Wildlife (Protection) Act (1972), the Air (Prevention and Control of Pollution) Act (1981) and the Environment (Protection) Act (1986), Biological Diversity Act, (2002). The responsible body for this is the Central Pollution Control Board.

Environmental Impact Assessment (EIA) studies need a significant amount of primary and secondary environmental data. Primary data are those collected in the field to define the status of the environment (like air quality data, water quality data etc.). Secondary data are those collected over the years that can be used to understand the existing environmental scenario of the study area. The environmental impact assessment (EIA) studies are conducted over a short period of time and therefore the understanding of the environmental trends, based on a few months of primary data, has limitations. Ideally, the primary data must be considered along with the secondary data for complete understanding of the existing environmental status of the area. In many EIA studies, the secondary data needs could be as high as 80% of the total data requirement. EIC is the repository of one-stop secondary data source for environmental impact assessment in India.

The Environmental Impact Assessment (EIA) experience in India indicates that the lack of timely availability of reliable and authentic environmental data has been a major bottleneck in achieving the full benefits of EIA. The environment being a multi-disciplinary subject, a multitude of agencies are involved in collection of environmental data. However, no single organization in India tracks available data from these agencies and makes it available in one place in a form required by environmental impact assessment practitioners. Further, environmental data is not available in enhanced forms that improve the quality of the EIA. This makes it harder and more time-consuming to generate environmental impact assessments and receive timely environmental clearances from regulators. With this background, the Environmental Information Centre (EIC) has been set up to serve as a professionally managed clearing house of environmental information that can be used by MoEF, project proponents, consultants, NGOs and other stakeholders involved in the process of environmental impact assessment in India. EIC caters to the need of creating and disseminating of organized environmental data for various developmental initiatives all over the country. EIC stores data in GIS format and makes it available to all environmental impact assessment studies and to EIA stakeholders.

In 2020, the Government of India proposed a new EIA 2020 Draft, which was widely criticized for heavily diluting the EIA. Many Environmental groups started a campaign demanding the withdrawal of the Draft, in face of these campaigns, the Government of India resorted to banning/blocking the websites of these groups.

4.11.1 EIA Governing Laws in India

The Environment Impact Assessment (EIA) Notification, 2006, is the governing legal instrument to grant green clearance for the establishment or expansion of an industry on the basis of the potential environmental impact of the project. The notification in recent times has been revised several times since its introduction in 1994. The draft of EIA Notification 2020 aims to increase transparency and streamline compliance by incorporating multiple notifications, amendments, circulars, court and tribunal directions, and so on.

The EIA Notification, issued under the Environment (Protection) Act, 1986, outlines the process and requirements for conducting an EIA for various categories of projects. The notification categorizes projects into categories: A and B based on their potential environmental impacts and clearance by the Central/State Government. Category A projects require environmental approval and do not undergo the screening procedure while Category B projects go through a Screening procedure. The Ministry of Environment, Forest, and Climate Change (MoEFCC) and the State Environmental Impact Assessment Authorities (SEIAAs) are responsible for implementing and overseeing the EIA process in India. In India, there are 39 categories of projects that require an environmental clearance (EC) process and are subject to EIA.

4.11.2 EIA Process

The EIA process involves multiple stakeholders, each with specific roles and responsibilities. These stakeholders include project proponents, government agencies, experts, local communities, and non-governmental organizations (NGOs). Project proponents are responsible for preparing the EIA report, while government agencies review and assess the report. Experts provide technical knowledge and guidance, while local communities and NGOs contribute through public consultation and participation.

The EIA process comprises several key steps to ensure a comprehensive assessment of potential environmental impacts. The 4 major stages notified in the 2006 notification are - Screening, Scoping, Public Consultation, and Appraisal.

Screening

First stage of EIA, which determines whether the proposed project, requires an EIA and if it does, then the level of assessment required.

Scoping

Once a project is identified for EIA, the scoping process follows. During scoping, key environmental concerns and potential impacts are identified and defined. This step helps in outlining the boundaries and focus areas for the subsequent environmental impact assessment.

Baseline Data Collection

Before conducting the actual assessment, comprehensive baseline data on the existing environmental conditions of the project area is collected. This data serves as a reference point for evaluating changes and impacts caused by the project.

Impact Prediction and Assessment

The project proponent, often with the assistance of environmental consultants, predicts and assesses potential impacts of the proposed project on various environmental components, such as air, water, soil, biodiversity, and socio-economic factors.

Mitigation Measures

Based on the identified impacts, the proponent proposes mitigation measures to minimize or eliminate adverse effects. These measures may include technological solutions, changes in project design, or implementation of environmental management plans.

Public Consultation

Public participation is a crucial aspect of the EIA process in India. The project proponent is required to conduct public consultations to gather opinions and concerns from local communities, NGOs, and other stakeholders. This input is considered during the decision-making process.

EIA Report Preparation

The project proponent compiles all the findings, including baseline data, impact assessments, and proposed mitigation measures, into a comprehensive Environmental Impact Assessment report. This document serves as the primary tool for decision-makers to evaluate the project's environmental implications.

Appraisal by Expert Appraisal Committee (EAC)

The EIA report is submitted to the Expert Appraisal Committee (EAC), a body of experts appointed by the regulatory authority. The EAC reviews the report and assesses the adequacy of the environmental impact assessment, including the proposed mitigation measures.

Decision-Making

Based on the EAC's recommendations and the EIA report, the regulatory authority makes a decision to grant environmental clearance, request additional information, or reject the project. The decision takes into account the potential environmental impacts and the adequacy of proposed mitigation measures.

Post-clearance Monitoring and Compliance

If environmental clearance is granted, the proponent is required to implement the proposed mitigation measures and adhere to environmental conditions stipulated in the clearance. Post-clearance monitoring ensures ongoing compliance and may include periodic environmental audits.

This comprehensive process is designed to ensure that development projects in India undergo a thorough evaluation of their potential environmental impacts and adhere to sustainable and environmentally friendly practices.

4.12 Environmental Profit & Loss Account (EP&L)

Environmental Profit & Loss Account (EP&L) helps measuring business impact on natural capital throughout our value chain - from the production and transformation of raw materials to the products' use and end of life - and assigning a monetary value to each of these steps.

To express environmental footprint in monetary terms, impacts are translated into a shared business language, with a view to facilitating understanding and comparative performance. The impacts in terms of GHG, air pollution, waste, water consumption, water pollution and land use etc. are considered.

The EP&L approach goes beyond standard environmental reporting, producing a richer, and much fuller picture of the impact of business activities.

The results should not be seen as a liability or a cost for business, rather, they represent a way of assessing the cost to society of environmental changes stemming from the activities of the business and its suppliers.

In other words, the Environmental Profit & Loss account is a method for placing a monetary (relating to money) valuation on a company's environmental impacts. Including the environmental and social impact derived from all its business operations and the entire supply chain. This scope on what parts of your business operations you want to measure is also called from 'cradle-to-grave'. An EP&L account is expressed in economical valuations (£, $ and €) instead of different environmental impact outcomes such as kg CO_2-eq or kg CFC-11-eq. This enables organizations to compare and consolidate different types of environmental impact (such as global warming potential, particulate matter or toxicities). Environmental impact can now be expressed in a single indicator.

Conceived by Puma Chairman, Jochen Zeitz, and launched by Puma and its parent company's sustainability initiative (PPR HOME), the first-ever E P&L was conducted on 2010 data and released in two phases. In May 2011 the valuation of Puma's 2010 Greenhouse Gas Emissions (GHG) and water usage was announced, followed in November 2011, by Puma's overall E P&L, which also included valuation results for other forms of air pollution, land conversion and waste. Simultaneously, the PPR Group announced in November 2011 that a Group E P&L would be implemented across its Luxury and Sport & Lifestyle brands by 2015.

The E P&L and the associated methodology were developed with the support of PricewaterhouseCoopers and Trucost. The E P&L used existing input-output models and developed new valuation methodologies, building on a large volume of work in the fields of environmental and natural resource economics such as the United Nations study on The Economics of Ecosystems and Biodiversity.

Kering, the parent company for Puma, has released its Environmental Profit and Loss Accounting methodology in an open source mode. Novo Nordisk is another company that has released its environmental profit and loss account and methodology report. The 2017 annual report of Philips mentioned that the company had an environmental impact of Euro 7.2 billion for that year. This assessment was made through an Environmental Profit and Loss Accounting process. The company mentioned that this monetary value has not considered various practices that has environmental impacts.

Some examples of the companies who use EP&L accounts to report their environmental impact among other are:

- Philips
- Kering Group (Gucci, Yves Saint Laurent, etc.)

- Vodafone
- Puma (part of Kering group)
- Novo Nordisk
- Wipro

4.13 Environmental Management Plan (EMP)

Environmental Management Plan (EMP) is a guidance document to measure and achieve compliance with the environmental protection and mitigation requirements of a project, which are typically requirements for project permits/approvals. EMP guidance documents can be presented at the project planning and approval application stage to inform regulatory agencies that the proponent has agreed to follow management strategies to avoid and mitigate environmental impacts during project works.

The primary objective of the EMP is to provide information to the Authority on a proposed/existing activity within the regional or local framework. The plan highlights on how the proposed/existing activity may influence on the relevant environmental factors and how those impacts may be alleviated and managed to be environmentally acceptable.

Say for example, if we consider the Construction Industry for the Environment Management Plan, it will be called a Construction Environmental Management Plan (CEMP), the CEMP is typically an amendment to the initial Environmental Management Plan that provides more specific mitigation measures for contractors to follow during construction phases of a project. Depending on the scope of a project, an individual Environmental Protection Plan (EPP) may be prepared for separate construction activities under one CEMP, or may be sufficient for smaller projects.

Keystone Environmental has completed several of these management plans taking into consideration specific municipal, provincial and federal construction requirements and environmental best management practices for a diverse range of projects, such as marine base infrastructure projects, linear utility and rail projects, and urban residential/commercial building developments.

4.14 Strategic Environmental Assessment (SEA)

Strategic environmental assessment consists of a range of analytical and participatory approaches that aim to integrate environmental considerations into policies, plans and programmes and evaluate the inter-linkages with economic and social considerations.

Effective SEA works within a structured and tiered decision framework, aiming to support more effective and efficient decision-making for sustainable development and improved governance by providing for a substantive focus regarding questions, issues and alternatives to be considered in policy, plan and programme (PPP) making.

Strategic environmental assessment (SEA) is a systematic decision support process, aiming to ensure that environmental and possibly other sustainability aspects are considered effectively in policy, plan and programme making. In this context, following Fischer (2007) SEA may be seen as:

- a structured, rigorous, participative, open and transparent environmental impact assessment (EIA) based process, applied particularly to plans and programmes, prepared by public planning authorities and at times private bodies,
- a participative, open and transparent, possibly non-EIA-based process, applied in a more flexible manner to policies, prepared by public planning authorities and at times private bodies,
- a flexible non-EIA based process, applied to legislative proposals and other policies, plans and programmes in political/cabinet decision-making.

Effective SEA works within a structured and tiered decision framework, aiming to support more effective and efficient decision-making for sustainable development and improved governance by providing for a substantive focus regarding questions, issues and alternatives to be considered in policy, plan and programme (PPP) making. SEA is an evidence-based instrument, aiming to add scientific rigour to PPP making, by using suitable assessment methods and techniques. Ahmed and Sanchez Triana (2008) developed an approach to the design and implementation of public policies that follows a continuous process rather than as a discrete intervention.

Relationship with Environmental Impact Assessment

For the most part, an SEA is conducted before a corresponding EIA is undertaken. This means that information on the environmental impact of a plan can cascade down through the tiers of decision making and can be used in an EIA at a later stage. This should reduce the amount of work that needs to be undertaken. A handover procedure is foreseen.

The SEA Directive only applies to plans and programmes, not policies, although policies within plans are likely to be assessed and SEA can be applied to policies if needed and in the UK certainly, very often is. The structure of SEA (under the Directive) is based on the following phases:

- "Screening", investigation of whether the plan or programme falls under the SEA legislation,
- "Scoping", defining the boundaries of investigation, assessment and assumptions required,

- "Documentation of the state of the environment", effectively a *baseline* on which to base judgments,
- "Determination of the likely (non-marginal) environmental impacts", usually in terms of Direction of Change rather than firm figures,
- Informing and consulting the public,
- Influencing "Decision taking" based on the assessment and,
- Monitoring of the effects of plans and programmes after their implementation.

The EU directive also includes other impacts besides the environmental, such as material assets and archaeological sites. In most western European states this has been broadened further to include economic and social aspects of sustainability.

SEA should ensure that plans and programmes take into consideration the environmental effects they cause. If those environmental effects are part of the overall decision taking it is called *Strategic Impact Assessment*.

4.15 Environmental Management System (EMS)

An environmental management system (EMS) is "a system which integrates policy, procedures and processes for training of personnel, monitoring, summarizing, and reporting of specialized environmental performance information to internal and external stakeholders of a firm". The most widely used standard on which an EMS is based is International Organization for Standardization (ISO) 14001.

The goals of EMS are to increase compliance and reduce waste, some of the specific features of EMS are mentioned below:

- Compliance is the act of reaching and maintaining minimal legal standards. By not being compliant, companies may face fines, government intervention or may not be able to operate.
- Waste reduction goes beyond compliance to reduce environmental impact. The EMS helps to develop, implement, manage, coordinate and monitor environmental policies. Waste reduction begins at the design phase through pollution prevention and waste minimization. Waste can be limited by 'reduce, reuse & recycle'.
- Reduce resource usage by minimizing Green house gases dependency and opting for more greener options like solar or wind power generation.
- Reduce pollution by reducing the usage of fossil fuels and making sure that the waste material is either processed before being dumped or is made sure that it is of least harm to the society directly.

- Serves as a tool, or process, to improve environmental performance and information mainly "design, pollution control and waste minimization, training, reporting to top management, and the setting of goals".
- Provides a systematic way of managing an organization's environmental affairs.
- Gives order and consistency for organizations to address environmental concerns through the allocation of resources, assignment of responsibility and ongoing evaluation of practices, procedures and processes.
- Creates environmental buy-in from management and employees and assigns accountability and responsibility.
- Sets framework for training to achieve objectives and desired performance.
- Helps understand legislative requirements to better determine a product or service's impact, significance, priorities and objectives.
- Focuses on continual improvement of the system and a way to implement policies and objectives to meet a desired result. This also helps with reviewing and auditing the EMS to find future opportunities.
- Encourages contractors and suppliers to establish their own EMS.
- Facilitates e-reporting to federal, state and provincial government environmental agencies through direct upload.

4.16 Environmental Due Diligence

Environment Due Diligence is the process of assessing the environmental conditions of a property in connection with a property merger or acquisition so that investors are aware of the potential environmental liabilities. In the present VUCA world, it has become imperative to fully understand the environmental risks before making investments or purchases in new properties or industrial sites. It is only through proper environmental due diligence that investigates potential liabilities, renovation needs, and hidden costs can make informed decisions.

The respective process can be at the request of land developers, lenders, attorneys, or private owners who intend to purchase, refinance, or occupy a property. This may include reviews of:

- Proximity to sensitive habitats
- Historical structure and materials
- Safe disposal of hazardous materials
- Operational procedures
- Potential soil and groundwater contamination

Environmental due diligence is a form of proactive environmental risk management. It is an essential liability protection measure to reduce risks and prevent unnecessary expenditure by accessing the potential environmental liabilities. Unfortunately, many projects fail or have their development stunted by lawsuits, fines, and ecological remediation without a proper environmental due diligence process. Without due diligence, you may not know what environmental liability you could potentially own.

Over the years India has developed several laws to safeguard the environment and society from the adverse impacts of different projects by laying out rules that the projects or property owners should abide by. However, the ideas of these laws were to identify the potential impacts of projects over the environment and habitat, even before its initiation. This pre-assessment was crucial in developing mitigation plans so that the projects carry out with minimal adverse impact on the ecosystem surrounding the area of operations. Further, the laws made the property/plant/project owners accountable to the violation of the established laws.

These laws, however, can also be seen as a benchmark for any stakeholder or investor to map out the environmental liability that the prospective property/project brings in. In other words, the investors could carry out an EED as against the applicable laws, before investing into the property. This process is certain to help the stakeholders in identifying the true cost of the property that they are planning to invest/buy in as the stakeholders will also consider the cost of making the property environmentally compliant.

Table: Environmental Due Diligence in Relevant Law

Act/Rule/Policy	Objective	Authority responsible	Applicability
Environmental Protection Act, 1986	To protect the environment	Ministry of Environment, Forest & Climate Change; State & Central Pollution Control Boards; Central Ground Water Authority	Applicable to almost all projects.
Environmental Impact Assessment	Required in developmental & expansion projects to study the impact of the activity on the environment	Ministry of Environment, Forest & Climate Change; State & Central Pollution Control Boards	Applicable to construction, developmental, and real estate projects

Act/Rule/Policy	Objective	Authority responsible	Applicability
Indian Forest Act, 1927; Forest (Conservation) Act, 1980; Forest (Conservation) Rules, 1981; National Forest policy	Protection of forests and keeping track of deforestation activities and maintaining ecological balance. A forest clearance certificate and tree felling license is required under these rules.	Ministry of Environment, Forest & Climate Change; State Forest Department	Applicable to projects linked to forests. e.g.: laying a pipeline through a forest, dam construction, etc.
Wildlife Protection Act, 1986	For the protection of National Parks & Sanctuaries for the protection of flora & fauna	National Board of Wildlife, Chief Wildlife Warden of State	If the transaction is related to Wildlife sanctuary, National Parks, etc.
Biological Diversity Act, 2002	Conservation of biological diversity, promote equitable sharing of benefits.	Ministry of Environment, Forest & Climate Change; National Biodiversity Authority; State Biodiversity Board	If the transaction deals with biodiversity.
Air (Prevention & Control of Pollution) Act, 1981	To control air pollution. Providing CTO (Consent to Operate) and CTE (Consent to Establish) certificates (NOC)	State Pollution Control Board	Applicable to all factories, manufacturing units and expansion activity under the transaction deal.
Water (Prevention & Control of Pollution) Act, 1974	To control Water Pollution. Providing CTO & CTE Certificates	State Pollution Control Board	Applicable to all factories, manufacturing units, and expansion activity under the transaction deal
Construction & Demolition Waste Rules, 2016	For proper disposal of waste arising from the construction & demolition of sites	Local Authority & State Pollution Control Board	Applicable to most of the transactions involving expansion & development

Act/Rule/Policy	Objective	Authority responsible	Applicability
E-waste (Management & Handling) Rules, 2016	For proper disposal of e-waste	State Pollution Control Board	Applicable to all major transactions, as e-waste is inevitable in every business activity
Hazardous and Other Waste (Management and Trans-boundary Movement) Rules, 2016	Ensure safe handling, conversion, processing, and treatment of hazardous waste. Permission is required under these rules if the company deals with hazardous substances.	State Pollution Control Board	Applicable to most of the transactions involving expansion & development
Noise Pollution (Regulation & Control) Rules, 2000	To control noise levels	State Pollution Control Board & Central Pollution Control Board	Required at any manufacturing facility, production houses, etc
Ozone Depleting Substances (Regulation & Control) Rules, 2000	Control & reduce the use of ozone-depleting substances	Ministry of Environment, Forest & Climate Change	Projects where air conditioning units play an important role

4.17 Summary of the Chapter

In this chapter we studied environmental risks to business, environmentally responsible investing, Indian regulatory mechanisms, key concepts like Climate Change, Carbon Accounting and Carbon Footprint calculation, decarbonisation solutions, Business and Biodiversity Conservations, Environmental Profit & Loss Account, Product design, Life Cycle Assessment, Circular Economy, Environmentally Responsible Procurement, Cleaner Production. It also dwelt upon key instruments like EIA, SIA, EMP, EMS, etc. As an important factor we tried to understand the current regulatory framework in India for measuring the environmental footprints of businesses, like extended producer responsibility, and carbon credits scheme, corporate environment responsibility, among others. How to address the challenges faced by businesses in complying with these novel environmental regulations and explore innovative interventions to effectively reduce the environmental footprints of businesses, foster dialogue between businesses, regulators, and environmentalists for better policy formulation.

SOCIAL DIMENSIONS OF ESG

CHAPTER 5

5.1 Social dimensions of ESG

From the barter system to present industrialised society and economy, we have witnessed a lot of changes in the way we behave individually and collectively through the organizations. If we see in the history, Business organizations came into existence with sole purpose of earning profits. There were many such management thinkers which propounded their theories around this idea. But gradually, businesses started realising the need to consider well-being of the people involved and affected by business activities.

If we consider the word 'social', it is by its literal meaning towards society or social structures or the way a society is organized. The society is woven by the individuals who remain organized through a web of social relationships. There are various social institutions, traditions, norms, structures and patterns which constitute our society. There are various problems of social structures and delinquent behaviours (both individual and organizational).

We might have heard the term individual delinquent behaviour, but have we ever thought about the term organizational delinquent behaviour? In the management books, we study about 'Organizational Behaviour' but what about 'Organizational Delinquent Behaviour'?

Other aspect through which organizations or businesses influence the society is through their structural interventions or their operations which cause some of the social problems.

Through these two ways businesses may impact society and its structure in negative manner. Against these negative impacts on society, businesses need to make corrective measures through various interventions such as discharging corporate social responsibility, implanting diversity and inclusion within organizational practices, building rapport with the local or nearby communities, engaging the local communities as stakeholder in the key decisions of the business which may potentially influence the communities, making interventions to assure welfare and wellbeing of employees and workers, fair practices in product or service development and taking its liability etc.

In this chapter, we will understand different measures which affect the social dynamics, what are the associated business risks and possible solutions, what strategies, policies, frameworks and action plans are to be adopted by a business for social acceptance. Usually, business literature talks about social licence to operate the business. The social licence to operate the business is nothing but the social acceptance, to mitigate the negative social impacts made by business operations, and to positively contribute in social development in local communities as well as for the nation at large.

Some of the pertinent questions like, how can a company manage its relationships with its workforce, the society in which it operates, and the political environment? The "S" in ESG — the social aspect tries to address these questions. S aspect of the ESG is comprised of issues like business and human rights, including employee relations, labour practices, diversity and inclusions, and working conditions. Another important aspect is Community relations, it includes not only maintaining harmonic relations but also fund projects in Local Communities to serve marginalized sections of society as a global practice. Bringing marginalized issues (e.g. ethics, human rights, stakeholder engagement, advocacy etc) into mainstream corporate plan and strategy are also of great importance.

Companies that can demonstrate real commitment to "S" factors are likely to see long-term benefits in terms of employee engagement, customer loyalty, investor confidence, and ultimately, sustainable profitability. In this chapter, an attempt has been made to deliberate on how the social risks may be converted or seen in terms of opportunities to a business to make positive interventions and build strategies for ESG aligned business interventions.

As we understand that to address, reduce and mitigate stakeholders' oppositions it is important to engage them in a company's decision-making process which affects its external environment in particular. Land acquisition for new projects and for operations of existing factories, Involuntary resettlement including the Forest land, agricultural land, loss of culture and tradition, and livelihoods as a result of resettlement, Land degradation, Water and Air Pollution in nearby communities, Gentrification and the adverse impact on Culture and Tradition in the local communities are some of the pressing issues in this context.

When we talk about the impact of Social Factors on the Businesses, we consider following facts:

- Brand Reputation
- Attracting Investments
- Stakeholder Relationships
- Setting up new projects
- Operations of factories

- Sales of products and
- Overall business success

Above are some of the 'Pulling' factors for the businesses to consider social aspects of ESG. On the other hand, there are various 'Pushing' factors which compel the business to take the necessary steps in adopting and implementing the required social aspects. The pushing factor comes from the stakeholders' expectations, regulatory compliance, consumer expectations, community pressure, investors demand, buyers' specific compliances, etc. In the figure below, we see some of the developments at the global level in the sphere of 'S' of ESG.

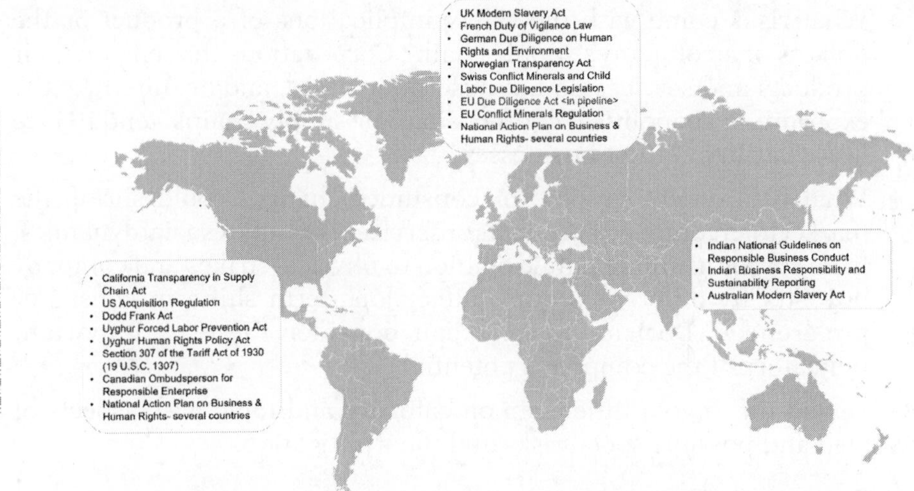

Figure 5.1: Global developments in Social Dimensions of ESG

5.2 Social Risks to a Business and Mitigation Strategies

A number of social factors can affect a company's financial performance, ranging from short-term to long-term challenges. These social factors several associated risks to businesses. Here we will try to understand various social risks to the businesses.

The business world recognizes that it impacts society and social equality through its power and influence. Many investors are looking into the social policies of the companies they choose for investments. ESG Risks related to social equity include a company's ability to fulfil commitments to support the community and social equity programmes for its internal and external stakeholders. Stakeholder expectations that are included in a business strategy and understood through an organizational risk assessment are more likely to reduce the risk to the company.

Who is impacted by Social Risks? Generally speaking, the social aspect of ESG includes internal and external stakeholders. These groups include employees, customers, vendors and suppliers, the nearby community, and possibly the global community.

A number of social factors can affect a company's financial performance, ranging from short- to long-term risks:

- How can a company's workforce requirements and composition present problems for the organization in the future? Labour strikes or consumer protests can directly affect a company's profitability by creating a scarcity of skilled employees or controversy that is damaging to a corporation's reputation.
- What risks come with the safety implications of a product or the politics of a company's supply chain? Corporations that ensure their products and services do not pose safety risks, and/or minimize the exposure to geopolitical conflicts in their supply chains, tend to face less volatility in their businesses.
- What future demographic or consumer changes could shrink the market for a company's products or services? Complex social dynamics, from surges in online public opinion to physical strikes and company boycotts by different groups, affect long-term shifts in consumer preferences. Decision-makers can consider these as important indicators of the company's potential.

Here we will try to go a little deep on category and topic wise aspects of associated and possible social risks and their mitigation.

5.2.1 Community Relations

Local communities play a significant role in the social aspect of ESG as they are directly impacted by a company's operations and activities. Engaging with and supporting local communities is crucial for building sustainable and responsible business practices. A community is the first entity affected by the business operations in multiple ways. We have seen in history, various community unrest and how these impact business operations. Community engagement in the business decisions and interventions a business designs for welfare and development of a community of vital importance to mitigate important risks foreseen. Below are some key observations related to communities' related social risks to businesses within the social dimension of ESG:

Community Engagement and Development are also important considerations. Businesses should actively engage with local communities, understand their needs, and develop initiatives that contribute to their well-being and development. This includes supporting education, healthcare, infrastructure development, and employment opportunities. We take an example here from the Tata Steel Rural Development Society, Tata Group, a prominent Indian conglomerate, has implemented various community development programmes. The Tata Steel Rural Development Society, for instance, focuses on education, healthcare, livelihoods, and infrastructure development in rural areas surrounding their operations by way for local community engagement.

Environmental Stewardship and Conservation in the local areas where companies are operating or having their factories/plants is also an important mitigation strategy. Communities feel unrest when they see that there is environmental degradation in the nearby areas. Hence, as a mitigative strategy, companies should prioritise environmental stewardship and minimise their impact on local ecosystems and natural resources. This includes responsible waste management, conservation efforts, and supporting local biodiversity, so as to minimise the negative effects on the local communities. Tanking an example of ITC e-Choupal, ITC Limited, has undertaken several initiatives focused on sustainable agriculture and environmental conservation. Their "e-Choupal" initiative empowers rural farmers through the use of digital technology, providing them with real-time information, training, and access to markets.

Cultural Preservation and Respect is another important mitigation of social risks. There are hundreds of examples not only from manufacturing plants but also from service sector industries where not considering cultural traditions and related aspects have resulted in negative business benefits. Hence, companies should respect and preserve the cultural heritage of local communities. This involves recognizing indigenous rights, supporting traditional crafts, and promoting cultural exchanges. Taking an example of Aditya Birla Group – Kalakriti, The Aditya Birla Group, an Indian multinational conglomerate, has initiatives that aim to preserve and promote Indian art and culture. The "Kalakriti" program focuses on reviving and promoting traditional Indian crafts, providing training and market access to artisans.

Effective Stakeholder Dialogue and Grievance Mechanisms are important to address and mitigate social risks to a business. Grievances redressal mechanisms both internal and external are important in this context. Companies should establish mechanisms for effective stakeholder dialogue, including local communities, to address concerns, grievances, and receive feedback. This promotes transparency, accountability, and responsiveness. Here, taking an example of HUL Shakti Advisory Council, Hindustan Unilever Limited (HUL) has implemented grievance redressal mechanisms, such as the HUL Shakti Advisory Council, which engages with rural women entrepreneurs to address their concerns and provide support.

5.2.2 Media and NGOs Relations

Non-Governmental Organisations (NGOs) and media groups play an important role in the social aspect of ESG by promoting transparency, accountability, and advocating for social causes. They often collaborate with companies to drive positive social change and hold them accountable for their actions.

Businesses cannot operate in isolation, engaging, collaboration and partnerships Media and NGOs are key stakeholder groups is important. Companies can collaborate with NGOs and media groups to address social issues, implement sustainable initiatives, and leverage their expertise and networks for positive impact. Citing an example, the Coca-Cola India Foundation has collaborated with multiple NGOs in India to implement water conservation and community development projects. They work with multiple non-governmental organisations to address water scarcity and promote water stewardship. Role of media groups in assessing the needs and showcasing the impact has been important factor.

In the context of designing and implanting Corporate Social Responsibility (CSR) initiative, NGOs as implementing agencies and media as monitoring entity play important roles. NGOs and media groups often play a crucial role in monitoring and evaluating a company's CSR initiatives, ensuring they align with societal needs and have a measurable impact. Taking an example from the Tata Sustainability Group, The Tata Group, through its various companies, has implemented several CSR initiatives in India. NGOs and media groups play a role in evaluating and reporting on these initiatives, ensuring transparency and accountability.

Stakeholder Advocacy and Reporting is another vital area. NGOs and media groups advocate for the interests of various stakeholders, including communities, workers, and the environment. They can raise awareness about social issues, highlight concerns, and push for responsible business practices. For instance, Greenpeace India, an environmental NGO, actively engages in advocacy and campaigns to address environmental issues in India. They work to raise awareness about climate change, air pollution, and sustainable development.

Media Coverage and Investigative Journalism are equally important. Media groups play a vital role in exposing social and environmental violations, holding companies accountable, and raising public awareness. Their reporting can influence public opinion and drive companies to improve their social practices. For example, the Centre for Science and Environment (CSE), an Indian environmental research and advocacy organisation, conducts investigations and publishes reports on various environmental issues. Their reports often influence policy changes and corporate actions.

5.2.3 Role of Regulators

Regulators also play a significant role in the social risk mitigation by establishing and enforcing rules, regulations, and standards that govern corporate behaviour and ensure social responsibility and sustainability. Their role is crucial in promoting transparency, accountability, and sustainable practices.

In respect of Legal Compliance and Reporting Requirements, regulators set mandatory requirements for companies to adhere to specific social and environmental standards. They may mandate reporting frameworks and guidelines for companies to disclose their ESG practices. There are various regulators like Ministry of Corporate Affairs, Securities and Exchange Board of India, various institutions under the Ministry of Labour & Employment and Ministry of Environment, Forest & Climate Change, etc. Here we take an example of SEBI Circular on Business Responsibility and Sustainability Reporting, the Securities and Exchange Board of India (SEBI) has introduced regulations that require listed companies to disclose their ESG performance as part of their annual reports (BRSR), enhancing transparency and encouraging responsible practices.

In the context of Corporate Governance, we may note that the regulators establish governance frameworks and guidelines to ensure companies operate ethically and responsibly, protecting the interests of stakeholders. These frameworks include principles related to board composition, executive compensation, and stakeholder engagement. For an example, the Ministry of Corporate Affairs, Govt. of India has notified under the Companies Act, certain governance related aspects including provisions for independent directors, audit committees, and shareholder rights, which promote accountability.

So far as consumer protection is concerned, regulators enforce laws and regulations to protect consumer rights, ensuring fair practices, product safety, and addressing consumer grievances. They play a vital role in safeguarding the interests of customers. Taking an example of the Consumer Protection Act, 2019, which was enacted by the Government of India, provides a comprehensive framework for consumer protection, addressing issues such as unfair trade practices, misleading advertisements, and product safety.

Regulators also establish environmental and social regulations to address sustainability challenges, promote environmental conservation, and protect social interests. These regulations may cover areas such as waste management, pollution control, and labour rights etc. For example, the Ministry of Environment, Forest and Climate Change (MoEFCC) in India sets regulations and guidelines to ensure environmental protection, such as the Environmental Impact Assessment (EIA) process for projects with potential environmental impacts on local community and on planet at large. There are many other regulations imposed on the businesses in the social sphere.

5.2.4 Customer Relations

Customer relation is another important aspect within the purview of social risks to a business. It focuses on a company's commitment to building strong relationships with its customers and ensuring responsible business practices. Aspects like Product Quality and Safety, Responsible Marketing and Advertising, Customer Satisfaction and Service, Responsible Marketing and Advertising, Responsible Product Development are considered in this mitigation strategy.

Companies are expected to provide high-quality products that meet or exceed customer expectations. This includes ensuring product safety, adhering to relevant regulations and standards, and conducting proper testing and quality control. According to an article in Forbes, "Toyota Recall: Five Years Later", In 2009, the Toyota recall crisis highlighted the importance of product quality and safety. Toyota faced significant backlash and reputational damage due to safety issues in their vehicles, which impacted customer trust and resulted in a massive recall. This case emphasises the significance of prioritising product quality and safety in customer relations.

Companies should engage in ethical and responsible marketing practices, ensuring transparency, accuracy, and avoiding misleading or deceptive advertising. They should also respect customer privacy and handle customer data responsibly. According to the "The Cambridge Analytica Files" - The Guardian, The Cambridge Analytica scandal involving Facebook in 2018 shed light on the misuse of customer data for targeted advertising. This case highlighted the importance of responsible handling of customer data and transparent advertising practices.

Companies should prioritise customer satisfaction by providing excellent customer service, addressing customer concerns and complaints promptly and fairly, and striving to meet customer needs. If we see for an example, Zappos, an online shoe and clothing retailer, is often cited as an example of exceptional customer service. Their customer-centric approach, including free shipping and a generous return policy, has contributed to high customer satisfaction and loyalty.

Companies should consider the social impact of their products, such as environmental sustainability, health implications, and social benefits. This includes incorporating sustainable materials, reducing waste, and offering products that contribute positively to society. According to the Patagonia - Our Footprint, Patagonia, an outdoor clothing and gear company, has been recognized for its commitment to responsible product development. They prioritise sustainability, fair trade, and durability, and actively communicate the environmental and social impact of their products to customers.

There are many guidelines for reporting on Customer Relations, like National Guidelines for Responsible Business Conduct (NGRBC), Global Reporting Initiative (GRI) Standards and United Nations Global Compact (UNGC), these standards provide guidelines for reporting on various sustainability topics, including customer relations.

5.2.5 Employee Relations

Employees are a key aspect of Social risk mitigation strategy and action plan, because they represent one of the most important stakeholder groups within a company. Their well-being, rights, and treatment are crucial in assessing a company's social performance. Fair Treatment and Labour Practices, Health and Safety, Employee Development and Well-being, diversity and inclusion, etc. are some of the important considerations.

With provisions like Fair treatment of employees, including equal opportunities, non-discrimination, and a safe working environment, including adherence to labour laws, fair wages, working hour regulations, and adequate benefits, companies are expected to provide a supportive and inclusive work culture that promotes diversity, equality of opportunity, and respect. For example, a company that actively promotes gender diversity and has implemented policies to address pay equity and prevent harassment would demonstrate a commitment to fair treatment of employees.

Ensuring the health and safety of employees within the workplace includes providing proper training, maintaining safe working conditions, and implementing measures to prevent accidents and occupational hazards. Companies are expected to comply with relevant health and safety regulations and proactively address employee well-being. For instance, a manufacturing company that invests in state-of-the-art safety equipment, conducts regular training programmes, and actively monitors and improves workplace safety conditions would exemplify a strong commitment to employee health and safety and will prevent risk of any mishappenings.

Company's support for employee growth, development, and overall well-being includes opportunities for training and skill enhancement, career advancement programmes, work-life balance initiatives, mental health support, and employee engagement programmes. For example, a company that offers flexible work arrangements, promotes work-life balance, provides wellness programmes, and encourages continuous learning and professional development would demonstrate a commitment to employee development and well-being.

Diversity & Inclusion refers to a company's efforts to foster a diverse workforce (women, differently abled, and LGBTQ+ etc.) and create an inclusive work environment where all employees feel valued and respected. Encourage diversity and enable it by having gender neutral washrooms, same sex partner benefits for employees at par with married spouses, or a gender neutral adoption policy and support. An example in the Indian context is Infosys, which has implemented various diversity and inclusion initiatives, such as unconscious bias training, gender balance programmes, and hiring practices that promote diversity.

5.2.6 Social Risks in Supply Chain

Suppliers play a critical role in the social dimensions of ESG because they have a direct impact on a company's social performance. Take for an example, any large manufacturing unit in automobile sector, you will find that only important portions are manufactured by them and rest most of the automobile components are manufactured by small industries which are supplier to the main large company. The main company only manufactures about 20-30% of the required product. Rest components are produced by supply chain partners or suppliers.

Interesting point here is that the main company may have all the best practices, policies, codes of conducts etc. in place but what about rest 70-80% manufacturing which is being done by suppliers? SEBI has recently mandated to a certain segment of companies to make disclosures on supply chain also but still these are a handful of companies.

Companies are expected to engage in responsible sourcing by selecting suppliers who adhere to ethical and sustainable practices. This includes assessing suppliers' labour conditions, environmental practices, and human rights records. Looking at an example, according to the Apple Supplier Responsibility Report, Apple Inc. has implemented a Supplier Code of Conduct that sets standards for labour and human rights, health and safety, environmental protection, and ethical conduct. The company regularly audits its suppliers and provides training and support to ensure compliance.

Transparency in the supply chain is crucial to identify and address any social risks or violations. Companies should aim for transparency by mapping their supply chain, understanding the origin of raw materials, and communicating openly with suppliers. Taking an example from the Nestlé Cocoa Plan, Nestlé, a global food and beverage company, has made efforts to increase supply chain transparency. They launched the "Nestlé Cocoa Plan," which includes a commitment to sourcing cocoa beans responsibly and ensuring fair treatment of farmers in their supply chain.

Companies can promote fair trade principles by establishing fair pricing and payment terms with suppliers. This includes ensuring that suppliers receive fair compensation for their products or services, enabling them to operate sustainably and support their workers. We take an example from the Fair Trade Certified™, The Fair Trade Certified™ programme certifies products that meet social, environmental, and economic standards. Companies like Ben & Jerry's, a well-known ice cream brand, use Fair Trade Certified ingredients to support fair prices and better working conditions for farmers.

Companies can collaborate with suppliers to promote social and environmental improvements. This includes providing support, training, and resources to help suppliers enhance their practices and meet sustainability standards. According to the Walmart Supplier Sustainability Assessment programme,

Walmart, a multinational retail corporation, launched the "Supplier Sustainability Assessment Programme" to assess and improve suppliers' sustainability performance. The programme includes capacity building initiatives to support suppliers in adopting more sustainable practices.

5.3 Business & Human Rights

5.3.1 Key Developments

India's endorsement of the United Nations Guiding Principles on Business and Human Rights in the UN Human Rights Council compelled it to develop a National Action Plan (NAP) on Business and Human Rights (BHR). In February 2019, Government of India published a zero draft of the NAP to contribute to achieving the targets of UNGPs, Agenda 2030 and promotion of Responsible Business Conduct. The Government of India has not limited its efforts till developing a National Action Plan, but it has also strengthen other tools and instruments to promote responsible business conduct and respect of human rights in business organizations in its value chain. Indian Labour Codes are the most awaiting and biggest labour reforms in the country. National Guidelines on Responsible Business Conduct (NGRBC) is one of the key milestones which have been aligned with the principles of UNGP and SDGs. There are other initiatives like mandating the Business Responsibility and Sustainability Reporting (BRSR) by top 1000 listed companies by market capitalization in India.

Now the question arises that how Indian efforts may be further strengthened and accelerated to intact, implement, monitor and review the NAP on BHR? Key institutions which are projected as responsible for NAP in India are Ministry of Corporate Affairs, Ministry of Foreign Affairs, Indian Institute of Corporate Affairs and the National Human Rights Commission. Different governing areas of each Ministry/Institution have contributed in producing the draft NAP in 2019 in India. However, now when there is time to review the NAP and to come up with revised action plan, the draft version is not finalised and launched yet in last four years. It is pertinent to mention that most of the South Asian countries have already developed and implemented NAP-BHR, hence it is important to review India's progress on it and come-up with suggestions and way ahead.

Some of the global developments in the arena of BHR are depicted in the image below:

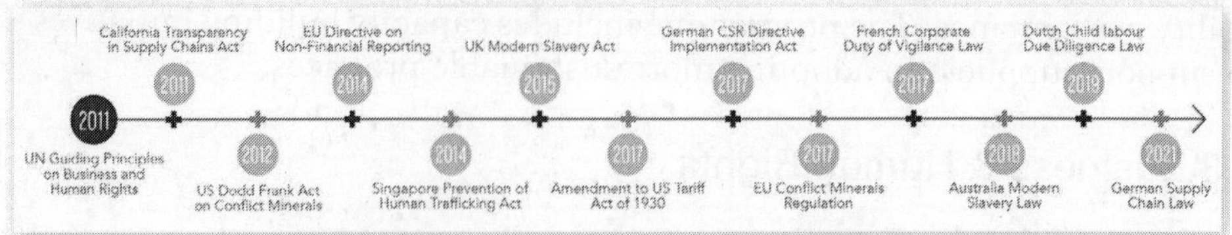

Figure 5.2: Global scenario of HBR

5.3.2 Role of Businesses

What role do business partners and investors have in driving the BHR agenda? Most business operate under a set of core values— expressed in mission statements, codes of conduct and other documents—that align with expectations around respect for human rights. Yet, in recent years public concern over human rights abuses in business operations and global supply chains has risen drastically. Governments, consumer protection groups, banks, industry trade groups, and journalists among others, are placing considerable pressure on companies doing business in Asia. Institutional and retail investors alike are increasingly interested in companies with reduced environmental, social and governance (ESG) risks. They are turning to corporate indexes to gauge the suitability of companies in the ESG asset class.

In today's world of immediate perception through information technology, it becomes unbearable to live with the knowledge of flagrant violations of Human Rights. We have made already the step of breaching the sacred "sovereign power" of the nation-state and interfering with national leaders not to commit the very worst of crimes against humanity. We are, even, very close to setting up international Courts of Justice.

In this climate it is understandable that many of us are in a hurry - "Where are the (strong) leaders who will put an end to these violations?"

5.3.3 United Nations Guiding Principles on Business and Human Rights

The United Nations Guiding Principles on Business and Human Rights (UNGPs) is an instrument consisting of 31 principles implementing the United Nations' (UN) "Protect, Respect and Remedy" framework on the issue of human rights and transnational corporations and other business enterprises. Developed by the Special Representative of the Secretary-General (SRSG) John Ruggie, these Guiding Principles provided the first global standard for preventing and addressing the risk of adverse impacts on human rights linked to business activity, and continue to provide the internationally accepted framework for enhancing standards and practice regarding business and human rights.

Unanimously endorsed by the Human Rights Council in 2011, the UNGPs are widely recognized as the world's most authoritative normative framework for addressing the adverse impacts of business on human rights. The UNGPs outline how the State and business share responsibility for human rights concerns, noting their complementary but differentiated roles. Composed of 31 principles, the UNGPs are divided into three "Pillars" consisting of:

(*i*) The State duty to protect human rights

(*ii*) The corporate responsibility to respect human rights

(*iii*) The requirement for the State and businesses to provide access to effective remedy for victims of business-related abuse

Many experts cite the emergence of the UNGPs as the most important development driving responsible business practices over the last 20 years. Importantly though, the UNGPs do not introduce new laws or regulations. The UNGPs provide, instead, inclusive approaches, policy coherence, minimum standards and a logical sequencing towards the assessment and management of human rights risks.

State duty to protect human rights

The first pillar of the Guiding Principles is the state's duty to protect against human rights abuses through regulation, policymaking, investigation, and enforcement. This pillar reaffirms states' existing obligations under international human rights law, as put forth in the 1948 Universal Declaration of Human Rights.

Corporate responsibility to respect

Businesses must act with due diligence to avoid infringing on the rights of others and to address any negative impacts. The UNGPs hold that companies have the power to affect virtually all of the internationally recognized rights. Therefore, there is a responsibility of both the state and the private sector to acknowledge their role in upholding and protecting human rights. In conducting due diligence, the UNGP encourage companies to conduct a Human Rights Impact Assessment through which they assess their actual and potential human rights impacts.

Access to remedy if these rights are not respected

The third pillar addresses both the state's responsibility to provide access to remedy through judicial, administrative, and legislative means, and the corporate responsibility to prevent and remediate any infringement of rights that they contribute to. Having effective grievance mechanisms in place is crucial in upholding the state's duty to protect and the corporate responsibility to respect. The UNGPs dictate that non-judicial mechanisms, whether state-based or independent, should be legitimate, accessible, predictable, rights-compatible, equitable, and transparent. Similarly, Company-level mechanisms are encouraged to operate through dialogue and engagement, rather than with the company acting as the adjudicator of its own actions.

5.3.4 National Action Plan on Business and Human Rights

There was a need to demonstrate more visibly India's implementation of the UNGPs based on UNHRC's 'Protect, Respect & Remedy' Framework and also make evident India's commitment to Sustainable Development Goals (SDGs). As required by the intergovernmental group of UNHRC formed in relation to Business and Human Rights, the Ministry of Corporate Affairs, Government of India with the Indian Institute of Corporate Affairs (IICA) has developed Zeroth Draft of National Action Plan on the subject matter by compiling the existing laws, policies, orders, etc. which will facilitate the businesses for respecting the human rights and complying with the various laws.

The Indian Institute of Corporate Affairs (IICA) has provided support to the Ministry of Corporate Affairs during negotiations in the United Nations. The United Nations Human Rights Council in Geneva through resolution 26/9, in 2014 established an Intergovernmental Working Group created to elaborate a "legally binding instrument to regulate, in international human rights law, the activities of transnational corporations and other business enterprises" (a draft treaty on business and human rights). The Working Group held three sessions, with its next session scheduled for October 2018 and the "Zero Draft" was released in 2018 and strongly focuses on the key issue of access to justice and remedy by those impacted by business operations.

This National Action Plan reaffirms India's commitments towards realization of human rights and promotion of socially responsible businesses. It provides an overview of India's legal framework setting out the State's duty to protect human rights, the corporate responsibility to respect human rights and access to remedy against business-related human rights. Main structure of the document is as under:

I. **Protect -** States' duty to protect against human rights abuse by third parties, including businesses.

II. **Respect -** Responsibility of businesses, as specialized organs of the society to comply with applicable laws and to respect human rights.

III. **Remedy -** The need to ensure better access to effective remedy for victims of business-related human rights abuses.

Relevance and Need

- **Goal**

  National Action Plan will provide an overview of India's legal framework setting out the State's duty to protect human rights, set the corporate responsibility to respect human rights, and access remedy against business-related human rights violations.

◆ **Inspiration**

The vision of India's NAP stems from the Gandhian principle of trusteeship that defines that the purpose of business is to serve all stakeholders.

◆ **Need**

Experts claim that the Covid-19 pandemic is a litmus test for the concept of stakeholder capitalism. The NAP becomes more relevant in the wake of Covid-19 in that the pandemic has exposed several systemic vulnerabilities in how businesses operate. The International Labour Organization (ILO) estimates that, due to Covid-19, 400 million Indian workers are at risk of sinking even deeper into poverty.

◆ **International Commitment**

The UN Guiding Principles on Business and Human Rights (of which India is a signatory) envisages the Protect-Respect-Remedy principle while the role of the State is to ensure that all three pillars of the principle are working effectively in reality. Further, the 2030 agenda for Sustainable Development Goals (SDG 8) focuses upon the realization of human rights in the business sector.

Main features of the 'Zero Draft'

(*a*) The Convention underlines the importance of **civil and criminal liability provisions** for natural and legal person liable for violations of human rights undertaken in the context of business activities of transnational character.

(*b*) Emphasizes States roles as primary duty bearers, and reinforces their main obligations to regulate, prevent, sanction and **prosecute business activities** which result in human rights abuses.

(*c*) Recognises the **primacy of Human Rights over all trade agreements.**

(*d*) Includes the liability for violation of Human Rights in its **supply chain.**

(*e*) Recognises that all businesses enterprises, regardless of their size, sector, operational context, ownership and structure shall respect all human rights, while focusing in other provisions on the specific challenges of transnational activities.

(*f*) The Convention stresses on the **States duty to strengthen and establish legislations** to ensure, companies of transnational character comply with and conduct due diligence procedures, comprising but not limited to, identifying, assessing, monitoring and reporting on human rights issues across it value chain. And these obligations also be the included in contractual matters with Companies with Transnational character.

(*g*) Includes a comprehensive definition of remedies, which specifically mentions **environmental remediation and ecological** restoration.

(*h*) Emphasis on the **reversal of burden of proof** for the purpose of fulfilling the victim's access to justice.

(*i*) The convention **defines jurisdiction** as where violation committed, or where the company has headquarters, substantial operations, has subsidiary, agency, instrumentality, branch, representative office or the like.

(*j*) Emphasis on International cooperation for fulfilment of treaty obligation, including mutual assistance in initiating and carrying out investigations, prosecutions and judicial proceedings

NAP - Way Forward

Access to remedy poses a major challenge in the effective implementation of NAP. The limitation of National Human Rights Commission to accept complaints against non-State actors such as companies is a big gap. Lack of operational level grievance mechanisms could be another stumbling block for rights holder to access remedy mechanisms. Setting up multi-stakeholder committees within industrial MSME clusters could be a crucial missing piece in the implementation of Pillar 3.

The NAP process is an opportunity for India to demonstrate leadership in achieving sustainable and inclusive growth and position itself as the world's largest sustainable and responsible economy. The NAP can serve as an important tool to guide Indian businesses to redefine its purpose and emerge out of this pandemic more humane. Some key recommendations for effective implementation are as under:

- All Educational Institutions must ensure that Business and Human Rights are included in the management curriculum.
- The Ease of Doing Business must include an indicator regarding human rights so that people rightfully do their businesses.
- Powers must be given to the National Human Rights Commission (NHRC) so that quick and efficient steps can be taken against the violators.
- The focus must be on building the Micro, Small, and Medium Enterprises(MSME) to help them adapt to the NAP draft as they cover a major part of the Indian business sector.
- In India, the technology sector has been growing manifolds over the past few years. Thus, NAP should ensure that the technology companies embed accountability on human rights issues.

- All National and State Commissions must issue strict guidelines ensuring that no incident of violation of human rights is ignored and left unattended.

5.3.5 Case Studies

Below are some of the case studies collected which depicts some of the human rights violations and its impact on the businesses:

In *Plachimada* v *Coca Cola,* as per the agreement struck by the company with the KSPCB (Karnataka State Pollution Control Board), up to 1.5 million litres of water were haggard commercially from 6 bore-wells to be found inside the factory compound. The permit granted Coca-Cola the right to extract groundwater to meet its production demands of 3.8 litres of water for a litre of cola. The water table receded, as did the quality of groundwater and from the region revealed a high concentration of calcium, and magnesium ions detailed sampling of the water was collected. In addition, the colloidal slurry that was generated as a by-product was initially sold to villagers as fertilizer and dangerous levels of toxic metals and the known carcinogen, cadmium was found. The health of local people have been put at risk in addition to the area's farming industry has been devastated.

In *Vishakha and others* v *State of Rajasthan* Public Interest Litigation was filed against State of Rajasthan and Union of India to put in force the fundamental rights under Articles 14, 19 and 21 of the Constitution of India for working women. The petition was filed subsequent to Bhanwari Devi, a social worker in Rajasthan was cruelly gang-raped for stopping child marriage. In this case, the matter of sexual harassment in working place was put forward before the court. It was decided by the court that the "International Conventions are important for the purpose of analysis of the guarantee of gender equality, right to work with human dignity in Articles 14, 15 19(1)(*g*) and 21 of the Constitution and the safeguards against sexual harassment inherent therein." Supreme Court of India defined sexual harassment and set guidelines for employers working in corporations.

The Bhopal gas tragedy, when the entire town slept, a highly toxic chemical named methyl Isocyanate-2 (MIC) escaped from the Union Carbide India Limited in 4th December 1984 in Bhopal killing and crippling thousands in its wake. Estimated 40 tonnes of toxic gases from the pesticide plant at Bhopal spread throughout the city. The reason for the accident was the runaway reaction of the MIC with water. As a repercussion of the leakage, people and animals dropped dead on the street in astonishing numbers. During this incident, there was no alarm sounding warnings were given out and neither was there any chance for preparation for evacuation. This aggravated the tragedy as an estimated number of 10,000 people died immediately while almost 50,000 were too ill to return to their jobs.

The *Mahanadi Coalfields Limited Controversy,* It is situated at Talcher coalfields in Angul district of Odisha. It is one of the prime and most profitable coal producing subsidiaries in India. The people complained that the productivity of the farmlands is negatively affected by pollutants such as coal dust and fly ashes. In addition to the biggest problem was opencast mines that are not filled by the workers get filled with water and become breeding grounds for mosquitoes, furthermore insufficient filling of land holes also a reason for land depression. Excessive mining activities take over agricultural lands, encroach on forest land and cause topsoil loss. It also affects the water table, soil micro-organism, vegetation coverage, drainage, etc. The sounds of blasting, motor vehicles and coal loaded trains on merry go round railway has been causing ground vibration, landslide, joint fractures and cracks in the mining area. It also adversely affects the health of insects, birds, animals and human beings those who are living in the locality.

5.3.6 Recommendations

To assess the current landscape of business and human rights in India, emphasizing the role of businesses and their impacts on human rights, we explore the progress achieved in aligning business practices with human rights principles, including case studies of best practices and successful initiatives and identify and analyze the persistent challenges and gaps in human rights awareness and its protection. Some key interventions in this context (among others) may be:

- ensuring human rights for employees and workers (Sexual Harassment, Discrimination at workplace, Child Labour, Forced Labour/ Involuntary Labour, Wages, or any other human Rights related issue.
- proactively disclosing on company website how many third party human rights complaints were received, the status of these complaints, and how the company engages to resolve them.
- considering people with disabilities.
- hiring practices, career progression, healthcare provision, and flexible working hours for employees.
- conduct a vulnerability mapping of rights holders to human rights risk.
- Identify right holders across value chain.

As the Business and Human Rights (BHR) issues are gaining traction in the business community in India, more and more investors, manufacturers, customers and other stakeholders are striving to adopt BHR principles in their areas of influence. This has resulted in an unwritten mandate for businesses to be BHR sensitive. However, there may be instances when violations also take place. Lack of awareness on BHR aspects and approaches among top leaderships and implementing actors in the companies is also an area of concern. Research and Capacity Building needs in Business and Human Rights in India have been recommended through various platforms.

5.4 Diversity & Inclusion

In the dynamic landscape of corporate responsibility and sustainability, Environmental, Social, and Governance (ESG) criteria have emerged as vital benchmarks for assessing a company's commitment to long-term success. Central to the "S" in ESG are Social factors, where the principles of Diversity and Inclusion (D&I) play a pivotal role. The evaluation of inclusion and diversity in corporates has become not just a measure of ethical practices but a strategic imperative for organizations seeking resilience and relevance in a rapidly evolving global market.

5.4.1 Global and National Perspectives on Diversity and Inclusion

Internationally, there is a growing acknowledgement that fostering diversity and inclusion is not just a moral obligation but also a business necessity. Companies are increasingly recognizing that diverse and inclusive workplaces lead to enhanced creativity, innovation, and overall organizational performance. Various global initiatives and frameworks, such as the United Nations Global Compact, emphasize the importance of integrating social sustainability, including diversity and inclusion, into corporate strategies.

On the national front, India has made significant strides in enacting regulations that support diversity and inclusion across various dimensions. In India, the commitment to diversity and inclusion is underscored by a robust legal framework. Constitutional provisions prohibit discrimination based on caste, religion, gender, or place of birth, while affirmative action measures, such as reservations for Scheduled Castes, Scheduled Tribes, and Other Backward Classes, aim to ensure inclusive representation. The Companies Act, 2013, mandates gender diversity on boards, and legislation like the Equal Remuneration Act, 1976, and the Sexual Harassment of Women at Workplace Act, 2013, contribute to fostering inclusive work environments. Additionally, reservation policies for persons with disabilities and the broader scope of Corporate Social Responsibility activities further reinforce India's commitment to diversity and inclusion.

As businesses navigate these global and national dynamics, the integration of diversity and inclusion into the fabric of corporate strategy becomes paramount. It is not merely a checkbox for compliance but a reflection of a company's commitment to social sustainability and its ability to thrive in an interconnected and diverse world.

5.4.2 The Business Case for Diversity & Inclusion

Diversity encompasses the range of visible and invisible differences among individuals, including but not limited to gender, race, ethnicity, age, sexual orientation, and abilities. Inclusion involves creating an environment where all individuals feel valued, respected, and have equal access to opportunities and resources.

The business case for diversity & inclusion lies in the transformative power of varied perspectives. Diverse teams bring a wealth of innovation and creative problem-solving, while reflecting the diversity of consumers enhances a company's ability to understand and respond to market demands effectively. In essence, diversity and inclusion are not just moral imperatives but strategic assets that drive competitiveness and sustainable success.

Social Capital and Human Capital

(*a*) **Social Capital:** The relationships, networks, and trust within a company, enhanced by diverse perspectives, contribute to sustainable business practices.

(*b*) **Human Capital:** Diverse and inclusive workplaces attract top talent, fostering a skilled and engaged workforce.

Employee Well-being and Productivity

(*a*) **Health and Well-being:** Inclusive policies and practices positively impact employee well-being, creating a healthier and more productive workforce.

(*b*) **Employee Engagement:** A sense of belonging and inclusivity fosters higher levels of employee engagement and commitment to the company's mission.

Risk Mitigation and Reputation Management:

(*a*) **Risk Mitigation:** Companies with diverse leadership are better equipped to anticipate and mitigate risks associated with a rapidly changing global business landscape.

(*b*) **Reputation Management:** Demonstrating commitment to diversity and inclusion enhances a company's reputation, making it more resilient to challenges.

5.4.3 Regulatory Compliance and Stakeholder Expectations in India

(*a*) **Constitutional Provisions:** The Indian Constitution provides a foundation for inclusive practices. Article 15 prohibits discrimination on grounds of religion, race, caste, sex, or place of birth. Article 16 ensures equal opportunities in public employment without discrimination based on caste, creed, or gender.

(*b*) **Affirmative Action and Reservations:** To address historical social imbalances, the Indian government has implemented affirmative action policies. Reservations in educational institutions and public employment for Scheduled Castes (SCs), Scheduled Tribes (STs), and Other Backward Classes (OBCs) aim to ensure their inclusive representation.

(*c*) **Companies Act, 2013:** The Companies Act, 2013, mandates certain companies to have at least one woman director on their board. This provision promotes gender diversity at the leadership level, recognizing the importance of women's representation in decision-making roles.

(*d*) **Equal Remuneration Act, 1976:** The Equal Remuneration Act ensures equal pay for men and women doing the same work or work of a similar nature. This promotes gender equality in compensation, contributing to a more inclusive work environment.

(*e*) **The Sexual Harassment of Women at Workplace (Prevention, Prohibition, and Redressal) Act, 2013:** This Act mandates the establishment of Internal Complaints Committees (ICC) in workplaces to address and prevent sexual harassment. Ensuring a safe and inclusive work environment for women is a crucial aspect of corporate responsibility.

(*f*) **Reservation Policies for Persons with Disabilities:** The Rights of Persons with Disabilities Act, 2016, mandates reservation in government jobs and educational institutions for persons with disabilities. This promotes inclusivity for individuals with diverse abilities.

(*g*) **Corporate Social Responsibility (CSR):** While not specifically focused on diversity, the Companies Act, 2013, requires certain companies to spend a portion of their profits on Corporate Social Responsibility activities. These activities often include initiatives that contribute to social inclusion and community development.

In aggregate, these legislative measures establish a framework that incentivizes companies to prioritize and integrate diversity and inclusion. Spanning dimensions such as gender, caste, and ability, India's legal landscape seeks to cultivate a corporate environment that is both equitable and representative. Corporations aligning with these regulations not only demonstrate legal compliance but also actively contribute to the cultivation of a socially responsible and sustainable business ecosystem.

5.4.4 Gender Equity

In recent years, the global discourse on gender equity has gained unprecedented traction, propelled by a multitude of factors spanning grassroots movements, international advocacy, and the evolving expectations of society. This shift, distinct from the traditional emphasis on gender equality, represents a nuanced approach to address the systemic imbalances that persist globally.

The demand for gender equity has found resonance through diverse channels. Women's rights activists, non-governmental organizations (NGOs), and global initiatives such as the He For She campaign and the UN Women's Empowerment Principles have collectively fuelled the momentum. Social media platforms, acting as powerful catalysts, have enabled individuals to share personal narratives, mobilize support, and challenge entrenched gender norms on a global scale.

Unlike the concept of gender equality, which advocates for equal treatment and opportunities, gender equity acknowledges historical disparities and necessitates targeted efforts to redress imbalances. It recognizes that achieving equality may require tailored interventions based on the unique challenges faced by different groups.

International organizations, particularly the United Nations, have spearheaded initiatives like the Sustainable Development Goals (SDGs), with Goal 5 specifically addressing Gender Equality. Simultaneously, governments worldwide have taken strides by implementing policies and action plans to bridge gender gaps in education, employment, and healthcare. The establishment of dedicated gender equality ministries underscores a growing commitment to fostering equity at the national level.

Businesses have also stepped into the arena of gender equity, recognizing the multifaceted benefits of diverse and inclusive workplaces. Beyond moral imperatives, businesses now perceive gender equity as a strategic advantage. Practices such as gender-neutral recruitment, mentorship programmes, and pay equity audits are becoming commonplace. Corporate social responsibility (CSR) initiatives increasingly include commitments to gender equity, reflecting a broader societal expectation for businesses to contribute positively to social issues.

In the context of Environmental, Social, and Governance (ESG) considerations, gender equity is emerging as a critical component of the 'Social' aspect. Investors, consumers, and regulators are scrutinizing companies based on their ethical and societal impact. Gender equity, therefore, becomes integral to a company's ESG framework, with diverse and inclusive practices influencing its standing in the eyes of stakeholders.

Within companies, the relevance of gender equity extends beyond ethical considerations. Diverse leadership and a gender-inclusive culture are recognized as drivers of innovation, better decision-making, and improved financial performance. In a landscape where societal expectations continually evolve, companies championing gender equity are not only fulfilling a moral obligation but also strategically positioning themselves to attract top talent, enhance brand reputation, and cultivate loyalty among diverse customer bases.

The evolution of the global conversation on gender equity reflects a maturation of societal values and expectations. From demanding basic rights to addressing entrenched disparities, the discourse has become integral to shaping a more inclusive and equitable world. Governments, international organizations, and corporations each play pivotal roles in driving tangible change, acknowledging that gender equity is not merely a societal obligation but a strategic imperative for navigating the complexities of the contemporary global landscape.

5.5 Human Rights Due Diligence

5.5.1 Evolution

The consideration of human rights within the Environmental, Social, and Governance (ESG) framework has undergone a profound evolution, mirroring the historical development of human rights principles and the establishment of global resolutions. Originating in the aftermath of World War II, the Universal Declaration of Human Rights (UDHR) in 1948 marked a seminal moment, articulating the inalienable rights inherent to all individuals. This declaration laid the groundwork for subsequent international treaties and conventions, establishing a comprehensive framework for the protection of human rights on a global scale.

In 2011, a significant milestone was reached with the endorsement of the UN Guiding Principles on Business and Human Rights by the United Nations Human Rights Council. This framework delineates the responsibilities of both states and businesses in preventing and addressing human rights abuses associated with corporate activities. Emphasizing the imperative of human rights due diligence, the Guiding Principles have become a cornerstone of responsible business conduct worldwide.

Complementing these global efforts, the Organisation for Economic Co-operation and Development (OECD) has crafted guidelines for multinational enterprises, offering recommendations on human rights due diligence. The European Union has also implemented the Non-Financial Reporting Directive, obliging large companies to disclose information pertaining to environmental, social, and human rights considerations.

Within the context of India, a nation committed to international human rights conventions, the integration of human rights due diligence into business practices is gradually taking shape. The Indian Constitution, adopted in 1950, embeds fundamental rights as a commitment to safeguarding the dignity and well-being of its citizens. In 2011, the release of the National Voluntary Guidelines on Social, Environmental, and Economic Responsibilities of Business provided a domestic framework for businesses to incorporate social and environmental considerations into their operations.

5.5.2 Key Trends

Recent discourse in India has also revolved around the development of a National Action Plan on Business and Human Rights, signaling a potential step forward in strengthening the emphasis on human rights due diligence in corporate activities. Despite these advancements, challenges persist, and the effective implementation of human rights due diligence in Indian businesses remains an ongoing and dynamic process.

As businesses navigate the complexities of ESG considerations, the historical evolution of human rights, coupled with present-day global principles and India's emerging regulatory landscape, underscores the significance of understanding and engaging with human rights due diligence. This intersection not only shapes responsible corporate behaviour but also contributes to a broader commitment to the sustainable and ethical advancement of societies worldwide.

Understanding Human Rights Due Diligence: Human rights due diligence, as articulated by the UN Guiding Principles, is a proactive and ongoing process that companies undertake to identify, assess, prevent, mitigate, and account for how they address their human rights impacts (UN Human Rights Council, 2011). It involves a comprehensive examination of a company's operations, supply chains, and business relationships to identify potential adverse human rights impacts and take appropriate actions to address them.

5.5.3 Key Components of Human Rights Due Diligence

Identification of Risks

Consistent with the UN Guiding Principles, companies need to systematically identify and assess potential human rights risks associated with their activities (UN Human Rights Council, 2011). This includes evaluating the impacts on employees, local communities, and other stakeholders throughout the value chain.

Stakeholder Engagement

Meaningful engagement with relevant stakeholders, as emphasized by the UN Guiding Principles, is essential for understanding the diverse perspectives on human rights issues (UN Human Rights Council, 2011). This engagement helps in identifying potential risks and in the development of effective mitigation strategies.

Integration into Policies and Practices

Human rights due diligence requires the integration of findings into corporate policies and practices, aligning with the UN Guiding Principles (UN

Human Rights Council, 2011). This involves updating codes of conduct, supplier guidelines, and operational procedures to ensure alignment with human rights principles.

Monitoring and Evaluation

Continuous monitoring and evaluation of human rights impacts, a key aspect of the UN Guiding Principles, are critical to ensure that the implemented measures are effective (UN Human Rights Council, 2011). This involves establishing key performance indicators (KPIs) and regularly reporting on progress.

Remediation

In cases where adverse human rights impacts are identified, companies must take prompt corrective action and provide remedies to those affected, as highlighted by the UN Guiding Principles (UN Human Rights Council, 2011). This may involve compensating affected parties, instituting policy changes, or ceasing specific business activities.

5.5.4 Benefits of Human Rights Due Diligence in ESG

Enhanced Reputation

Companies that prioritize human rights due diligence build a positive reputation, earning trust from consumers, investors, and other stakeholders, in line with the principles outlined by the UN (UN Human Rights Council, 2011).

Risk Mitigation

Identifying and addressing human rights risks helps mitigate legal, operational, and reputational risks, consistent with the risk management framework emphasized in the UN Guiding Principles (UN Human Rights Council, 2011).

Market Competitiveness

Demonstrating a commitment to human rights can enhance a company's competitiveness in the market, as consumers and investors increasingly seek socially responsible businesses, echoing the expectations set by the UN (UN Human Rights Council, 2011).

5.5.5 Global Frameworks for mapping Human Rights and Due Diligence

United Nations Guiding Principles on Business and Human Rights (UNGPs)

The UNGPs, endorsed by the UN Human Rights Council in 2011, are a foundational framework. Developed by John Ruggie, they consist of three pillars: the state duty to protect human rights, the corporate responsibility to respect human rights, and access to remedy for victims of human rights abuses. The UNGPs emphasize the importance of human rights due diligence as a core element of responsible business conduct.

International Labour Organization (ILO)

Tripartite Declaration of Principles Concerning Multinational Enterprises and Social Policy: This ILO declaration provides guidance on social policy for multinational enterprises. It covers various aspects of labour and employment, including non-discrimination, freedom of association, and the elimination of forced labor. The declaration encourages businesses to adhere to these principles in all their operations.

OECD Guidelines for Multinational Enterprises

The Organisation for Economic Co-operation and Development (OECD) provides guidelines for multinational enterprises, which include recommendations on human rights due diligence. The guidelines encourage companies to respect human rights, contribute to sustainable development, and engage in transparent reporting.

Global Reporting Initiative (GRI)

The GRI provides a sustainability reporting framework that includes human rights indicators. Organizations using the GRI framework are required to report on their human rights due diligence processes, impacts, and performance. This helps in enhancing transparency and accountability.

ISO 26000 - Guidance on Social Responsibility

The International Organization for Standardization (ISO) developed ISO 26000 to provide guidance on social responsibility. While not a certifiable standard, it includes principles and guidelines on human rights due diligence, encouraging organizations to consider the social impacts of their activities.

UN Global Compact

The UN Global Compact is a voluntary initiative encouraging businesses to align their operations with ten universally accepted principles in areas such as human rights, labor, environment, and anti-corruption. Signatories commit to implementing these principles and reporting on their progress.

Equator Principles

While primarily focused on the financial industry, the Equator Principles provide a framework for assessing and managing environmental and social risks in project financing. Human rights considerations, including due diligence, are integral to these principles.

Business and Human Rights Resource Centre (BHRRC)

The BHRRC operates as a global resource for tracking the human rights performance of companies. It offers tools, resources, and assessments to encourage businesses to integrate human rights due diligence into their operations.

Integrating human rights due diligence into ESG practices is not just a legal or ethical imperative, it is a strategic necessity for businesses in the modern world, aligning with the UN Guiding Principles on Business and Human Rights. By systematically addressing human rights impacts, companies contribute not only to the well-being of individuals and communities but also to the overall sustainability of their operations. As ESG considerations continue to gain prominence, human rights due diligence, guided by the UN principles, will play an increasingly pivotal role in shaping responsible and resilient businesses.

5.5.6 OECD Due Diligence Guidance for Responsible Business Conduct

We often use OECD Due Diligence Guidance for Responsible Business Conduct to carryout human rights due diligence in India. Here we will present this framework in detail. The guidance is also available separately for different industry sectors.

Businesses can play a major role in contributing to economic, environmental and social progress, especially when they minimise the adverse impacts of their operations, supply chains and other business relationships. The OECD Guidelines for Multinational Enterprises recommend that enterprises conduct due diligence in order to identify, prevent or mitigate and account for how actual and potential adverse impacts are addressed.

The OECD Due Diligence Guidance for Responsible Business Conduct provides practical support to enterprises on the implementation of the OECD Guidelines for Multinational Enterprises by providing plain-language explanations of its due diligence recommendations and associated provisions. Implementing these recommendations can help enterprises avoid and address adverse impacts related to workers, human rights, the environment, bribery, consumers and corporate governance that may be associated with their operations, supply chains and other business relationships. The Guidance includes additional explanations, tips and illustrative examples of due diligence.

This Guidance also seeks to promote a common understanding among governments and stakeholders on due diligence for responsible business conduct. The UN Guiding Principles on Business and Human Rights, as well as the ILO Tripartite Declaration of Principles Concerning Multinational Enterprises and Social Policy, also contain due diligence recommendations, and this Guidance can help enterprises implement them.

The objective of the OECD Due Diligence Guidance for Responsible Business Conduct is to provide practical support to enterprises on the implementation of the OECD Guidelines for Multinational Enterprises by providing plain language explanations of its due diligence recommendations and associated provisions. Implementing these recommendations helps enterprises avoid and address adverse impacts related to workers, human rights, the environment, bribery, consumers and corporate governance that may be associated with their operations, supply chains and other business relationships. The due diligence process by OECD has six key steps:

- ◆ Embed responsible business conduct into policies and management systems
- ◆ Identify and assess actual and potential adverse impacts associated with the enterprise's operations, products or services
- ◆ Cease, prevent and mitigate adverse impacts
- ◆ Track implementation and results
- ◆ Communicate how impacts are addressed
- ◆ Provide for or cooperate in remediation when appropriate

The OECD Guidance Document on Due Diligence for Responsible Business Conduct provides following steps and practical action points:

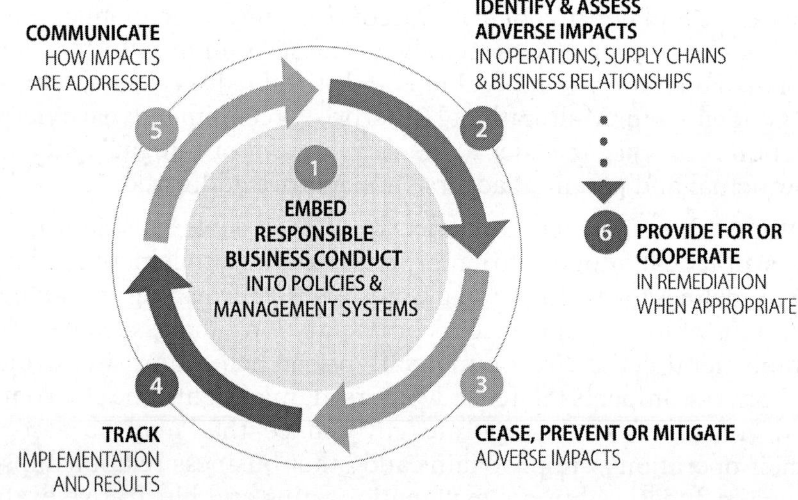

(Source: OECD)

Figure 5.3: Due Diligence Process & Supporting Measures

STEP – 1: Embed Responsible Business Conduct into Policies and Management Systems

The practical actions to articulate the company's commitments may be followed as per the below points:

- ◆ Review and update existing policies on RBC issues (e.g. labour, human rights, environment, disclosure, consumer protection, governance, anti-bribery and corruption) to align with the principles and standards of the OECD Guidelines for MNEs.

- Develop specific policies on the enterprise's most significant risks, building on findings from its assessment of risk, in order to provide guidance on the enterprise's specific approach to addressing those risks. Consider making the enterprise's due diligence plans part of these policies.
- Make the enterprise's policies on RBC issues publicly available, e.g. on the enterprise's website, at the enterprise's premises, and when relevant, in the local languages.
- Communicate the policies to the enterprise's own relevant employees and other workers, e.g. during staff orientation or training and periodically as needed to maintain awareness.
- Update the enterprise's policies as risks in the enterprise's operations, supply chain and other business relationships emerge and evolve.

To embed the business' policies on Responsible Business Conduct issues into management systems, following practical action points may be followed:

- Assign oversight and responsibility for due diligence to relevant senior management and assign board level responsibilities for RBC more broadly.
- Assign responsibility for implementing aspects of the policies across relevant departments with particular attention to those workers whose actions and decisions are most likely to increase or decrease risks.
- Develop or adapt existing information and record-keeping systems to collect information on due diligence processes, related decision-making and responses.
- Establish channels of communication, or utilise existing channels of communication, between relevant senior management and implementing departments for sharing and documenting information on risk and decision-making.
- Encourage alignment across teams and business units on relevant aspects of the enterprise's RBC policies. This could be done for example by creating cross-functional groups or committees to share information and decision-making about risks, and including business units that can impact observance of the RBC policies in decision-making.
- Provide training to workers to help them understand and implement relevant aspects of RBC policies and provide adequate resources commensurate with the extent of due diligence needed.
- Develop incentives for workers and business units that are compatible with the enterprise's RBC policies.

- Develop, draw from or adapt existing complaint procedures for workers to raise issues or complaints related to RBC issues (e.g. labour practices, corruption, corporate governance).
- Develop processes to respond to or, where appropriate, provide remedies in situations where the RBC policy is not observed (e.g. through additional fact-finding, capacity building or disciplinary actions/sanctions).

Practical actions for incorporating Responsible Business Conduct expectations and policies into engagement with suppliers and other business relationships may be as under:

- Communicate key aspects of the RBC policies to suppliers and other relevant business relationships.
- Include conditions and expectations on RBC issues in supplier or business relationship contracts or other forms of written agreements.
- Develop and implement pre-qualification processes on due diligence for suppliers and other business relationships, where feasible, adapting such processes to the specific risk and context in order to focus on RBC issues that have been identified as relevant for the business relationships and their activities or area(s) of operation.
- Provide adequate resources and training to suppliers and other business relationships for them to understand and apply the relevant RBC policies and implement due diligence.
- Seek to understand and address barriers arising from the enterprise's way of doing business that may impede the ability of suppliers and other business relationships to implement RBC polices, such as the enterprise's purchasing practices and commercial incentives.

STEP – 2: Identify and assess actual and potential adverse impacts associated with the enterprise's operations, products or services

Key practical action points to carry out a broad scoping exercise to identify all areas of the business, across its operations and relationships, including in its supply chains, are as under:

- Create an initial, high-level picture of the enterprise's areas of operation and types of business relationships to understand what information will be relevant to gather.
- Gather information to understand high-level risks of adverse impacts related to the sector (e.g. products and their supply chains, services and other activities), geography (e.g. governance and rule-of-law, conflict, pervasive human rights or environmental adverse impacts) or enterprise-specific risk factors (e.g. known instances of corruption, misconduct, implementation of standards for RBC). Sources might

include reports from governments, international organisations, civil society organisations, workers' representatives and trade unions, national human rights institutions (NHRIs), media or other experts.

- Where gaps in information exist, consult with relevant stakeholders and experts.
- Consider information raised through early warning systems (e.g. hotlines) and grievance mechanisms.
- Identify the most significant RBC risk areas and prioritise these as the starting point for a deeper assessment of potential and actual impacts.
- Review the findings of the scoping exercise on a regular basis.
- Update the scoping exercise with new information whenever the enterprise makes significant changes, such as operating in or sourcing from a new country; developing a new product or service line that varies significantly from existing lines; changing the inputs of a product or service; restructuring, or engaging in new forms of business relationships (e.g. mergers, acquisitions, new clients and markets).

Practical action points to carry out iterative and increasingly in-depth assessments of prioritised operations, suppliers and other business relationships

- Map the enterprise's operations, suppliers and other business relationships, including associated supply chains, relevant to the prioritised risk.
- Catalogue the specific RBC standards and issues applicable to the risk being assessed, including relevant provisions from the OECD Guidelines for MNEs, as well as domestic laws and relevant international and industry-specific frameworks on RBC issues. c. Obtain, when appropriate and feasible, relevant information about business relationships beyond contractual relationships (e.g. sub-suppliers beyond "tier 1"). Establish processes individually or collaboratively to assess the risk profile of more remote tiers of the relationship, including by reviewing existing assessments, and engaging with mid-stream actors and "control points" in the supply chain to assess their due diligence practices against this Guidance.
- Assess the nature and extent of actual and potential impacts linked to prioritised operations, suppliers or other business relationships (*i.e.* which RBC issue is impacted and in what ways, the scope of the impact, etc.). Where available, use information from the enterprise's own, or third parties', environmental impact assessments (EIA), environmental and social impacts assessments (ESIA), human rights impact assessments (HRIA), legal reviews, compliance management systems regarding corruption, financial audits (for disclosure),

occupational, health and safety inspections; and any other relevant assessments of business relationships carried out by the enterprise or by industry and multi-stakeholder initiatives, including environmental, social and labour audits, corruption assessments and KYC processes.

- Identify activities that may not be carried out in an appropriate legal and institutional framework sufficient to protect the rights of all persons and enterprises involved.
- Consider the RBC risks prior to a proposed business activity (e.g. an acquisition, restructuring, new market entry, new product or service development) projecting how the proposed activity and associated business relationships could have adverse impacts on specific RBC issues.
- Reassess impacts at regular intervals as needed: prior to major decisions or changes in the activity (e.g. market entry, product launch, policy change, or wider changes to the business); in response to or in anticipation of changes in the operating environment (e.g. rising social tensions); and periodically throughout the life of an activity or relationship.
- For human rights impacts, consult and engage impacted and potentially impacted rightsholders, including workers, workers' representatives and trade unions, to gather information on adverse impacts and risks, taking into account potential barriers to effective stakeholder engagement. Where directly consulting with rightsholders is not possible, consider reasonable alternatives such as consulting credible, independent expert resources, including human rights defenders, trade unions and civil society groups. Consult potentially impacted rightsholders both prior to and during projects or activities that may affect them (e.g. through site-level assessments).
- In assessing impacts related to human rights, pay special attention to potential adverse impacts on individuals from groups or populations that may have a heightened risk of vulnerability or marginalisation, and to different risks that may be faced by women and men.
- For enterprises with multiple entities within an enterprise group, support local entities to carry out their own assessments.

To assess the enterprise's involvement with the actual or potential adverse impacts identified in order to determine the appropriate responses, following practical action points may be considered:

- Consult with business relationships, other relevant enterprises and other relevant stakeholders.
- Consult with impacted stakeholders and rightsholders or their legitimate representatives.

- Seek relevant internal or external expertise as needed.
- If impacted stakeholders or rightsholders disagree with the enterprise's assessment of its involvement with any actual or potential adverse impact, cooperate in good faith with legitimate mechanisms designed to help resolve the disagreements and provide remediation.
- To prioritise the most significant Responsible Business Conduct risks and impacts for action, following practical action points are considered:
- Identify which potential or actual impacts may be addressed immediately, at least to some degree (e.g. update contract terms with suppliers, amend audit protocols to focus on risks that may have been previously missed during audits).
- Prioritise for action any activities that are causing or contributing to adverse impacts on RBC issues, based on the enterprise's assessment of their involvement with adverse impacts.
- For impacts involving business relationships, assess the extent to which business relationships have appropriate policies and processes in place to identify, prevent and mitigate relevant RBC risks themselves.
- Where it is not possible to address all real and potential adverse impacts directly linked to the enterprise's operations, products or services by business relationships (or to address them to the full extent desirable), evaluate the likelihood and severity of the identified impacts or risks to understand which issues should be prioritised for action.
- Consult with business relationships, other relevant enterprises and impacted or potentially impacted stakeholders and rightsholders on prioritisation decisions.
- Seek relevant internal or external expertise as needed.

STEP – 3: Cease, prevent and mitigate adverse impacts

To develop and implement plans that are fit-for-purpose to prevent and mitigate potential (future) adverse impacts, the practical action points below may be considered:

- Assign relevant senior responsibility for ensuring that activities that cause or contribute to adverse impacts cease, and for preventing activities that may cause or contribute to adverse impacts in the future.
- In the case of complex actions or actions that may be difficult to stop due to operational, contractual or legal issues, create a roadmap for how to stop the activities causing or contributing to adverse impacts, involving in-house legal counsel and impacted or potentially impacted stakeholders and rightsholders.

- Update the enterprise's policies to provide guidance on how to avoid and address the adverse impacts in the future and ensure their implementation.
- Provide training that is fit-for-purpose for the enterprise's relevant workers and management.
- Draw from the findings of the risk assessment to update and strengthen management systems to better track information and flag risks before adverse impacts occur.
- Consult and engage with impacted and potentially impacted stakeholders and rightsholders and their representatives to devise appropriate actions and implement the plan.
- In the case of collective or cumulative impacts (*i.e.* where the enterprise is only one of several entities contributing to the adverse impact occurring) and, where appropriate, seek to engage with other involved entities to cease the impacts and prevent them from recurring or to prevent risks from materialising, e.g. through industry initiatives and engagement with governments.
- In cases where the enterprise is contributing to adverse impacts or risks that are caused by another entity, it should take necessary steps to cease or prevent its contribution as described above, also building and using leverage to mitigate any remaining impacts to the greatest extent possible.

To develop and implement plans to seek to prevent or mitigate actual or potential adverse impacts on RBC issues which are directly linked to the enterprise's operations, products or services by business relationships, below are the suggestive points:

- Assign responsibility for developing, implementing and monitoring these plans.
- Support or collaborate with the relevant business relationship(s) in developing fit-for-purpose plans for them to prevent or mitigate adverse impacts identified within reasonable and clearly defined timelines, using qualitative and quantitative indicators for defining and measuring improvement (sometimes referred to as "corrective action plans").
- Use leverage, to the extent possible, to prompt the business relationship(s) to prevent or mitigate adverse impacts or risks.
- If the enterprise does not have sufficient leverage, consider ways to build additional leverage with the business relationship, including for example through outreach from senior management and through commercial incentives. To the extent possible, cooperate with other actors to build and exert collective leverage, for example through

collaborative approaches in industry associations, or through engagement with governments.

- To prevent potential (future) adverse impacts and address actual impacts, seek to build leverage into new and existing business relationships, e.g. through policies or codes of conduct, contracts, written agreements or use of market power.
- For human rights impacts, encourage entities causing or contributing to adverse impacts to consult and engage with impacted or potentially impacted rightsholders or their representatives in developing and implementing corrective action plans.
- Support relevant suppliers and other business relationships in the prevention or mitigation of adverse impacts or risks, e.g. through training, upgrading of facilities, or strengthening of their management systems, striving for continuous improvement.
- Consider disengagement from the supplier or other business relationship as a last resort after failed attempts at preventing or mitigating severe impacts; when adverse impacts are irremediable; where there is no reasonable prospect of change; or when severe adverse impacts or risks are identified and the entity causing the impact does not take immediate action to prevent or mitigate them. Any plans for disengagement should also take into account how crucial the supplier or business relationship is to the enterprise, the legal implications of remaining in or ending the relationship, how disengagement might change impacts on the ground, as well as credible information about the potential social and economic adverse impacts related to the decision to disengage.
- If an enterprise decides to remain in a relationship, it should be prepared to account for its ongoing risk mitigation efforts and be aware of the reputational, financial or legal risks of the continuing connection.
- Encourage relevant authorities in the country where the impact is occurring to act, e.g. through inspections, enforcement and application of existing laws and regulations

STEP – 4: Track implementation and results

Tracking the implementation and effectiveness of the enterprise's due diligence activities:

- Monitor and track implementation and effectiveness of the enterprise's own internal commitments, activities and goals on due diligence, e.g. by carrying out periodic internal or third party reviews or audits of the outcomes achieved and communicating results at relevant levels within the enterprise.

- Carry out periodic assessments of business relationships, to verify that risk mitigation measures are being pursued or to validate that adverse impacts have actually been prevented or mitigated.
- For human rights impacts the enterprise has, or may, cause or contribute to, seek to consult and engage impacted or potentially impacted rightsholders, including workers, workers' representatives and trade unions.
- Seek to encourage periodic reviews of relevant multi-stakeholder and industry initiatives of which the enterprise is a member, including their alignment with this Guidance, and their value to the enterprise in helping it identify, prevent or mitigate adverse impacts linked to its business, taking into account the independence of these initiatives.
- Identify adverse impacts or risks that may have been overlooked in past due diligence processes and include these in the future.
- Include feedback of lessons learned into the enterprise's due diligence in order to improve the process and outcomes in the future.

STEP – 5: Communicate how impacts are addressed

To communicate externally relevant information on due diligence policies, processes, activities following practical action points may be considered:

- Publicly report relevant information on due diligence processes, with due regard for commercial confidentiality and other competitive or security concerns, e.g. through the enterprise's annual, sustainability or corporate responsibility reports or other appropriate forms of disclosure. Include RBC policies, information on measures taken to embed RBC into policies and management systems, the enterprise's identified areas of significant risks, the significant adverse impacts or risks identified, prioritised and assessed, as well as the prioritisation criteria, the actions taken to prevent or mitigate those risks, including where possible estimated timelines and benchmarks for improvement and their outcomes, measures to track implementation and results and the enterprise's provision of or co-operation in any remediation.
- Publish the above information in a way that is easily accessible and appropriate, e.g. on the enterprise's website, at the enterprise's premises and in local languages.
- For human rights impacts that the enterprise causes or contributes to, be prepared to communicate with impacted or potentially impacted rightsholders in a timely, culturally sensitive and accessible manner, the information above that is specifically relevant to them, in particular when relevant concerns are raised by them or on their behalf.

STEP – 6: Provide for or cooperate in remediation when appropriate

For cooperating in their remediation, following practical action points may be considered:

- Seek to restore the affected person or persons to the situation they would be in had the adverse impact not occurred (where possible) and enable remediation that is proportionate to the significance and scale of the adverse impact.
- Comply with the law and seek out international guidelines on remediation where available, and where such standards or guidelines are not available, consider a remedy that would be consistent with that provided in similar cases. The type of remedy or combination of remedies that is appropriate will depend on the nature and extent of the adverse impact and may include apologies, restitution or rehabilitation (e.g., reinstatement of dismissed workers, recognition of the trade union for the purpose of collective bargaining), financial or non-financial compensation (for example, establishing compensation funds for victims, or for future outreach and educational programmes), punitive sanctions (for example, the dismissals of staff responsible for wrongdoing), taking measures to prevent future adverse impacts.
- In relation to human rights impacts, consult and engage with impacted rightsholders and their representatives in the determination of the remedy.
- Seek to assess the level of satisfaction of those who have raised complaints with the process provided and its outcome(s).

In respect to legitimate remediation, OECD Guidance suggests following practical action points:

- Cooperate in good faith with judicial or non-judicial mechanisms. For example, if a specific instance is submitted to an NCP or through initiatives that provide other types of grievance mechanisms involving the conduct of the enterprise. If the actual adverse impact caused constitutes a criminal or administrative offense, the enterprise may be subject to criminal prosecution or administrative sanctions.
- Establish operational-level grievance mechanisms (OLGM), for example in-house worker complaint mechanisms or third-party complaint systems. This may involve setting up a complaints process including: a roadmap for remediation and resolving complaints; timelines for resolving grievances; processes to respond to complaints if agreement is not reached or if impacts are particularly severe; determining the scope of the OLGM's mandate; consulting with relevant stakeholders on appropriate forms of OLGMs and ways to

resolve complaints that are culturally appropriate and accessible; staffing and resourcing the OLGM; and tracking and monitoring the performance of the OLGM. For human rights impacts, align OLGMs with core criteria of legitimacy, accessibility, predictability, equitability, compatibility with the OECD Guidelines for MNEs, transparency and dialogue-based engagement.

- Engage with workers' representatives and trade unions to establish a process through which they can raise complaints to the enterprise, for example, through grievance mechanisms set forth in any collective agreements or through Global Framework Agreements.

5.6 Corporate Social Responsibility

The infinite universe has been graced with the existence of organized life on earth. Key components of the organized human life are regularization of the social behaviour, regularization of the business activities and Government systems. To govern the social behaviour various laws are in existence, besides sociological, social work and psychological norms and institutions. Businesses provide necessary commodities, services and infrastructure to us, regularization of the business practices is also done through various laws and norms. Government systems provide machinery for law making and execution of it. Businesses/Corporates started exploiting the available resources in order to deliver necessary and luxurious goods and services to the society. Core motto for most of the businesses became profit maximization. Organized efforts were made by the Government of India to navigate/regularise the corporate behaviour more responsibly, figure below depicts Government initiatives in this respect:

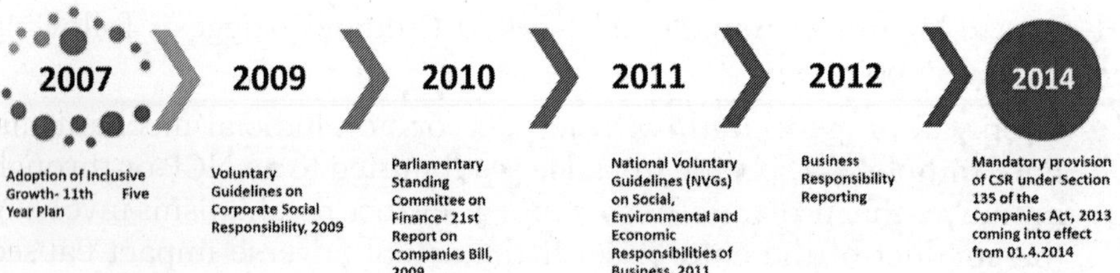

(Source: https://csr.gov.in/page-history.php)

Figure 5.4: Historical perspective of CSR Legislation

Corporate Social Responsibility (CSR) in India has distinguished features when compared with the CSR practices in almost rest of the world. In the post-2014 era, CSR in India is considered as a mandatory spend in accordance with the section 135 of the Companies Act, 2013. Whereas, CSR practices in rest of the world are considered as integration of the responsible business behaviour in each step of the business in terms of Environment, Social and

Governance initiatives besides charitable/developmental contributions. However, Government of India has released National Guidelines on Responsible Business Conduct (NGRBC) also in 2019, but the definition of CSR in India is governed by the section 135 of the Companies Act, 2013. Hence, CSR and Responsible Business Conduct may be seen two different aspects in India whereas in almost rest of the world both are considered same.

5.6.1 Section 135 of the Companies Act, 2013

CSR in India as defined in the Companies Act, 2013 is as under:

Corporate Social Responsibility (CSR) means and includes but is not limited to:—

- Projects or programmes relating to activities specified in Schedule VII to the Act; or Concept and Evolution of Corporate Social Responsibility and Sustainable...
- Projects or programmes relating to activities undertaken by the board of directors of a company (Board) in pursuance of recommendations of the CSR Committee of the Board as per declared CSR Policy of the company subject to the condition that such policy will cover subjects enumerated in Schedule VII of the Act'.

Government of India introduced special sections in the Companies Act, 2013 by which it became mandatory for the corporates having annual net worth of INR 500 Crore or more, net profit of INR 5 Crore or more, or turnover of INR 1000 Crore or more, to spent 2% of their net average profit in last three consecutive years on the corporate social responsibility initiatives. Government of India has also introduced Schedule VII in the Companies Act, 2013 detailing about the suggestive activities to be taken by the corporations under the CSR.

The provisions given in the Companies Act, 2013 under section 135 are as under:

- Every company having net worth of rupees five hundred crore or more, or turnover of rupees one thousand crore or more or a net profit of rupees five crore or more during any financial year shall constitute a Corporate Social Responsibility Committee of the Board consisting of three or more directors, out of which at least one director shall be an independent director.
- The Board's report under sub-section (3) of section 134 shall disclose the composition of the Corporate Social Responsibility Committee.
- The Corporate Social Responsibility Committee shall:
  - Formulate and recommend to the Board, a Corporate Social Responsibility Policy which shall indicate the activities to be undertaken by the company as specified in Schedule VII;

- Recommend the amount of expenditure to be incurred on the activities referred to in clause (*a*); and
- Monitor the Corporate Social Responsibility Policy of the company from time to time.

◆ The Board of every company referred to in sub-section (1) shall:

- After taking into account the recommendations made by the Corporate Social Responsibility Committee, approve the Corporate Social Responsibility Policy for the company and disclose the contents of such Policy in its report and also place it on the company's website, if any, in such manner as may be prescribed; and
- Ensure that the activities included in Corporate Social Responsibility Policy of the company are undertaken by the company.

◆ The Board of every company referred to in sub-section (1), shall ensure that the company spends, in every financial year, at least two per cent of the average net profits of the company made during the three immediately preceding financial years, in pursuance of its Corporate Social Responsibility Policy:

- **Provided** that the company shall give preference to the local area and areas around it where it operates, for spending the amount earmarked for Corporate Social Responsibility activities:
- **Provided further** that if the company fails to spend such amount, the Board shall, in its report made under clause (o) of sub-section (3) of section 134, specify the reasons for not spending the amount.

Sometimes people inquire if the eligible CSR amount is to be calculated bases on average net profit before tax or average net profit after tax. The Ministry of Corporate Affairs has clariid that computation of the net profit for section 135 is as per section 198 of the Companies Act, 2013 which primarily is net profit before tax.

5.6.2 Schedule VII

Schedule VII of the Companies Act, 2013 enlists the activities which may be included by the Companies in their Corporate Social Responsibility Policy. Activities like - Eradicating extreme hunger and poverty; Promotion of education; Promoting gender equality and empowering women; Reducing child mortality and improving maternal health; Combating Human Immunodeficiency Virus, Acquired Immune Deficiency Syndrome, Malaria and other diseases; Ensuring environmental sustainability; Employment enhancing vocational skills; Social business projects; Contribution to the Prime Minister's National Relief Fund or any other fund set up by the Central Government or the State Governments for socio-economic development and relief and funds for the welfare of the Scheduled Castes, the Scheduled Tribes, other backward classes, minorities and women; and Such other matters as may be prescribed, were initially listed.

There have been several clarifications/amendments/additions/substitutions in the Schedule VII from time to time. *Vide* GSR 130E on 28.02.2014, for items (i) to (ix) in the original Schedule VII and entries relating thereto, the following items and entries were substituted:

1. Eradicating hunger, poverty and malnutrition, promoting preventive health care and sanitation and making available safe drinking water
2. Promoting education, including special education and employment enhancing vocation skills, especially among children, women, elderly, and the differently abled and livelihood enhancement projects
3. Promoting gender equality, empowering women, setting up homes and hostels for women and orphans; setting up old-age homes, day care centres and such other facilities for senior citizens and measures for reducing inequalities faced by socially and economically backward groups
4. Ensuring environmental sustainability, ecological balance, protection of flora and fauna, animal welfare, agro-forestry, conservation of natural resources and maintaining quality of soil, air and water
5. Protection of national heritage, art and culture including restoration of buildings and sites of historical importance and works of art; setting up public libraries; promotion and development of traditional and handicrafts
6. Measures for the benefit of armed forces veterans, war widows and their dependents
7. Training to promote rural sports, nationally recognised sports, Paralympics sports and Olympic sports
8. Contribution to the Prime Minister's National Relief Fund or any other fund set up by the Central Government for socio-economic development and relief and welfare of the Scheduled Castes, the Scheduled Tribes, other backward classes, minorities and women
9. Contributions or funds provided to technology incubators located within academic institutions which are approved by the Central Government
10. Rural development projects

Further, *vide* GSR 568E on 06.08.2014, Government amended the Schedule VII as under:

> (1) In Schedule VII, after item (x), the following item and entry shall be inserted, namely: (xi) slum area development.

> Explanation For the purposes of this item, the term 'slum area' shall mean any area declared as such by the Central Government or any State Government or any other competent authority under any law for the time being in force."

In October 2014, Government amended Schedule VII as under:

> In item (*i*), after the words "and sanitation", the words "including contribution to the Swachh Bharat Kosh set-up by the Central Government for the promotion of sanitation" shall be inserted;
>
> In item (*iv*), after the words "and water", the words "including contribution to the Clean Ganga Fund setup by the Central Government for rejuvenation of river Ganga;" shall be inserted.

5.6.3 CSR Rules

Further, the Government of India has also framed model rules in year 2014 on the subject to clarify the matters of complex nature. These rules are known as 'The Companies (Corporate Social Responsibility Policy) Rules, 2014. The rules were published on 27.02.2014 and were effective from 01.04.2014. The rules focus on all important aspects given under the section 135 of the Companies Act, 2013 like CSR activities to be undertaken by the eligible Companies, CSR Committee, CSR Policy, CSR Expenditure, CSR Implementing Partners, Programme/Project under the CSR expenditure – exclusions and inclusions, Human Resources, Calculation of Net Profit, CSR Reporting, Display of CSR Activities, and other general observations.

Several clarifications have been notified to the Companies (Corporate Social Responsibility Policy) Rules, 2014 from time to time, 18.06.2014, 12.09.2014, 17.09.2014 etc. The Rules were also amended from time to time. The Companies (Corporate Social Responsibility Policy) Amendment Rules, 2021 have been described in the later part of this chapter.

5.6.4 The Companies (Amendment) Act, 2019

The Companies (Amendment) Act, 2019 came into effect on July 31, 2019 *vide* Gazette Notification No. 22 of 2019. In order to ensure accountability and better enforcement to strengthen the Corporate Social Responsibility and compliance management, the government introduced a Bill to amend the Companies Act to restructure provisions about unspent funds for CSR and impose penalty on firms and officials not adhering to these provisions. Amendments brought through the Companies (Amendment) Act, 2019 are presented below, explanation in these amendments has also been presented in the later part:

> In section 135 of the principal Act,— (a) in sub-section (5), after the second proviso, the following proviso shall be inserted, namely:— "Provided also that if the company spends an amount in excess of the requirements provided under this sub-section, such company may set off such excess amount against the requirement to spend under this sub-section for such number of succeeding

financial years and in such manner, as may be prescribed."; (b) for sub-section (7), the following sub-section shall be substituted, namely:— "(7) If a company is in default in complying with the provisions of sub-section (5) or sub-section (6), the company shall be liable to a penalty of twice the amount required to be transferred by the company to the Fund specified in Schedule VII or the Unspent Corporate Social Responsibility Account, as the case may be, or one crore rupees, whichever is less, and every officer of the company who is in default shall be liable to a penalty of one-tenth of the amount required to be transferred by the company to such Fund specified in Schedule VII, or the Unspent Corporate Social Responsibility Account, as the case may be, or two lakh rupees, whichever is less."; (c) after sub-section (8), the following sub-section shall be inserted, namely:— "(9) Where the amount to be spent by a company under sub-section (5) does not exceed fifty lakh rupees, the requirement under sub-section (1) for constitution of the Corporate Social Responsibility Committee shall not be applicable and the functions of such Committee provided under this section shall, in such cases, be discharged by the Board of Directors of such company."

Highlights on some of the key provisions of the amendment Act and their explanation are presented below:

The Act mandates that companies with a profit of more than INR 5 crore, turnover of INR 100 crore, and net worth of more than INR 500 crore have to spend at least two percent of their three years' annual average net profit towards CSR activities. Earlier, if companies were not able to spend entire eligible CSR amount in the given financial years, they were expected to declare reason for not spending the amount in their annual report. Now, companies are obliged to transfer their unspent CSR funds to one of the funds prescribed under Schedule VII of the Act within six months of the end of the financial year.

If the CSR funds are committed to certain ongoing projects, the company must transfer the amount to an unspent account with a scheduled bank within 30 days from the end of the financial year. A special account in this respect is to be opened by the company in a scheduled bank. This amount is to be utilized for mentioned ongoing projects within three financial years. If the company fails to spend this amount within three financial years, it must transfer it to one of the funds mentioned in Schedule VII of the Act.

In case of any violation of the CSR provisions, the company is liable to a minimum penalty fee of INR 0.5 lakh which may extend to INR 25 lakh. Further, every defaulting officer of the company may be liable to imprisonment for up to three years, or a fine up to INR 5 lakh or both.

Allaying industry concerns, Finance and Corporate Affairs Minister after amendments in the Companies Act, expressed that violations of CSR norms under the companies law will be treated only as civil liability and not as a criminal offence (confirmed in media reports). After expression of concerns over penal provisions for non-compliance with Corporate Social

Responsibility (CSR) requirements in the amended Companies Act, 2013, the Ministry of Corporate Affairs plans to review the sections concerned under the Companies Act.

Finance and Corporate Affairs Minister has also assured the industry that the government will review the criminal penal provisions on Corporate Social Responsibility contained in the recent amendments to the Companies Act. It has also been conveyed that CSR notices with retrospective effect "were unacceptable" and that a stop may be putted to them. Amendments to the Companies Act have empowered the government to put the officers concerned in jail for up to three years, besides imposing monetary fines if they do not adhere to CSR norms. After the new amendments, firms will have to spend on CSR, and the earlier practice of explaining to shareholders about not doing so has been discontinued.

5.6.5 The Companies (Amendment) Act, 2020

Government of India has introduced certain amendments to the Companies Act, 2013 and the amended Act is known as the Companies (Amendment) Act, 2020. It was notified on 28.09.2020. Amendments pertaining to the Section 135 are as under:

> In section 135 of the principal Act,— (a) in sub-section (5), after the second proviso, the following proviso shall be inserted, namely:— "Provided also that if the company spends an amount in excess of the requirements provided under this sub-section, such company may set off such excess amount against the requirement to spend under this sub-section for such number of succeeding financial years and in such manner, as may be prescribed."; (b) for sub-section (7), the following sub-section shall be substituted, namely:— "(7) If a company is in default in complying with the provisions of sub-section (5) or sub-section (6), the company shall be liable to a penalty of twice the amount required to be transferred by the company to the Fund specified in Schedule VII or the Unspent Corporate Social Responsibility Account, as the case may be, or one crore rupees, whichever is less, and every officer of the company who is in default shall be liable to a penalty of one-tenth of the amount required to be transferred by the company to such Fund specified in Schedule VII, or the Unspent Corporate Social Responsibility Account, as the case may be, or two lakh rupees, whichever is less."; (c) after sub-section (8), the following sub-section shall be inserted, namely:— "(9) Where the amount to be spent by a company under sub-section (5) does not exceed fifty lakh rupees, the requirement under sub-section (1) for constitution of the Corporate Social Responsibility Committee shall not be applicable and the functions of such Committee provided under this section shall, in such cases, be discharged by the Board of Directors of such company."

5.6.6 Companies (Corporate Social Responsibility Policy) Amendment Rules, 2021: Challenges and Solutions

Some of the recent amendments pertaining to the CSR in the Companies Act have brought many questions in the minds of the CSR policy makers and practisers in the Companies as well as implementing partners. The notification of the Companies (Corporate Social Responsibility Policy) Amendment Rules, 2021 *vide* notification GSR 40(E) 22.01.2021. A lot of reviews and explanations have been issued and published on aspects of what has been changed in new amendments but very less has been written on the dilemma CSR stakeholders are facing out of amendments. Purpose of the chapter is not to elaborate the changes made in the Act and Rules, we explain here some of the generic questions arising after the amendments which the author has came across, views given on different aspects are author's personal. These questions may be related to the definition of ongoing CSR project, creation of capital assets under CSR, definition of the public authority, CSR activities targeted for the wards of their employees, registration as per CSR-1 Form, projects through Central or State Government agencies, undertaking impact assessments of long running projects, Annual Action Plan, and calculation of Set off amount, among others.

In respect of definition of the ongoing CSR projects, as per Clause 2(*h*)(*i*) 'Ongoing Project' means a multi-year project undertaken by a Company in fulfilment of its CSR obligation having timelines not exceeding three years excluding the financial year in which it was commenced, and shall include such project that was initially not approved as a multi-year project but whose duration has been extended beyond one year by the board based on reasonable justification. It is clarified that ongoing projects of any company, which initially was not approved as multi-year project by the Board, will come under the definition of the ongoing projects as per the recent amendments. Company will have to reframe the ongoing projects in terms of maximum timeline of 3 years in a project mode and will have to get these approved by Board. In case the project is envisaged to be completed in 10 years (for example), the project under CSR, should be defined and categorised in a way that it achieves the targets in phased manner. For example, if a CSR project targets to train 10000 youth in 10 years, it should formulate three years long project with target of 3400 youth in first three years in specified targeted locations.

As such, looking at the diverse nature of the CSR projects, many changes may be envisaged in the way of implementation. The amendments as per Clauses (4) (6) states that in case of ongoing project, the Board of a Company shall monitor the implementation of the project with reference to the approved timelines and year-wise allocation and shall be competent to make modifications, if any, for smooth implementation of the project within the overall permissible time period. It also clarified that any unspent amount shall be transferred to Unspent CSR Account for the project as per section 135(6) of the Act. Any modifications in the ongoing projects/programmes are to be dealt with the Clauses (4) (6) of the Rules.

In respect of creation of capital assets under CSR, Public Sector Undertakings (PSUs) find the definition of the Public Authority ambiguous. In accordance with the Right to Information Act, PSUs are treated as the public authorities. Companies also find it difficult to be ascertain about the definition of the 'capital asset'. They also pose a question that if a PSU is considered as a public authority, can it keep the Capital asset created through CSR funds with itself or not.

As such the amended rules node to the definition of a Public Authority as defined in clause (*h*) of section 2 of the Right to Information Act, 2005. Amended Rules further states that the CSR amount may be spent by a company for creation or acquisition of a capital asset, which shall be held by – (*a*) a company established under section 8 of the Act, or a Registered Public Trust or Registered Society, having charitable objects and CSR Registration Number under sub-rule (2) of rule 4; or (*b*) beneficiaries of the said CSR project, in the form of self-help groups, collectives, entities; or (*c*) a public authority. Now, since the amended CSR Rules itself indicate that a public authority may held the creation or acquisition of the public assets, there is no surprise if the PSUs ask if they can hold the public assets created under their own CSR funds. However, it is clarified in terms of intent of the amended rules further clarified with the section 3.5 of the Report of High-Level Committee on CSR, which states that "...In keeping with the intent of the legislation, CSR amount should be spent by the company, *i.e.* it must not be lying with the company. However, if a company creates an asset by spending CSR funds, the asset shall continue to hold the value till it depreciates or gets liquidated. An asset, by definition, inheres the potential for giving future economic benefits. Therefore, the creation of an asset by the company in its name, especially appreciable assets, would tantamount to non-spending of the CSR monies. This means that an asset created out of CSR funds must not be held by the company in its name or in the name of any other incorporated or unincorporated entity of which it is the ultimate beneficiary. Further, it is important to understand the utilization of the assets so created". In view of the above, it is clarified that a company cannot create assets on its own name.

Companies do often remain in dilemma about CSR activities targeted for the wards of their employees, if these may be treated as a CSR activity or not. It is clarified that CSR activities cannot be targeted towards wards of employees. These activities may be targeted towards communities in general, if wards of the employees are part of that community, they may receive benefits among and alongwith other beneficiaries in targeted community but the objective of the particular CSR project may not be towards benefit of the wards of employees.

If a company itself implements any CSR project does it require filling the CSR-1 Form on MCA website? The answer is 'No'. As per Clause (4)(2)(*a*), Every entity, covered under sub-rule (1), who intends to undertake any CSR activity, shall register itself with the Central Government by filing the form CSR-1 electronically with the Registrar, with effect from the 1st day of April, 2021:

Provided that the provisions of this sub-rule shall not affect the CSR projects or programmes approved prior to the 1st day of April, 2021. (*b*) Form CSR-1 shall be signed and submitted electronically by the entity and shall be verified digitally by a Chartered Accountant in practice or a Company Secretary in practice or a Cost Accountant in practice. (*c*) On the submission of the Form CSR-1 on the portal, a unique CSR Registration Number shall be generated by the system automatically. The intent of this clause is towards registration of implementing partners with the MCA. Hence, in the Form also, no option of the Company implementing CSR by itself has been given. The Form CSR 1 is specifically for Implementing Partners.

If a company undertakes projects through Central or State Government agencies, is it mandatory for these agencies to fill CSR-1 Form? The answer is 'Yes'. Central of State Government Agencies are registered entities (these might be registered as Society or Trust etc.), or might be established under an Act of Parliament or State Legislature. These categories fall under the Clause (4)(2)(*a*) of the Rules and are recipients of the CSR Funds. Hence, Registration by filling CSR 1 Form may be required by these entities.

If a company implements hundreds of CSR activities every year, whether the details mentioned in CSR Rule 5 are to be filled with regards to all the CSR activities separately under Annual Action Plan? The answer is 'Yes'. As per Clause (5) "The CSR Committee shall formulate and recommend to the Board, an annual action plan in pursuance of its CSR policy, which shall include the following, namely:- (*a*) the list of CSR projects or programmes that are approved to be undertaken in areas or subjects specified in Schedule VII of the Act; (*b*) the manner of execution of such projects or programmes as specified in sub-rule (1) of rule 4; (*c*) the modalities of utilisation of funds and implementation schedules for the projects or programmes; (*d*) monitoring and reporting mechanism for the projects or programmes; and € details of need and impact assessment, if any, for the projects undertaken by the company:

Provided that Board may alter such plan at any time during the financial year, as per the recommendation of its CSR Committee, based on the reasonable justification to that effect." It is further clarified that according to the Companies Act, 2013, any CSR Activity is to be carried out in Project/

programme mode. If each of the 900 activities of the company are in project/ programme mode. Details of each project/programme shall be part of the annual action plan.

In respect of undertaking impact assessments of long running projects such as Schools, Hospitals, etc. which may be perpetual in nature, it is to state that as per Clause (8)(3)(*a*) of the amended rules, every company having average CSR obligation of ten crore rupees or more in pursuance of sub-section (5) of section 135 of the Act, in the three immediately preceding financial years, shall undertake impact assessment, through an independent agency, of their CSR projects having outlays of one crore rupees or more, and which have been completed not less than one year before undertaking the impact study. Hence, it is clarified that the Impact Assessment can be carried out any time after completion of one year of the project completion.

In respect of calculation of Set off amount, it is clarified that as per Clause (7)(3) Where a company spends an amount in excess of requirement provided under sub-section (5) of section 135 , such excess amount may be set off against the requirement to spend under sub-section (5) of section 135 up to immediate succeeding three financial years subject to the conditions that – (*i*) the excess amount available for set off shall not include the surplus arising out of the CSR activities, if any, in pursuance of sub-rule (2) of this rule. (*ii*) the Board of the company shall pass a resolution to that effect. Hence, the excess amount spent by a company in particular financial year against the total eligible CSR amount, is considered as the set off amount. The excess amount available for set off shall not include the surplus arising out of the CSR activities.

5.6.7 Other contemporary challenges & recommendations

Apart from above challenges in terms of amendments in law, some of the fundamental challenges are observed in terms of skills and capacity building of CSR workforce in India. Not only skills and capacity enhancement, but the aspects of involvement of various categories of professionals (management, accounts, communication, human resources etc.) in CSR implementation seems a challenge in drawing expected results from the CSR interventions.

All the Schedule VII activities are traditional fields of Social Work profession. Hence, Social Workers are well equipped to deal/implement CSR projects/ programmes in India. Engagement of more and more social workers in planning and implementation of CSR initiatives is to be ensured. Necessary amendments in the law may also be suggested to make employment of professional social workers mandatory in execution of the CSR projects by companies. Social Workers are also experts in the Social Welfare Administration as a method of Social Work, hence, instead of management and other such professionals, responsibility of execution of CSR projects should be given to professionally trained social workers.

Corporate Social Responsibility has emerged as the third pillar of the social development in last one decade in India. The CSR Mandate brought by the Ministry of Corporate Affairs through amendments in the section 135 of the Companies Act, 2013. Businesses have been committed to the social causes since ages but the new era of mandatory CSR in India has putted the corporate contributions as the corporate social revolution.

Since 2014, after introducing mandatory provisions related to CSR, Businesses in India have significantly contributed in the thematic development in accordance with the Schedule VII of the Companies Act. It is important to mention that Rs. One Trillion have been spent so far by the companies as their CSR initiatives.

Through strategic CSR interventions, companies are addressing long pending social problems not only by putting money but with expertise in time bound project management approach. CSR Fund Pooling has been brought out in the law by the ministry. However, the same is to be adopted by the companies and mechanisms for efficient implementation are to be developed. Inter-Corporate Coordination for this purpose is very important.

There is a need to strengthen the State level CSR Authorities and also conceptualizing such structures at District level for better planning and coordination. To facilitate the Intra-Corporate coordination for planning and execution of developmental initiatives of Govt., Corporate, and CSOs, a Partnership Guidelines standard is also needed.

There is also a need for localizing the CSR planning with SDG indicators, particularly at the district levels. Relevant stakeholders from various Govt. departments, district administration, Companies and NGOs operating in a particular district should come at a platform to plan and execute programmes in partnerships. The impact assessment of the interventions should also be measured against the baseline indicators based on Sustainable Development Goals.

Looking at the future, CSR should not be limited to 2% spend but beyond companies need to look beyond also. Aspects associated with the CSR, need to be integrated in core business philosophies and policies. Only then the businesses will be considered as responsible businesses caring for people, planet and profits. We also need to develop modalities for development communication for generating awareness among businesses and stakeholders.

As we all have witnessed that the Covid-19 has posed a lot of questions and opportunities for us to excel in our public healthcare systems, it has also created new avenues for CSR interventions, necessary changes in the law have already been incorporated by the Government. Government is also promoting the technology incubation through CSR initiatives, many solutions have been witnessed for social upliftment through theses incubators supported under various CSR initiatives.

The Government has introduced the National CSR exchange portal to establish an interactive digital platform for CSR Stakeholders. It serves as an e-marketplace hosting PAN India social welfare projects where stakeholders such as Implementing agencies can put up their ongoing projects and companies can select projects for CSR Spending as per their preferences and *vice versa*.

Corporate Social Responsibility (CSR) in India has distinguished features when compared with the CSR practices in almost rest of the world. In the post-2014 era, CSR in India is considered as a mandatory spend in accordance with the Section 135 of the Companies Act, 2013. Whereas, CSR practices in rest of the world are considered as integration of the responsible business behaviour in each step of the business in terms of Environment, Social and Governance initiatives besides charitable/developmental contributions. However, Government of India has released National Guidelines on Responsible Business Conduct (NGRBC) also in 2019, but the definition of CSR in India is governed by the Section 135 of the Companies Act, 2013. Hence, CSR and Responsible Business Conduct may be seen two different aspects in India whereas in almost rest of the world both are considered same.

Some of the fundamental challenges in CSR implementation are observed in terms of skills and capacity building of CSR workforce in India. Not only skills and capacity enhancement, but the aspects of involvement of professionals from diverse backgrounds including management, accounts, communication, human resources etc. in CSR implementation seems a challenge in drawing expected results from the CSR interventions. As all the Schedule VII activities seem traditional fields of Social Work. Hence, it is observed that professional Social Workers are well equipped to deal/implement CSR projects/programmes in India. Management approaches to CSR implementation need to incorporate Humanitarian and Democratic Matrix.

The Companies Act, 2013 has introduced systematic corporate participation into social development in India, mandating 2% contribution from corporates to society. With this law, NGOs will have a decisive role in determining the benefits of corporate involvement for meaningful social change. Harnessing this available opportunity will require infrastructure, research, collaboration and most importantly trust between partners. The trust deficit between NGOs and CSR partners in India is a key obstacle to the success of NGO– CSR collaborations in the social sector. There is a requirement of good practices that could be adopted to enable good partnerships with transparency, accountability, effective and efficient programme delivery. Partnerships play a major role in pooling complementary knowledge, skills, resources, capacities and potential of the partners to deliver sustainable impactful services and solutions Partnership standards enable processes and good practices that bring in transparency, effective and efficient management techniques, tools and aids that not only build confidence and trust among partners but also enhance quality of services and accountability of partners to communities and other stakeholders.

The popular statement - “You can’t manage what you can’t measure” is much relevant in terms of business sustainability/CSR reporting. Measuring the adverse impact a business is making on social, economic and environmental spheres through its existence and processes, and also measuring the initiatives being taken by the business in terms of protecting and taking remedial measures is utmost important. CSR and Sustainability Reporting is a way through which companies can disseminate their efforts towards social, economic and environmental sustainability and can win trust of different segments of business stakeholders. Theme based Impact Measurement standards in CSR are required.

Indian businesses have been voluntarily committed towards philanthropy since ages but after 2013, since CSR provisions included in the Companies Act, CSR practices are evolving as a specialized professional manner. Now the corporates need and are looking for more impactful, long lasting and innovative activities touching more lives through their CSR interventions. This can be possible only when their CSR activities, though catering to a certain geography or community, align with much wider objectives and goals for the wellbeing of the nation and the world. Having sustainable business practices besides CSR activities and linking to the (Sustainable Development Goals) SDGs and (Nationally Determined Contributors) NDCs is the need of the hour for businesses to reap the benefits of such initiatives. “Better Business, Better World”, a report by the Business and Sustainable Development Commission reveals that sustainable business models could offer a compelling growth strategy, opening up an economic prize of at least US$1 trillion by 2030 for the Indian private sector and over 73 million new jobs could be created in India by 2030.

The High Level Committee on the Corporate Social Responsibility, in its report released in August 2019, has presented an analysis of the alignment of Sustainable Development Goals with the CSR activities as given in the Schedule VII of the Companies Act, 2013. The analysis not only maps the SDGs against each of the relevant activities as given under the Schedule VII but it also provides an analysis of the activity wise expenditure made by companies under CSR after notification of the mandatory CSR in India.

It is need of the hour that the Companies need to broaden the horizon of their CSR policies and activities to align with global or national priorities and goals. Aligning CSR activities with global sustainability goals encapsulated within the 17 UN SDGs and the Paris Accord driven NDCs provide, businesses the opportunity to achieve these social and business objectives. Few of the benefits are as below:

5.6.8 Aligning CSR with SDGs

Today, CSR has become an effective tool to work in line of Sustainable Development Goals with a strong focus on social performance indicated in the CSR projects of the business organizations. Companies have made their contribution to the society which has catered to the needs of millions of people and enhanced their quality of life. In the Financial Year 2021-22 alone, Rs. 6,46,382 lakh was spent on Education, Livelihoods and support to differently-abled. Other development sector also witnesses a large contribution through CSR.

Aligning CSR activities with SDGs and NDCs establish direct contributions to national and global targets of social, environmental and economic development/growth. A good economy or socially developed communities expand the market and people's purchasing power increases, which ensure further growth of markets. The measurable contribution with larger goals can enhance corporate reputation, which can add great value to help establish a responsible brand. The socially conscious millennial consumer is vying for responsible brands and do not hesitate to spend extra bucks to buy the product with such a reputation. Sustainable business practices and ethical business are increasingly becoming mandatory requirements to enter and grow in the mature markets globally. Adopting sustainability practices aligned with CSR initiatives can help grow business globally.

For social upliftment, businesses need to come together to alleviate structural social problems. There are immense problems in our country. After the freedom Government started working on alleviation of suffering of people from marginalized and disadvantaged sections of society. Non-Governmental Organizations also came into existence to compliment the efforts of the Government. In the recent past, in last one decade, a third pillar in the sphere of social development has also emerged, that is Indian Corporates. This was due to making CSR mandatory under the Companies Act, 2013. Through their CSR interventions, companies have made a great change in the country in last 8 years and they are expected to bring more changes in future. For this collaborative efforts of corporates are required in different sectoral interventions. That will be real businesses connect.

5.7 Product Liability

Product liability in terms of safety and quality are integral components of the "Social" aspect of ESG because they directly impact consumers, their well-being, and their trust in a company. In the Indian context, ensuring product safety and quality is crucial for companies to meet the expectations of stakeholders and maintain sustainable business practices.

Firstly, product safety involves designing, manufacturing, and distributing products that do not pose any harm to consumers. Indian companies are expected to comply with various laws and regulations, such as the Bureau of Indian Standards (BIS) certification, Food Safety and Standards Authority of India (FSSAI) Regulations for food products, and the Drugs and Cosmetics Act for pharmaceuticals and cosmetics. Adhering to these standards ensures that products meet specific safety requirements and undergo proper testing before reaching consumers.

For instance, in the food and beverage industry, companies are responsible for ensuring the safety of their products by conducting quality checks, adhering to hygiene standards, and providing accurate labeling. In 2019, the Food Safety and Standards Authority of India introduced the Food Safety and Standards (Labelling and Display) Regulations, which mandate clear and accurate labelling of packaged food products to enhance consumer safety and transparency.

Secondly, product quality relates to the overall performance, durability, and reliability of goods and services. Indian companies are increasingly recognizing the importance of delivering high-quality products that meet customer expectations. This includes factors such as durability, functionality, efficiency, and customer support.

For example, in the automotive sector, companies strive to enhance the quality of their vehicles by implementing robust manufacturing processes, conducting rigorous quality control checks, and addressing customer feedback promptly. Tata Motors, a prominent Indian automobile manufacturer, among others has been emphasizing product quality and safety in its vehicles through continuous improvement initiatives, advanced safety features, and adherence to global quality standards.

Companies that prioritize product safety and quality demonstrate their commitment to consumer well-being and long-term sustainability. By ensuring their products meet stringent safety standards and providing high-quality offerings, they foster trust among consumers, reduce the risk of product-related incidents, and maintain their reputation in the market.

In conclusion, within the "Social" aspect of ESG, product safety and quality play a vital role in the Indian context. By complying with safety regulations, conducting rigorous testing, and delivering high-quality goods and services, companies contribute to consumer well-being, build trust, and uphold sustainable business practices. This commitment to product safety and quality strengthens the social impact of companies and enhances their overall ESG performance.

5.8 Displacement, Rehabilitation & Resettlement

As we understand that to address, reduce and mitigate stakeholders' oppositions it is important to engage them in a company's decision-making process which affects its external environment in particular. Land acquisition for new projects and for operations of existing factories, Involuntary resettlement including the Forest land, agricultural land, loss of culture and tradition, and livelihoods as a result of resettlement, Land degradation, Water and Air Pollution in nearby communities, Gentrification and the adverse impact on Culture and Tradition in the local communities are some of the pressing issues in this context.

In the context of land acquisition, resettlement and rehabilitation while establishing a new plant or commercial projects or during expansion of existing projects, stakeholders' engagement becomes a necessary tool. As a socially conscious enterprise, a business should be very sensitive to the needs of the Project Affected Persons (PAPs) unsettled by the construction of a plant. The population getting affected by such projects/plants need to be given special attention to protect their rights, minimise their losses and to help them to restore a secure means of livelihood.

5.8.1 Land acquisition

Land acquisition in the process of acquiring land for industrialization, development of infrastructural facilities or urbanization of the private land by Government or private organizations. The Land Acquisition Act, 1894 was replaced in 2013 by The Right to Fair Compensation and Transparency in Land Acquisition, Rehabilitation and Resettlement Act, 2013. The amendment bill – Right to Fair Compensation and Transparency in Land Acquisition, Rehabilitation and Resettlement (Amendment) Bill was passed in 2015.

5.8.2 Rehabilitation & Resettlement

Land acquisition and displacement alter the social, economic, cultural and environmental status of the affected population. The Rehabilitation and Resettlement Bill, 2007 provides for benefits and compensation to people displaced by land acquisition purchases or any other involuntary displacement.

A business should always pay greater attention to developing rehabilitation strategies focusing on the effective Rehabilitation and Resettlement (R&R) of Project affected persons and also community development works in and around the projects. The business should be passionate about ensuring that sense of displacement felt in the local communities is minimal.

Growing industrialization and large development projects involve the significant land acquisition and displacement of people from their land. Resettlement & Rehabilitation Plan (R&R Plan) helps to systematize the land acquisition process so as to achieve the satisfaction of the landowners and aids effective execution/development of the project with maximized social acceptability. Components like Rehabilitation & Resettlement Policy Analysis, Initial Social Assessments, Baseline Surveys and Preparation of Resettlement Action Plan should be dwelt upon by businesses.

5.8.3 Resettlement & Rehabilitation Management (RRM)

For protecting the rights of project affected population by land acquisition, minimize socio-economic losses and helping restore a secure means of livelihood, companies are required to formulate a Rehabilitation Policy. Based on the policy, Management of displacement, resettlement, and rehabilitation activities are carried out by an organization. The term is commonly known as the Resettlement & Rehabilitation Management (RRM). Below are the suggestive key steps in RR Management:

Classification of project affected families

As a first step, classification of project affected families is done based on suggestive criteria of fully affected or partially affected depending upon the percentage of land acquired from them.

Categorizing R & R Plans for different categories

Different resettlement and rehabilitation plans should be developed for different affected groups of families, hence categorization of affected families is second step. The categorization may be in terms of fully affected to be displaced with basic infrastructure, amenities and partially affected would be paid cash compensation.

Settling Rehabilitation packages

After calculation of the categories of families in different segments of displacement, a rehabilitation packages for settling the unrest as per eligibility of families is to be defined. Modes of *ex-gratia* payments are also to be defined.

Social Assessment

Initial social assessment are needed to understand the extend of families to be affected as a result of an upcoming acquisition. Baseline Surveys to be done to collect owner details of corresponding plots and identification of zones to rehabilitate the families. Relevant ownership documents of the areas of interest are to be procured from respective land departments

5.8.4 Challenges in RR Management

Before discharging the benefits to the affected families, it is important to acquire ownership details, kinship & marriage documents of the people to be displaced. It is also pertinent to highlight to understand the needs and requirements of the Project affected people by the company, multiple consultations are needed with the affected communities and relevant stakeholders. The RR management may only be treated successful once it considers above points. However, some of the key challenges in this process may be envisaged as under:

- Limited provision for visualization of relocation plots.
- Collection of Record of Rights (RoR), names of owners, property details etc. from the land departments and tagging against each plot becomes a hassle.
- Often difficult to identify the family tree and kinship resulting in duplicate compensations.
- Documents against each plot are haphazard to maintain.
- It is tiresome to maintain Excel Sheets/Hardcopy documents of Awardee details with resettlement/compensation/training package.
- Tracking employments created one by one gives way to erroneous data.
- Manually generating reports is tedious.

5.8.5 Solutions

A pertinent question is what are the solutions to challenges in Resettlement and Rehabilitation Management and how R & R Proceedings can be eased for implementation. We see that companies have adopted a lot of initiatives including adoption of a centralized software, the software acts as a decision support system for granting rehabilitation, resettlement and fair compensation to the families that have been unsettled or displaced due to projects execution. Using of a software and other automation tools results in displaying of all relevant information on a single click, along with graphics, maps and other integrated features. It eases the analysis of the data gathered, customising the solutions, updating and tracking the beneficiaries. The data is also entered as per the GIS map, it displays digitized R&R colony map for relocation of the displaced families for easy visualization. Village wise analysis of number of Project Affected Families (PAF) or Project Displaced Families (PDF). The Document Management System (DMS) within the software helps in storage of all relevant documents against each affected family.

By adopting these solutions, tracking of tasks and activities related to all procedural milestones of R & R becoming easier. Software integration with finance systems helps in easy disbursement of payments for compensation and relocation assistance. Dynamic reports on Rehabilitation details like occupation, training, and income details of the project affected families. It also helps in handling of pending, assigned, resolved grievances along with details and actions taken.

5.9 BRSR and Human Rights Disclosures

Business Responsibility and Sustainability Reporting (BRSR) is used as a base of analysis of ESG adoption by the eligible companies. As per the SEBI's notifications, now top listed companies have started disclosing their ESG practices. There is need for research which analyses all 1000 BRSR Reports starting from the Financial Year 2022-23 as a base year on all the disclosure principles. It will set the baseline for these 1000 top listed companies in India to enable to track their future performance on various principles of BRSR. It will also gauge into quality of reporting specifically on some of the pressing social issues of today including on child labour, forced labour, gender and other issues.

There is also a need for the analysis in areas of classification according to sector, ownership, markets, export-domestic, thematic issues etc. The analysis will form a Baseline for potential tracking future performance of 1000 companies. Baseline report of 1000 disclosure will also gauge the quality of reporting on Child Labour and Forced labour in supply chains. Later on, the research should focus on the development of detailed thematic indicators on assessing grievous human rights issues such as child bonded labour, bonded labour and human trafficking for forced labour and Business and Human Rights risks through formal and informal labour market intermediaries in supply chains.

The concurrent research findings disseminated to Investors (international and Domestic), Public Procurement, Business Federations/membership organisations, ESG rating providers, Financial Institutions will help to take responsible decisions. One of the similar kinds of study based on Business Responsibility Reporting (BRR) has recently been conducted by the Partners in Change and the Indian Institute of Corporate Affairs.

The Business Responsibility and Sustainability Reporting (BRSR) in its Principle-5 'Businesses should respect and promote human rights' has stipulated following aspects to be disclosed by the eligible companies:

BRSR PRINCIPLE 5 Businesses should respect and promote Human Rights Essential Indicators

1. Employees and workers who have been provided training on human rights issues and policy(ies) of the entity, in the following format:

Category	FY___ Current Financial Year			FY___ Previous Financial Year		
	Total (A)	No. of employees/ workers covered (B)	% (B/A)	Total (C)	No. of employees/ workers covered (D)	% (D/C)
Employees						
Permanent						
Other than permanent						
Total Employees						
Workers						
Permanent						
Other than permanent						
Total Workers						

2. Details of minimum wages paid to employees and workers, in the following format:

Category	FY___ Current Financial Year					FY___ Previous Financial Year				
	Total (A)	Equal to Minimum Wage		More than Minimum Wage		Total (A)	Equal to Minimum Wage		More than Minimum Wage	
		No. (B)	% (B/A)	No. (C)	% (C/A)		No. (E)	% (E/D)	No. (F)	% (F/D)
Employees										
Permanent										
Male										
Female										
Other than Permanent										
Male										
Female										
Workers										
Permanent										
Male										
Female										
Other than Permanent										
Male										
Female										

3. Details of remuneration/salary/wages, in the following format:

	Male		**Female**	
	Number	**Median remuneration/ salary/wages of respective category**	**Number**	**Median remuneration/ salary/wages of respective category**
Board of Directors (BoD)				
Key Managerial Personnel				
Employees other than BoD and KMP				
Workers				

4. Do you have a focal point (Individual/Committee) responsible for addressing human rights impacts or issues caused or contributed to by the business? **(Yes/No)**

5. Describe the internal mechanisms in place to redress grievances related to human rights issues.

6. Number of Complaints on the following made by employees and workers:

	FY Current Financial Year			**FY Previous Financial Year**		
	Filed during theyear	**Pending resolution at the end of year**	**Remarks**	**Filed during the year**	**Pending resolution at the end of year**	**Remarks**
Sexual Harassment						
Discrimination at workplace						
Child Labour						
Forced Labour/ Involuntary Labour						
Wages						
Other human rights related issues						

7. Mechanisms to prevent adverse consequences to the complainant in discrimination and harassment cases.

8. Do human rights requirements form part of your business agreements and contracts?

(Yes/No)

9. Assessments for the year:

% of your plants and offices that were assessed (by entity or statutory authorities or third parties)
Child labour
Forced/involuntary labour
Sexual harassment
Discrimination at workplace
Wages
Others – please specify

10. Provide details of any corrective actions taken or underway to address significant risks/concerns arising from the assessments at Question 9 above.

Leadership Indicators

1. Details of a business process being modified/introduced as a result of addressing human rights grievances/complaints.
2. Details of the scope and coverage of any Human rights due-diligence conducted.
3. Is the premise/office of the entity accessible to differently abled visitors, as per the requirements of the Rights of Persons with Disabilities Act, 2016?
4. Details on assessment of value chain partners:

	% of value chain partners (by value of business donewith such partners) that were assessed
Sexual Harassment	
Discrimination at workplace	
Child Labour	
Forced Labour/Involuntary Labour	
Wages	
Others – please specify	

5. Provide details of any corrective actions taken or underway to address significant risks/concerns arising from the assessments at Question 4 above.

5.10 Summary of the Chapter

In this chapter, we have studied key concepts pertaining to the social dimensions of the ESG, how and what factors are responsible for business risks and how to mitigate those risks. We deliberated in details on some of the pressing issues like Corporate Social Responsibility, Business and Human Rights, Diversity & Inclusion, among others. Business Responsibility & Sustainability Reputing has specific indicators on social related disclosures like Business and Human Rights, Consumers, Communities, CSR etc., a brief analysis of trends in reporting by listed companies has also been presented, we have also touched upon important considerations in displacement, resettlement and rehabilitation.

CHAPTER 6

GOVERNANCE DIMENSIONS OF ESG

6.1 Evolution of Responsible Governance

Good Governance has always been an issue that stimulated fundamental thinking right from ancient times. Origin of good governance may be traced back to Kautilya's Arthashastra which maintains that for good governance, all administrators, including the king were considered servants of the people and there is a complete link between good governance and stability. Kautilya elaborates on the four fold duty of a king as follows:

- **Raksha** - literally means protection, in the corporate scenario it can be equated with the risk management aspect.
- **Vridhi** - literally means growth, it is equated to stakeholder value enhancement.
- **Palana** - literally means maintenance/compliance, in the present scenario it can be equated to compliance to the law in letter and spirit.
- **Yogakshema** - literally means well being and in Arthashastra it means social security system. In the present context it can be equated to corporate social responsibility.

In the corporate scenario, the substitution of the state with the corporation, the king with the CEO or the board of corporation, and subjects with the shareholders, bring out the quintessence of corporate governance, because central to the concept of corporate governance is the belief that public good should be ahead of private good and that the corporation's resources cannot be used for personal benefit. It is the duty of the king to protect the wealth of the state and its subjects, to enhance the wealth, to maintain it and safeguard it and the interests of the subjects.

The term 'Corporate Governance' is primarily concerned with the running and regulation of an enterprise for generating wealth for all the stakeholders. The separation of ownership and control gives rise to agency problems in listed companies because of the separate entity concept which a corporation or a company possesses distinct from the members who pool in their money towards the capital of the company and delegate its management to specialist managers. The persons pooling in their resources are the shareholders of the company and the specialist managers are more commonly known as the Directors. One way of reducing agency costs is to have effective corporate governance mechanisms.

There is no universal definition for Corporate Governance. In the narrowest sense, Noble laureate Milton Friedman defined Corporate Governance as "the conduct of business in accordance with shareholders' desires, which generally is to make as much money as possible, while conforming to the basic rules of the society embodied in law and local customs." It signifies establishing a system whereby directors are entrusted with responsibilities and duties in relation to the direction of a company's affairs. It is primarily concerned with ways of bringing the interests of the investors (the principals) and the managers (the agents) into line and ensuring that firms are run for the benefit of all stakeholders rather than primarily only for shareholders. It is based on a system of collective Board responsibility and accountability. Corporate governance is the 'acceptance by management of the inalienable rights of shareholders as the true owners of the corporation and of their own role as trustees on behalf of the shareholders without prioritizing the interest of any of the other stakeholder. It is about commitment to values, about ethical business conduct and about making a distinction between personal and corporate funds in the management of a company.

Apart from studying the issues arising out of separation of ownership and control, the theme of corporate governance includes

1. Issues of accountability and Fiduciary Duty to ensure good behaviour and protect shareholders, essentially advocating the implementation of guidelines and mechanisms to ensure good behaviour and protect shareholders.
2. The Economic Efficiency view, that is, the aim of corporate governance systems should be to optimize economic result.
3. Stakeholder view, which calls for more attention and accountability to players other than the shareholders, e.g. the employees or the environment.

Quality of such governance depends on the integrity of the management; ability of the board; adequacy of the process; commitment level of individual board members; quality of corporate reporting; and the participation of stakeholders in the management. Corporate governance therefore calls for transparency in decision-making, accountability which follows from transparency because responsibilities could be fixed easily for actions taken or not taken, and the accountability is for the safeguarding the interests of the stakeholders and the investors. The term corporate governance has now come to mean two things, the processes by which companies are directed and controlled and a field in economics, which studies the many issues arising from the separation of ownership and control.

Recent corporate governance scandals in India, United States and Europe some of which have triggered the largest insolvencies in history have caused a crisis of confidence in the corporate sector, and among the investors.

The rise of the institutional investor has brought with it some increase of professional diligence which has led to improve regulation of the stock market. Corporate governance systems have evolved over centuries, often in response to corporate failure or systemic crises. The first well documented failure of governance was the South Sea Bubble in the 1700s, which revolutionized business laws and practices in England. Similarly much of the securities law in the United States was put in place following the stock market crash of 1929. There has been no shortage of other crisis such as the secondary banking crisis of the 1970s in the United Kingdom and the US savings and loan debacle of the 1980s.

We have witnessed a long way of evolution and growth in concepts and practices of governance related aspects in corporate arena, from the Kautilya to present age practices of responsible governance. The phases of evolution have gone through the rapid industrialization, various calamities, globalization, financial crisis, technological innovations, etc. The governance structures have adopted changes in its journey what it is in present shape, conceptually as well as in practice. Various international organizations came-up with the corporate governance guidelines and updated those from time to time. Governments in different countries also constituted various committees and issued guidelines, regulations, compliances and disclosure requirements.

In the new age of responsibility, where it is essential for everyone to be responsible towards their actions to protect the planet earth and to sustain it as a more liveable planet to our next and upcoming generations, it becomes more important for the businesses not only to make efforts for sustainability of businesses but to contribute to the wider sustainability of the planet, its eco-system, biodiversity, economic and social structures etc. Here from a border perspective, business sustainability is a small component of the planet's sustainability. When there are broken economies, disorganized social structures, there is no life on the planet, no survival, then how the businesses will continue?

We all are taught and we understand about long term strategy making for the businesses, not only for five to ten years but for one hundred years and beyond. In those strategic thinking, from raw ideas about sustainability of earth to the refined objectively achievable targets and KPIs for businesses are integral part for any business leader. As the time is changing very rapidly, businesses are now more and more expected and pressurised from a diverse group of stakeholders to adopt responsible and sustainable practices, the framework of strategic thinking has also to be redefined.

6.2 Governance in ESG

6.2.1 What is G in ESG

We have seen a transition on Governance from the Kautilya to present age responsible governance. Here we will try to understand the importance of G in ESG. Many studies and rating agencies have highlighted the ESG disclosure framework for scoring with more emphasis of G part *i.e.* the Governance. It is because the effective governance aspects also ensure the compliance with E & S aspects of ESG.

Investors eagerly look for company's ESG considerations to be assured that company's accounting and reporting systems are reliable and transparent. Investors also consider how a company handles its shareholders and their opportunity to vote on significant issues. Investors do reassurance that the company is not engaging in unlawful actions and that conflicts of interest are avoided when selecting board members. Such aspects of the responsible governance system in a company give additional advantages to attract more investments, more loyalty among the consumers, communities and other stakeholders.

The "G" in ESG stands for decision-making governance considerations, these governance factors range from sovereign policymaking to the allocation of rights and obligations among various organizational stakeholders, such as the board of directors, management, shareholders and stakeholders. The aim of a business, the function and composition of boards of directors, and the remuneration and monitoring of senior executives has become key topics in corporate governance frameworks.

6.2.2 Embedding ESG into Corporate Strategies

According to a Brookings study, companies embed sustainability and related ESG considerations into their corporate strategies through three related mechanisms:

Strategic integration

'Strategic integration' is the first step, whereby companies incorporate ESG alongside financial returns into corporate strategy.

Operational integration

'Operational integration' takes this a step further by outlining specific ESG goals and targets, which are set to hold the company accountable to progress within a given time frame.

Organisational integration

Lastly and most importantly is 'organisation integration', a complex process whereby ESG leadership and buy-in is established from the mailroom to the boardroom.

6.2.3 Importance of G in ESG

Companies around the world are increasingly recognising the importance of embedding Environmental-Social-Governance (ESG) considerations into their strategy, risk management and governance practices for their long-term value creation. If ESG strategies are built on practical, material targets, which require oversight to ensure companies stay on track and make progress towards their stated goals, it is more likely that the company may better embed, relate, implement, measure and disclose its initiatives in the domain of ESG. Governance in a company in general and governance of Social and Environmental aspects as stipulated under various standards ESG Frameworks, plays an important role to set the targets and to achieve those diligently.

The institutional investors while considering a company for investment, look for that company's ESG integration and disclosures, they specifically look to ensure that company's accounting and reporting systems are reliable and transparent. Investors also consider how a firm handles its shareholders and their opportunity to vote on significant issues. They want reassurance that the company isn't engaging in unlawful actions and that conflicts of interest are avoided while selecting and on-boarding the board members.

MacKenzie Compbell has presented in an article that that basis of ESG is on the stakeholder capitalism model of fostering shared value generation, then governance is critical to long-term success. Stakeholder capitalism is built on the foundation of good governance. ESG risks and opportunities abound, and they can only be avoided or taken advantage of by sound corporate governance decisions.

Governance choices are made based on quantifiable outcomes, as 'E' and 'S' become more mainstream and better monitored, and the board sees success in social and environmental policies, environmental and social performance will logically become an integral component of good governance. The three ESG factors *i.e.* the environmental, social and governance is interlinked. Governance is also the crucial part of ESG as it will ensure that the material elements of 'E' and 'S' are effectively governed.

Investors are employing all ESG factors in their search for potential growth opportunities and material risks. However, in recent years, environmental issues gained much attention due to the reason of climate change, global warming, carbon emissions etc.

Importance of Governance mechanism for 'Environmental' aspects of ESG

Strategic Alignment

Effective governance of corporates ensures that environmental sustainability is integrated into a company's long-term strategy. This alignment is essential for addressing long-term environmental risks and opportunities. Boards of directors and executive leadership play a critical role in setting this strategic direction.

Risk Mitigation

Environmental risks can have significant financial and reputational implications. Responsible governance structures help identify and manage environmental risks effectively, providing a framework for addressing issues such as climate change, resource scarcity, and regulatory compliance.

Transparency and Accountability

Robust governance mechanisms promote transparency by requiring companies to disclose their environmental performance and metrics. This transparency is essential for investors, stakeholders, and the public to assess a company's commitment to sustainability. It also holds companies accountable for their environmental impact.

Ethical Leadership

Ethical leadership, a key aspect of good governance, influences a company's commitment to environmental responsibility. Ethical leaders prioritize sustainability initiatives, set an example for employees, and foster a culture of environmental stewardship within the organization.

Stakeholder Engagement

Responsible governance mechanisms provide a platform for stakeholder engagement, including dialogues with environmental organizations, local communities, and regulators. This engagement helps companies understand diverse perspectives on environmental issues and make informed decisions.

Importance of Governance for 'Social' aspects of ESG

Ethical Conduct

Responsible governance sets the tone for ethical conduct within an organization. Ethical behaviour, promoted by strong governance, ensures that companies consider the social impacts of their actions, including how they treat employees, customers, and the communities in which they operate.

Stakeholder Engagement

Governance mechanisms facilitate engagement with various stakeholders, including employees, customers, and local communities. This engagement helps companies understand and address social issues that may arise, such as labour practices, diversity and inclusion, and community development.

Risk Management

Governance structures help identify and manage social risks effectively. By assessing and mitigating risks related to labour practices, human rights, and customer satisfaction, companies can protect their reputation and financial stability.

Employee Well-being

Responsible governance influences how companies treat their employees. Fair compensation, work-life balance, and safe working conditions are aspects of social performance that are underpinned by governance practices.

Community Impact

Effective governance ensures that companies consider the social impact of their operations on local communities. This can include overall community development approach including education, healthcare, and infrastructure development etc.

6.2.4 Benefits of focusing on 'Governance' in ESG

Below are some of the benefits which are visible or envisaged by focusing more on the Governance aspects within ESG:

Better Financial performance

A company's financial performance improves through responsible governance practices. A solid ESG offering enables businesses to enter new markets and develop into current ones driving shareholder value. When governments have faith in corporate actors, they are more inclined to provide access, permissions, and licenses that open up new development prospects.

Reduced regulatory pressure

Reduced regulatory and legal compliance pressure is witnessed by the companies once they adhere to the embedding, compliance and disclosures on ESG parameters identified for the company. Companies with a better external-value offering can attain greater strategic independence while reducing regulatory pressure. Indeed, we've found that strong ESG framework helps firms lower their risk of adverse government action across industries and locations. It may also get the required encouragement from the government and other stakeholders.

Investor confidence

We see through several research studies conducted that investors confidence is boosted by good and responsible governance practices. Good corporate governance or the responsible corporate governance encompasses a wide variety of activities such as board and management structures, as well as a company's rules, standards, information disclosure, audits and compliance.

Investors, intend to understand if a company's book keeping is accurate and transparent and whether its business operations are ethical. They also prefer corporations with a board of directors that is both accountable and diverse, as well as practices that encourage shareholder's participation.

Governance methods may be screened in the same way as environmental and social factors. Negative screens can be used to exclude organizations whose governance rules and practices put them at an unacceptable risk level. It might be a firm that engages in legally or morally dubious acts or one that fails to appropriately handle long-term business risks, such as those posed by climate change.

6.3 Redefined Strategic Thinking

Some of the important changes which are expected for adoption by new age organizations to embrace ESG, which shall aid in redefining the strategic thought process of leaders involved is important to understand. Authors present following areas of redefined strategic thinking by the governance structure for business sustainability:

6.3.1 Redefined Corporate Purpose

From "profit maximization purpose" to "purpose before profit" is a shift corporates increasingly adopting at the core of their existence. The redefined corporate purpose of value creation should be based on the key philosophy of Responsibility as stipulated in the first chapter by the authors in this book "The New Theory of Responsibility".

Paul Polman's statement - "Making Business with Purpose the Purpose of Business" is pertinent to mention in this context. Sustainable businesses are redefining the corporate ecosystem by designing models that create value for all stakeholders. The Corporate Governance has this important role of redefining the core purpose of business existence.

Approach of Originality as described by the authors in earlier in this book is pertinent to follow while defining or redefining the corporate purpose. Atrey's Tree Model is an example of adopting responsible business conduct in each aspect of the business operations.

6.3.2 Rethink how corporate performance is conceived and assessed

- Shifting focus from rights to duties in governance.
- Evaluating global expectations and standards for responsible governance, encompassing sustainable development, human rights

and environmental protection and businesses' role in meeting these expectations.

- The impact of CSR initiatives, driven under the Companies Act, in contributing to good corporate governance.
- Fostering accountable corporate governance through successful citizen, customers, shareholders and community led initiatives.
- Corporate alignment with the United Nations' Sustainable Development Goals and the associated progress and challenges.

6.3.3 A shift towards Cross-Sectoral Leadership

Sustainability requires involvement of multi stakeholder approach (*i.e.* community members, organisational, governments etc.) to complex issues. A single organisation may not have the required expertise, skills or capacity to effectively address these problems alone, which means that a complex leadership challenge require cross sector collaboration, partnerships and leadership to achieve success. Cross sector leaders possess require experience for coordinating with different sectors to lead their organisation towards success, whether that means building a sustainable model or bringing a new product to market that solves a tough social dilemma.

Cross-Sectoral Leadership requires following essential skills —

- Team Building
- Managing Conflict
- Understanding Impact on stakeholders
- Communication
- Innovative Culture
- Navigating Complexity

6.4 Corporate Governance in Indian Law

Corporate governance refers to the set of systems, principles and processes by which a company is directed and governed to fulfil its goals and objectives in a manner that adds to the value of the company and is also beneficial to all the stakeholders for long term. Corporate governance is most often viewed as both the structure and the relationships which determine corporate direction and performance. The board of directors is typically central to corporate governance. Its relationship to the other primary participants, typically shareholders and management, is critical. Additional participants include employees, customers, suppliers, and creditors. The corporate governance framework also depends on the legal, regulatory, institutional and ethical environment of the community

Participants in Corporate Governance - Corporate governance is the relationship among various participants in determining the direction and performance of corporations. The participants include the regulatory body (e.g. the Chief executive officer, the board of directors, management, shareholders and auditors) and other stakeholders (e.g. employees, suppliers, creditors, customers and the community at large). In corporations, the shareholder delegates decision rights to the manager to act in the principal's best interests. As a result of this separation of ownership from control between the two parties, a system of corporate governance controls is significant. The Board of directors also plays a vital role as its their responsibility to endorse the corporation's strategy, develop directional policy, appoint, supervise and remunerate senior executives and to ensure accountability of the organization to its owners and authorities. All parties to corporate governance have a direct or indirect interest in the effective performance of the organization. Directors, workers and management receive salaries, benefits and reputation, while shareholders receive capital return. Customers receive goods and services; suppliers receive compensation for their goods or services. In return these individuals provide value in the form of natural, human, social and other forms of capital.

Companies Act 2013 - The Companies Act 2013 (Act) promises to substantively raise the bar on governance and in a comprehensive form purports to deal with some very relevant themes. However, it appears to be quite pervasive and thrusts greater responsibility and obligation on the Board of Directors and Management in Indian Companies. The Act has introduced significant changes regarding the board composition and has a renewed focus on board processes which over a period of time would institutionalize good corporate governance and not make governance over-dependent on the presence of certain individuals on the board. The Act is a progressive and forward looking which promises improved corporate governance norms, enhanced disclosures and transparency, facilitation of responsible entrepreneurship, increased accountability of company managements and auditors, protection of interest of investors particularly small and minority investors, better shareholder democracy, facilitation of Corporate Social Responsibility (CSR) and stricter enforcement processes. A responsible management has to; therefore, ensure that the business sub serves various groups effectively and efficiently. These days, it is not enough for a company to merely be profitable; it also needs to demonstrate good corporate citizenship through environmental awareness, ethical behaviour and sound corporate governance practices.

The Companies Act, 2013 has the provisions in order to protect the interest of the stakeholders which includes shareholders, creditors, employees, etc., and the remedies through class action suits, special courts and NCLT and NCLAT in case their rights are being hampered. Also, section 135 talks about

Corporate Social Responsibility and provides for mandatory contribution towards social welfare activities by the corporates. Also, section 166(2) requires directors to not only promote the objects of the company for the benefit of its members and company but also act in good faith towards its employees, the shareholders, the community and for the protection of environment. The concept of Independent Directors has been made stringent to provide for better compliance of law. Thus, the Companies Act, 2013, which is the guiding law for all corporates, itself, follows the Ruggie's three pillar framework of Protect, Respect and Remedy.

Further Clause 49 of SEBI and SEBI Listing Obligations and Disclosure Requirements (LODR) Regulations aims to enhance the quality of corporate governance in listed entities by empowering shareholders and improving transparency and disclosures under following broad heading:

Figure 6.1: Enhancing quality of Corporate Governance

6.5 Responsible Governance

Responsible governance refers to a form of governance in which those in positions of authority or power act ethically, transparently, and in the best interests of the people or entities they serve.

Responsible governance plays a crucial role in the corporate world, as it is essential for the ethical and sustainable operation of businesses. To Promote Ethical Business Practices, Compliance with laws and regulations, Sustainability, CSR, Shareholder rights and engagement, Diversity and Inclusion, Risk Management, Stakeholder Management, Long term Value creation.

Businesses, as key stakeholders, are instrumental in steering India's journey toward responsible governance. They are expected to operate with ethical and transparent practices, champion sustainable initiatives, and engage responsibly with the community. At the heart of this transformation is the recognition that the corporate sector holds a significant duty to society—a duty that goes beyond profit motives to encompass a profound sense of corporate social responsibility.

6.5.1 Benefits of Responsible Governance

The benefits of responsible governance includes as follows:

- Responsible governance leads to congruence of interests of board, management including owner managers and shareholders.
- Responsible governance provides stability and growth to the company.
- Responsible governance system builds confidence among investors.
- Responsible governance reduces perceived risks, consequently reducing cost of capital.
- Well governed companies enthuse employees to acquire and develop company specific skills.
- Adoption of responsible corporate practices promotes stability and long-term sustenance of stakeholders' relationship.
- Potential stakeholders aspire to enter into relationships with enterprises whose governance credentials are exemplary.
- Sound corporate governance also decreases the "likelihood of a domestic financial crisis" and the severity if such a crisis does occur.
- Responsible governance can play a role in reducing corruption, and decreased corruption significantly enhances a country's developmental prospects.

6.5.2 Principles of Responsible Governance

Key Principles of Responsible Governance may be considered as under:

Impact Leadership

Impact Leadership or the purpose driven Leadership is about an ability to ignite excellence within oneself and others to address intricate challenges in the evolving realm of responsible governance. Impact Leadership is one where a leader prioritises their purpose and values over anything else when making decisions on behalf of the organisation keeping in mind the greater good of the community, society and planet.

Accountability

Accountability means being responsible for what you do and provide a satisfactory reason for the same. Being accountable is more than just complying with the letter of law thus accountability is critical in responsible governance as it extends to shareholders, employees and wider community in which the organisation operates.

Transparency

In the competitive and technology driven business environment, while corporate require greater autonomy of operation and opportunity for self-regulation with optimum compliance costs, there is a need to bring about transparency through better disclosures and greater responsibility on the part of corporate owners and management for improved compliance. In response to such changing corporate climate, the Companies Act, 2013 and other allied rules and regulations has been amended from time to time so as to provide more transparency in corporate governance and protect the interests of multiple stakeholders.

Responsibility

In good governance, responsibility aims to serve the common good and ensure equity and participation. It will also ensure that the organisation processes and practices foster explicit acceptance of authority to act on behalf of the organization.

Fairness and Justice

It means protecting the rights of all shareholders and ensuring fair treatment of company's various stakeholders and ensure a remediation mechanism to ensure timely justice.

Ethical Conduct

The governance structure should set the right tone for the entire company with top ethical behaviour. Management cannot act one way and expect others to act the other way. The irregularities committed by senior management typically override the internal controls of the reporting system. Because management may override controls, or can influence others to perpetrate or conceal fraud, the need for a strong culture of good ethics in business operations is extremely important.

Participation

It means giving a voice to stakeholders including employees, labour unions, communities, civil society organisations, shareholders and others with special consideration to vulnerable groups.

Predictability

It is very important for organisations to show that it care about its stakeholders and value their inputs. Building stakeholder confidence is a gradual process that requires organisations to demonstrate transparency, openness and commitments towards ethical conduct through out their operations.

Sustainability

Organisations can achieve sustainability by ensuring that they take into account the interest of all stakeholders including environment and society in decision making. It means having a clear role for the Board and management in defining and managing the sustainability policy and ensuring its ability to meet the present needs without compromising the needs of future generation.

Respect for Human Rights

Organizations are expected to imbibe the core principles of Business and Human Rights into their policies and practice. Board has a responsibility to ensure that appropriate human rights policies are in place.

6.5.3 Shift from Rights to Duties

The shift from "Rights to Duties" in the responsible business represents a transition in how businesses approach their roles and responsibilities in society. Traditionally, the focus has been on the rights of businesses, which include the right to make a profit, operate without undue interference, and protect intellectual property. While these rights are important, there has been a growing recognition of the need to balance them with a heightened sense of duty and responsibility toward various stakeholders and the broader community. This shift involves several key changes: Social and Environmental Responsibility, Ethical Considerations, Stakeholder-Centric Approach, Long-term Perspective, Compliance with Laws and Regulations, CSR, etc.

In an era marked by rapid globalization, shifting demographics, and heightened social consciousness, the concept of responsible governance transcends its conventional understanding. It encompasses the critical shift from an exclusive emphasis on individual rights to a more comprehensive framework that equally prioritizes collective duties. For India, a nation distinguished by its extraordinary diversity and complex socio-cultural tapestry, understanding the nuances and imperatives of this transition is not just essential but profoundly transformative.

India's cultural and philosophical traditions have long extolled the significance of duty, with the concept of "dharma" embedded in its heritage. Against this backdrop, responsible governance takes on a distinctive flavour, shaped by the nation's traditional values and its response to contemporary global expectations.

6.5.4 Key Issues in India w.r.t Responsible Governance

A. *Balancing Economic Development and Sustainability* - Responsible governance must prioritize economic development while adhering to global environmental responsibilities and sustainability goals. Achieving this balance is a significant challenge, as it requires harmonizing growth with environmental protection.

B. *Individual Rights vs. Collective Duties* - Balancing individual rights with collective duties poses a complex challenge. Indian governance institutions need to find an equilibrium that respects individual freedoms while ensuring the welfare and rights of the collective

C. *Government and Non-State Actors* - With the rise of non-state actors and multinational corporations, the role of the government in ensuring responsible governance in areas beyond its jurisdiction is a pressing concern. Coordinating efforts and regulating non-state actors is complex.

D. *Transparency and Accountability* - Ensuring transparency and accountability in governance practices is a critical aspect of responsible governance. Implementing mechanisms for oversight and accountability is an ongoing challenge.

E. *Environmental Sustainability* - Ensuring responsible governance in the context of global expectations requires addressing environmental sustainability. India faces challenges related to climate change, pollution, resource management and biodiversity conservation.

6.5.5 G-20 recommendations on Responsible Business

A. The evolving global landscape, characterized by economic growth, technological advancements and international collaboration, necessitates reinvigorated multilateralism and reforms to address interconnected challenges and enhance global governance's effectiveness, transparency and accountability.

B. The G20 endorses the revised G20/OECD Principles of Corporate Governance to strengthen policy and regulatory frameworks supporting sustainability and access to capital markets, contributing to economic resilience.

C. These principles guide policymakers in improving the legal and institutional framework for corporate governance, promoting market confidence, economic efficiency, sustainable growth and financial stability.

D. The Principles also facilitate companies' access to finance, protect investors and enhance the sustainability and resilience of corporations, thereby benefiting the broader economy.

E. They aim to improve access to financial markets, support investor confidence through transparency and address evolving investor expectations.

F. The Principles acknowledge the growing role of institutional investors and recommend stewardship codes, conflict-of-interest disclosure, and corporate debt considerations.

6.6 Duties of the Board

Usually a Board may have three kinds of duties - the Contractual duty, Statutory duty and the Fiduciary duty. Out of these Fiduciary duties of the board are most important duties to be discharged by the Board of Directors. These duties may also be relevant to the other officers in a company. Several scholars define Fiduciary duties in different ways, most common duties are - Duty of Care and Duty of Loyalty.

6.6.1 Duty of Care (Prudence)

Duty of care in the context of the relationship between directors and shareholders is a duty to stay informed and exercise ordinary care and prudence in management of the organization. Duty of care requires a director to act in good faith, with ordinary care and in a manner he reasonably believes to be in the best interest of the company.

Broadly, the term good faith describes "that state of mind denoting honesty of purpose, freedom from intention to defraud, and, generally speaking, means being faithful to one's duty or obligation." (Black's Law Dictionary)

"Ordinary care" requires the director to display the degree of care that is reasonably expected of him having regard to his knowledge and experience. Ordinary care implies that the director is not expected to take special care. The standard of care is the care that a person of ordinary prudence would exercise in the same or similar circumstances. However, if a director has a special expertise (e.g., accounting expertise, legal expertise, etc.), ordinary care means that degree of care that a person with the same expertise would exercise in the same or similar circumstances.

A director can satisfy the duty of care only if he is reasonably informed with respect to the decisions he is required to make. He should have a clear understanding of the purpose (vision and mission) of the company. He should carefully read the Memorandum of Association, Articles of Association and other governance documents. He should have an understanding of the policies of the company and factors that should be considered in making the right choice in the best interest of the company. He should actively seek the information necessary to make an informed and independent decision. The director should regularly attend board meetings to develop familiarity and knowledge about the company, its business model, business environment and policies. While a director may rely on outside experts, he must nevertheless exercise her own independent judgment in making decisions as to what is in the corporation's best interests.

6.6.2 Business Judgment Rule

According this rule a decision maker is not liable for errors or mistakes in judgment if he acted in good faith with reasonable skill and prudence in a manner he reasonably believed to be in the best interest of the corporation. Courts do not take a second look to the decision of the board of directors and hold director liable unless it is established that the director has failed to act diligently.

6.6.3 Duty of Loyalty

The duty of loyalty requires undivided loyalty to the company. The duty of loyalty can be breached either by making a self-interested transaction or taking a corporate opportunity or by disclosing confidential business information.

A director should not exploit to his own use the corporate opportunity. Where the opportunity properly belongs to the company, the director has an obligation to disclose the opportunity and offer the opportunity to the company. An opportunity properly belongs to the company where the company has a legitimate interest or expectancy in the particular opportunity and has financial resources to take advantage of that opportunity.

According to the Stanford Social Innovation Review:

The duty of loyalty is one of a board's three essential legal duties, a legal perspective aimed at avoiding self-dealing and conflicts of interest. In practice, however, the duty of loyalty is often interpreted as the responsibility to think *only* of the organization when making governing decisions. This interpretation unnecessarily focuses board members on loyalty to the organization as a corporate entity. Instead, boards should focus their loyalty to the organization's purpose or reason for being, fidelity to the reason that the organization exists and—by extension—to the people and communities its work impacts. What is best for purpose and community is not always synonymous with what's best for the organization.

The Board is not only responsible for protecting minority interest against the opportunistic behaviour of the manager; it is also responsible for the business sustainability and growth. An effective board ensures that the organization reaches its objectives by explicitly assuming responsibility for:

- Corporate strategy
- Identifying, assessing and evaluating business risks
- Succession planning
- Performance evaluation
- Communications policy
- Integrity of internal controls and management information systems
- Developing the organization's approach to corporate governance

6.7 Building Effective Boards

There are several aspects to be considered for building better and effective Boards. Here we will discuss some of the important aspects like avoiding Homogeneity Trap, Effective Conflict Resolution Process, Alignment on Major Strategic Issues, Business Judgment Rule, Process Management, Behaviour-change strategies for the Board Members etc.

6.7.1 Avoid Homogeneity Trap

Boards only see what they're presented with and can easily become passive recipients of agendas created by powerful CEOs and senior executives. Corporate failure raises questions as to what the board knew and what more it could have done. As a Board member, you are expected to take responsibility, despite not being a day-to-day decision maker. You have responsibility for a company but limited means to really understand it and that understanding is often mediated by management. How aware are you of what's really happening in the company you're responsible for governing? Having industry specialists on the board is important, but a lack of diversity of thought can lead to homogeneity that creates myopathy. Consider bringing in new board members to make the group more diverse, and bring in guest speakers who will challenge your assumptions and bring fresh perspectives.

6.7.2 Effective Conflict Resolution Process

The board has the duty of stimulating the flow of ideas, identifying key issues affecting the business, and making informed decisions. This often calls for deliberation and debates. Conflict will arise and managing conflict is a skill every board member is expected to excel in. It is important to be Purpose-Oriented, before undertaking conflict resolution, board members and the organization's executive should identify the key issues they face and their impact on the organization. Keep the focus on finding a solution that benefits the company, not personal agendas or individual interests.

6.7.3 Alignment on Major Strategic Issues

According to Harvard Business Review, boards go through four distinct developmental stages' foundational, developed, advanced and strategic. It's essential for high-performing boards to have agreement and alignment with senior management on where the company is within those four stages and where they want to go next. Getting into alignment requires having a joint sense of clarity of purpose, alignment on the company's strategy, good team dynamics within the board and with the executives, and a strong board that is capable of objectively evaluating themselves.

6.8 The Purpose Driven Board Leadership

Leadership is defined as the action or an act of guidance of leading a group of people or an organisation. It is a practical skill and a research area that helps individuals to influence or lead teams, organisations, or individuals. Great leaders are created through an endless cycle of self-study, training, preparing and experience.

Great leaders are persistently working and concentrating on improving their administration aptitudes; they are not settling for the *status quo*. Authority is a cycle by which an individual impacts others to achieve a target and co-ordinates the association such that it makes it more durable and cognizant. Leaders complete this cycle by applying their administration ascribes, for example, - convictions, values, morals, character, information and abilities.

According to the Harvard Business Review:

> With the idea that a company's purpose is about far more than making money gaining ground, the hard-charging, profit-optimizing hero-leader model has lost much of its appeal.

6.8.1 The Purpose

In the context of Sustainability or adopting ESG Framework in Business, a leader has to be clear about 'The Purpose' of the core existence of the Business a leader is steering.

> The only purpose of the business is the business with purpose.

As we have already studied in the Principles of the Responsible Governance earlier in this chapter, the Impact Leadership or the purpose driven Leadership is about an ability to ignite excellence. A leader prioritises their purpose and values over anything else when making decisions on behalf of the organisation keeping in mind the greater good of the community, society and the planet.

According to the Stanford Social Innovation Review, a new orientation to the board's leadership role is described as "Purpose-Driven Board Leadership," a mindset characterized by four fundamental principles, mutually reinforcing and interdependent, that define the way that the board sees itself and its work.

6.9 Fundamental Principles of Purpose Driven Board Leadership

Purpose before organization

Prioritizing the organization's purpose, versus the organization itself.

Respect for ecosystem

Acknowledging that the organization's actions can positively or negatively impact its surrounding ecosystem, and a commitment to being a respectful and responsible ecosystem player.

Equity mindset

Committing to advancing equitable outcomes, and interrogating and avoiding the ways in which the organization's strategies and work may reinforce systemic inequities.

Authorized voice and power

Recognizing that organizational power and voice must be authorized by those impacted by the organization's work.

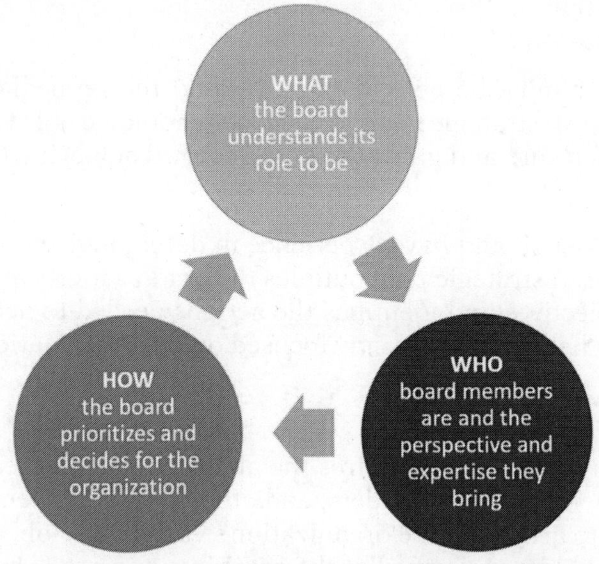

(Source: ssir.org)

Figure 6.2: Relationship between board role, composition and decision making

Further, according to the SSIR study, traditionally, boards are understood to be "mission-driven," which means the board is responsible for ensuring that the organization does good work that advances its cause. But while being mission-driven is centred on the organization's role in doing good, we believe boards need to re-centre on purpose: the fundamental reason that the organization exists.

The vision, mission and values are seen as more narrowly-defined elements of purpose:

Vision: the desired future state

Mission: an organization's role in working toward its vision

Values: the principles and beliefs that guide how an organization enacts its mission

Purpose: an organization's reason for being in the world, which is a melding of the concepts of mission and values in pursuit of vision.

6.10 Characteristics for effective Board Leadership

Board Leadership is considered as a critical component for organizational success. Effective board leadership is vital for achieving long-term success. A strong board leader creates a culture of accountability, promotes transparency, and fosters collaboration among board members. According to a study, the following are some essential characteristics that make for effective board leadership:

Visionary Thinking

A board leader must be able to think beyond the immediate challenges and set long-term strategic goals. The leader should be able to envision the organization's future and guide the board toward achieving that vision.

Strategic Planning

The board leader should have experience in developing and implementing strategic plans. A strategic plan outlines the organization's mission, vision, goals, and objectives and identifies the actions needed to achieve them. A strategic plan helps the board stay focused on the organization's long-term goals.

Effective Communication

Effective board leadership requires the ability to communicate effectively with board members, stakeholders, and other key constituents. The leader must be able to articulate the organization's vision, mission, and goals and keep all stakeholders informed of the organization's progress.

Collaborative Leadership

A board leader should be able to foster a culture of collaboration and teamwork among board members. A collaborative leader recognizes the strengths and weaknesses of each member and leverages those strengths to achieve the organization's goals.

Commitment to Excellence

A board leader must be committed to excellence and continuous improvement. The leader should strive to create a culture of excellence within the board and the organization and encourage board members to do the same.

Accountability

A board leader should hold themselves and other board members accountable for their actions and decisions. The leader should ensure that the board operates in compliance with the organization's policies, values and vision.

6.11 Corporate Anti Corruption drive in India

There are no general laws like the Prevention of Corruption Act (PCA) that specifically prohibit private commercial corruption and bribery in India. Organisations may have internal codes of conduct that prohibit corruption.

India's legislation governing companies, being the Companies Act, 2013 has introduced stringent provisions pertaining to fraud, which has been defined to include following and does not require there to be a wrongful gain or a wrongful loss:

> *'any act, omission, concealment of any fact or abuse of position committed by any person . . . with intent to deceive, to gain undue advantage from, or to injure the interests of the company or its shareholders or its creditors or any other person'*

According to a study, recommendations have been made that Acts of private bribery and concealment thereof could be considered to constitute a fraud on or by the company, which may be punishable with imprisonment ranging from six months to 10 years and a fine, depending on the amount involved in the fraud. However, for fraud that is below a de minimums limit, 1 million rupees or 1 per cent of the turnover of the company, whichever is lower and not involving public interest, the punishment is imprisonment for up to five years, a fine of up to 5 million rupees or both.

Directors, in their directors' responsibility statement under the Companies Act, are required to provide certain confirmations that are relevant, and also provide details of any fraud reported by auditors, other than those which are mandatorily reportable to the government. The Companies Act also obliges auditors, in the course of performance of their duties as an auditor, cost accountants in practice in the course of conducting cost audit, and company secretaries in practice in the course of conducting secretarial audit to report any suspected fraud to the Central Government.

Listed companies and certain types of unlisted companies are mandated to establish a vigilance mechanism for reporting concerns and to provide safeguards for whistle-blowers. There is a disclosure mechanism for disclosure of fraud in the auditor's report for all companies, and in certain instances to the stock exchanges for listed companies.

Particulars of some high-profile corruption-related proceedings in India are set out below. Since public updates with regard to matters under investigation or pending trial are not published, most publishable information is available from media sources and a few publicly reported judicial decisions concerning certain ancillary proceedings have been presented below:

6.11.1 2G Spectrum scam

This case concerned the allotment of telecoms bandwidth spectrum by the government to several small and unknown telecoms players at giveaway prices. Soon after, the spectrum was sold to larger telecoms players at a very high premium. A report by the Comptroller and Auditor General of India (CAG) estimated the loss to the public exchequer at 1,760 billion rupees. In 2011, the CBI, after investigating the matter, initiated proceedings against the telecoms minister A Raja, senior bureaucrats, the companies awarded the spectrum and their key officials, alleging offences under the PCA and the Indian Penal Code, 1860. Later, M K Kanimozhi, a member of Parliament, was added as an accused. In 2012, the Supreme Court passed an order cancelling the impugned licences and directed that the spectrum be re-allotted by auction process. On 21 December 2017, a special court constituted to conduct the trial in the matter acquitted the accused. The CBI subsequently filed an appeal against the acquittal before the High Court of Delhi. The Court rejected appeal in April, 2022.

6.11.2 Punjab National Bank scam

A diamond business has recently been accused of defrauding the Punjab National Bank of 114,000 million rupees through the family members, companies and partnership firms of the persons operating the business. The complaint by the Punjab National Bank to the CBI reveals that the fraud had been perpetrated for years through collusion between bank officials and the accused persons along with their affiliates, and involved the issuance of bank guarantees to overseas branches of other Indian lenders, on behalf of the accused and their affiliates. These guarantees were allegedly used to raise buyer's credit for the accused persons' firms to pay for imports and various other purposes. The CBI has filed two charge sheets against the accused, who include bank officials, alleging various offences under the Indian Penal Code, 1860, the PCA and the Prevention of Money Laundering Act, 2002 (PMLA). The two main accused are reported to have fled the country, and as per various media reports, extradition proceedings are ongoing against both main accused.

6.11.3 Action by MCA on shell companies

The Ministry of Corporate Affairs (MCA) is taking strong action against non-functional companies, commonly known as shell companies, as part of its ongoing efforts to combat illegal activities. MCA is planning to further intensify its crackdown on these companies, which are often used for illegal money transactions.

To ensure better compliance and discipline, the MCA is now planning to implement physical verification processes for non-functional or non-compliant firms. This means that these companies will be subjected to closer scrutiny by the Registrar of Companies (RoC), compelling them to take compliance more seriously.

In the past three years, a significant number of companies, approximately 127,952, were removed from records, according to a statement by Minister of State for Corporate Affairs, Rao Inderjit Singh, in the Lok Sabha. The MCA has been actively working since 2016 to crack down on shell companies.

The MCA21 portal, designed for various filings under the Companies Act and the LLP Act, will play a crucial role in identifying and taking action against shell companies. Its comprehensive database will aid in tracking non-compliant firms and supporting the crackdown.

6.12 Board Committees

Board committees allow a subset of directors with appropriate skills to spend additional time focusing attention on their assigned subject matter. These committees, however, do not relieve the full board of its responsibility for these matters, they merely allow for specialization and help streamline the operations (and the meetings) of the full board. The committee chairs assist the board by providing a report with the committees' recommendations on how the board can best discharge its responsibilities.

The Companies Act, 2013 has prescribed formation of board committees for various tasks. As per the Companies Act, 2013, constitution of four committees is mandatory:

(1) Audit Committee

(2) Nomination and Remuneration Committee

(3) Stakeholder Relationship Committee

(4) CSR Committee

The Committees are envisaged to act as the main pillars of corporate governance system in corporations. By prescribing formation of these board committees the Act has now fixed accountability on these board committees for crucial activities of the corporation.

Section 177 of the Companies Act, 2013 lays down rules for composition, roles and responsibilities of Audit Committee for oversight of financial activities and important disclosures. The objective of the committee is to strengthen the finance and control systems of an organisation. Even though, formation of audit committee is not a new concept but the scope and responsibility has increased manifold. The organization and its shareholders rely on select audit committee members' decision to have adequate control and oversee areas such as risk, compliance, financial reporting and corporate resources.

The challenge to boards and senior management is to balance risk with acceptable reward, to create value without hurting the enterprise. Corporate governance and enterprise-wide risk management are interconnected. Risk management, like corporate governance, involves both conformance and performance aspects: ensuring that past and present issues are well handled while also looking to the future1.

It is important to make financial and also non-financial disclosures. The purpose of the disclosing non-financial information in addition to financial information is to provide the context necessary to understand the firm's financial condition, changes in financial condition, and results of operations. The audit committee should ensure the numbers are backed by activities of the company and the attached non-financial statement should provide adequate narrative.

In addition to above mentioned committees that are mandatory under Companies Act, 2013, organisations are also constituting various other committees such as ESG Committee, Ethics Committee, Risk Managment Committee, etc.

ESG Committee

Constituting ESG Committee is an important step to begin the journey of ESG. An ESG Committee has overall responsibility for the effective operation of a company's ESG policy, and has delegated responsibility for overseeing its implementation. The committee reviews data from across the business and then filters and summarises it for the board. The ESG Committee is responsible for writing the ESG content in the company's annual report and producing all information relating to ESG disclosures. Also before constituting ESG Committee, Businesses/Organisations must understand ESG Maturity Framework to ensure that businesses are doing things in the right order and at the right time.

6.13 Risk Management Strategies

Understand the approaches to assess and mitigate risks, ensuring that governance mechanisms are robust and effective.

While ESG problems are gaining popularity and becoming commonplace in business, the governance aspect is sometimes disregarded. However, while receiving less emphasis, it provides the foundation for long-term value generation and underlies any organization's capacity to meet its environmental and social objectives.

While the growth of ESG has aided in the emergence of a new age of stakeholder capitalism based on the notion of long-term value creation for everybody, the emphasis has mostly been on the 'E' and, more recently, the 'S' aspects. Environmental imperatives and popular social movements have brought these concerns to the top of the business agenda in recent years.

On the other hand, governance has a lower profile, as it is seen as the domain of the board of directors rather than a sphere of influence for all stakeholders. Only shareholders may expect to be involved in and influence governance choices, and only indirectly, or as a last resort, through a shareholder revolt. Governance has been included with varying degrees of effectiveness, but it hasn't captivated the imagination of stakeholders or garnered widespread public attention, except in catastrophic failure scenarios.

Governance is critical to business performance, stakeholder confidence, and building a long-term value creation. The following aspects of Governance may be considered:

Diversity in the boardroom

There are several benefits to having a diverse board. It provides a broader viewpoint, makes more sound judgments, encourages innovation, is more nimble, and better reflects the company's investors, consumers, and community. A diversified board is beneficial to the company's bottom line.

Compliance

Information disclosure, auditing, accounting and regulatory compliance are all aspects of governance. Failure to meet these duties can jeopardize the company's reputation, income and long-term viability.

Creating and executing policy

Governance assesses whether or not a company is operating ethically, pursuing policies that are in the best interests of its stakeholders, and not having a harmful influence on the environment. Without the 'G', the 'E' or 'S' cannot be effectively complied with.

Compensation for executives

The Companies Act, 2013 requires the appointment of every director (including a managing director) along with the complete details of the remuneration package including prerequisites to be tabled separately and approved individually at shareholders' meetings. However, under section 197 of Companies Act, there are generous overall limits as to what such companies can pay their executive and non executive directors.

6.14 Governance disclosures under the NGRBC

With the evolving landscape of mandatory and voluntary rules and regulations, organisations are expected to comply with the spirit of the law and also adapt voluntary guidelines and make disclosures in implementing the same throughout their operations.

Principle 1 of the National Guidelines on Responsible Business Conduct (NGRBC) stipulates about the aspects to be adopted and disclosed towards responsible governance.

6.14.1 Principle - 1 of NGRBC on Governance

Principle 1: Businesses should conduct and govern themselves with integrity and in a manner that is ethical, transparent and accountable.

The principle ensures ethical behaviour in all operation, functions and processes, is the basic of businesses that are guiding their governance of economic, social and environmental responsibilities. It considers that businesses are an integral part of society and they will hold themselves accountable for the effective adoption, the implementation and the making of disclosures on their performance.

This Principle recognizes that ethical behaviour in all operations, functions and processes, is the cornerstone of businesses guiding their governance of economic, social and environmental responsibilities. The Principle emphasizes that disclosures on business decisions and actions that impact stakeholders form the fundamental basis of operationalizing responsible business conduct and should be accessible to all relevant stakeholders. It recognizes that businesses are an integral part of society and that they will hold themselves accountable for the effective adoption, implementation, and the making of disclosures on their performance with respect to the Core Elements of these Guidelines. The Principle further emphasizes that the governance structure of the business should ensure this, in line with SDG 16.

6.14.2 NGRBC Core Elements on Governance

The Principle 1 has further nine Core Elements as under:

(*a*) The governance structure should develop and put in place structures, policies and procedures that promote this Principle, prevent its contravention and effect prompt and fair action against any transgressions.

(*b*) The Governance Structure should ensure that the Principles of these Guidelines are understood, adopted and implemented throughout the operations of their business.

(*c*) The Governance Structure should also promote the adoption of this Principle across the value chain of their business.

(*d*) The Governance Structure should disclose and communicate transparently and enable access to information about the policies, procedures, performance (financial and non-financial), and decisions of their enterprise, that impact their stakeholders, especially those that are most at risk to business impacts and communities that are vulnerable and marginalized.

(*e*) The Governance Structure should take responsibility for meeting all its statutory obligations in line with the spirit of the law, enabling fair competition and ensuring it treats all its stakeholders in an equitable manner.

(*f*) The Governance Structure should ensure that the business avoids complicity with the actions of any third party that violates any of the Principles contained in these Guidelines.

(*g*) The Governance Structure should put in place appropriate structures, policies and procedures to address conflicts of interest involving its members, employees and business partners.

(*h*) The Governance Structure should put in place appropriate structures, codes, policies and procedures to ensure that the business does not engage in illegal and abusive practices, bribery and corruption, and ensure timely and fair action in case such transgressions are detected.

(*i*) The Governance Structure should ensure that the business contributes to public finances by timely and complete payment of all applicable taxes in the letter and spirit of the laws and regulations governing such payments.

6.14.3 NGRBC Disclosure Questions related to Governance

The Governance, Leadership, Policy, Stakeholders, Oversight and Communications related disclosure questions in the NGRBC Disclosure Format are as under:

Disclosures on Policy and Management Processes

- Names of the policy/policies that covers each Principle.
- Core Elements related to the Principle that the policy/policies cover.
- Policy/policies relating to each principle that has been translated into guidelines and procedures.
- Extent to which manpower, planning and financial resources have been allocated for the implementation of the policy/policies relating to each Principle.

Disclosures on Governance, Leadership & Oversight

- Names of the policies that have been approved by the Board/top management.
- Name of the specified committee(s) of the Board/Director/Officer and processes to oversee the implementation of the policy/policies.
- The process for board/top management to review performance against the above policies and incorporating inputs.
- Process for board/top management to review compliance with statutory requirements of relevance to the Principles and rectify any non-compliances.
- Frequency of the reviews of the business's alignment with the Principles and Core Elements conducted by the board/top management.

Disclosures on Stakeholders Engagement

- Description of the process to identify your business's key stakeholders.
- Description of the process to engage with your stakeholders on the Principles.
- Description of the processes to identify groups that are vulnerable and marginalized stakeholders.
- Description of the processes to identify issues related to inclusion and impact of adopting the Principles on vulnerable and marginalized stakeholders.

Disclosures on Communications

- Description of process to communicate to stakeholders, the impact of your policies, procedures, decisions and performance that impact them.

- Description of how the business communicates the results of stakeholder engagement in the public domain.
- Description of the process of communicating performance against these Guidelines to relevant stakeholders.
- Note on how disclosures and reporting helped in improving business performance/strategy.

Essential Indicators of the Principle-1

- Month/year of last review by Governance Structure/top management of performance of the business across the Principles and Core Elements of the Guidelines?
- % Coverage of leadership team by awareness programmes on the Guidelines: *a.* In reporting year *b.* Total to date.
- % of suppliers and distributors (by value), in the year: *a.* Covered by awareness programmes for the Guidelines? *b.* Had responsible/s.
- Number of meetings/dialogues with minority shareholders that were organized in the year?
- Number of complaints received on any aspect of the NGRBC in the year from: *a.* Shareholders/investors *b.* Lenders.
- Number of the above complaints pending resolution at close of year?
- Value of non-disputed fines/penalties imposed on your business by regulatory and judicial institutions in the year?
- Number of complaints/cases of corruption and conflicts of interest that were registered in the year?
- Details of unmet obligations (fiscal, social, etc.) arising out of any benefits or concessions provided by the Central, State, or Local Governments

Leadership Indicators of the Principle-1

- % Coverage of all employees by awareness programmes for the Guidelines: *a.* In reporting year *b.* Total to date.
- % of suppliers and distributors (by value) covered by social and environmental audits: *a.* In reporting year *b.* Total to date.
- Was report on responsible business conduct made, in the year: *a.* As per mandatory/global reporting frameworks. *b.* Available in the public domain. *c.* Assured by a third party.
- Details of non-disputed fines/penalties imposed on your business by regulatory and judicial institutions in the year available in public domain.

- Provide examples (up to three) of corrective action taken on the above fines/penalties imposed.
- Provide examples (up to three) of corrective action taken on the complaints/cases of corruption and conflicts of interest to prevent recurrence.

6.14.4 Role of Governance Structure in remaining NGRBC Principles

The NGRBC principles are aligned with the objectives of the United Nation Guiding Principles (UNGPs) based on UNHRC's 'Protect, Respect & Remedy' Framework and Sustainable Development Goals (SDGs). It also highlights 'the governance structure to ensure. . .compliance with all the core elements', thus it is critical for the board/top management to ensure integration, practice and disclosures on all the Principles of the Guideline *viz.*

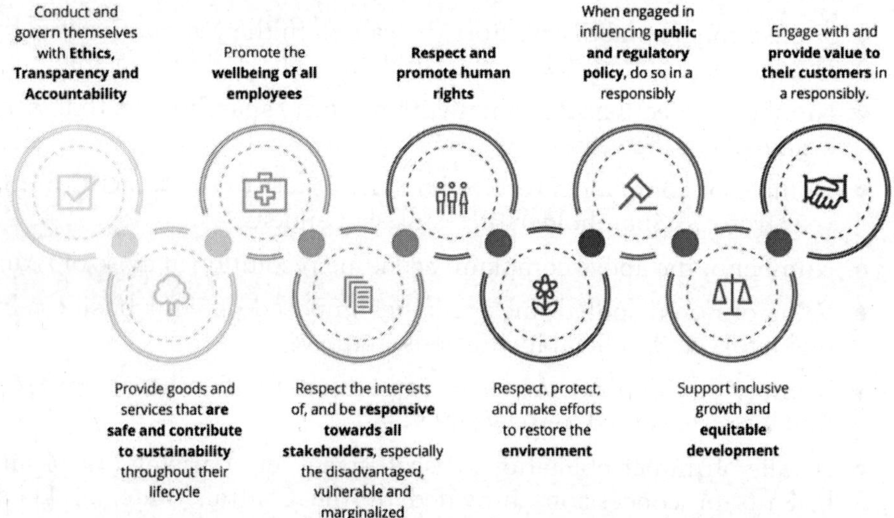

Figure 6.3: Nine Principles of NGRBC

6.15 G20/OECD Principles of Corporate Governance

The G20/OECD Principles of Corporate Governance provide guidance to help policy makers evaluate and improve the legal, regulatory and institutional framework for corporate governance, with a view to supporting market confidence and integrity, economic efficiency, sustainable growth and financial stability.

As the main international benchmark for good corporate governance, the Principles have a global reach and reflect the experiences and ambitions of a wide variety of jurisdictions with varying legal systems and at different stages of development. They are also one of the Financial Stability Board's Key Standards for Sound Financial Systems.

It is pertinent to mention that these Principle have been recently revised in 2023 to reflect recent evolutions in capital markets and corporate governance policies and practices.

Six Principles are as under:

I. Ensuring the basis for an effective corporate governance framework

The corporate governance framework should promote transparent and fair markets, and the efficient allocation of resources. It should be consistent with the rule of law and support effective supervision and enforcement.

II. The rights and equitable treatment of shareholders and key ownership functions

The corporate governance framework should protect and facilitate the exercise of shareholders' rights and ensure the equitable treatment of all shareholders, including minority and foreign shareholders. All shareholders should have the opportunity to obtain effective redress for violation of their rights at a reasonable cost and without excessive delay.

III. Institutional investors, stock markets, and other intermediaries

The corporate governance framework should provide sound incentives throughout the investment chain and provide for stock markets to function in a way that contributes to good corporate governance.

IV. Disclosure and transparency

The corporate governance framework should ensure that timely and accurate disclosure is made on all material matters regarding the corporation, including the financial situation, performance, sustainability, ownership and governance of the company.

V. The responsibilities of the board

The corporate governance framework should ensure the strategic guidance of the company, the effective monitoring of management by the board, and the board's accountability to the company and the shareholders.

VI. Sustainability and resilience

The corporate governance framework should provide incentives for companies and their investors to make decisions and manage their risks, in a way that contributes to the sustainability and resilience of the corporation.

6.16 Responsibilities of Board as per G20 - OECD

The G-20 OECD Guidelines on Corporate Governance define the responsibilities of the Board as under:

- Board members should act on a fully informed basis, in good faith, with due diligence and care, and in the best interest of the company and the shareholders, taking into account the interests of stakeholders.
    - Board members should be protected against litigation if a decision was made in good faith with due diligence.
- Where board decisions may affect different shareholder groups differently, the board should treat all shareholders fairly.
- The board should apply high ethical standards.
- The board should fulfil certain key functions, including:
    - Reviewing and guiding corporate strategy, major plans of action, annual budgets and business plans; setting performance objectives; monitoring implementation and corporate performance; and overseeing major capital expenditures, acquisitions and divestitures.
    - Reviewing and assessing risk management policies and procedures.
    - Monitoring the effectiveness of the company's governance practices and making changes as needed.
    - Selecting, overseeing and monitoring the performance of key executives, and, when necessary, replacing them and overseeing succession planning.
    - Aligning key executive and board remuneration with the longer term interests of the company and its shareholders.
    - Ensuring a formal and transparent board nomination and election process.
    - Monitoring and managing potential conflicts of interest of management, board members and shareholders, including misuse of corporate assets and abuse in related party transactions.
    - Ensuring the integrity of the corporation's accounting and reporting systems for disclosure, including the independent external audit, and that appropriate control systems are in place, in compliance with the law and relevant standards.
    - Overseeing the process of disclosure and communications
- The board should be able to exercise objective independent judgment on corporate affairs.

- Boards should consider assigning a sufficient number of independent board members capable of exercising independent judgment to tasks where there is a potential for conflicts of interest. Examples of such key responsibilities are ensuring the integrity of financial and other corporate reporting, the review of related party transactions, and nomination and remuneration of board members and key executives.
- Boards should consider setting up specialised committees to support the full board in performing its functions, in particular the audit committee - or equivalent body - for overseeing disclosure, internal controls and audit-related matters. Other committees, such as remuneration, nomination or risk management, may provide support to the board depending upon the company's size, structure, complexity and risk profile. Their mandate, composition and working procedures should be well defined and disclosed by the board which retains full responsibility for the decisions taken.
- Board members should be able to commit themselves effectively to their responsibilities.
- Boards should regularly carry out evaluations to appraise their performance and assess whether they possess the right mix of background and competences, including with respect to gender and other forms of diversity.

◆ In order to fulfil their responsibilities, board members should have access to accurate, relevant and timely information.

◆ When employee representation on the board is mandated, mechanisms should be developed to facilitate access to information and training for employee representatives, so that this representation is exercised effectively and best contributes to the enhancement of board skills, information and independence.

6.17 Global Best Practices

Since the economist Milton Friedman famously stated, "the social responsibility of business is to increase its profits," shareholder primacy has been the bedrock of business operations. However, in light of ever-increasing global challenges such as climate change, environmental risks, growing inequality, and so on, business leaders have been compelled, and have found it to be in their best interests, to re-imagine the role of businesses in society and to see them as more than just economic units for generating wealth. Perhaps this is what prompted the Business Roundtable (BRT), an influential association of CEOs from the largest corporations in the United States of America, to issue a statement in 2019 that redefined the purpose of a corporation. The statement's 181 signatories reaffirmed their companies' commitment to all stakeholders. Also, the World Economic Forum issued the 'Davos Manifesto: The Universal Purpose of a Company in the Fourth Industrial Revolution' at its annual meeting in 2020. The statement asserted, among other things, a shift towards stakeholder capitalism and emphasised that a company's performance must be measured not only on the return to shareholders, but also on how it achieves its environmental, social, and good governance objectives. Therefore, it is evident that even globally there is a growing recognition and emphasis on stakeholder model of governance.

In this context, non-financial, sustainability reporting provides an opportunity to businesses to communicate in an open and transparent way with stakeholders. Sustainability reporting is an emerging business trend that entails disclosing and communicating an entity's non-financial - environmental, social and governance (ESG) performance and impact.

6.18 Future Directions

The Sustainable Future is an ongoing series that explores big questions for companies as they prepare to lead their organisations. This question also explores the how organisations approach establishing strong governance over their ESG strategy.

While the social component of ESG is still in its infancy in corporate adoption, the maturation of both social and environmental considerations will result in these issues being treated by business as usual, requiring the same level of reporting and regulatory framework as any other area of governance.

The expansion of legislation and its integration into boardroom procedures will drive this, and so will the impact of all the many stakeholder groups asking that their ESG requirements be recognized. Since the green paper on corporate governance reform in 2016, there has been a growing expectation that board responsibilities involve soliciting and reporting stakeholder feedback.

The green paper did not need particular stakeholder engagement approaches and did not result in a governance revolution. However, there was a deliberate effort to include stakeholder representation on the board of directors and proven procedures for routinely interacting with stakeholders and reporting on such discussions.

These ambitions will be inscribed in the future of governance, making it a more visible and beneficial component for all human as well as non-human stakeholders such as natural resources and other species.

The most effective changes to establish strong ESG governance includes:

- Establishment of clear, measurable goals.
- Establishment of a ESG board committee overseeing ESG.
- Appointment of an executive ESG leader.
- Cross-functional ESG management team.
- Identifying human centric and planet centric stakeholders.
- ESG target achievement as part of assessing management performance.
- Publishing of interim ESG targets and/or transition plans.
- An ESG strategy etc.

Sustainability is one of the greatest challenges facing the world today specifically as a result of climate change, equality issues, and other major social and environmental concerns.

ESG - Driven New World

The concept of Environmental, Social and Governance (ESG) has gained significant traction in recent years as a framework for assessing sustainability and societal impacts of business entities. The ESG ecosystem refers to the interconnected network of stakeholders, including companies, investors, regulators, government and civil society organizations, that play critical roles in promoting and implementing sustainable practices.

The G20 summit provides us with a unique opportunity to collectively redefine our priorities, reimagine our strategies, and forge partnerships that will steer us towards a more sustainable and resilient future.

ESG: Creating Value and Sustainability for Future

- The G20 recognises the importance of collective action in tackling environmental challenges and climate change while promoting transitions towards more flexible, transparent and cleaner energy systems. The OECD supports the G20 Presidency's work, building on its extensive expertise in green growth, clean and climate-resilient infrastructure, fossil fuel subsidies, energy regulation, green finance and investment, environmental taxation and Environmental, Social and Governance (ESG).
- Business entities are increasingly being held accountable for sustainability of their performance by all stakeholders. This is prompting a growing number of companies to incorporate ESG considerations into their operations and reporting on their initiatives for sustainable performance through various frameworks and reporting standards.

- Regulators have also started playing an important role by setting standards and guidelines for sustainable practices, and by enforcing those. This can help to ensure that companies are held accountable and that investors have access to reliable and comparable ESG data.
- The G20 summit provided us with a unique opportunity to collectively redefine our priorities, reimagine our strategies, and forge partnerships that will steer us towards a more sustainable and resilient future.

Key dialogues that India need to refocus

- **Tracking per-capita emissions**

  India can champion the tracking of per-capita emissions as an indicator of climate action. With India having the lowest per-capita emissions among G20 nations, efforts to reduce per-capita emissions can lead to a sharper decline in aggregate national emissions.

- **Mainstreaming circular economy principles**

  The concept of a circular economy, which aims to turn used goods into reusable products, is essential for sustainability. India needs to address its challenges in waste management and air pollution control. By implementing effective land, water, and air pollution control measures, including greening public procurement practices, India can create a conducive environment for circular economy initiatives.

- **Allocated funds for climate-techs and green techs**

  India should drive action on the funding to impact-based start-ups which are solving dire issues faced by our and G20 countries'. These start-ups can give economic support and create solutions for non-economic events which can help create a much more balanced world. India can collaborate with other vulnerable economies to create a collective solution bank through these upcoming ventures and solutions.

- **Addressing net-zero targets**

  While net-zero targets have gained popularity, there is still a long way to go for G20 countries to phase out coal use and reduce reliance on fossil fuels. India, with its commitment to a 2070 net-zero target and increased investments in renewable energy, can lead the dialogue on coal phase-outs and energy transition. By advocating for concrete roadmaps and policies, India can encourage G20 nations to align with net-zero goals. India started this dialogue with renewable energy and bio-fuel adaptation push but a concretised output can help us stay away from one of the biggest emission categories.

Governance of Sustainability

'International Union of Conservation of Nature' defines the Governance of Sustainability as the set of written and unwritten rules that link ecological citizenship with institutions and norms of governance. It is a complex topic because it addresses the three issues of globalization, democracy and sustainability. It further narrates that no form of governance can succeed if there is no common bond between those who govern and those who are being governed.

No form of governance can succeed if there is no common bond between those who govern and those who are being governed.

Governance is instrumental to the implementing sustainability in organisations and to become a future 'change agent' who can develop and inform governance solutions to complex environmental and social sustainability challenges. Governance solutions to the complex issues of Environmental and Social (E&S) Sustainability are important to consider as ESG risks and opportunities abound, and they can only be avoided or taken advantage of by sound decisions of responsible governance.

6.19 Summary of the Chapter

We had gone through the evolution of Responsible Governance starting from the Kautilya. Dynamics of the Governance in ESG were discussed by way of defining 'G' in ESG and embedding ESG into Corporate Strategies. Importance & benefits of 'G' in ESG have helped to understand its relevance in attaining targets and compliance of other two factors of ESG *i.e.* E&S. The abstract aspects of strategic thinking have been redefined in terms of redefined Corporate Purpose and rethinking how corporate performance is conceived and assessed, and a shift towards Cross-Sectoral Leadership. Corporate Governance in Indian Law has been narrated. Aspects of Responsible Governance have been presented in terms of its benefits, principles, a shift from Rights to Duties alongwith key Issues in India w.r.t Responsible Governance. G-20 recommendations on Responsible Business have also been presented.

Duties of the Board including the Duty of Care (Prudence), Business Judgment Rule and Duty of Loyalty were explained. Aspects for building Effective Boards in terms of avoiding Homogeneity Trap, effective Conflict Resolution Process and alignment on major Strategic Issues have been incorporated. Fundamentals of the Purpose Driven Board Leadership and Characteristics for effective Board Leadership have also been studied in this chapter. We have also gone through Corporate Anti-Corruption drive in India, Board Committees, Risk Management Strategies and Governance disclosures under the National Guidelines on Responsible Business Conduct. We concluded the discussions with future directions for Governance dimensions of ESG.

ESG KEY TRENDS, CHALLENGES AND WAY FORWARD

CHAPTER 7

7.1 Key Trends in India

India is the world's third-largest emitter of greenhouse gases and a signatory to the Paris Agreement that aims to limit global warming by keeping a global temperature rise this century well below 2 degrees Celsius above pre-industrial levels and to pursue efforts to limit the temperature increase even further to 1.5 degrees Celsius. **At COP-26**, Hon'ble Prime Minister Shri Narendra Modi announced that by 2030, India will reduce the carbon intensity of its economy by more than 45% and meet 50% of its energy requirements from renewable energy by 2030, **reduce India's total projected carbon emission by 1 billion tonnes by 2030** in the aspirations to become carbon neutral by 2070, **while as per United Nations, it is going to be the most populous country by 2028**. It is important to understand the equations between the targets and challenges we have been facing together. **Indian companies stand to lose Rs 7.14 lakh Crore to the impact of climate change** if they do not take mitigation measures over the next five years, according to the Carbon Disclosure Project's (CDP) 2020 annual report. **Indian Government has set a target to make India a 5 trillion-dollar economy by 2025, further to meet its goals of net-zero by 2070, India will need close to $10 Trillion**, according to an analysis by climate and energy research firm CEEW. Though some major companies in India have agreed to go carbon neutral by 2030 or so, but to achieve such environmental goals, the need of the support of companies beyond the top 1000 listed seems inevitable.

Due to the COVID-19 pandemic, the Indian economy was severely affected. According to the Reserve Bank of India, it will take over 12 years for the Indian economy to overcome the COVID-19 losses. In the recovery, investment in the Indian companies would definitely play an important role and to attract such investments, Indian companies would need to have **high ESG scores** as Investors are day by day becoming more interested in looking at the ESG factors of a company before investing and the first step towards having such high scores is to go for sustainability reporting. There has been a renewed focus on sustainability due to COVID-19.

Investors' awareness intensification has been supported by a research from Goldman Sachs, which has highlighted a 75% increase in the number of companies in the S&P 500 discussing key Environmental and Social terms from 2010 to 2017 on their earnings calls, with a peak of 41% from 2016 to 2017. Such interest led to great inflows of money to these types of sustainable products. According to Morningstar, assets under management in ESG funds have risen 60% from USD 655 billion in 2012 to USD 1.05 billion in October 2018.

The **Principles for Responsible Investment annual report 2021** shows that among 2771 signatories that were required to report to the PRI in 2021 (excluding new signatories), 82% of the reporting asset owners said they incorporated ESG factors into their selection, appointment, and monitoring processes and 86% reported implementing ESG requirements in their requests for proposals, investment management agreements, limited partnership agreements, and other appointment processes. As of 31 March 2021, the **collective Asset Under Management represented by all 3826 PRI signatories** (3404 investors and 422 service providers) **is just over US $121 Trillion**. Global investment based on ESG strategies stood at nearly $30.6 Trillion in 2018, and ESG assets are on track to exceed $53 trillion by 2025 and represent more than a third of the $140.5 Trillion in projected total Assets under Management (AuM), according to Bloomberg Intelligence. As per the DJSI (Dow Jones Sustainability Index), assessing the ESG performances of businesses on a global level has seen an increase in the participation rate by 33 per cent in 2021 against 19 per cent in 2019, which implies that businesses that generate higher profit margins could risk losing capital flows due to the low ESG scores. The data from Morningstar India shows that the fund size of ESG funds stood at Rs. 12,447 crore as of March 2022.

Not just for environmental and economic reasons, sustainable practices and disclosures are important, but such initiatives will also help **solving many social problems that India faces,** because to enhance the ESG score the companies would start working on these issues as a push factor. Inclusion of small businesses for sustainability reporting is needed **for instance, on the issue of unemployment, the inclusion of smaller companies is essential because globally, 50% of employment is generated through small businesses.** A Confederation of Indian Industry (CII) survey in 2019 reveals that the MSME sector created the most number of jobs in the country in the last four years. Removal of unemployment in itself leads to alleviation of other social issues like caste system, drug addiction, gendered violence/discrimination, poverty, malnutrition etc. ESG investing could also play an important role in advancing the **interests of the LGBTQ+ community**, especially when in India such people are discriminated against. For ascertaining the proper implementation of **Sexual Harassment of Women in workplace and other social justice causes, ESG will be helpful**. After the Puttaswamy Judgment, privacy has become a Fundamental Right and an important aspect of privacy is data privacy but **according to research by UK-based VPN company Surfshark, India stood third in the list of Countries with the greatest number of data breaches in 2021** and in the first quarter of 2022, India stands on the fifth position. To secure this right, ESG reporting by all companies will become important.

The letter G in ESG stands for governance so inevitably, corporate governance would be improved by compulsion of such reporting and disclosures. Governance focused corporates focus on accountability, transparency and corporate responsibility to balance business decisions and to serve multiple stakeholders equitably. Citing an example, due to poor management and bad financial decisions, Jet Airways worsened its financial position and officially shut down its services in April 2019 due to a lack of funds. If there had been a proper reporting framework, Jet Airways could have been saved. Jet Airways is one of the top 1000 listed companies and then also the governance was problematic, so one can easily assume the condition of governance in smaller companies, who are not obligated to go for Business Responsibility and Sustainability Reporting disclosures.

Going forward, Sustainability adoption and reporting is beneficial for the businesses in multiple ways. **In 2019, Accenture conducted a survey of more than 1,000 CEOs in 99 countries and 21 industries. They found that** just 26% of CEOs in 2019 cited "no clear link to business value" as a barrier to sustainability. In addition, 40% of CEOs said that sustainability is driving revenue growth and 35% realized value through cost reduction. Leaders said that an unprecedented shift in public expectations is driving them to get ahead on sustainability to build trust and competitiveness in their markets and 76% of CEOs say citizen trust will be critical to business competitiveness in their industry in the next five years. On the contrary, they found that only 21% of all surveyed CEOs feel business is currently playing a critical role in contributing to the Global Goals. **A report by Oxford University and Arabesque Partners "From the Stockholder to the Stakeholder" makes a compelling case for the fact that firms can as David Vogel says 'do well while doing good'**. An article titled 'Sustainability Assessment and Reporting for Non-profit Organizations: Accountability "for the Public Good"' explains why not just for-profit companies but non-profit organizations should also publish sustainability reports and how it is beneficial for them. In one of the **Mckinsey and Company's** podcast "inside the strategy room" episodes called **'Why is ESG here to stay', Robin Nuttall mentions that there have been more than 2,000 academic studies on ESG and financial performance, of which around 70% find a positive**

relationship between ESG scores on the one hand and financial returns. Women leaders would be a way to up ESG score and according to the International Finance Corporation, companies with more women board members were associated with better financial performance. On average, ASEAN companies that had boards with more than 30% female membership had an average return on equity of 6.2%, compared to 4.2% for companies with no women on the board.

There are several ESG reporting frameworks, some are generic like GRI while some are sector-specific and even investor/buyer-specific. In India it is observed that the companies publish about 10-20 ESG related reports to cater to sector-specific and buyer specific needs, etc., and there was no indigenously developed standard for ESG reporting until 2020, when Ministry of Corporate Affairs brought a report on Business Responsibility and Sustainability Reporting (BRSR), recommending for two types- lite and comprehensive, on which later, Securities Exchange Board of India (SEBI), issued the format. **BRSR is today seen as only proposed solution to these problems, its application actually being a solution is to be tested.** Apart from need of an Indian ESG reporting standard, assurance and auditing of these reports is also a need of the hour, to ensure reliability of the data, for which several **Indian companies go to foreign auditing firms which may lead deteriorating the image of the country as being non-serious about ESG along with outflow of money from India, which needs to be observed and quantified.**

Thus, a question arises as to effectiveness and efficiency of the ESG reporting and auditing framework pan-India, for which **there is a need to look into BRSR framework as a benchmark (in India and internationally) for ESG reporting; the scope of extending BRSR to companies beyond top 1000 listed companies and the ESG auditing framework in India.**

We see that these days the word **'Sustainable' is used as a prefix with every term within corporate eco-system**. Sustainable Human Resource, Sustainable Supply Chain, Sustainable Logistics, Sustainable Production, Sustainable Consumption, Sustainable Business, and Sustainable Development Goals also among others. Here the question arises, why it is so important to use 'sustainable' with everything we do, particularly in the context of Business. Sustainability is a business imperative and should be core to the strategy and operations of every business. The reasons for this are both ethical and financial. Government of India through Indian Institute of Corporate Affairs (IICA) which is an autonomous organization under the Ministry of Corporate Affairs, launched National Guidelines for Responsible Business Conduct (NGRBC) in 2019. The guidelines laid down the basic requirements for businesses to function responsibly, thereby ensuring a wholesome and inclusive process of economic growth.

The overarching nine principles of the guidelines have been linked to the UNGPs and SDGs. The NGRBC urges businesses to conduct business responsibly and sustainably and to encourage and support their suppliers, vendors, distributors, partners and other stakeholders to adopt the guidelines. The NGRBC is designed to be a common framework for all businesses irrespective of their size, scope, sector, ownership, structure or location. It has been designed in such a way that every business in India, including SMEs, can easily adopt the guidelines and put them into practice. Based on the NGRBCs, SEBI has introduced the Business Responsibility and Sustainability Reposting (BRSR) Framework and has also mandated it on top 1000 listed companies (by market capitalization). It is of significance that BRSRs owing to their adoption of NGRBC principles include and recognise some of the salient issues in the Indian context. Value chain, labour welfare, and women's participation in economic activity - recognised as the three key pillars for inclusive development - are within the influence of companies and have been explicitly emphasised in the proposed BRSR formats. Also, Sustainable production, with a focus on raw material procurement, waste disposal, and recycling are recognised challenges and has been incorporated into the BRSR.

The growing salience of non-financial disclosures along with the annual financial disclosures ensures that businesses explicitly recognise their environmental and social responsibilities. In the Indian context, National Guidelines on Responsible Business Conduct sets the foundation for understanding responsible business conduct.

Indian Institute of Corporate Affairs (IICA), a think tank under the Ministry of Corporate Affairs, Govt. of India through its School of Business Environment has been working in the areas of Responsible Business-related aspects by supporting to the Governments, Corporates and other stakeholders in policy, advocacy, research and capacity building initiatives. School of Business Environment in IICA has recently launched Certified ESG Professional: Impact Leader Programmes, and other courses in Strategic CSR and Business and Human Rights. IICA also is in process of developing sector specific guidelines for adaptation of NGRBC. Ministry of Corporate Affairs with the IICA has developed Zeroth Draft of National Action Plan on the subject matter by compiling the existing laws, policies, orders, etc. which will facilitate the businesses for respecting the human rights and complying with the various laws.

The Securities and Exchange Board of India (SEBI) has mandated Business Responsibility and Sustainability (BRSR) reporting on top 1000 listed companies by market capitalization. The foundation of BRSR is inspired by the Ministry of Corporate Affairs' Report on Business Responsibility Reporting (BRR) and National Guidelines on Responsible Business Conduct (NGRBC). In the sphere of Corporate Social Responsibility (CSR), the Ministry of Corporate Affairs has introduced a legislation under section 135 of the Companies Act, 2013 with effect from 1st April 2014. To facilitate and incentivise corporates for complying with CSR provisions in true spirit, MCA has launched the National CSR Data Portal to reflect the Government commitment towards leveraging digital technology for smart governance.. Good governance of corporates requires a constant emphasis on ethics, transparency and accountability in the operations of corporates. With this objective, the Ministry of Corporate Affairs has mandated various disclosures by the corporates, defined specific service standards so as to ensure accountability of corporates to all stakeholders. The Ministry of Corporate Affairs has facilitated ease of doing business in the country by strengthening the enforcement framework. Government lays strong emphasis on the reinforcement of 'minimal government & maximum governance', public trust and ease of doing business. The Government has repealed over 25000 compliances and nearly 1500 union laws. Next phases will include initiatives like Ease of Doing Business (EoDB 2.0) and Ease of Living and the government following the goal of 'trust-based governance' to improve the productive efficiency of capital and human resources.

Among many other initiatives of the Government Lifestyle for Environment (Mission LIFE) is also one of the important initiatives of Govt. of India through the NITI Aayog. It is an India led global mass movement to nudge individual and community action to protect and preserve environment. It is also a time when we all should start looking beyond the SDGs, the post 2030 agenda.

A country's collective performance in ESG is positively linked with per capita GDP also, Hon'ble Finance Minister of India in the budget for 2022-2023 demonstrated a continuing effort by the Government of India towards a more sustainable resilient economy. The underlying objective of the Government is also to create a space where India emerges as one of the fastest growing nations in the world to integrating a strong ESG framework across industries while aligning with the 17 UN Sustainable Development Goals. Government encourages the ESG propaganda which projects a framework of global acceptance, making India a liberal and attractive nation for trade and global supply chains.

Our Hon'ble Prime Minister Shri Narendra Modi announced the 'Amrit Kaal' for the nation on 75th Independence Day celebration under Azadi Ka Amrit Mahotsava. Government's aim to fulfil vision India@100 by achieving specified milestones in Amrit Kaal includes - Focus on growth and all inclusive welfare, promoting technology development, energy transition and climate action, virtuous cycle starting from private investment, crowded in by public capital investment.

There have been various national and international developments in the past decade that have nudged businesses to be sustainable and more responsible. There is also a demand from the investors, consumers, and communities at large for the businesses to be responsible. Businesses' responsibility towards various internal and external stakeholders, ethical and transparent procedures in supply chains and production processes, responsible branding etc. are some of the issues businesses are more actively considering to incorporate these days.

Global and National legislative compliances also encourage companies to adopt responsible practices in various dimensions like labour, human rights, environment, consumers related, community concerns, employee wellbeing, etc. Government of India's commitment towards inclusive development incorporating social and ecological wellbeing and promoting responsible business conduct may be seen through various initiatives of the Ministry of Corporate Affairs.

India is one of the fastest growing emerging market economies with a young population and burgeoning innovation and business ecosystem. India strives to become a USD 5 trillion economy by 2025, to achieve this goal as well as to achieve the Sustainable Development Goals by 2030, it is important to focus on environment, inclusive and equitable development particularly in the era of climate crisis. Business organizations' responsible conduct is key to achieve these goals.

7.2 Contemporary issues that impact the future of businesses

We have discussed a lot of issues pertaining to the ESG in this book, in this chapter also certain specific data and trends have been presented. Broad trends for businesses which are addressed through the ESG Framework includes as under:

- Climate Crisis - Impact on Business
- Natural Resources Scarcity - water, forest produce, minerals
- Growing Inequality
- Increasingly Unmanageable Pollution - water, air and solid waste
- Informalisation of the workforce
- Each of these will be discussed in detail

7.2.1 Climate Change Impacts on business

Climate change is one of the most critical global challenges of our times. Below are some of the Climate Change effects:

Extreme weather events

Droughts, floods, cyclones & storms, heat & cold waves are very likely to become frequent and unpredictable as weather patterns change. Modelling studies show for instance that in the state of Gujarat, annual rainfall may increase slightly over time but the number of rainy days will reduce; this could result in floods (as the same quantity of rain falls in a fewer number of days) and droughts as the number of dry days increase. The signs are already there - floods in Chennai, Uttarakhand, Mumbai with increasing frequency, super-cyclones in Odisha, forest fires etc.

Sea level rise

As global temperature rise, the melting of glaciers will accelerate. And this will result in sea-levels rising and the submergence of coastal areas (the Sundarbans for example) and island states (such as neighbouring Maldives). This process has already begun and cities like New York are already contemplating build sea-walls even as its President dismisses Climate Change as a hoax!

Threat to food security

As temperatures rise, agriculture yields tend to drop and pest attacks tend to increase. Taken together with the impacts of extreme weather events discussed above, the agriculture productivity in countries like India is expected to drop significantly, thus impacting its food security. At the same time, countries in the temperate regions are likely to see productivity increases and the possibility of a second crop as the weather turns tropical.

Ocean acidification

The earth's oceans are a big sink for CO_2 and this enables marine life to flourish. However, the greater CO_2 absorption makes it more difficult for marine organisms, such as coral and some plankton, to form their shells and skeletons, and existing shells may begin to dissolve.

Biodiversity loss

The rapidity of the increase in CO_2 concentration does not allow ecosystems to adapt fully. This is further exacerbated by fragmented habitats due to human action and all of this is accelerating habitat loss and species extinction.

7.2.2 Natural Resources Scarcity and its Impact on Business

Water

Freshwater only makes 2.5% of the total volume of the world's water, which is about 35 million km3. But considering 70% of that freshwater is in the form of ice and permanent snow cover and that we only have access to

200,000 km3 of freshwater overall, it isn't surprising that demand for water could soon exceed supply.

Oil and Natural gas

The fear of reaching peak oil continues to haunt the oil industry. The BP Statistical Review of World Energy in June measured total global oil at 188.8 million tonnes, from proved oil resources at the end of 2010. This is only enough to oil for the next 46.2 years, should global production remain at the current rate. A similar picture to oil exists for natural gas, with enough gas in proven reserves to meet 58.6 years of global production at the end of 2010.

Phosphorus

Without this element, plants cannot grow. Essential for fertiliser, phosphate rock is only found in a handful of countries, including the US, China and Morocco. With the need to feed 7 billion people, scientists from the Global Phosphorus Research Initiative predict we could run out of phosphorus in 50 to 100 years unless new reserves of the element are found.

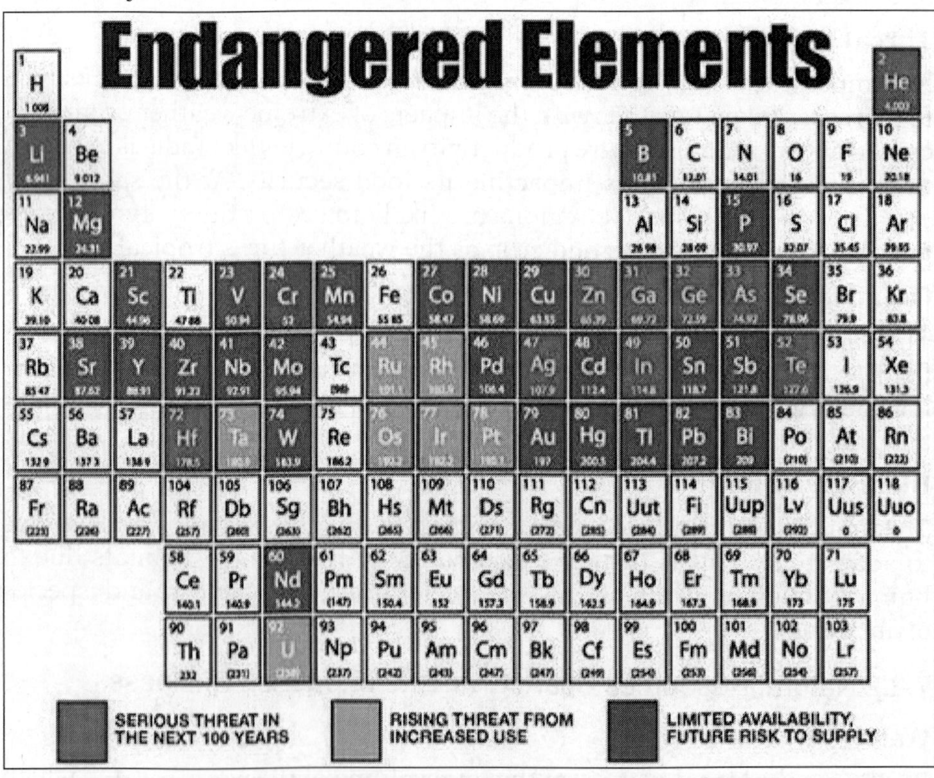

(Source: Chemistry Innovation Knowledge Transfer Network)

Figure 7.1: Endangered elements

Studies show that nearly 40% of the 118 elements that are used in manufacturing various products by businesses - from the chemist's arsenal to a variety of consumer products, are facing depleting supplies. The analysis by Mike Pitts revealed that 44 of such rare elements are facing limited supply, or are under the threat of becoming scarce or inaccessible. These include all of the rare earth elements, as well as zinc, gallium, germanium, helium, silver, and even phosphorus. We also observe that Scandium and terbium are just two of the 17 rare earth minerals that are used in everything from the powerful magnets in wind turbines to the electronic circuits in smartphones.

Mike Pitts, Chemistry Innovation Knowledge Transfer Network, UK, has developed a new type of periodic table to show the availability and distribution of the elements in nature and to indicate which elements are at risk and may become scarce, as shown in the figure above.

7.2.3 Growing Inequality

Since the human life emerged on the planet earth, lot of development in multiple spheres has been witnessed. When human race took its existence on the planet, almost all the human could have been equal in terms of ownership on earth's resources. But gradually, humans identified their needs for better living and also started living in the groups. This resulted in requirement of basic necessities through dependency on inter-group dynamics. Humans also identified their core skills and started working accordingly, some identified their skills in growing food grains, others in making huts and etc. This was the phase which resulted in birth of the barter system. Gradually, industries took place and started organized productions of required commodities and services. We are grown rapidly in the science and technology, information technology, social patterns, industrial development, artificial intelligence and other related innovations and advancements.

With these innovations and technological advancements, few people or groups were able to cope-up and accumulated maximum resources available on earth, while some others were deprived from minimal required resources for their survival. We developed different types of socio-political system in different parts of the globe. The systems we created for ourselves were expected to provide equality, economic and social justice to each one of us. We will not discuss here pros and cons of the socio-political systems, but the fact is that those inequalities continued and grown more rapidly.

Today, we see that inequalities can be viewed from different perspectives, all of which are related. Most common metric is *Income Inequality*, which refers to the extent to which income is evenly distributed within a population. Related concepts are *lifetime Inequality* (inequality in incomes for an individual over his or her lifetime), *Inequality of Wealth* (distribution of wealth across households or individuals at a moment in time), and *Inequality of Opportunity* (impact on income of circumstances over which individuals have no control, such as family socio-economic status, gender, or ethnic background). All of these inequality concepts are related and offer different yet complementary insights into the causes and consequences of inequality, hence providing better guidance to governments when designing specific policies aimed at addressing inequality.

According to the International Monetary Fund, over the past three decades, more than half of the countries and close to 90 per cent of advanced economies have seen an increase in income inequality, as measured with the Gini coefficient. We may discuss and compare the income inequalities through different perspectives like the income inequality between countries, income inequality within countries etc.

Apart from the income inequalities, we also consider inequality of opportunities, growing inequalities due to climate change and urbanization, gender pay gap, vulnerability of differently-abled persons, inequality within households, uneven progress of women and girls.

Despite progress in some regions, income and wealth are increasingly concentrated at the top. An Oxfam report shows that in the 10 years since the financial crisis, the number of billionaires has nearly doubled, and the fortunes of the world's super-rich have reached record levels. In 2018, the 26 richest people in the world held as much wealth as half of the global population (the 3.8 billion poorest people).

According to the United Nations, inequalities are not only driven and measured by income, but are determined by other factors - gender, age, origin, ethnicity, disability, sexual orientation, class and religion. These factors determine inequalities of opportunity which continue to persist, within and between countries. In some parts of the world, these divides are becoming more pronounced. Meanwhile, gaps in newer areas, such as access to online and mobile technologies are emerging. The result is a complex mix of internal and external challenges that will continue to grow over the next twenty-five years.

Today, wherever people live, they don't have to look far to confront inequalities. Inequality in its various forms is an issue that will define our time. Confronting inequalities has moved to the forefront of many global policy debates as a consensus has emerged that all should enjoy equal access to opportunity. '**Leave no one behind**' serves as the rallying cry of the 2030 Agenda for Sustainable Development.

7.2.4 Increasingly Unmanageable Pollution - water, air and solid waste

According to the World Bank, industrialization, use of pesticides and nitrogen-based fertilizers, crop residues in agriculture, urbanization, forest fires, desert dust, and inadequate waste management have intensified environmental health risks and pollution, especially in low- and middle-income countries.

At the same time, the global economy relies on deeply intertwined supply chains, sustained by more than 100 billion tons of raw materials entering the system each year. Intensive material consumption depletes natural resources and causes negative environmental impacts at every stage of the product lifecycle including production, use phase, and end-of-life. Global waste is expected to increase to 3.4 billion tons by 2050.

According to the European Environment Agency, globally, levels of air pollution and releases of nutrients from agriculture and wastewater remain high, causing acidification and eutrophication in ecosystems, and losses in agricultural yield. In the coming decades, overall pollution levels are projected to increase strongly, particularly in Asia. Pollution is linked to three main human activities: Fossil-fuel combustion, primarily by industry and transport; the application of synthetic fertilisers and pesticides in agriculture; and the growing use and complexity of chemicals.

Air Pollution

Air pollution is the leading environmental risk to health, causing 7 million premature deaths each year.

This is equivalent to the number of people that have died from COVID-19 since March 2020.

A World Bank publication found that air pollution cost the globe an estimated $8.1 trillion in 2019, equivalent to 6.1 per cent of global GDP. More than 95 per cent of deaths caused by air pollution occur in low- and middle- income countries. In individual countries, the economic burden of pollution associated with premature mortality and morbidity is also significant, equivalent to 5 to 14 per cent of countries' GDPs.

Air pollution is the leading environmental risk to health, causing 7 million premature deaths each year.

The figure below depicts Historical and projected trends in ozone concentrations for Europe, North America, East and South Asia, from year 1950 to 2050.

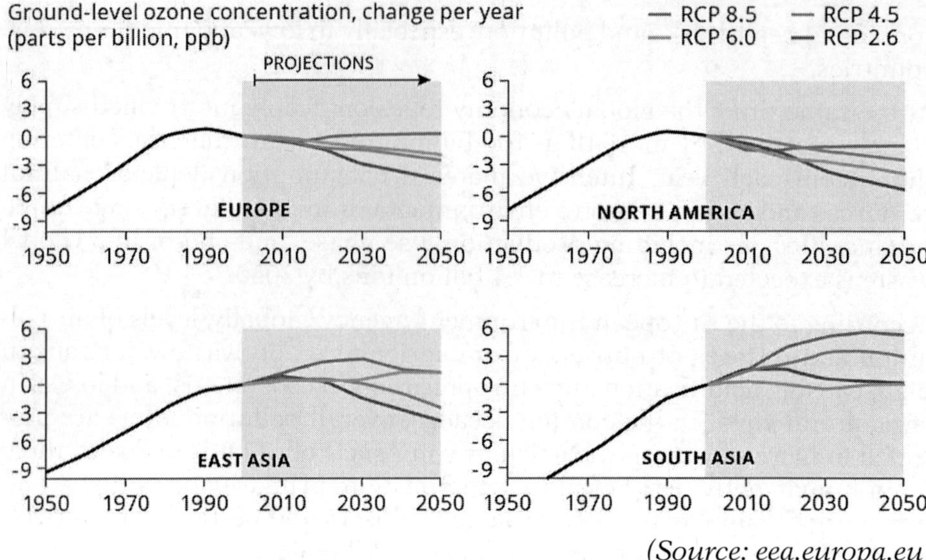

(Source: eea.europa.eu)

Figure 7.2: Future changes in anthropogenic precursor emissions

Water Pollution

Water pollution is the contamination of water sources by substances which make the water unusable for drinking, cooking, cleaning, swimming, and other activities. Pollutants include chemicals, trash, bacteria and parasites. All forms of pollution eventually make their way to water. Air pollution settles onto lakes and oceans. Land pollution can seep into an underground stream, then to a river, and finally to the ocean. Thus, waste dumped in a vacant lot can eventually pollute a water supply. Oil pollution, Radioactive substances, Sewage and wastewater, and Agricultural are the key cause of water pollution.

This widespread problem of water pollution is jeopardizing our health. Unsafe water kills more people each year than war and all other forms of violence combined. Meanwhile, our drinkable water sources are finite: Less than 1 per cent of the earth's freshwater is actually accessible to us. Without action, the challenges will only increase by 2050, when global demand for freshwater is expected to be one-third greater than it is now.

Both industrial and agricultural activities have contributed to water contamination in India. Discharge of untreated or inadequately treated industrial effluents into water bodies leads to the contamination of surface and groundwater sources.

As per the Central Pollution Control Board (CPCB), 61 percent of urban sewage is discharged into rivers and other water bodies without treatment. The Yamuna River in Delhi, for example, receives substantial pollution from domestic sewage and industrial waste, leading to severe contamination.

Ganga is one of the most polluted rivers in the world. About 80 per cent of the pollution in the river comes from untreated domestic sewage and industrial effluents.

Groundwater contamination is impacting both rural and urban areas. A study by the CPCB reported that 276 districts in India have groundwater contaminated with fluoride, arsenic, and nitrate beyond the permissible limits. Excessive use of chemical fertilizers and pesticides in agriculture contributes to groundwater pollution. Industrial activities release various pollutants into ground water and water bodies, contributing to water pollution.

Solid-Waste Pollution

Solid waste contamination occurs when solid wastes are present in the environment (air, water and soil), making them less suitable or unsuitable for living creatures. Solid waste pollution is also caused by spoiled agricultural and dairy products from farmers, orchards and dairies.

Some of the examples of Solid Waste are Tyres, Scrap metal, Demolition, wastes, Asbestos, Vehicle Scraps, Electronic appliances etc. Some of the major factors that contribute to solid waste pollution are Commercial establishments, Residential houses, Debris from construction and demolition, Debris from roads (such as asphalt and scrap metal), Scrap from vehicles, and Agriculture. Apart from these improper waste management is also one of the causes of solid waste pollution.

The solid waste management sector in India has witnessed significant growth in recent years due to the government's push towards cleanliness and sanitation. Increasing population and rapid urbanization have resulted in a substantial increase in the amount of waste generated, leading to the need for efficient and sustainable waste management practices. The government's Swachh Bharat Abhiyan (Clean India Mission) has provided a boost to the sector, resulting in a surge in demand for waste management solutions. The market for solid waste management in India is expected to grow at a CAGR of 7.5% during the forecast period (2021-2026), driven by factors such as increasing urbanization, rising awareness of waste management, and growing investments in waste management infrastructure.

A study featured in the Journal of Urban Management (December 2021) reports that the 62 MT of waste generated annually includes 7.9 MT of hazardous waste, 5.6 MT of plastic waste, 1.5 MT of e-waste, and 0.17 MT of biomedical waste. The Indian Central Pollution Control Board (CPCB) recently projected that annual waste generation in India will increase to 165 MT by 2030. Hazardous, plastic, e-waste, and bio-medical waste generated is expected to increase proportionately, as well.

7.2.5 Informalisation of the workforce

The informalisation of the Workforce refers to a situation where the workforce in the informal sector increases to the total workforce of the country. According to the composition of the workforce in India, it has been divided into two categories, Formal or Organised Sector and Informal or Unorganised Sector.

According to the International Labour Organisation approximately 60 per cent of the world's population participates in the informal sector. Although this is mostly prevalent in emerging and developing economies, it is also an important part of advanced economies. In developing countries like India, a large share of the population typically depends upon the informal economy.

Majority of Work Force in India is estimated 450 million informal workers comprise 90% of its total workforce, with 5-10 million workers added annually.

According to a report, the practical realities are that informal workers work under worse working conditions with little job security, deprived of perks or protections and with low wages. The protections guaranteed to workers under different legislations are difficult to comply with by the informal sector, and they also escape the purview of the monitoring. Recent Initiatives taken by Government are as under:

Atmanirbhar Bharat Abhiyan

Atmanirbhar Bharat Abhiyan (or Self-reliant India Mission) with an economic stimulus package — worth Rs. 20 lakh crores aimed towards cutting down import dependence by focussing on substitution while improving safety compliance and quality goods to gain global market share.

Labour Codes: The Parliament passed three labour codes - on industrial relations; occupational safety, health and working conditions; and social security - proposing to simplify the country's archaic labour laws and give impetus to economic activity without compromising with the workers' benefits. The new labour codes that have been passed by parliament to take care of the informal urban segment of the informal economy *i.e.* the gig economy, workers now are the worst affected in a pandemic like situation.

E-Shram Portal: The Ministry of Labour & Employment has developed e-Shram portal for creating a National Database of Unorganized Workers (NDUW) for optimum realization of their employability and extend the benefits of the social security schemes to them. It is the first-ever national database of unorganised workers including migrant workers, construction workers, gig and platform workers, etc.

Udyam Portal: It is the only Government Portal for registration of MSME (Udyam). The Ministry of Micro, Small and Medium Enterprises maintains this portal. It gives the details and steps relating to registration and makes the registration process easy for any person. It provides free of cost and paperless registration.

Pradhan Mantri Shram Yogi Maan-dhan: PM-SYM is a Central Sector Scheme administered by the Ministry of Labour and Employment and implemented through Life Insurance Corporation of India and Community Service Centers (CSCs). This scheme seeks to benefit around 42 crore workers from the unorganized sector of the country.

PM SVANidhi: The Ministry of Housing and Urban Affairs (MoHUA) has launched Pradhan Mantri Street Vendor's Atma Nirbhar Nidhi (PM SVANidhi), for providing affordable loans to street vendors. The scheme would benefit vendors, hawkers, thelewale and people involved in goods and services related to textiles, apparel, artisan products, barbers shops, laundry services etc. in different areas.

MGNREGA

MGNREGA is one of the largest work guarantee programmes in the world. The primary objective of the scheme is to guarantee 100 days of employment in every financial year to adult members of any rural household willing to do public work-related unskilled manual work. Unlike earlier employment guarantee schemes, the act aims at addressing the causes of chronic poverty through a rights-based framework.

Deendayal Antyodaya Yojana National Urban Livelihoods Mission: The mission was launched in 2014 and is being implemented by the Ministry of Housing & Urban Affairs. It aims to uplift urban poor by enhancing sustainable livelihood opportunities through skill development and other such initiatives.

One Nation One Ration Card: The government of India introduced the One Nation One Ration Card Scheme (ONORC). ONORC allows a beneficiary to access his food entitlements from anywhere in India irrespective of the place where the ration card is registered.

Though several measures have been taken by the Government of India to provide social security to informal sector workers, various schemes and provisions in the law have been introduced, their effective implementation is to be ensured.

7.2.6 Impact on Businesses

Now we will try to understand how the issues discussed above may adversely impact businesses. There are different perspectives to look at different issues and challenges, for examples extreme heat conditions will make it very difficult for workers to maintain productivity and likely to increase the possibility of heat strokes, both of which will impact business outputs. Drought-like conditions, which will be exacerbated by climate change, may result in factories that depend upon water to run below capacity during the pre-monsoon months, a situation that some already face at present. Floods, cyclones and sea-level rise will impact business continuity. Industry sectors that depend upon agriculture produce as a raw material (tea, coffee, food processing to name a few) will find themselves very vulnerable. And as all these effects will significantly impact communities, especially those that are marginalised and excluded, regulations may become tighter.

At the same time, Climate Change also offers new business opportunities. Several businesses such as renewable energy and electric vehicles (EVs) to name have grown immensely as a result of the negative consequences of burning fossil fuels; that they also have a positive impact on pollution is an important co-benefit. The market for a whole range of decarbonisation saving solutions has also grown in response to climate crisis.

Looking from the investors' perspectives, Global sustainability challenges such as flood risk and rising sea levels, privacy and data security, demographic shifts, and regulatory pressures, are introducing new risk factors for investors that may not have been seen previously. As companies face rising complexity on a global scale, investors tend to revisit traditional investment approaches and are moving towards ESG based investments.

7.3 ESG Today

We have seen the evolution of Sustainable Development related initiatives through some of the important events in the history like - the United Nations Sustainable Development Summit New York, United Nations Conference on Sustainable Development Rio+20 Rio de Janeiro, the World Summit on Sustainable Development Rio+10 Johannesburg, the Millennium Summit New York, the Earth Summit Rio de Janerio, and the Brundtland Commission Report-Our Common Future. However, the concept of ESG emerged as inclined towards a more focused financially relevant investment discipline affecting the environment, society and corporate governance. Considering ESG specific conceptual evolution, we had studied the Socially Responsible Investing (SRI), the Community Reinvestment Act (CRA), Forum for Sustainable and Responsible Investment, Who Cares Wins, and Principles for Responsible Investment (PRI).

Today, not only from the perspective of investors but different stakeholders put pressure on businesses to be responsible towards their actions and impact. Though the ESG was adopted as a framework to report Sustainability Initiatives and Impacts by Businesses for attracting investments, but its role and scope has broadened in past few years. In today's 'Age of Responsibility', it is a prerequisite for businesses to be responsible towards their actions and impact. ESG Provides a framework by which Businesses adopt, integrate, implement, monitor, measure, and report their ESG initiatives and impacts to a wider stakeholder group.

Sustainable Development is Fundamental Right of the people. The Supreme Court of India held that sustainable development is to be treated as an integral part of life under article 21 of the Constitution of India. Hence, complying with the principle of sustainable development is a constitutional mandate. Today ESG has also become an unwritten mandate for companies. Not only global investors and buyers demand businesses to adopt sustainable practices in the business value chains but the customers also demand products and services which have sustainable background. Sustainability is not limited to protection of environment as it is generally understood but it consists of social and governance aspects of company's performance too.

ESG principles became more integrated into business strategies, with growing recognition of their importance for long-term financial performance and societal impact.

Today, not only the businesses but the Governments, quasi-Government organizations and other organizations are also intending to adopt ESG. The landscape of ESG regulation intensified, with initiatives like the EU's Corporate Sustainability Reporting Directive (CSRD) and initiatives from the International Sustainability Standards Board (ISSB)'s IFRS S1 and S2. ESG factors plays a more prominent role in investment decisions, leading to significant flows of capital towards sustainable companies and technologies. Every major public policy issue is potentially coming under the umbrella of ESG.

7.4 The Way Ahead

We have divided and presented the discussion on the ESG way ahead in following sub-topics:

7.4.1 Concept of Sustainability Champions

To revolutionize the Responsible Business Conduct or adoption of ESG Framework into the core business philosophy and action, several measures have been envisaged. One of those is to prepare and promote the sustainability champions. There are two dimensions of this discussion, one at individual level within a company and another identifying the companies and MSMEs as sustainability champions. While we talk about identifying sustainability champions within a company, we propose nurturing the identified employees in the specialised or generic domains of ESG, prepare a policy in the company for capacity building of employees on ESG, rewarding the good ESG practices by way of competitive spirit. On the other hand, promotion of the companies and MSMEs is equally important.

7.4.2 From Becoming a Great Leader to Becoming a Green Leader

Leadership plays a pivotal role in achieving excellence. When the world is facing unprecedented challenges which are important to address to survive life on the planet earth, role of leaders become more pertinent. Leaders in all walks of life need to adopt ESG principles into their core actions and interventions. ESG is pertinent not only of business leaders but also to the Government agencies, Non-governmental organizations and other such entities. Until a shift from normal way of living to ESG way of living is adopted, the goals of the sustainability are hard to achieve. The ESG way of leadership is coined here as Green Leadership. While a leader takes initiatives to preserves and restore the environment, make efforts to ensure social justice and follows responsible governance practices, the leader may be termed as a Green Leader. In the times to come, this concept and practice needs to be promoted so as to achieve the organizational goals of being responsible as well as being profitable.

7.4.3 Connecting Indian Entities to Global Business

Indian entities need to be responsible, they have to adopt responsible business conduct, only then they may compete the global business requirements. Being responsible is not a choice now it is an unwritten mandate. Investors, Buyers and Customers progressively demand the companies to be more responsible towards environment, society and economy. Standard governance practices are also expected from them.

Ministry of Corporate Affairs has issued National Guidance on Responsible Business Conduct (NGRBC) which is an extension of the National Voluntary Guidelines on Social, economic and Environmental Responsibilities of Business. The NGRBC has been mandated as Business Responsibility and Sustainability Reporting (BRSR) by SEBI on 1000 listed companies. More and more such initiatives in India will attract global investors, buyers and customers.

Problems being faced by businesses operating in India are that they have to follow compliances under various International Standards on Sustainability, different buyers and investors have different requirements in different Industry sectors. India lacks its own generic as well as sector specific globally recognized sustainability standards.

To connect the Indian entities to Global business, it is important that world sees India's commitment towards responsible business conduct. For this, such Indian origin standards are prerequisite. A mechanism for ESG/Sustainability self-assessment, assurance, audit, rating and index is need of hour. School of Business Environment, Indian Institute of Corporate Affairs under the aegis of the Ministry of Corporate Affairs is actively working on these aspects.

7.4.4 The Ethical Way of Living - Key to collective responsible behaviour

As we have studies in the "New Theory of Responsibility" and "Solar System Model of ESG" propounded in this book, reflect on how the ethics or ethical behaviour are at the core of responsible conduct. This responsible conduct is also seen at the level of the organizations or businesses and hence called the Responsible Business Conduct. Here we reiterate how a person who follows and imbibe ethical conduct and values becomes responsible towards every action he or she takes. We have seen that organizational responsibilities in terms of Environment, Social and Governance are discharged collectively by ethically oriented individuals coupled with the right intent policies, rules and norms in an organization. In that context, ethically motivated individuals both at the level of leadership roles as well as those who implement the policies, play an important role in discharging organizational responsibilities of E, S & G.

7.4.5 The Last Word "Ubuntu"

Ubuntu is an African philosophy that places emphasis on '**being human through other people**'. It has been succinctly reflected in the phrase - **I am because of who we all are**. One cannot be happy until other are suffering is the key essence. As individuals also, we have a great responsibility on our shoulders, until individual mindsets don't change, massive revolutions are challenging. All of us also have to discharge our Individual Responsibilities only than our country will be prosperous and will attain goals of inclusive and sustainable development.

7.4.6 Towards a new beginning

As we enter in the new era of responsibility, we have more and more responsibilities to discharge as per our positioning in our individual and organizational lives. To cater these needs the authors have already started writing upcoming books on ESG Disclosure requirements and Role of Leadership in adopting and implementing ESG framework. These books are mere a guiding aid to the motivated individual to adopt the frameworks required to sustain a fulfilling life and existence of planet earth. Being in the corporate sector, our role becomes more prominent in designing such policies, strategies, plans and targets for our businesses which not only contribute to the goals of Environmental-Social-Governance but also positively contribute in the growth of the business in multifold manner.

We would like to thank our readers for continuously trusting us and providing positive feedbacks on our earlier books, 'Benchmarking ESG & CSR: a Compendium of Best Practices in Environmental-Social-Governance and Corporate Social Responsibility', and 'Exploring Corporate Social Responsibility: Fundamentals and Implementation'. We trust that the present piece of writing 'Demystifying ESG: A Comprehensive Guide for Environmental-Social-Governance Integration and Practice' will also serve as per the expectations of the readers and will help in your journey to adopt, integrate and practice ESG.

*- **Dadhich & Atrey***

The end is a new beginning...

BIBLIOGRAPHY AND REFERENCES

Acaroglu, L. (2018, April). *How do ESG and Sustainability Fit Together?* Retrieved from medium.com: https://medium.com/disruptive-design/how-do-esg-and-sustainability-fit-together-f8d91b605003

Akash. (2023, April 03). *ESG in Action: Case Studies of Companies Making a Difference*. Retrieved from vakilsearch.com.

Alpha Sense. (2023, May 8). *How to Use Alpha Sense for ESG Benchmarking*. Retrieved from www.alpha-sense.com: https://www.alpha-sense.com/blog/product/how-to-esg-benchmarking/

Amendment to Schedule VII of the Companies Act, 2013 (2014, October 24). G.S.R. Notification, Ministry of Corporate Affairs, Government of India.

Amity Institute of Social Sciences, Amity University. (2017). *Conference Proceedings of the National Social Work Conference.* Noida: Author.

Anand, S. (2023, May 18). *Less than a third of Indian businesses confident of ESG preparedness: Deloitte Survey.* Retrieved from livemint.com: https://www.livemint.com/news/india/deloitte-india-s-esg-preparedness-survey-only-27-of-indian-businesses-feel-confident-about-meeting-esg-requirements-11684405627826.html

Anand, S. (2023, November 17). *India tightens climate goals with new carbon credit trading compliance draft*. Retrieved from energy.economictimes.indiatimes.com: https://energy.economictimes.indiatimes.com/news/renewable/india-tightens-climate-goals-with-new-carbon-credit-trading-compliance-draft/105275822

Ansari, S. (2023, May 25). *Procurement Perspectives: Traditional vs. Leading Approaches.* Retrieved from linkedin.com: https://www.linkedin.com/pulse/procurement-perspectives-traditional-vs-leading-the-procurementholic/?utm_source=share&utm_medium=member_android&utm_campaign=share_via

Assets of ESG funds rise 5x in four years to Rs. 12,450 crore, shows data. (n.d.). Business News, Finance News, India News, BSE/NSE News, Stock Markets News, Sensex NIFTY, Budget 2022. https://www.business-standard.com/article/markets/assets-of-esg-funds-rise-5x-in-four-years-to-rs-12-450-crore-shows-data-122042400997_1.html.

Atrey, R. R. (2012). *ISO 26000 - Theory and Practice.* In Mittal, S. (Ed.), CSR and Competitiveness. New Delhi: Allied Publishers.

Atrey, R. R. (2017). *Exploring Corporate Social Responsibility - Fundamentals and Implementations.* New Delhi: Studera Press.

Atrey, R. R. (2020). *Exploring Corporate Social Responsibility - Fundamentals and Implementations, 2nd Edition.* New Delhi: Studera Press.

Atrey R. R. (2020). Corporate Social Responsibility (CSR) in Indian Context: An analysis of relevant provisions of the Companies Act, International and National Instruments, Theories and Models. International Journal of Social Science and Economic Research, 5(7), 1748-1773.

Axel Gosseries, Gaëll Mainguy. (2008). Retrieved from journals.openedition.org: https://journals.openedition.org/sapiens/165?lang=en

Baruah, A. (2023, June 18). *ESG metrics of IT services companies turn crucial in winning deals*. Retrieved from business-standard.com: https://www.business-standard.com/companies/news/esg-metrics-of-it-companies-turning-crucial-in-winning-deals-123061800428_1.html

BBC News. (2016, October 2). *India ratifies Paris climate agreement*. Retrieved from bbc.com: https://www.bbc.com/news/world-asia-india-37536348

BBC News. (2021, November 2). *COP26: India PM Narendra Modi pledges net zero by 2070.* Retrieved from COP26: India PM Narendra Modi pledges net zero by 2070: https://www.bbc.com/news/world-asia-india-59125143

BDC. (n.d.). *What is ESG and what does it mean for your business?* Retrieved from www.bdc.ca: https://www.bdc.ca/en/articles-tools/sustainability/environment/what-esg-and-what-does-mean-business

Board Gender Diversity in ASEAN. (n.d.). International Finance Corporation. https://www.ifc.org/wps/wcm/connect/21f19cfe-9cce-4089-bfc1-e4c38767394e/Board_Gender_Diversity_in_ASEAN.pdf?MOD=AJPERES.

Bosselmann, K. E. (2008). *Governance for sustainability : issues, challenges, successes*. Retrieved from iucn.org: https://www.iucn.org/resources/publication/governance-sustainability-issues-challenges-successes#:~:text=Governance%20for%20sustainability%20is%20defined,of%20globalization%2C%20democracy%20and%20sustainability

Bureau of Energy Efficiency. *Detailed Procedure for Compliance Mechanism under CCTS.* Bureau of Energy Efficiency.

Business Responsibility & Sustainability Reporting Format. (2021, May 10). Securities and Exchange Board of India. https://www.sebi.gov.in/sebi_data/commondocs/may-2021/Business%20responsibility%20and%20sustainability%20reporting%20by%20listed%20entitiesAnnexure1_p.PDF

Business Standard. (2022, April 24). *Assets of ESG funds rise 5x in four years to Rs. 12,450 crore, shows data.* Retrieved from Business-standard.com: https://www.business-standard.com/article/markets/assets-of-esg-funds-rise-5x-in-four-years-to-rs-12-450-crore-shows-data-122042400997_1.html

BYJU'S. (2023). *List of Environment Conventions & Protocols*. Retrieved from byjus.com: https://byjus.com/free-ias-prep/environment-conventions-protocols/

BYJU'S. (2023). *National Action Plan on Business and Human Rights*. Retrieved from byjus.com: https://byjus.com/free-ias-prep/national-action-plan-business-human-rights/

Byrne, D. (2023). *What is ESG benchmarking?* Retrieved from thecorporategovernanceinstitute.com: https://www.thecorporategovernanceinstitute.com/insights/lexicon/what-is-esg-benchmarking/

Campbell, M. (2022, July 14). *What is the G in ESG: Governance Explained*. Retrieved from vationventures.com: https://www.vationventures.com/research-article/the-g-in-esg

CDP India. (2021). *Disclosure: Imperative For a Sustainable India CDP India Disclosure Report 2021.* India: CDP India.

CDP India Disclosure Report 2021. (n.d.). CDP. https://cdn.cdp.net/cdp-production/cms/reports/documents/000/006/164/original/CDP_AnnualDisclosureReport2021_V7.pdf?1650447997.

CEEW. (2021, November 18). *Council on Energy, Environment and Water, integrated, International, Independent*. Retrieved from ceew.in: https://www.ceew.in/press-releases/india-will-require-investments-worth-over-usd-10-trillion-achieve-net-zero-2070-ceew

Center for Climate and Energy Solutions. (2019). *Global Emissions*. Retrieved from c2es.org: https://www.c2es.org/content/international-emissions/

CFA Institute. (2023). *ESG Investing and Analysis*. Retrieved from www.cfainstitute.org: https://www.cfainstitute.org/en/rpc-overview/esg-investing

CFA Institute. (2023). *Introduction to Corporate Governance and Other ESG Considerations*. Retrieved from cfainstitute.org: https://www.cfainstitute.org/en/membership/professional-development/refresher-readings/introduction-corporate-governance-esg-considerations

Change, U. N. (n.d.). *Conference of the Parties (COP)*. Retrieved from unfccc.int: https://unfccc.int/process/bodies/supreme-bodies/conference-of-the-parties-cop

CNBCTV18.com. (2021, December 14). *Major Indian companies committed to go carbon-free; check out here on when they plan to achieve the goal*. Retrieved from cnbctv18.com: https://www.cnbctv18.com/business/companies/major-indian-companies-committed-to-go-carbon-free-check-out-here-on-when-they-plan-to-achieve-the-goal-11808892.htm

Col. Rajeev Kumar, M. R. (2021). *Outlast: How ESG Can Benefit Your Business*. Harper Business, 2021.

Companies (Account) Amendment Rules (2016). Ministry of Corporate Affairs, Government of India.

Companies (Corporate Social Responsibility Policy) Amendment Rules, 2016 (2016, May 23). Ministry of Corporate Affairs, Government of India.

Companies (Corporate Social Responsibility Policy) Rules, 2014 (2014, February 27). Gazette Notification of Government of India

COP26: India PM Narendra Modi pledges net zero by 2070. (2021, November 1). BBC News. https://www.bbc.com/news/world-asia-india-59125143.

Curwood, S. (2021, May 20). *Imagining Gaia, the Earth, as 'one great, living organism'*. Retrieved from theworld.org: https://theworld.org/stories/2021-05-20/imagining-gaia-earth-one-great-living-organism

Dadhich & Atrey (2020). An analytical study of the CSR Reporting in India – aligning, measuring and reporting CSR with Global and National Goals, International Journal of Science & Research (IJSR)

Dadhich, G. & Atrey, R.R. (2020). An analytical study of the CSR Reporting in India – Aligning, Measuring and Reporting CSR with Global and National Goals. *International Journal of Science and Research, 9(10),* 1145-1155.

Dadhich, G. & Atrey, R.R. (2021). An analytical study of the role of Business in promoting Inclusive Growth and Equitable Development in India. *International Journal of Management, Sociology & Humanities 12(1),* 287-296.

Dadhich, G. & Atrey, R. R. (2022). *Benchmarking ESG & CSR: A Compendium of best prcatices in Environmental-Social-Governance (ESG) and Corporate Social Responsibility (CSR) in India.* New Delhi: Taxmann Publications (P.) Ltd.

Dadhich, G., Atrey, R.R. & Mishra, D. (2021). *India's commitment and allegiance to international stance on Responsible Business Conduct*. In Srivastava, A.K. & Tripathi V.R. (Ed.), Corporate Governance – Emerging Dimensions. Bangalore: Thomson Reuters.

Data breach statistics by country: Q1 2022. (2022, May 16). (n.d.). Surfshark. https://surfshark.com/blog/data-breach-statistics-by-country.

Data breach statistics by country in 2021. (n.d.). Surfshark. https://surfshark.com/blog/data-breach-statistics-by-country-in-2021.

David A. Cifrino. (2023, June 29). *The Rise of International ESG Disclosure Standards*. Retrieved from corpgov.law.harvard.edu: https://corpgov.law.harvard.edu/2023/06/29/the-rise-of-international-esg-disclosure-standards/

Deloitte. (2021). *What is ESG? ESG Explained.* Retrieved from deloitte.com: https://www2.deloitte.com/ce/en/pages/global-business-services/articles/esg-explained-1-what-is-esg.html

Deloitte. (2023). *Scope 1, 2 and 3 emissions*. Retrieved from www2.deloitte.com: https://www2.deloitte.com/uk/en/focus/climate-change/zero-in-on-scope-1-2-and-3-emissions.html

Denchak, M. (2023, January 11). *Water Pollution: Everything You Need to Know.* Retrieved from nrdc.org: https://www.nrdc.org/stories/water-pollution-everything-you-need-know

Department of Economic and Social Affairs, United Nations. (n.d.). *Department of Economic and Social Affairs, Sustainable Development*. Retrieved November 2023, from sdgs.un.org: https://sdgs.un.org/about

Divecha, G. (2023, July 11). *Uncovering the S in ESG.* Retrieved from www.businesworld.in: https://www.businessworld.in/article/Uncovering-The-S-In-ESG-/11-07-2023-483834/

Divecha, G. (2023, November 18). *Uncovering S in ESG*. Retrieved from businessworld.in: https://www.businessworld.in/article/Uncovering-The-S-In-ESG-/11-07-2023-483834/

DJSI/CSA annual review. (n.d.). S&P Global. https://www.spglobal.com/esg/csa/djsi-csa-annual-review.

Doshi, J. (2023, October 27). *The new facets of corporate governance - sustainability, technology and ethical leadership*. Retrieved from moneycontrol.com: https://www.moneycontrol.com/news/opinion/the-new-facets-of-corporate-governance-sustainability-technology-and-ethical-leadership-11494521.html/amp

Dr. Heera Lal, D. K. (2023, August 10). *Zoomed Out | Carbon Credit Trading Scheme — India's bold step towards net zero*. Retrieved from cnbctv18.com: https://www.cnbctv18.com/views/carbon-credit-trading-scheme-17473261.htm

Dr. Kathrin Berensmann, D. N. (2016). *Green Finance: Actors, Challenges and Policy Recommendations.* Germany: German Development Institute.

Drishti IAS. (2023, March 13). *Daily Updates - ESG and India.* Retrieved from www.dridhtiias.com: https://www.drishtiias.com/daily-updates/daily-news-analysis/esg-and-india

Ecolytics Team. (2023, March 9). *What's the Difference Between ESG and Sustainability?* Retrieved from www.ecolytics.io: https://www.ecolytics.io/blog/whats-the-difference-between-esg-and-sustainability#:~:text=ESG%20 criteria%20are%20a%20subset,other%20social%20or%20governmental%20 practices

Editorials, D. n. (2021, April 03). *National Action Plan on Business and Human Rights*. Retrieved from drishtiias.com: https://www.drishtiias.com/daily-news-editorials/national-action-plan-on-business-and-human-rights

Emerick, D. (n.d.). *What is the Social in ESG*. Retrieved from esgthereport.com: https://www.esgthereport.com/what-is-esg/the-s-in-esg/

Empower asset owners. (2021). PRI. https://www.unpri.org/annual-report-2021/delivering-our-blueprint-for-responsible-investment/responsible-investors/empower-asset-owners.

Enhance our global footprint. (2021). PRI. https://www.unpri.org/annual-report-2021/how-we-work/building-our-effectiveness/enhance-our-global-footprint.

Environment, C. f. (n.d.). *CSE @ COP 28*. Retrieved from cseindia.org: https://www.cseindia.org/

Environmental & Social Management System (ESMS). (2020). *Environmental and Social Impact Assessment (ESIA)*. IUCN.

ESG assets may hit $53 trillion by 2025, a third of global AUM. Bloomberg. (n.d.). https://www.bloomberg.com/professional/blog/esg-assets-may-hit-53-trillion-by-2025-a-third-of-global-aum/.

ESG Measures that Matter: Q&A with Deutsche Post DHL Group's CFO Melanie Kreis, Excerpts from Gartner Business Quarterly, Proven Guidance for C-Suite Action, Michael Ramsey, Fourth Quarter, 2021, Gartner

Esha Gupta, A. R. (n.d.). The Importance of "ESG" and its application in India. *Lexforti Legal Journal [ISSN: 2582:2942] Volume II – Issue IV*, 19.

European Environment Agency (2020, May 11). *Increasing environmental pollution (GMT 10)*. Retrieved from eea.europa.eu: https://www.eea.europa.eu/soer/2015/global/pollution

Fair Trade USA. (n.d.). *Improving Lives, Protecting the Planet*. Retrieved from fairtradecertified.org: https://www.fairtradecertified.org/

Fall of Jet Airways due to poor corporate governance. (2021, August 4). iPleaders. https://blog.ipleaders.in/fall-jet-airways-due-poor-corporate-governance/.

Farina, A. (2000, April). *The Cultural Landscape as a Model for the Integration of Ecology and Economics*. Retrieved from researchgate.net: https://www.researchgate.net/publication/200668061_The_Cultural_Landscape_as_a_Model_for_the_Integration_of_Ecology_and_Economics

FDIC, Division of Depositor and Consumer Protection. (n.d.). *Community Reinvestment Act*. Retrieved from www.fdic.gov: https://www.fdic.gov/regulations/resources/director/presentations/CRA.pdf

Ferrarini, G. (2021, March 22). *Corporate Purpose: Sustainability as a Game Changer*. Retrieved from blogs.law.ox.ac.uk: https://blogs.law.ox.ac.uk/business-law-blog/blog/2021/03/corporate-purpose-sustainability-game-changer

File, C. (2023, April 06). *Practices and Metrics for Corporate Governance*. Retrieved from sustainalytics.com: https://www.sustainalytics.com/esg-research/resource/corporate-esg-blog/examining-the-g-in-esg-the-role-best-practices-and-metrics-for-corporate-governance

From the Stockholder to the Stakeholder. (n.d.). Arabesque. https://arabesque.com/research/From_the_stockholder_to_the_stakeholder_web.pdf.

Garima Dadhich, R. R. Atrey (2020, October 10). *An Anlytical Study of the CSR Reporting in India - Aligning, Measuring and Reporting CSR with Global And National Goals* . Retrieved from ijsr.net: https://www.ijsr.net/getabstract.php?paperid=SR201018115937

Gartner. INC. (2023). *Environmental, Social and Governance (ESG)*. Retrieved from www.gartner.com: https://www.gartner.com/en/finance/glossary/environmental-social-and-governance-esg-

Gautam, N. (2023, September 01). *SEBI's Got Indian Thoughts on ESG Push*. Retrieved from outlookbusiness.com: https://www.outlookbusiness.com/strategy-4/feature-17/sebis-got-indian-thoughts-on-esg-push-6841

Geetey, T. (2021, August 2). *Fall of Jet Airways due to poor corporate governance*. Retrieved from blog.ipleaders.in: https://blog.ipleaders.in/fall-jet-airways-due-poor-corporate-governance/

GEF. (n.d.). *How does sustainable finance attract investors and catalyze private investment?* Retrieved from news.globallandscapesforum.org: https://news.globallandscapesforum.org/40996/what-is-sustainable-finance/#:~:text=The%20two%20main%20financial%20instruments,amount%20of%20capital%20they%20invest

GEP. (2023, April 28). *Three Pillars of Sustainability: A Brief Guide*. Retrieved from gep.com: https://www.gep.com/blog/strategy/three-pillars-of-sustainability-brief-guide

GEP. (n.d.). *From source to destination and back, Driving efforts and insights for a sustainable supply chain*. Retrieved from gep.com: https://www.gep.com/supply-chain-sustainability

GLG. (2023, January 26). *Environmental, Social & Governance Law India 2023*. Retrieved from iclg.com: https://iclg.com/practice-areas/environmental-social-and-governance-law/india

Global, S. &. (2020, February 24). *What is the "S" in ESG?* Retrieved from spglobal.com: https://www.spglobal.com/en/research-insights/articles/what-is-the-s-in-esg

Global Legal Group. (n.d.). *Environmental, Social & Governance Law India 2023*. Retrieved from iclg.com: https://iclg.com/practice-areas/environmental-social-and-governance-law/india

Global Reporting Initiative. (2023). *About GRI*. Retrieved from globalreporting.org: https://www.globalreporting.org/about-gri

Global Reporting Initiatives. (2023). *The global standards for sustainability impacts*. Retrieved from www.globalreporting.org: https://www.globalreporting.org/standards/

Gopani J. (2020), ESG Investing: Why is it even more relevant for investors in the current scenario?, Financial Express, June 19, 2020

Government of India. (2023). *Ministry of Environment, Forest and Climate Change*. Retrieved from moef.gov.in: http://moef.gov.in/moef/

Greenhouse Gas Protocol. (n.d.). *Guidance GHG Protocol develops guidance to provide clarity on how specific sectors can apply GHG Protocol standards*. Retrieved from ghgprotocol.org: https://ghgprotocol.org/guidance-0

Greenpeace. (n.d.). *Our Campaigns*. Retrieved from Greenpeace.org: https://www.greenpeace.org/india/en/

Group, G. L. (2023, January 26). *Environmental, Social & Governance Law India 2023*. Retrieved from iclg.com: https://iclg.com/practice-areas/environmental-social-and-governance-law/india

Group, M. (2023, March 12). *Explained | The rise of the ESG regulations*. Retrieved from thehindu.com: https://www.thehindu.com/opinion/op-ed/explained-the-rise-of-the-esg-regulations/article66610907.ece

GSR – 130(E) Notification (2014, February 28). Ministry of Corporate Affairs, Government of India.

GSR – 261(E) Notification (2014, March 31). Ministry of Corporate Affairs, Government of India.

GSR – 568(E) Notification (2014, August 6). Ministry of Corporate Affairs, Government of India.

GSR – 644(E) Notification (2014, September 12). Ministry of Corporate Affairs, Government of India.

GS Sustain ESG Series A Revolution Rising - From Low Chatter to Loud Roar. (n.d.). Goldman Sachs. https://goldmansachs.com/insights/pages/new-energy-landscape-folder/esg-revolution-rising/report.pdf.

Gupta, D. N. (2023, July 25). *Water contamination: Still a serious national challenge*. Retrieved from timesofindia.indiatimes.com: https://timesofindia.indiatimes.com/blogs/voices/water-contamination-still-a-serious-national-challenge/

Harvard Business Review on Greening Your Business Profitability. (2011). Boston: Harvard Business Review Press.

Hayes, A. (2023, July 27). *How to Tell If a Company Has High ESG Scores*. Retrieved from investopedia.com: https://www.investopedia.com/company-esg-score-7480372

Henisz, w. (2021, December 13). *Beyond Business: Humanizing ESG*. Retrieved from knowledge.wharton.upenn.edu: https://knowledge.wharton.upenn.edu/article/beyond-business-humanizing-esg/

Hobbs, A. (2023, February 21). *How corporate governance can help build a more sustainable world*. Retrieved from ey.com: https://www.ey.com/en_in/public-policy/how-corporate-governance-can-help-build-a-more-sustainable-world

HV, H. (2023, May 25). *Don't ignore the 'S' in ESG*. Retrieved from thehindubusinessline.com: https://www.thehindubusinessline.com/opinion/dont-ignore-the-s-in-esg/article66893567.ece

Ilibrary, O. (2023, September 11). *G20/OECD Principles of Corporate Governance 2023*. Retrieved from OECD-ilibrary.org: https://www.oecd-ilibrary.org/governance/g20-oecd-principles-of-corporate-governance-2023_ed750b30-en

IMF. (2022). *Income Inequality Introduction to Inequality*. Retrieved from imf.org: https://www.imf.org/en/Topics/Inequality/introduction-to-inequality#:~:text=Over%20the%20past%20three%20decades,Gini%20coefficients%20exceeding%20two%20points

Inc, A. (2023). *Supplier Responsibility Designed by Apple in California. Made by people everywhere.* Retrieved from apple.com: https://www.apple.com/supplier-responsibility/

India, R. B. (2022, July 27). *Report of the Survey on Climate Risk and Sustainable Finance.* Retrieved from m.rbi.org.in: https://m.rbi.org.in/scripts/PublicationReportDetails.aspx?ID=1215

Intergovernmental Panel on Climate Change. (2022). *Sixth Assessment Report.* ipcc.

International Institute for Sustainable Development. (December 2009). *A Brief Analysis of the Copenhagen Climate Change Conference An IISD Commentary.* iisd.

IPCC. (2023). *AR6 Synthesis Report Climate Change 2023.* ipcc.

Jain, C. U. (2023, January 05). *Corporate Fraud in India & Outside India under Companies Act, 2013*. Retrieved from legalwindow.in: https://www.legalwindow.in/corporate-fraud-in-india/

Joon, C. (2023, June 28). *Environmental Impact Assessment (EIA) and Its Significance*. Retrieved from drishtiias.com: https://www.drishtiias.com/blog/environmental-impact-assessment-eia-and-Its-significance

Karmakar, S. (2023). *What is Land Acquisition*. Retrieved from cyberswift.com: https://www.cyberswift.com/blog/what-is-land-acquisition/

Kyte, R. (2023, June 08). *Republicans' anti-ESG attack may be silencing insurers, but it isn't changing their pro-climate business decisions*. Retrieved from thecoversation.com: https://theconversation.com/republicans-anti-esg-attack-may-be-silencing-insurers-but-it-isnt-changing-their-pro-climate-business-decisions-206922

Landgraf, A. (2022, May 13). *A deep dive into the social aspect of ESG*. Retrieved from esg.conservice.com: https://esg.conservice.com/the-social-aspect-of-esg/

Logo, D. B. (2023). *What is the "E" in ESG?* Retrieved from https://www.deutschewealth.com/: https://www.deutschewealth.com/en/our-capabilities/esg/what-is-esg-investing-wealth-management/environmentally-responsible-investing-e-in-esg-environmental.html

Market Business News. (2023). *What is ESG? Definition and meaning.* Retrieved from marketbusinessnews.com: https://marketbusinessnews.com/financial-glossary/esg-definition-meaning/

Mark S. Bergman, Ariel J. Deckelbaum, and Brad S. Karp,. (2023, November 04). *Harvard Law school Forum on Corporate Governance.* Retrieved from corpgov.law.harvard.edu: https://corpgov.law.harvard.edu/

McKinsey & Company. (2022, November 28). *What is net zero?* Retrieved from mckinsey.com: https://www.mckinsey.com/featured-insights/mckinsey-explainers/what-is-net-zero

Mehndiratta, M. (2023, March 22). *Section 134 of the Companies Act, 2013.* Retrieved from blog.ipleaders.in: https://blog.ipleaders.in/section-134-of-the-companies-act-2013/#:~:text=According%20to%20Rule%208%20of,investments%20made%20in%20this%20regard

MILNE Library. (n.d.). *Chapter 10: Leadership on the Board*. Retrieved from milnepublishing.geneseo.edu/: https://milnepublishing.geneseo.edu/guidelines-for-improving-the-effectiveness-of-boards/chapter/chapter-10/

Ministry of Corporate Affairs. (2013). *The Companies Act, 2013.* New Delhi: Ministry of Corporate Affairs.

Ministry of Environment, F. a. (2022, November 15). *India delivers National Statement at COP 27.* Retrieved from pib.gov.in: https://pib.gov.in/PressReleasePage.aspx?PRID=1876119

Ministry of Environment, Forest and Climate Change. *Final Minutes of the 10th EAC meeting held on 29th August 2016.* Ministry of Environment, Forest and Climate Change.

Historical GHG Emissions. (n.d.). Climatewatch. https://www.climatewatchdata.org/ghg-emissions?end_year=2019&source=CAIT&start_year=1990.

How ESG reporting landscape is evolving in India. (2020, December 22). EY US - Building a better working world. https://www.ey.com/en_in/climate-change-sustainability-services/how-esg-reporting-landscape-is-evolving-in-india.

India ratifies Paris climate agreement. (2016, October 2). BBC News. https://www.bbc.com/news/world-asia-india-37536348.

India will require investments worth over USD 10 trillion to achieve net-zero by 2070: CEEW-CEF. (2022, April 5). CEEW. https://www.ceew.in/press-releases/india-will-require-investments-worth-over-usd-10-trillion-achieve-net-zero-2070-ceew.

Introduction to ESG, *Posted by Mark S. Bergman, Ariel J. Deckelbaum, and Brad S. Karp, Paul, Weiss, Rifkind, Wharton & Garrison LLP, on Saturday, August 1, 2020 posted on Harvard Law School – Forum for Corporate Governance*

Invest India.(2020, November). Retrieved from investindia.gov.in: https://www.investindia.gov.in/invest-india-sustainability-framework

Jones, K. R., & Mucha, L. (2014). Sustainability Assessment and Reporting for Non-profit Organizations: Accountability "for the Public Good." Voluntas: International Journal of Voluntary and Non-profit Organizations, 25(6), 1465–1482. http://www.jstor.org/stable/43654676.

Justice *K.S. Puttaswamy and Anr.* vs. *Union of India* (UOI) (2017) 10 SCC 1

Justice K.S. Puttaswamy and Anr. *vs*. Union of India (UOI) and Ors., (2019) 1 SCC 1 (S. C. 2019).

Kenton, W. (2022, May 10). *What is the Community Reinvestment Act (CRA)? Definition.* Retrieved from investopedia.com: https://www.investopedia.com/terms/c/community_reinvestment_act.asp

Kerner, S. M. (2023). *Definition ESG Score.* Retrieved from techtarget.com: https://www.techtarget.com/sustainability/definition/ESG-score

Khakee, A. (2014, June). *An unbalanced model for sustainable urban development.* Retrieved from researchgate.net: https://www.researchgate.net/publication/263764197_An_unbalanced_model_for_sustainable_urban_development

Ministry of Science & Technology. (2023, September 28). *India is committed to achieve the Net Zero emissions target by 2070 as announced by PM Modi, says Dr. Jitendra Singh.* Retrieved from pib.gov.in: https://pib.gov.in/PressReleaseIframePage.aspx?PRID=1961797#:~:text=Jitendra%20Singh%2C%20has%20said%20India,Prime%20Minister%20Shri%20Narendra%20Modi

Kiprijanovska, E. (n.d.). *What is Governance within ESG?* Retrieved from esgpro.co.uk: https://esgpro.co.uk/what-is-governance-within-esg/

Lev, H. (2021, June 03). *Getting started with sustainability benchmarking.* Retrieved from esg.conservice.com: https://esg.conservice.com/getting-started-sustainability-benchmarking/

Lin, B. (2023, January 31). *India transforms its ESG landscape to be future-ready.* Retrieved from timesofindia.indiatimes.com: https://timesofindia.indiatimes.com/blogs/voices/india-transforms-its-esg-landscape-to-be-future-ready/

Livemint. (2022, April 29). *India's economy to take 12 years to overcome Covid losses: RBI*. Retrieved from livemint.com: https://www.livemint.com/news/india/india-s-economy-to-overcome-covid-losses-in-fy35-recovery-remains-stimulus-dependent-rbi-11651238870034.html

M&H. (n.d.). *Understanding ESG:Governance Factors*. Retrieved from mhes.com: https://mhes.com/understanding-esg-governance-factors/

Mar, V. d. (2023, October 1). *Sustainability & ESG insights September 23: Big SEC fines and the urgent need for ESG data and software.* Retrieved from linkedin.com: https://www.linkedin.com/pulse/sustainability-esg-insights-september23-big-sec-fines-de-la-mar/?utm_source=share&utm_medium=member_android&utm_campaign=share_via

Ministry of Corporate Affairs. (2018). *National Guidelines on Responsible Business Conduct.* Indian Institute of Corporate Affairs. New Delhi: Ministry of Corporate Affairs.

Ministry of Corporate Affairs. (2020). *Report of the Committee on Business Responsibility Reporting.* New Delhi: Ministry of Corporate Affairs.

Montezzana, M. (2023, January 10). *What are ESG Principles and How to Apply them in an Organization*. Retrieved from voxy.com: https://voxy.com/blog/esg-principles/

Morisson, R. (2021, May 05). *Environmental, Social, and Governance Theory.* Retrieved from cei.org: https://cei.org/studies/environmental-social-and-governance-theory/

Murray, S. (2023, June 22). *In-house lawyers grapple with ESG demands*. Retrieved from ft.com: https://www.ft.com/content/6e094e6d-b97d-45dd-941f-39f5b5fa1f14

Mygov. (2023). *Lifestyle For Environment: About the LiFE Campaign*. Retrieved from mygov.in: https://www.mygov.in/life/

Namit Agarwal, A. P. (2020, April 14). *India's Business & Human Rights National Action Plan*. Retrieved from ihrb.org: https://www.ihrb.org/other/governments-role/commentary-indias-national-action-plan

National CSR Network. (2023, April 11). *How does ESG reporting change the CSR landscape?* Retrieved from linkedin.com: https://www.linkedin.com/pulse/how-does-esg-reporting-change-csr-landscape-national-csr-network/?utm_source=share&utm_medium=member_android&utm_campaign=share_via

Nestle. (2023). *Our Vision for a Brighter Future*. Retrieved from nestlecocoaplan.com: https://www.nestlecocoaplan.com/

Nickolas, S. (2022, August 15). *How is a Capitalist System Different Than a Free Market System?* Retrieved from investopedia.com: https://www.investopedia.com/ask/answers/042215/what-difference-between-capitalist-system-and-free-market-system.asp

Nola Taylor Tillman, M. B. (2023, May 14). *https://theworld.org/stories/2021-05-20/imagining-gaia-earth-one-great-living-organism*. Retrieved from space.com: https://www.space.com/17661-theory-general-relativity.html

Patagonia.inc. (2023). *Everything we make has an impact on the planet.* Retrieved from patagonia.com: https://www.patagonia.com/our-footprint/

NTPC. (2022). *Rehabilitation & Resettlement*. Retrieved from ntpc.co.in: https://www.ntpc.co.in/about-us/corporate-functions/corporate-citizenship/rehabilitation-resettlement

OECD. (2023, June 08). *OECD Guidelines for Multinational Enterprises on Responsible Business Conduct*. Retrieved from oecd-ilibrary.org: https://www.oecd-ilibrary.org/finance-and-investment/oecd-guidelines-for-multinational-enterprises-on-responsible-business-conduct_81f92357-en

OECD. (2023, September 11). *G20/OECD Principles of Corporate Governance 2023*. Retrieved from oecd-ilibrary.org: https://www.oecd-ilibrary.org/governance/g20-oecd-principles-of-corporate-governance-2023_ed750b30-en;jsessionid=dNWx7Ua78AT7Gf_p9O1HiF0zP55fBfnK_wkDJyES.ip-10-240-5-83

OECD. (n.d.). *OECD Due Diligence Guidance for Responsible Business Conduct*. Retrieved from oecd.org: https://www.oecd.org/investment/due-diligence-guidance-for-responsible-business-conduct.htm

KPMG. (15, July, 2023). *SEBI framework on BRSR Core and value chain – disclosures and assurance by listed.* KPMG.

Kristen L.M., 2019, Top 10 ESG Issues for 2019, Environmental, Social, Governance, AMP Capital, Australia, March 2019

Luis Serven, A.S. (1993). *Striving for Growth after Adjustment, The Role of Capital Formation.* Washington D. C.: The World Bank.

Major Indian companies committed to go carbon-free; check out here on when they plan to achieve the goal. (2021, December 14). cnbctv18.com. https://www.cnbctv18.com/business/companies/major-indian-companies-committed-to-go-carbon-free-check-out-here-on-when-they-plan-to-achieve-the-goal-11808892.htm.

Meyer, L. (2021, May 4). *Intergenerational Justice*. Retrieved from plato.stanford.edu: https://plato.stanford.edu/entries/justice-intergenerational/ (2021). *Mitigating ESG Risk.* Squire Patton Boggs.

Ministry of Corporate Affairs (2016). CSR Expenditure of 7334 Companies for the Financial Year 2014-15.

Ministry of Corporate Affairs (2019). Report of the High Level Committee on Corporate Social Responsibility 2018.

Ministry of Corporate Affairs (2019). The Gaps & the Bridges: the Saga of Best CSR Initiatives in India.

Ministry of Corporate Affairs, Government of India (2009), Corporate Social Responsibility Voluntary Guidelines, 2009

Ministry of Corporate Affairs, Government of India (2011), National Voluntary Guidelines on Social, Environmental & Economic Responsibilities of Business

Ministry of Corporate Affairs, Government of India (2018), National Guidelines on Responsible Business Conduct

Mishra, P. D. (1994). *Social Work Philosophy and Methods.* New Delhi: Inter - India Publications.

MOOC.fi, University of Helsinki. (n.d.). *Sustainable development and sustainability as normative concept*. Retrieved from courses.mooc.fi: https://courses.mooc.fi/org/uh-inar/courses/introduction-to-sustainability/chapter-1/sustainable-development-and-sustainability-as-normative-concept

MSME firms created up to 14.9 million new jobs per annum in four years: CII survey. (n.d.). Business Today. https://www.businesstoday.in/latest/economy-politics/story/msme-firms-created-up-to-14-million-new-jobs-in-four-years-cii-survey-173880-2019-03-08.

Mukund Rajan, R.K. (2021). *Outlast How ESG Can Benefit Your Business.* Noida, India: Harper Business.

Nations, U. (n.d.). *Peace, dignity and equality.* Retrieved from un.org: https://www.un.org/en/global-issues/climate-change

Office of the Comptroller of the Currency. (n.d.). *Community Reinvestment Act (CRA).* Retrieved from occ.treas.gov: https://www.occ.treas.gov/topics/consumers-and-communities/cra/index-cra.html

Oliveira, R.V. (2022, August 22). *Irreplaceable Goods: Bridging Sustainability and Intergenerational Sufficientarianism*. Retrieved from tandfonline.com: https://www.tandfonline.com/doi/full/10.1080/21550085.2022.2112488

Pai, D. S. (2023, August 28). *India's Climate Journey: Setting Course for the 21st Century*. Retrieved from yourstory.com: https://yourstory.com/socialstory/2023/08/india-climate-journey-cleantech-decarbonisation

Paterra, M. (2022, June 29). *Making ESG work through good governance*. Retrieved from impact.economist.com: https://impact.economist.com/sustainability/net-zero-and-energy/big-question-esg-governance?utm_medium=cpc.adword.pd&utm_source=google&utm_campaign=a.io_apac_generic&utm_content=conversion.non-brand.anonymous.apac_in_en_generic_prosp_non-brand_google_subs

Patrick, S. (2022, November 28). *To Prevent the Collapse of Biodiversity, the World Needs a New Planetary Politics*. Retrieved from carnegieendowment.org: https://carnegieendowment.org/2022/11/28/to-prevent-collapse-of-biodiversity-world-needs-new-planetary-politics-pub-88473

Pattanayak, B. (2023, October 05). *In a first, senior IBBI functionaries endorse focus on ESG in insolvency resolution*. Retrieved from economictimes.indiatimes.com: https://economictimes.indiatimes.com/news/economy/policy/in-a-first-two-ibbi-members-endorse-focus-on-esg-in-insolvency-resolution/articleshow/104168133.cms?from=mdr

Pau, L. G. (2023, April 04). *5 ways organizations can address the social factors of ESG*. Retrieved from techtarget.com: https://www.techtarget.com/sustainability/feature/5-ways-organizations-can-address-the-social-factors-of-ESG

PIB. (2021, December 1). *(Frequently Asked Questions (FAQs), National Action Plan on Climate Change (NAPCC)*. Retrieved from static.pib.gov.in: https://static.pib.gov.in/WriteReadData/specificdocs/documents/2021/dec/doc202112101.pdf

Poddar, N. (2021, April 14). *Whether expense towards Corporate Environment Responsibility (CER) be eligible as CSR spending?* Retrieved from vinodkothari.com: https://vinodkothari.com/2021/04/whether-expense-towards-corporate-environment-responsibility-cer-be-eligible-as-csr-spending/

Pranab Dhal Samanta, B. G. (2020, October 31). *New India believes in market forces, will be the most preferred investment destination: PM Modi*. Retrieved from economictimes.indiatimes.com: https://economictimes.indiatimes.com/news/politics-and-nation/we-should-assess-our-coronavirus-fight-against-the-metric-of-how-many-lives-we-are-able-to-save-pm-narendra-modi/articleshow/78922895.cms

PRI Association. (2021). *Annual Report Enhance our global footprint*. London: PRI Association.

Principles for Responsible Investment. (n.d.). *About the PRI*. Retrieved from unpri.org: https://www.unpri.org/about-us/about-the-pri

Pryde, N. (2023, March 7). *ESG in 2023 : Who Cares Wins?* Retrieved from www.dlapiper.com: https://www.dlapiper.com/en/insights/publications/2023/03/esg-in-2023-who-cares-wins

PWC. (2023). *ESG trends in 2023*. Australia.

PWC. (October 2023). *What's New Draft Ecomark Certification Rules, 2023 open to feedback and suggestions – MoEF & CC.* pwc.

P'RAYAN, A. (2023, September 02). *Why a teacher should use principles of Ubuntuism in the classroom*. Retrieved from thehindu.com: https://www.thehindu.com/education/why-a-teacher-should-use-principles-of-ubuntuism-in-the-classroom/article67250999.ece/amp/

Qiang Ma, P. M. (2023, October 19). *The hidden cost of carbon*. Retrieved from pwc.com: https://www.pwc.com/gx/en/issues/esg/the-hidden-cost-of-carbon.html?WT.mc_id=GMO-ESG-NA-FY24-NZT-NZCP-T68-CI-TAX-ART-GMOS0008-EN-OSLI-T1

Quist, Z. (2023, November 20). Retrieved from ecochain.com: https://ecochain.com/blog/life-cycle-assessment-lca-guide/#:~:text=Gate%2Dto%2Dgate,larger%20level%20Life%20Cycle%20Assessment

Qureshi, Z. (2023, May 16). *Rising inequality: A major issue of our time*. Retrieved from brookings.edu: https://www.brookings.edu/articles/rising-inequality-a-major-issue-of-our-time/

Rade, A. (2023, June 26). *Deep dive: Scope 2 emissions.* Retrieved from sustain.life: https://www.sustain.life/blog/scope-2-emissions

Rade, A. (2023, May 26). *Deep dive: Scope 1 emissions.* Retrieved from sustain.life: https://www.sustain.life/blog/scope-1-emissions

Raghupathy, J. (2023, May). *Jaganathan Raghupathy, Sustainability Consultant & Trainer*. Retrieved from linkedin.com: https://www.linkedin.com/posts/jaganathanraghupathy_esg-sustainability-csr-activity-7070305018423250944-X8hv/?utm_source=share&utm_medium=member_android

Ramin Farzam, W. B. (2023). *Beyond Environmental Impact: The Case of Social in ESG*. Retrieved from www2.deloitte.com: https://www2.deloitte.com/nl/nl/pages/sustainability/articles/beyond-environmental-impact-the-case-of-social-in-esg.html

Ramos, M. (2022, November 3). *What is supply chain sustainability?* Retrieved from ibm.com: https://www.ibm.com/blog/what-is-supply-chain-sustainability/

Rathi, C. A. (2022, November 26). *Analysis on: Business responsibility and sustainability reporting (BRSR)*. Retrieved from caclubindia.com: https://www.caclubindia.com/amp/articles/business-responsibility-and-sustainability-reporting-brsr-48012.asp

MSME firms created up to 14.9 million new jobs per annum in four years: CII survey. (n.d.). Business Today. https://www.businesstoday.in/latest/economy-politics/story/msme-firms-created-up-to-14-million-new-jobs-in-four-years-cii-survey-173880-2019-03-08.

Mullick & Kumar (2020), SDGs still remain relevant for accelerating focused sustainability actions by Indian businesses, Discussion Paper, The Energy Resource Institute (TERI)

National Guidelines on Responsible Business Conduct 2018. Ministry of Corporate Affairs, Government of India.

National Stock Exchange (NSE) of India (2019) Business Responsibility Reporting in India: Disclosures & Practices

National Voluntary Guidelines on Social, Environmental & Economic Responsibilities of Business 2011. Ministry of Corporate Affairs, Government of India.

New India believes in market forces, will be the most preferred investment destination: PM Modi. (2020, October 29). The Economic Times. https://economictimes.indiatimes.com/news/politics-and-nation/we-should-assess-our-coronavirus-fight-against-the-metric-of-how-many-lives-we-are-able-to-save-pm-narendra-modi/articleshow/78922895.cms.

OECD (2023), OECD Guidelines for Multinational Enterprises on Responsible Business Conduct, OECD Publishing, Paris, https://doi.org/10.1787/81f92357-en.

PM Modi explains how India will become $5 trillion economy in 5 years. (2019, July 6). India Today. https://www.indiatoday.in/india/story/pm-modi-varanasi-5-trillion-economy-budget-1563362-2019-07-06.

Promoting Clean Energy Usages through Accelerated Localization of E-Mobility Value Chain, NITI Aayog, Asian Development Bank, Boston Consulting Group, May 2022

Reading in Science and Spirituality. (July 2010). New Delhi: Sri Sathya Sai International Centre for Human Values.

Recykal. (n.d.). *A Guide to EPR Compliance in India*. Retrieved from recykal.com: https://recykal.com/blog/a-guide-to-epr-compliance-in-india/#:~:text=Extended%20Producer%20Responsibility%20(EPR)%20Plan,%2C%20recycling%2C%20and%20awareness%20raising

Report of the Committee on Business Responsibility Reporting. (2020, May 8). Ministry of Corporate Affairs. https://www.mca.gov.in/Ministry/pdf/BRR_11082020.pdf.

Revankar, S. (2023). *Understanding ESG and Sustainability.* Roorkee, Uttarakhand, India: String Production.

Reyer, R. B. (1975). *Adaptive Processing For Landsat Data.* Houston, Texas: Environmental Research Institute of Michigan.

Robeco. (n.d.). *Sustainable Investing ESG Definition.* Retrieved from robeco.com: https://www.robeco.com/en-me/glossary/sustainable-investing/esg-definition

Robeyns, I. A. (2023). *Stanford Encyclopedia of Philosophy, The Capability Approach*. Retrieved from plato.stanford.edu: https://plato.stanford.edu/entries/capability-approach/

Ronald J. Burke, G. M. (2011). *Corporate Reputation- Managing Opportunities and Threats.* Gower Applied Business Research.

Rupinder Malik, A. S. (2023, June 05). *India: ESG Comparative Guide.* Retrieved from mondaq.com: https://www.mondaq.com/india/corporate commercial-law/1231978/esg-comparative-guide

Ruthsdotter, B. E. (2023). *History of the Women's Rights Movement*. Retrieved from nationalwomenshistoryalliance.org: https://nationalwomenshistory alliance.org/history-of-the-womens-rights-movement/

S & P Global. (2023). *DJSI Annual Review 2022.* Retrieved from spglobal.com: https://www.spglobal.com/esg/csa/djsi-csa-annual-review

S. Christian Albright, W.L. (2015). *Business Analytics - Data Analysis and Decision Making.* Cenage Learnings.

S. Ramachandran, D. S. (2022, January 17). *An explainable product design can ensure ESG goals are achieved*. Retrieved from forbesindia.com: https://www.forbesindia.com/blog/environment-and-sustainability/an-explainable-product-design-can-ensure-esg-goals-are-achieved/

Sayeda, S. (2023, November 10). *Earth Forward Dialogues continue: ESG visionaries explore discussions on sustainable strategies at Candor TechSpace Sector 48, Gurugram*. Retrieved from m.economictimes.com: https://m.economictimes.com/news/company/corporate-trends/earth-forward-dialogues-continue-esg-visionaries-explore-discussions-on-sustainable-strategies-at-candor-techspace-gurugram/amp_articleshow/105112920.cms

Sean Lees. *Training Facilitation Guide Human Rights Due Diligence.* UNDP.

Securities and Exchange Board of India (2012), Circular – Business Responsibility Reports (BRR), August 13, 2012

Securities and Exchange Board of India. (2021). *Business Responsibility & Sustainability Reporting Format.* Mumbai: SEBI.

Segal, M. (2023, November 02). *Over 80% of Companies to Increase Budgets for Environmental Sustainability Goals Over Next Year: Honeywell Survey*. Retrieved from esgtoday.com: https://www.esgtoday.com/over-80-of-companies-to-increase-budgets-for-environmental-sustainability-goals-over-next-year-honeywell-survey/

Sharma, D. S. *LAW Topic Name -Polluter Pays.* Meerut: ILS, CCSU campus, Meerut.

Sharma, R. (2022, September 06). *ESG Framework In India – Explained, pointwise.* Retrieved from https://forumias.com/blog/esg-framework-in-india/#Conclusion: https://forumias.com/blog/esg-framework-in-india/#Conclusion

Shylla Sawhney, G. d. (2022, May 24). *Taking ESG reporting to the next level.* Retrieved from www.thehindubusinessline.com: https://www.thehindubusinessline.com/opinion/taking-esg-reporting-to-the-next-level/article65457659.ece

Singal, N. (n.d.). *The ESG Imperative.* Retrieved from www.businesstoday.in: https://www.businesstoday.in/interactive/longread/the-esg-imperative-indian-businesses-future-ready-265-20-06-2023

Smith, A. (2022). *The Wealth of Nations.* New Delhi : Rupa Publications India Pvt. Ltd.

Solomon, D. S. (2020). *Challenges of Green Finance and Sustainable Economic Development in India.* Lucknow, U.P., India.

Standard, B. (2023, February). *ESG reporting by Indian corporates has improved by 160%, shows research.* Retrieved from Business Standard: https://mail.google.com/mail/u/0/#inbox/KtbxLxgBxdXqRljTszhTsKXksJvZZChSRL?projector=1&messagePartId=0.1

Stanford Encyclopedia of Philosophy. (December, 2020). *The Capability Approach.* Stanford University: The Metaphysics Rsearch Lab, Depatment of Philosophy, University of Stanford.

Steve Gagnon, S.E. (n.d.). *Question and Answers, Does Gravity Affects Atom.* Retrieved from education.jlab.org: https://education.jlab.org/qa/atomgravity_01.html#:~:text=Gravity%20affects%20atoms%20the%20same,creating%20a%20much%20stronger%20pull

Stowe, L. (2023, June 24). *7 Steps to Getting Started on Your ESG Strategy.* Retrieved from eqm.ai: https://eqm.ai/insights-trends/start-your-esg-strategy-7-steps/

Sun Consulting. (2022, October 10). *What is ESG? Definition & Theory.* Retrieved from senyumnegeri.id: https://senyumnegeri.id/what-is-esg-definition-theory/

Sundar, P. (2013). *Business & Community.* Sage Publications.

Surfshark. (2021, December 20). *Data breach statistics by country in 2021.* Retrieved from surfshark.com: https://surfshark.com/blog/data-breach-statistics-by-country-in-2021

Surfshark. (2022, April 13). *Data breach statistics by country: first quarter of 2022*. Retrieved from surfshark.com: https://surfshark.com/blog/data-breach-statistics-by-country

Surfshark. https://surfshark.com/blog/data-breach-statistics-by-country.

Swiss Sustainable Finance. (n.d.). *European Union*. Retrieved from sustainablefinance.ch: https://www.sustainablefinance.ch/en/resources/regulation/european-union-3182.html

Swiss Sustainable Finance. (n.d.). *Sustainable investing standards*. Retrieved from sustainablefinance.ch: https://www.sustainablefinance.ch/en/resources/what-sustainable-finance/sustainable-investing-standards.html#anchor_SFIXEP

Swiss Sustainable Finance. (n.d.). *What is Sustainable Finance*. Retrieved from sustainablefinance.ch: https://www.sustainablefinance.ch/en/resources/what-is-sustainable-finance-_content---1--1055.html#:~:text=Sustainable%20finance%20refers%20to%20any,clients%20and%20society%20at%20large

Task Force on Climate-related Financial Disclosures. (2023). *Task Force on Climate-related Financial Disclosures*. Retrieved from www.fsb-tcfd.org: https://www.fsb-tcfd.org/about/

Tata. (2023). *Project Aalingana: Embracing Sustainability*. Retrieved from tata.com: https://www.tata.com/sustainability

Tata Motors (2020), Tata Nexon becomes the first Indian car to be published on the International Dismantling Information System (IDIS)

The cocacola Company. (n.d.). *Sustainability News*. Retrieved from Coca-cola.com: https://www.coca-cola.com/in/en

The Companies Act, 2013. Retrieved from http://www.mca.gov.in

The Core Writing team, H. L. (2023). *Climate Change 2023 Synthesis Report Summary for Policymakers*.ipcc.

The Corporate Environmental Responsibility Team Infrastructure Service. (2022). *Corporate Environmental Responsibility at FAO*. New York: Food and Agriculture Organization of the United Nations.

The Decade To Deliver A Call To Business Action. The United Nations Global Compact —Accenture Strategy CEO Study on Sustainability 2019. (n.d.). Accenture. https://www.accenture.com/_acnmedia/pdf-109/accenture-ungc-ceo-study.pdf.

The Impact Investor. (2023, October 10). *What Are ESG Principles? Key Factors for ESG Investing*. Retrieved from https://theimpactinvestor.com/esg-principles/: https://theimpactinvestor.com/esg-principles/

The Institute of Chartered Accountants of India. (2021). *E-BOOK Corporate Governance in India*. Chennai: Southern India Regional Council, The Institute of Chartered Accountants of India.

Theories of Inter Generational Justice: A Synopsis, ISSN: 1993-3819, SAPIENS, Institut Veolia, 2008

The World Bank. (2023). *Pollution*. Retrieved from worldbank.org: https://www.worldbank.org/en/topic/pollution#:~:text=Industrialization%2C%20use%20of%20pesticides%20and,%2D%20and%20middle%2Dincome%20countries

Thomas, G. (2015). *Contemporary Methods of Social Work*. New Delhi: Shipra Publication.

Today, I. (2019, July 06). *PM Modi explains how India will become $5 trillion economy in 5 years*. Retrieved from indiatoday.in: https://www.indiatoday.in/india/story/pm-modi-varanasi-5-trillion-economy-budget-1563362-2019-07-06

Torsten Ehlers, B. M. (2020, September 14). *Green bonds and carbon emissions: exploring the case for a rating system at the firm level*. Retrieved from bis.org: https://www.bis.org/publ/qtrpdf/r_qt2009c.htm

U.S. Environmental Protection Agency. (1997). *The Economics of Sustainability*. U.S.A.: U. S. Environmental Agency.

UNFPA INDIA. United Nations Population Fund. https://www.unfpa.org/data/IN.

United Nations. (2023). *Inequality – Bridging the Divide*. Retrieved from un.org: https://www.un.org/en/un75/inequality-bridging-divide#:~:text=Income%20inequality%20within%20countries%20is%20getting%20worse&text=Today%2C%2071%20percent%20of%20the,to%20m-onth%2C%20year%20to%20year

United Nations. (n.d.). *United Nations Climate Action, The Paris Agreement*. Retrieved from un.org: https://www.un.org/en/climatechange/paris-agreement

United Nations Environment Programme Finance Initiative. (2023). *The UN-convened network of banks, insurers and investors accelerating sustainable development*. Retrieved from unepfi.org.

United Nations Global Impact. (2023). *The Power of Principles*. Retrieved from unglobalcompact.org: https://unglobalcompact.org/what-is-gc/mission/principles/

United States Environmental Protection Agency. (2023, August). *Scope 1 and Scope 2 Inventory Guidance*. Retrieved from epa.

gov: https://www.epa.gov/climateleadership/scope-1-and-scope-2-inventory-guidance#:~:text=Scope%201%20emissions%20are%20direct,boilers%2C%20furnaces%2C%20vehicles

United States Environmental Protection Agency. (n.d.). *Sources of Greenhouse Gas Emissions*. Retrieved from epa.gov: https://www.epa.gov/ghgemissions/sources-greenhouse-gas-emissions

University of Helsinki MOOC Center. (2012). *Sustainable development and sustainability as normative concept.* Retrieved from courses.mooc.fi: https://courses.mooc.fi/org/uh-inar/courses/introduction-to-sustainability/chapter-1/sustainable-development-and-sustainability-as-normative-concept

UNPRI. (2021). *Principles for Resposible Investment Annual Report*. London: PRI Association.

US SIF. (2023). *US Sustainable Investment Forum*. Retrieved from ussif.org: https://www.ussif.org/about

Verghese, B. K. (2023, July 13). *Is SEBI's BRSR Core Utilitarian Or Distractive?* Retrieved from planet.outlookindia.com: https://planet.outlookindia.com/opinions/is-sebi-s-brsr-core-utilitarian-or-distractive--news-415631

Verschelden, A. (2022, February). *Why Conducting an ESG Baseline Assessment is Essential for Every Company*. Retrieved from getgoodlab.com: https://getgoodlab.com/resources/esg-baseline-assessment/#:~:text=The%20materiality%20assessment%20informs%20which,your%20organization%20and%20its%20stakeholders

Verschelden, A. (2022, February 01). *Why Conducting an ESG Baseline Assessment is Essential for Every Company*. Retrieved from getgoodlab.com: https://getgoodlab.com/resources/esg-baseline-assessment/

Viral Thakker, The Economic Times. (2023, May 22). *How prepared are Indian companies with respect to ESG? Viral Thakker explains.* Retrieved from economictimes.indiatimes.com: https://economictimes.indiatimes.com/markets/expert-view/how-prepared-are-indian-companies-with-respect-to-esg-viral-thakker-explains/articleshow/100415626.cms

Visser, W. (2011). The Age of Responsibility, CSR 2.0 and the New DNA of Business. Wiley, a John Wiley & Sons Ltd. Publication

Wallestad, A. (2021, March 10). *The Four Principles of Purpose-Driven Board Leadership*. Retrieved from ssir.org: https://ssir.org/articles/entry/the_four_principles_of_purpose_driven_board_leadership#

Water *Pollution.* (2023). Retrieved from hsph.harvard.edu: https://www.hsph.harvard.edu/ehep/82-2/#:~:text=Water%20pollution%20is%20the%20contamination,make%20their%20way%20to%20water

Why ESG is here to stay. (2020, May 26). McKinsey & Company. https://www.mckinsey.com/business-functions/strategy-and-corporate-finance/our-insights/why-esg-is-here-to-stay.

Wikipedia. (2021, May). *US SIF.* Retrieved from en.wikipedia.org: https://en.wikipedia.org/wiki/US_SIF

Wikipedia. (2023). *Life-cycle assessment*. Retrieved from en.m.wikipedia.org: https://en.m.wikipedia.org/wiki/Life-cycle_assessment

Wikipedia. (2023). *Supply Chain Sustainability*. Retrieved from en.wikipedia.org: https://en.wikipedia.org/wiki/Supply_chain_sustainability

Wikipedia. (n.d.). *Environmental impact assessment*. Retrieved from en.m.wikipedia.org: https://en.m.wikipedia.org/wiki/Environmental_impact_assessment

Wikipedia. (n.d.). *United Nations Guiding Principles on Business and Human Rights*. Retrieved from en.wikipedia.org: https://en.wikipedia.org/wiki/United_Nations_Guiding_Principles_on_Business_and_Human_Rights

WILSON, A. V. (2023, October 31). *How CEOs and leaders can 'stand their ground' and resist the backlash on diversity, inclusion, and ESG*. Retrieved from fortune.com: https://fortune.com/2023/10/31/diversity-dei-esg-backlash-ceo-initiative/amp/

Word Press (2007), Ten Points Charter, Manmohan Singh, Excerpt from Prime Minister Manmohan Singh's speech on May 24, 2007

World Bank SME finance. (n.d.). World Bank. https://www.worldbank.org/en/topic/smefinance.

World Business Council for Sustainable Development (2019), Business and Human Rights Ambitions and Actions in India, WBCSD & CII-ITC

World Economic Forum -WEF (2020), White Paper - Measuring Stakeholders Capitalism: Towards Common Matrix and Consistent Reporting of Sustainable Value Creation

World Investment Report 2023. (2023). *Capital Markets and Sustainable Finance.*

Zach Christensen, H. L. (n.d.). *Inequality: Global trends*. Retrieved from devinit.org: https://devinit.org/resources/inequality-global-trends/

http://www.fsb-tcfd.org/about

http://www.globalreporting.org/about-gri

http://www.un.org/en/climatechange/paris-agreement

http://www.unepfi.org/

http://www.unpri.org/about-us/about-the-pri

https://amzn.eu/d/00MvWQP

https://blog.ipleaders.in/section-134-of-the-companies-act-2013/#:~:text=According%20to%20Rule%208%20of,investments%20made%20in%20this%20regard

https://carnegieendowment.org/2022/11/28/to-prevent-collapse-of-biodiversity-world-needs-new-planetary-politics-pub-88473

https://cei.org/studies/environmental-social-and-governance-theory/

https://cfpub.epa.gov/watertrain/pdf/modules/economics_of_sustainability.pdf

https://corpgov.law.harvard.edu/2020/08/01/introduction-to-esg/

https://corpgov.law.harvard.edu/2023/06/29/the-rise-of-international-esg-disclosure-standards/

https://corporatefinanceinstitute.com/course/environmental-social-governance/

https://courses.mooc.fi/org/uh-inar/courses/introduction-to-sustainability/chapter-1/sustainable-development-and-sustainability-as-normative-concept

https://csr.gov.in/page-history.php

https://en.wikipedia.org/wiki/National_Voluntary_Guidelines_on_Social,_Environmental_and_Economic_Responsibilities_of_Business

https://en.wikipedia.org/wiki/US_SIF

https://enterclimate.com/blog/overview-of-the-environment-protection-amendment-rules-2023/

https://eqm.ai/insights-trends/start-your-esg-strategy-7-steps/

https://esg.conservice.com/getting-started-sustainability-benchmarking/

https://esgpro.co.uk/what-is-governance-within-esg/

https://hbr.org/2022/11/its-time-to-focus-on-the-g-in-esg

https://iclg.com/practice-areas/environmental-social-and-governance-law/india

https://m.economictimes.com/markets/expert-view/how-prepared-are-indian-companies-with-respect-to-esg-viral-thakker-explains/articleshow/100415626.cms

https://m.economictimes.com/news/economy/policy/in-a-first-two-ibbi-members-endorse-focus-on-esg-in-insolvency-resolution/articleshow/104168133.cms

https://marketbusinessnews.com/financial-glossary/esg-definition-meaning/

https://mca.gov.in/content/mca/global/en/home.html

https://medium.com/disruptive-design/how-do-esg-and-sustainability-fit-together-f8d91b605003

https://mhes.com/understanding-esg-governance-factors/

https://pib.gov.in/Pressreleaseshare.aspx?PRID=1568750

https://plato.stanford.edu/entries/capability-approach/

https://plato.stanford.edu/entries/justice-intergenerational/

https://sdgs.un.org/about

https://senyumnegeri.id/what-is-esg-definition-theory/

https://theimpactinvestor.com/esg-principles/

https://unccelearn.org/course/view.php?id=139&page=overview

https://www.alpha-sense.com/blog/product/how-to-esg-benchmarking/

https://www.barrons.com/articles/13-esg-investing-trends-to-watch-for-in-2020-51580385602

https://www.bdc.ca/en/articles-tools/sustainability/environment/what-esg-and-what-does-mean-business#

https://www.businesstoday.in/interactive/longread/the-esg-imperative-indian-businesses-future-ready-265-20-06-2023

https://www.businessworld.in/article/Four-Primary-Challenges-Hindering-Adoption-Of-ESG-In-India/24-06-2022-433877/

https://www.businessworld.in/article/Uncovering-The-S-In-ESG-/11-07-2023-483834/

https://www.cfainstitute.org/en/membership/professional-development/refresher-readings/introduction-corporate-governance-esg-considerations

https://www.cfainstitute.org/en/rpc-overview/esg-investing

https://www.classcentral.com/course/esg-risks-opportunities-58758

https://www.coursera.org/learn/esg-and-climate-change?irclickid=QyN1oUTGpxyIUC2xiNQX-y8yUkAVifR9%3AWLYz40&irgwc=1&utm_medium=partners&utm_source=impact&utm_campaign=259799&utm_content=b2c

https://www.coursera.org/learn/sustainability

https://www.csr.gov.in

https://www.deutschewealth.com/en/our-capabilities/esg/what-is-esg-investing-wealth-management/corporate-governance-g-in-esg-governance.html

https://www.dlapiper.com/en/insights/publications/2023/03/esg-in-2023-who-cares-wins

https://www.drishtiias.com/daily-updates/daily-news-analysis/esg-and-india

https://www.ecolytics.io/blog/whats-the-difference-between-esg-and-sustainability#:~:text=ESG%20criteria%20are%20a%20subset,other%20social%20or%20governmental%20practices

https://www.fdic.gov/regulations/resources/director/presentations/CRA.pdf

https://www.financialexpress.com/money/esg-investing-why-is-it-even-more-relevant-for-investors-in-the-current-scenario/1996623/

https://www.gartner.com/en/finance/glossary/environmental-social-and-governance-esg-

https://www.google.com/amp/s/iclg.com/practice-areas/environmental-social-and-governance-law/india/amp

https://www.google.com/amp/s/timesofindia.indiatimes.com/blogs/voices/india-transforms-its-esg-landscape-to-be-future-ready/

https://www.google.com/amp/s/timesofindia.indiatimes.com/blogs/voices/rise-of-the-esg-regulations/

https://www.google.com/amp/s/www.businesstoday.in/amp/latest/corporate/story/indias-esg-jobs-witness-223-surge-since-2019-study-384235-2023-06-05

https://www.google.com/amp/s/www.livemint.com/news/india/deloitte-india-s-esg-preparedness-survey-only-27-of-indian-businesses-feel-confident-about-meeting-esg-requirements/amp-11684405627826.html

https://www.google.com/amp/s/www.thehindu.com/opinion/op-ed/explained-the-rise-of-the-esg-regulations/article66610907.ece/amp/

https://www.google.com/amp/s/www.thehindubusinessline.com/opinion/taking-esg-reporting-to-the-next-level/article65457659.ece/amp/

https://www.iica.nic.in

https://www.insightsonindia.com/2020/08/13/what-is-business-responsibility-reporting/

https://www.investopedia.com/ask/answers/042215/what-difference-between-capitalist-system-and-free-market-system.asp

https://www.investopedia.com/terms/c/community_reinvestment_act.asp

https://www.linkedin.com/posts/jaganathanraghupathy_esg-sustainability-csr-activity-7070305018423250944-X8hv?utm_source=share&utm_medium=member_android

https://www.linkedin.com/pulse/how-does-esg-reporting-change-csr-landscape-national-csr-network?utm_source=share&utm_medium=member_android&utm_campaign=share_via

https://www.linkedin.com/pulse/procurement-perspectives-traditional-vs-leading-the-procurementholic?utm_source=share&utm_medium=member_android&utm_campaign=share_via

https://www.linkedin.com/pulse/sustainability-esg-insights-september23-big-sec-fines-de-la-mar?utm_source=share&utm_medium=member_android&utm_campaign=share_via

https://www.livelaw.in/amp/articles/incorporating-environment-social-and-governance-norms-into-indian-corporations-230878

https://www.livemint.com/news/india/deloitte-india-s-esg-preparedness-survey-only-27-of-indian-businesses-feel-confident-about-meeting-esg-requirements-11684405627826.html

https://www.mca.gov.in

https://www.mca.gov.in/Ministry/pdf/NationalGuildeline_15032019.pdf

https://www.mondaq.com/india/corporatecommercial-law/1231978/esg-comparative-guide

https://www.occ.treas.gov/topics/consumers-and-communities/cra/index-cra.html

https://www.outlookbusiness.com/strategy-4/feature-17/sebis-got-indian-thoughts-on-esg-push-6841

https://www.researchgate.net/publication/325599995_Triple_Bottom_Line_The_Pillars_of_CSR

https://www.robeco.com/en-me/glossary/sustainable-investing/esg-definition

https://www.sciencedirect.com/science/article/abs/pii/S0921800914000895

https://www.sciencedirect.com/science/article/abs/pii/S0921800921000094#:~:text=The%20capability%20approach%20is%20considered,Seckler%20and%20Volker%2C%202021

https://www.singhico.com/esg-integration.html

https://www.springer.com/series/2881

https://www.stern.nyu.edu/sites/default/files/assets/documents/NYUSternCSBSustainabilityMateriality_2019_0.pdf

https://www.sustainalytics.com/esg-research/resource/corporate-esg-blog/examining-the-g-in-esg-the-role-best-practices-and-metrics-for-corporate-governance

https://www.tatamotors.com/press/tata-nexon-becomes-the-first-indian-car-to-be-published-on-the-international-dismantling-information-system-idis/

https://www.techtarget.com/sustainability/definition/ESG-score

https://www.teriin.org/sites/default/files/2020-05/Discussion%20Paper-SDGs%20and%20Business_April2020.pdf

https://www.thecorporategovernanceinstitute.com/insights/lexicon/what-is-esg-benchmarking/

https://www.un.org/sustainabledevelopment/development-agenda/

https://www.ussif.org/about

https://www2.deloitte.com/ce/en/pages/global-business-services/articles/esg-explained-1-what-is-esg.html

https://www-knowesg-com.translate.goog/featured-article/what-is-esg-performance-and-how-to-measure-it?_x_tr_sl=en&_x_tr_tl=hi&_x_tr_hl=hi&_x_tr_pto=rq

https://yourstory.com/socialstory/2023/08/india-climate-journey-cleantech-decarbonisation